ARMING THE WORLD

ARMING THE WORLD
American Gun-Makers in the Gilded Age

GEOFFREY S. STEWART

LYONS
PRESS

Essex, Connecticut

An imprint of Globe Pequot, the trade division of
The Rowman & Littlefield Publishing Group, Inc.
4501 Forbes Blvd., Ste. 200
Lanham, MD 20706
www.rowman.com

Distributed by NATIONAL BOOK NETWORK

British Library Cataloguing in Publication Information available

Library of Congress Cataloging-in-Publication Data
Names: Stewart, Geoffrey S., author.
Title: Arming the world : American gun-makers in the Gilded Age / Geoffrey S. Stewart.
Description: Essex, Connecticut : Lyons Press, [2024] | Includes bibliographical references and
    index. Summary: "The story of the development of American arms manufacturing and how
    ingenuity and inventiveness made the United States the major arms supplier to the world
    beginning in the mid-nineteenth century"— Provided by publisher.
Identifiers: LCCN 2023037064 (print) | LCCN 2023037065 (ebook) | ISBN 9781493078585
    (hardcover) | ISBN 9781493078592 (epub)
Subjects: LCSH: Firearms industry and trade—United States—History—19th century.
Classification: LCC HD9744.F553 U68 2024 (print) | LCC HD9744.F553 (ebook) | DDC
    338.4/768340097309034—dc23/eng/20231207

LC record available at https://lccn.loc.gov/202303706
LC ebook record available at https://lccn.loc.gov/2023037065

♾️™ The paper used in this publication meets the minimum requirements of American National
Standard for Information Sciences—Permanence of Paper for Printed Library Materials, ANSI/
NISO Z39.48-1992.

To Sandra

Contents

CONTENTS

Acknowledgments

There is no simple way to acknowledge all of the support and help I have received with this project. Suffice it to say that many dozens of people have enabled me to research and write this book. For helping me many years ago, I owe thanks to James and Margaret Sims, David Cross of the Rhode Island Tool Company, Nathaniel Shipton of the Rhode Island Historical Society, Laura Kajute and Irene Marotta of the Olin Corporation Library in New Haven, Sam Alvis of Remington Arms, and the dozens of librarians and archivists who helped me in so many ways.

I also would like to acknowledge the assistance of Dr. Julian Bennett of Bilkent University in Ankara, Turkey, who kindly shared with me his superb work on the Peabody-Martini rifle and the Russo-Turkish War; Professor Keith Brown of the Melikian Center at Arizona State University, whose insights into the broader cultural and historical implications of weapons are profoundly important; and Tarik Tansu Yiğit, whose meticulous work on the post–Civil War American presence in Egypt and knowledge of sources was extraordinarily helpful. Professor Yiğit teaches in the Department of American Culture and Literature, Baskent University, Ankara, Turkey, and, at the time of this writing, is a visiting scholar at the Weatherhead Research Cluster on Global Transformations at Harvard University.

I owe thanks to the archivists and staffs of the Connecticut Museum of Culture and History, the Rhode Island Historical Society, and the Manuscript Collection of the University of Rhode Island, all of whom were helpful in my more recent efforts to access original source material. Thanks are due as well to those who fund and maintain the indispensable online resources that have collected, digitized, indexed, and preserved an inspiring range of secondary and original sources. These include the Canadian Research Knowledge Network, Google Books, Hathi Trust, the Internet Archive, the Library of Congress, the New York Public Library, and the Wikipedia Foundation.

I wish to acknowledge the friendship, teaching, and guidance of the late Norman Rich (1921–2020), my debts to whom cannot be repaid. Finally, I could not have accomplished this task without the help, support, and love of my wife, Sandra Baker, to whom this work is dedicated.

INTRODUCTION

For every author, a book is a personal journey, and this one began with a phone call to a florist in 1972.

During my junior year at Brown University in Providence, Rhode Island, my favorite professor, the late Norman Rich, delivered an intriguing lecture about the Russo-Turkish War of 1877–1878. At the pivotal battle of Plevna, the Turks held off a vastly superior force thanks to the deadly effectiveness of their rifles. Surprisingly, the guns used in this distant fight had been made in Providence. This deserved some investigation, Norman thought. He had heard of these guns before and had some questions. Why were the rifles manufactured in Rhode Island and, for that matter, how had the bankrupt Turks found the money to pay for them? Scholars suspected that England was somehow involved.

The local historical society had little beyond the original contracts, showing that Turkey had ordered 600,000 rifles in 1873 from a long-defunct firm called the Providence Tool Company. An old newspaper clipping—full of fascinating details—said that the company's president had been John Brayton Anthony and that he died in 1904. I began searching for his family, looking up everyone named "Anthony" in the phone book, ringing the doorbell of the house where he used to live, and tracking down the owner of Providence Tool's old factory. I dug up John Anthony's obituary from the microfilm archives of the *Providence Journal*, but still had no luck tracking down his descendants.

A few days later, I remembered a detail from the obituary, namely that John Anthony had been an avid churchman and the senior warden for many years of Providence's Grace Episcopal Church. Maybe, I supposed, his grandchildren still went there. I put a dime in the dormitory pay phone and dialed the church. The kindly church secretary pondered my request, but concluded that no one in the congregation fit the bill. So, it seemed, I had reached the end of the road.

But as I was hanging up the phone, she exclaimed "Wait!" I froze, handset in midair. "There is a plaque on the wall of the nave dedicated to John Anthony," she said, "and every Easter someone lays flowers there." She knew no more, but suggested that I call the head of the church's Flower Committee. The Flower Committee chair could confirm only the broad details, since the flowers were placed anonymously. Perhaps I might call the church's florist?

I have long since forgotten the name of the florist, but he was a friendly Italian man who knew all about it. On second thought, though, he concluded that—since the donors gave the flowers anonymously—he could not reveal their names. But he added that if he had time, he would try to call them up and tell them what I was looking for. At this, my heart sank, but I had done everything I could, and I turned to other things.

Two weeks later, the pay phone rang down the hall, and one of my dorm-mates said it was for me. I put the handset to my ear, and the voice on the other end of the line said, "Mr. Stewart, my name is James Sims. I believe I have the papers that you are looking for."

James Sims, his wife, and their unmarried son lived in a tidy bungalow near the Brown football stadium. They invited me to come by on Sunday. I knocked on the door and was greeted by a small man in his seventies, dressed in a coat and tie. He introduced me to his silent wife and led me into their small dining room. There on the table sat an old cardboard box. When I lifted the top folder, there was a sprinkling of shiny confetti. "Those are gold coins," Margaret Sims said. "John Anthony was my grandfather. My grandmother and aunts stayed at the Sultan's palace in Constantinople, and the Turks tossed these little coins to newlyweds, like we throw rice today."

The sad and touching story that emerged about Margaret Sims and the Anthony papers is too long to tell here. For the balance of the semester, however, the Simses let me come to their house every Sunday afternoon to read John Anthony's papers. I was not allowed to photocopy the documents, but I was permitted to transcribe them by hand into a notebook I kept and still have. After many weeks, I completed these labors, and James Sims asked if he could drive me back to campus. In the car he explained why he had responded to the florist's call. For intensely personal reasons, reopening history was a wrenching decision for his wife. "But this was the only important thing our family has ever done," he told me, "and Margaret wanted the world to know what John Anthony accomplished."

At Norman Rich's urging, I applied for a small grant to continue my work during the summer of 1972. There, I learned that Providence Tool and Turkey were just the tip of the proverbial iceberg. With my parents' second car, I drove to Hartford to research the Colt archives, New Haven to read the Winchester records, Ilion for Remington, and various small New England towns where gun-makers had once thrived. Husbanding my grant money, I spent a week in Washington, DC, at the National Archives and even went to London to see what was in the diplomatic collection at the hoary Public Record Office on Chancery Lane. In keeping with the methods of the day, I ended up with boxes of three-by-five-inch note cards, sheaves of faint photocopies, and files of half-written drafts and miscellaneous notes. All of this came together in a master's thesis I wrote in the spring of 1973.

I had hoped to continue this work, but with the Vietnam War still fresh in everyone's minds, no one was interested in my research on guns. So I went off to law school, never forgetting the captivating stories that so deserved telling. Retirement offered me the opportunity to finish my work, and so I wrote this book.

Over the intervening fifty years, a variety of sources have become available that were unknown back then, and there has been much written by scholars and collectors of antique weapons alike that round out and add important detail to the story of the American arms industry before and after the Civil War. However, there has been no general treatment of the subject since Felicia Deyrup's brilliant *Arms Makers of the Connecticut Valley* in 1948, and much new information has since surfaced. Obviously, the broader the scope, the narrower the depth, but I have tried to supply important details wherever possible to document my work and help those who follow.

A Note about Money and Exchange Rates

Unless otherwise indicated, all of the prices, values, and sums mentioned in this book are in the amounts and currencies of the time. Because of inflation, these numbers would be far higher if given in 2024 dollars.

Translating the purchasing power of the nineteenth-century dollar into modern currency is difficult and imprecise. The dollar rose and fell in value depending upon political events of the day, wartime inflation, and, most of all, the supply of gold. As a very general rule, though, a dollar in the mid-nineteenth century was worth about $25 to $30 in today's money, although this could vary materially if payment was promised in gold, or if the United States was at war or experiencing one of its periodic financial panics.

The relative values of different currencies were generally fixed in gold by the 1870s, resulting in an exchange rate of 5 US dollars to the British pound (£) and 5 French francs (F) to the US dollar. Thus, a British pound ostensibly was worth 25 French francs. There were 20 shillings to the British pound, so a shilling equaled 25 US cents.

Other currencies are more difficult to convert. It appears that the Imperial Russian ruble (₽) was worth $1.50 in these years. Egypt's currency was the Egyptian pound (E£), which was officially equivalent to the British pound, although the value of Egyptian currency fell as the Khedivate encountered financial difficulties. Turkey used the Turkish gold lira which, again, was nominally worth about one British pound, but its transactions with foreign firms generally were denominated in British pounds or US dollars.

CHAPTER I

Brother Jonathan at the Crystal Palace

At the midpoint of the nineteenth century, Great Britain's leaders resolved to show the world just how far progress had come among the world's civilized nations. A commission of Victorian notables organized an ambitious spectacle called *The Great Exhibition of the Works of Industry of All Nations*. As its name suggested, the Great Exhibition was intended to display the accomplishments of "All Nations." Yet there was little doubt that its overarching purpose was to play to the national pride of Britain itself, the birthplace of the Industrial Revolution and now the world's wealthiest country.

The Great Exhibition of 1851 was housed in a building called the Crystal Palace, a remarkable greenhouse-like structure 1,848 feet long, 456 feet wide, and 135 feet high and enclosing almost a million square feet. About half of the exhibition space was given over to Britain and its colonies. After that came spaces allotted in a generally descending order to the powers of continental Europe. The United States was given 50,000 square feet at the east end of the exhibition hall, as distant from the British exhibits as possible.[1]

America's physical isolation reflected its general irrelevance. While Britain's list of exhibited items included James Nasmyth's famous steam hammer, rare diamonds, and all manner of Victorian accomplishments, the American entries seemed to have come from the hinterlands. The United States exhibition featured specimens of roofing slate, rice, tobacco, "Indian corn," preserved peaches, corn-husk mattresses, lead ore, and "American forest autumn leaves, in their natural colours." The

I

French, meanwhile, "showed Sèvres porcelain and Gobelins tapestries; chemicals and carpets, machinery and metal; musical as well as philosophical instruments," while the Queen of Spain exhibited her crown jewels and the Austrians "sent over a superb collection of glass, furniture, precious works in gold and silver; silver plate, inlaid flooring" and "objects in ivory, bronze, tortoiseshell and horn." "It is a wonderful place—vast, strange, new and impossible to describe," Charlotte Brontë wrote her father. "It seems as if only magic could have gathered this mass of wealth from all the ends of the earth."[2] She was not, obviously, speaking of the American end of the building.

This simplicity of the American exhibits confirmed to most Britons their dismal view of the United States. Caricatured as "Brother Jonathan"—a clumsy, witless, ill-educated, and bumptious fool—America was remote and irrelevant, useful mainly as a source of cotton and a market for Britain's finished goods. It did not help matters that the country's southern regions still embraced the barbarous practice of human slavery, nor that the United States and Britain had fought two declared wars in the past seventy years and only recently had patched up another dispute.

European disdain for America was confirmed by the fact that the US government was too cheap to subsidize the country's offerings at the Crystal Palace and, thereby left to their own devices, the American entries were disorganized, late, crude, and generally disappointing. In fact, but for the generous intervention of the London-based American banker George Peabody, the United States exhibition may not have come off at all. The London *Times* wrote that "the American department was the poorest and least interesting of all foreign countries." So ill-attended was the American exhibition that the London press sneeringly referred to it as the "Prairie."[3]

Queen Victoria presided over the Great Exhibition's opening on May 1, 1851. In the first few weeks, high admission fees discouraged everyone but the wealthy from attending, and they made no effort to conceal their condescension to the Americans. Yet within weeks several almost-random events startled even the smuggest Englishman. Whatever its shortcomings in luxury items, the United States had made disconcerting progress elsewhere.[4]

One the American exhibitors was the New York firm of Day & Newell, which had recently developed an advanced "parautoptic lock." Day & Newell sent a representative, one Alfred C. Hobbs, to the exhibition to promote the lock. Hobbs was something of a loudmouth, but he also happened to be a skilled locksmith. At the time, the most celebrated lockmaker in Britain was Chubb & Son: in fact, the Bank of England used Chubb locks and, at the Great Exhibition itself, Queen Victoria's crown jewel—the famed Koh-i-Noor diamond—was exhibited in a case protected by a Chubb lock. On July 21, Hobbs brazenly challenged Chubb & Son to come see him pick their lock. Chubb ignored Hobbs's obnoxious note as a publicity stunt, but shortly before noon the next day in the presence of eleven witnesses, Hobbs successfully picked one of Chubb's six-tumbler locks in twenty-five minutes, and then did it again in seven.[5]

Even more sacred was the famous Bramah lock. The lock had been constructed in 1784 by the English mechanical genius Joseph Bramah. Bramah's lock was an intricate device that used an array of tricks to defeat any lockpick. So confident was Bramah & Co. that they had for years displayed the lock in their shop window with the sign "The artist who will make an instrument that will pick or open this lock, will receive 200 guineas the moment it is produced." Hobbs publicly took on Bramah's challenge on July 23, a dare Bramah & Co. gamely accepted. The Bramah lock was indeed complicated, and it took Hobbs fifty-one hours, spread over sixteen days, to pick it. Despite grumbling about the unrealistic conditions surrounding Hobbs's success, Bramah & Co. nevertheless conceded the results and graciously paid Hobbs his 200 guineas.[6]

Hobbs was nothing if not persistent. He soon issued a public challenge daring anyone to try to pick his own Day & Newell lock, offering a $1,000 reward. After thirty days of trying, England's best locksmiths gave up. Soon the Bank of England replaced its Chubb locks with the Day & Newell lock, and Hobbs moved to London to start his own lock company.[7]

Britain's pride soon suffered another indignity. As part of the Great Exhibition's festivities, the commodore of the Royal Yacht Squadron invited his counterpart at the New York Yacht Club to come to the Isle of Wight to compete in a regatta open to all comers. The New Yorkers crossed the Atlantic in a new schooner—appropriately enough named *America*—which had an innovative design and a professional crew. The race was held the morning of August 22 among fifteen boats. *America* won handily. According to one popular account, while watching *America* tear by, Queen Victoria asked who was in second place. The famous reply was "There is no second, Your Majesty."

Any further doubts about technological progress in the United States were dispelled by yet another American invention. This was the McCormick Reaper, an ungainly looking contraption ridiculed in the British press as a "cross between a flying machine, a wheelbarrow and [a circus] chariot." In a carefully organized trial on July 24, the McCormick machine successfully cut a seventy-four-yard path through a sodden wheat field in about a minute. This shook the foundations of English agriculture and caused the British public to take a second look at these American inventions. It "gave a new turn to affairs, and on the return of the Reapers to the Palace, crowds were continually examining them, and the American department from this time to the closing of the exhibition, was no longer the 'Prairie ground,' but thronged with inquiring visitors."[8]

There, these inquiring visitors encountered one of the great self-promoters of American business, Samuel P. Colt. A native of Hartford, Connecticut, Colt had traveled across the United States in his younger days as "Dr. Coult," giving demonstrations of laughing gas and performing a rendition of Dante's *Divine Comedy* using wax sculptures and fireworks. Colt may have been something of a huckster, but he was no fool. A few years earlier, he had worked with Samuel Morse to develop and lay underwater telegraph cables. In 1842, Colt impressed the US Navy by successfully destroying a moving vessel with his remotely operated underwater mine, although any chances of selling the device to the navy were scuttled when ex-president John Quincy Adams condemned it as an "unchristian contraption."[9]

Colt had an abiding interest in the concept of a gun with revolving chambers. The idea was an old one, but he sufficiently improved upon prior art that he received British and American patents in the mid-1830s. Colt's original models of the gun were impractical, useless, and dangerous to the user, but in fits and starts he improved it until by the late 1840s the Colt revolver was a practical gun. By the time of the Great Exhibition, Colt products were reliable, cheap, and appealingly deadly.

Ever the promoter, Colt used the occasion of the Great Exhibition to present a handsome boxed set of extravagantly chased and inlaid revolvers to various British grandees, including Britain's Master General of the Ordnance and Prince Albert himself. A frequent visitor to Colt's exhibit was the ancient Duke of Wellington, still venerated for his victory over Napoleon at Waterloo thirty-six years earlier. As a matter of principle, the duke generally opposed progress in any form, but he was often found at Colt's exhibit "forcefully asserting the advantages of repeating firearms to an audience of officers and friends." Prince Albert, too, came by, enjoying the pleasure of blasting away with Colt's handgun.[10]

By the end of the Great Exhibition, the American exhibit was no longer an embarrassing sideshow. London's *Daily News* wrote that "[f]ormerly, the crowds used to cluster most in the French and Austrian section, while the region of the stars and stripes was almost deserted—now the domain of Brother Jonathan is daily filled with crowds of visitors." Another British journal wrote: "[I]t is beyond all denial, that every practical success of the season belongs to the Americans. . . . Their reaping machine has carried conviction to the heart of the British Agriculturist. Their revolvers threaten to revolutionize military tactics, as completely as the original discovery of gunpowder."[11]

The public's fascination with revolvers, reapers, and locks overshadowed what might have been the most important display of American technology. This was an exhibit of six ordinary-looking rifles made a few years earlier by the firm of Robbins & Lawrence from Windsor, Vermont. Robbins & Lawrence's catalogue entry modestly described their offering as "Rifles: with their various parts made to *interchange.*" This last word was intriguing to the officers from the British Ordnance Board who dropped by the Robbins & Lawrence exhibit. For years, they had known that the United States was making steady progress toward the mass production of muskets with machinery, and the proof of success would be whether the process was precise enough to produce guns with interchangeable parts.

Now it seemed that a small firm in a remote Vermont village was offering them for sale.[12]

Before long, the British government dispatched experts to the United States to see what this was all about. What they learned was that the United States was pulling ahead of the rest of the world, and not just in gun-making. Uniquely, the United States had mechanized the making of countless products and had done so with such thoroughness that Europeans soon called mass production itself "the American System of Manufactures." But it had started with guns.

CHAPTER 2

Muskets

Since the seventeenth century, soldiers had carried into battle a portable weapon that came to be known as a musket. With time, the gun took a standard form: generally speaking, it was about five feet long, weighed nearly ten pounds, had a wooden stock and wrought-iron barrel, and cost somewhere between $12 and $17 to make. Usually, the barrel had a fitting at the muzzle allowing the soldier to fix a bayonet there, which turned the musket into a type of spear.[1] But, bayonet or not, the musket remained a "firearm": its purpose was to convert the chemical energy of burning gunpowder into the kinetic energy of a bullet, and then deliver that bullet at a distant target. Military tactics turned upon the capabilities and shortcomings of muskets; the musket was a seed around which armies crystallized.

For years, muskets did not change much. In fact, the famous British Brown Bess musket, first issued around 1722, was still in use in 1838. Part of this was because of the gun's simple durability: a musket was expected to survive thousands of discharges and, in normal service, last ten to twelve years. But another reason was that the form of the gun was a function of the ammunition it used, and ammunition stayed the same for a long time. Constrained by laws of physics, muskets fired a spherical lead bullet—a "musket ball"—whose diameter was determined by its weight, its weight by the size of its gunpowder charge, the size of the gunpowder charge by the stoutness of the gun barrel, and the stoutness of the gun barrel by how heavy a gun a foot soldier could bear.[2] Optimizing these variables resulted in a .65- to .69-caliber musket

7

ball that weighed between about 390 and 500 grains and used a powder charge of one-third to one-half of the weight of the musket ball.*

The process of loading and firing a musket was cumbersome. These were muzzle-loading weapons where the soldier poured the powder into the mouth of the barrel and then pushed the ball down into the base of the barrel—known as the "firing chamber"—with a ramrod. To make the gun easier to load, the inside of the barrel was completely smooth, and so these muskets were called "smoothbores." A muzzle-loading musket could be loaded and fired about twice a minute. Originally, the gunpowder was ignited using a complicated flint-and-steel mechanism known as a "flintlock," where the friction between a piece of flint and a steel frizzen produced a spark that set off the powder charge. Beginning in the 1820s, flintlocks were progressively replaced with an alternative called a percussion lock.† These percussion arms were more reliable than the flintlocks they supplanted, but otherwise not much different. Instead, it seemed that the musket would remain essentially unchanged, as it already had for over a century.

GUN-MAKING

The fabrication of muskets was a craft practiced by gunsmiths in communities where gun-making often had deep roots. Muskets were difficult to make, and gunsmiths served long apprenticeships. And there were specialties within the trade: blacksmiths forged gun barrels, stockers carved gunstocks, lorimers made the miscellaneous parts of the gun known as "furniture," and locksmiths made and assembled the components of the gunlock. This was handwork. Even when machinery was an option, few gunsmiths were prepared to invest in it because, unfortunately, peace

---

* *Caliber* is a synonym for *diameter* and is expressed in decimals of inches unless otherwise noted. Bullets and gunpowder charges were measured in grains, an ancient weight based on the mass of a single kernel of barley, wheat, or other cereal. There are 437.5 grains in an ounce.

† Percussion locks relied upon the chemical properties of unstable explosive compounds known as fulminates to create the spark. Fulminates were packed into copper caps that looked like tiny hats. After pouring the gunpowder down the musket barrel and ramming down the musket ball, a soldier stuck one of these percussion caps on the top of a cone-shaped nipple that was set into the musket's breech. The nipple was hollow and vented directly into the musket's firing chamber. When the soldier pulled the trigger, the musket's hammer smashed the percussion cap, setting off the fulminate which, in turn, sent its spark into the firing chamber to ignite the main powder charge.

could happen at any time. In fact, given the ups and downs of the business, many gun-makers had sidelines to tide them over between wars.

The embodiment of this approach was found in England, which subscribed to an archaic method of handcrafting muskets known generally as the "Birmingham System," after the city where the nation's gun business was centered. Gun-makers there were organized into "trades" that made the main components of the musket, such as the barrel, ramrod, stock, bayonet, and lock. The British Army's Ordnance Board was in charge of procurement and, once it decided upon its needs, the board let contracts to each trade for the requisite number of components. These artisans generally worked from home workshops laboring, as one British government official put it in 1853, in "wretched cellars and garrets." The various parts were assembled into the larger components of the gun and then went to "setters-up" in London who furnished miscellaneous small parts and then assembled—"set up"—the gun. Because each part of the gun was unique, the setters-up did much filing and other handwork to make everything fit together.[3] As convoluted as the process was, it resulted in high-quality muskets at a good price; on the other hand, it was deeply resistant to change and, as events would prove, limited in what it could produce.

The European gun trade adhered to this guild-like system for years. The gun-making centers of Birmingham, Liege, Charleville, Potsdam, and Tula reliably met the Great Powers' needs, even during the great Napoleonic wars of the early nineteenth century. Like the standardized muskets themselves, the craft of arms-making seemed to be a settled matter. In fact, when a French gunsmith named Honoré Blanc attempted in the late eighteenth century to modernize the production of muskets, his work foundered upon the hostility of the entrenched gun trade.[4]

But these traditions were about to come under irresistible pressure. Within the space of a dozen years, there were two revolutions in the world of firearms, each of which made older weapons obsolete and imposed new demands upon gun-makers. Both times, the revolution was driven by a breakthrough in ammunition. The first was the perfection of the bullet known generally as the Minié ball; the second the development of the one-piece metallic cartridge. The capabilities of the new ammunition opened the way to rifled muskets and then to rifles that loaded from the breech instead of the muzzle.

For reasons having nothing to do with either revolution, gun factories in the United States already had perfected a way of mass-producing arms known there as "armory practice."[5] The two revolutions in small-arms technology played directly into this strength, and the American advantage was further magnified by the fact that American methods encouraged gun-makers to develop new designs that would have been impractical in an artisanal culture. And, as if there were a need for anything more, the Civil War occurred in the middle of it all, and—at least in the North—government spending paid for the gun industry's rapid expansion and subsidized its research and development.

The revolution in breech-loading rifles began at the same time that the Civil War ended. This began an era in American history of growth, wealth, and pride in the country's newfound power that came to be known as the Gilded Age after a novel of the same title Mark Twain published in 1873. With their enormous productive capacity and a range of breech-loader designs, American gun-makers were in a unique position to take advantage of the world's need to rearm itself with new and deadlier weapons. This book is the story of the people who took that opportunity and their unexpected encounters with history.

CHAPTER 3

Armory Practice

CRYSTAL PALACE VISITORS MARVELING AT THE COLT REVOLVERS AND inspecting the Robbins & Lawrence rifles may have wondered how a backwater like America had come so far. Scholars have identified any number of causes: the shortage of skilled labor, an abundance of unskilled labor, the ready availability of waterpower, free public education, a multitude of native mechanical geniuses, the British blockade in the War of 1812, the concentration of capital in the country's northeastern states, a shortage of arable land in New England, and so on.[1] Whatever caused it, the American System of Manufactures arose from the unique way the arms industry developed in the United States.

It began, fittingly, with George Washington and Alexander Hamilton. In his first address to Congress, Washington emphasized that the United States should promote its domestic industries, especially the arms industry, as a matter of national security.[2] Congress asked Hamilton to look into it, and in December 1791, he offered a blueprint of the steps the federal government could take to build the country's industrial capacity. Possibly the most audacious of these was Hamilton's proposal that the federal government should build and operate its own munitions factories. After thinking about it, Congress agreed, and it authorized Washington in 1794 to establish as many as "three or four arsenals with magazines, as he shall judge most expedient" and appropriated $59,000 to pay for it.[3] Washington decided that only two federal armories were needed, and he personally selected sites for both. In the North, he chose land outside the village of Springfield, Massachusetts, near the banks of the

Connecticut River. In the South, Washington designated the old settlement of Harper's Ferry, Virginia, at the confluence of the Potomac and
Shenandoah Rivers. Both places had sources of waterpower and were
upstream of rapids that blocked the passage of enemy warships.

The United States had, from the beginning, a hybrid military. There
was a small standing army, the size of which Congress set by statute.
Beyond that, each state had a paramilitary force of its own—a militia—
under the control of the state governor or legislature, yet also subject
to federal regulation and service in emergencies. From this emerged a
hybrid arms industry. Springfield and Harper's Ferry made muskets for
the standing army and let out contracts to private firms for muskets,
rifles, and pistols as the army needed. The state militias, funded by the
federal government after 1808, looked to the private sector. At first, these
guns were made with traditional artisanal methods. However, largely due
to the influence of Eli Whitney—who had promised disingenuously in
1798 to revolutionize gun-making by making guns with interchangeable
parts using "machinery moved by water"—the federal government progressively mechanized Springfield and Harper's Ferry and encouraged
private firms to do the same.[4] Organizing this effort became easier when,
on the eve of the War of 1812, Congress created the Army Quartermaster and Ordnance Departments to centralize the procurement and
inspection of artillery, small arms, ammunition, and other matériel.[5]

Originally, the idea of using machinery to make muskets and pistols
was seen as a way to cut costs. But speeding up the production of gun
parts made little sense if the machinery spat out a jumble of raw parts
that had to be reworked. Thus, a concomitant of producing gun parts by
machine was the principle that each of those parts would be sufficiently
identical that muskets could be quickly and easily assembled. By dint
of being identical, each of these parts also could be exchanged with one
another, and the term "interchangeable parts" became a shorthand for
the larger idea that parts of a gun would be made by machine instead
of by hand. Almost out of the blue, the notion of interchangeability
became the official policy of the United States in February 1815, when
Congress passed a law "for the better regulation of the Ordnance Department." Among its other provisions, it put the federal armories under the

authority of the chief of the Ordnance Department and directed him "to draw up a system of regulations . . . for the *uniformity of manufactures of all arms*."[6] It so happened that the chief of the Ordnance Department given this sweeping authority was a well-connected military engineer named Decius Wadsworth, who was an admirer and acolyte of Eli Whitney.

With this, the Ordnance Department set off on a decades-long course to mechanize the manufacture of muskets and other weapons. It began, of course, at the two federal armories. However, the department also was in charge of procuring muskets, rifles, and pistols from private arms-makers, and it imposed upon them the same requirements of uniformity that it required of the federal armories. Because profit margins were thin, the private firms became creative in finding faster and cheaper ways to manufacture guns, and their inventiveness found its way back to the federal armories and then onwards to other sectors of the American economy. Over the years, an ecosystem of sorts developed, especially in New England, between the Ordnance Department and the private armories.

Besides being a convenient abbreviation for the more complex subject of machine-based manufacture, interchangeability was the best way to test whether the machines were doing their job. The ultimate measure of success in using machinery to make arms was whether different batches of guns were completely and practically interchangeable with one another. At Harper's Ferry, the Maine-born John Hall operated the Rifle Works (a somewhat unwelcome step-child of the main armory) that produced limited numbers of Hall's breech-loading rifle in 1834 that met this standard. Springfield and Harper's Ferry themselves achieved interchangeability a few years later in their mass production of the Model 1842 Springfield musket.[7] Private contractors adhered to these same strictures; in fact, the six Model 1841 rifles Robbins & Lawrence exhibited at the Crystal Palace interchanged not only with each other, but also with M1841s made at Harper's Ferry and by any number of other government contractors.

With this accomplished, the United States' break from the traditional methods of Europe was all but complete. There was no particular reason this should have happened: the United States did not fight more wars than other countries; its military doctrines were not much different; its resources for gun-making were neither better nor worse; its muskets were copied from European guns anyway; and American muskets did not break down more often than their foreign counterparts. Nevertheless, America and America alone had resolved to make guns this way.

THE MECHANICAL MENAGERIE

The details of how the United States reached its goal of mass-producing arms has been well-told in scholarly and popular books.[8] At the great risk of oversimplification, it can be said that mechanization of arms-making depended upon three things. One was the almost-obsessive reliance upon gauges to measure parts, the second was the use of specialized machine tools to make the identical part over and over, and the third was a strict regime of quality control.

Gauges are tools used to assure that finished parts have the correct dimensions. They can take all forms, but gauges usually are thin steel plates, a few inches long, with precisely cut curves, notches, insets, and other geometries that are complementary to the shapes of the part they are intended to test. By putting the gauge against the edges of the part, an inspector can see at a glance whether the part does or does not match the gauge or, to use a more technical term, is "within tolerance." Gauges, of course, had long been in use, but what made the American adaptation of them unique was their pervasiveness. Special types of gauges were developed to enable arms inspectors to test more and more dimensions of more and more parts; beyond that, the use of gauges was pushed down to the production line so that machinists could check tolerances in real time. So thorough had the use of gauges become that by the time the Model 1842 musket was put into production at Springfield, the armory was using fifty-six different gauges to test it.[9]

The second thread was the development of new machine tools; that is, tools that operate with mechanical power. Among the most ancient of powered tools was the lathe, which is a machine where the workpiece spins around while a worker uses a cutting tool to turn it into something like a round table leg or stairway baluster. About 1818, the Massachusetts inventor Thomas Blanchard developed an ingenious metal-cutting lathe that could shape gun barrels even when they had asymmetric or angular features. Blanchard then invented an even more astounding "stocking machine" that could carve the highly irregular form of a gun stock out of a rough walnut blank in a matter of minutes. Other "mechanics"—as they were called—invented an array of other machine tools. Richard Lawrence, Frederick Howe, and their coworkers at Robbins & Lawrence developed or improved drills, rifling machines, and metal lathes, to name just a few things. Colt's chief mechanic, Elisha K. Root, pioneered any number of other machines, including new types of drop forges that replaced the time-worn practice of hand-making iron parts with hammers and steel swages. Much of this built upon the innovations of John Hall, who spent years laboring at Harper's Ferry to perfect his eponymous breech-loading rifle. Among his many other achievements, Hall demonstrated that manufacturing something as complicated as a gun required heavier and more stable machine tools, demanded higher cutter speeds, and needed increasingly specialized equipment and tools. Hall also was instrumental in yet another way: he was perhaps the first to recognize that once you decided to make gun parts with machine tools, you would have to redesign the parts so that machine tools could make them.[10]

At the bottom of all of this was the continuous development and adaptation of that most American of machine tools, the milling machine. In a sense, the milling machine was the flip side of the lathe. As just mentioned, in a lathe the workpiece spins rapidly while the artisan forms it with a cutter; with a milling machine, by contrast, the workpiece is fixed to a worktable while the rotating cutting tool (the "mill") imposes its shape upon it. (An easy way to imagine how this happens is to look at the nearest piece of window or floor molding and think how a spinning cutter could turn a flat board into such a curved piece of millwork.) At first, milling machines were used to remove excess iron from forged parts, but toolmakers and inventors then found that they could do almost anything with them. The ornate curves of a lock plate or hammer could quickly be milled by using a cutter shaped in the negative silhouette of the desired form; when done repeatedly with different cutters, all three dimensions of the part could be milled away.

Soon there were adaptations of the milling machine, such as the inventive variant known as the profiling machine. Unlike basic milling machines, the cutters on profiling machines were not fixed in place. Instead, the cutter's spindle was connected by a pantograph to a dummy spindle that acted like a tracer. Adjoining the workpiece was a template, or "former," in the shape of the finished part. When the machinist pushed the dummy spindle around the circumference of the template, the cutting tool moved in lockstep around the edge of the workpiece, creating a duplicate. Ingenious Yankees improved profiling machines so that they had multiple spindles and a lazy-Susan-like worktable that allowed a single machinist to complete one part after another without the need to change tools or repeatedly set up the workpiece.[11] Later, using cams and other means of mechanical logic, some profiling machines became "self-acting" (the term used before the more modern adjective "automatic" came into common parlance).

The glue that held the system together was a regime of constant inspection. Using their sets of gauges, inspectors checked every part to confirm that it had the right dimensions. Parts that failed were scrapped unless they could be reworked. In some cases, the offending machinist was personally charged for the cost of the lost work, including the time and effort of everyone who had previously worked on the part up until the time he had ruined it. This, of course, sounds like a recipe for industrial strife. We can easily imagine heated arguments between workers on the shop floor and the inspectors who were, after all, an arm of management. But there are few recorded instances of this happening; the dispute was between the worker and the gauge itself, and there was little use arguing with a piece of metal.

CHAPTER 4

The Machinery Committee Visits

DESPITE THE FACT THAT BRITAIN WAS THE CRADLE OF THE INDUS-
trial Revolution, its Board of Ordnance was still beholden to the archaic
Birmingham System, and the Birmingham gun-makers used their
political clout to keep it that way. But thirty-five years had passed since
the Napoleonic Wars and, with demand for military arms so low, the
Birmingham trade had withered. In May 1851, just a few weeks before
the Great Exhibition opened, the Board of Ordnance solicited offers to
manufacture a new rifled musket, but the Birmingham gun-makers could
not complete delivery of the initial batch of 23,000 rifles until November
1853, by which time the board had decided to replace it anyway. When
the board asked for bids for the new model rifle—destined to be the
Pattern 1853 Enfield—Birmingham's offers were so high that the board
rejected them all. Even after the board negotiated a better deal, it learned
that the Birmingham armorers could not commit to delivering the new
guns on time.[1]

The six rifles Robbins & Lawrence sent to the Crystal Palace were
proof that there was an alternative. And, as if there were any doubt, Samuel Colt himself soon invaded the English market. In May 1852, on the
heels of his success at the Crystal Palace, Colt won permission from the
British government to lease a building on the River Thames in Pimlico
for construction of an armory. Bringing over machinery and workmen
from Hartford, Colt had his armory up and running in a year. Visits by
Britain's most respected engineers confirmed "the fearless and masterly
manner" in which Colt had implemented the American System. The

celebrated engineer Sir James Nasymth complimented the "quaker-like rigidity of form" found in the American machinery and cautioned Parliament that Britain was "very far behind in carrying out what we know to be good principles."[2] If Samuel Colt could mass-produce guns in England, so too could and should the British.

In October 1853, the Board of Ordnance tasked the Superintendent of Machinery at the Royal Woolwich Arsenal, John Anderson, to look into producing muskets entirely by machines. Anderson reported that although it was possible to do so, the required machinery did not exist in England. Since the Americans seemed to have figured out how to mechanize musket production, the smartest thing to do would be to buy "a simple set of their machinery" and copy it. The board jumped at the idea. It resolved in late 1853 "to introduce the American system, by which arms might be produced much more perfectly, and at a great diminution of cost" and appointed Nasymth to chair a committee to implement it. The board included in its 1854 budget £150,000 to modernize the Royal Small Arms Factory at Enfield and formed a "Committee on the Machinery of the United States" to cross the ocean to buy the necessary equipment.[3] Over the determined opposition of the Birmingham gun trade, Parliament finally approved the idea and sent the Machinery Committee on its way.

The committee arrived in the United States on April 26, 1854, and stayed until August. It covered an impressive amount of ground, visiting all of the major US government arsenals in the Northeast, as well as perhaps a dozen private factories. Among others, the Machinery Committee met with Secretary of War Jefferson Davis, Samuel Colt, Eliphalet Remington, and the most brilliant of the Ordnance Department's officers, Major Alfred Mordecai. Everywhere they went, the group found interesting inventions. At the Boston Navy Yard there was a "peculiar shaped screw auger, for boring hard wood"; in Springfield a "machine for sifting sand"; and in Pittsburgh a curious "[m]achine for boring a square hole."[4]

But the Machinery Committee's main job was to buy machinery to produce the new P1853 rifle-musket. Springfield Armory embodied the American System, and the committee lost no time in going there. They were welcomed and shown around by its proud superintendent, Major

James Wolfe Ripley. Perhaps flattered by the attention, Ripley courteously, "though perhaps not wisely," let the British see whatever they wanted. To prove the perfection of the armory's work, Ripley invited the committee to tear down and then reassemble random parts from ten muskets made in the ten years between 1844 and 1853. Going further, he showed his visitors the newly designed Burton bullet and made recommendations as to machinery, vendors, and just about everything else. Ripley also sent the committee to nearby Chicopee, where the Ames Manufacturing Company made products ranging from swords to machinery, including the intriguing Blanchard lathes that the armory used to carve its gunstocks. The committee soon placed an order with Ames for a suite of fifteen Blanchard machines.[5]

The British relied upon Ripley for more than pointers on where to buy machine tools. They brought with them two prototypes of their P1853 rifle-musket and asked for his thoughts. Ripley and his staff scrutinized the new gun and suggested improvements, including shrinking the size of the stock, redesigning the bayonet blade, and changing the "arrangement of the trigger-plate and trigger-guard" to simplify the gun's manufacture. Perhaps in gratitude for the Americans' helpfulness, the committee's Colonel Burn made a gift of one of the P1853s to the Ordnance Department before he returned to England in August 1854.[6] Two years later, when the United States unveiled its new Springfield Model 1855 rifle-musket, it bore an uncanny similarity to the British gun.

The Machinery Committee was able to see for itself how Americans made guns. The British had, of course, pioneered mechanization, but they had never implemented it on the scale it was practiced in the United States. A major reason was that British workers resisted using machines, partly out of fear for their jobs and partly from artisanal pride.[7] In America, by contrast, workers seemed to welcome anything that relieved tedium of work, if only because it freed them to do more interesting things.

The key to it all was substituting mechanical power for manual work. In the United States, almost everything was driven by water or steam; indeed, that is why the lathes, milling machines, drills, and drop-forges were called "machine tools" in the first place. This power was distributed inside the factory through a system of spinning metal rods known as "line shafts." The line shafts were mounted on brackets in parallel rows in the factory ceiling and held in greased bearings to reduce friction. Every few yards there was a large pulley mounted on the shaft. Heavy leather belts connected these pulleys to matching pulleys on each of the factory's machine tools, passing the rotation of the line shaft to the machinery. A common lubricant for the shaft bearings was animal fat. Because the heat of friction essentially fried the tallow or lard, factories often smelled like kitchens and melted grease dripped down on the factory floor. Everyone wore hats to protect themselves; the factory floor being no less hierarchical than anywhere else, ordinary workers wore flat-brimmed hats and foremen wore bowlers. Machinists also often wore aprons to protect themselves from the metal chips flying from their mills and the spray of the whale oil used as a cutting lubricant.[8] Between the roar of the shafting, the spattering grease, the racket from the machines, the soot from forges, and the haze of oil and iron dust rising from the cutting tools, the factory floor was noisy, dirty, smelly, and, in the summer, insufferably hot.

When finished, the individual gun parts were dropped into bins and taken to the fitting room for final assembly. There, stationed at long tables, usually under the windows for the better light, rows of "fitters" put the guns together. Historically, this had been a wearisome job, with fitters patiently filing away excess iron until, after some trial and error, the parts of the gun all fit. Interchangeability eliminated most of this. Although there might still be some hand-filing or grinding, it now took a fitter only about three minutes to assemble a musket.[9]

Mechanization ineluctably led to the division of labor. With time, the price of machine tools fell—a basic milling machine, for example, cost $300 in 1854—so it often made economic sense to install rows upon rows of drill presses, drop-forges, barrel lathes, or profilers, each machine and worker assigned only one slice of the production process. This specialization of work on the factory floor freed the United States from the needs and demands of skilled gunsmiths. Almost anyone could tend to the machines, and often one worker ran several.[10] In America, the work of making guns no longer was an art—the skill and precision were built into the machines.

ROBBINS & LAWRENCE

After wrapping up its business in Springfield, the Machinery Committee took the train to Hartford. Unable to buy machinery from Samuel Colt—there was none to spare, he said—the group rode a mile up Rifle Avenue to the armory being built to manufacture a new breech-loading gun. This was the soon-to-be-famous Sharps rifle, a single-shot breech loader patented a few years earlier by inventor Christian Sharps.

Born in 1811, Sharps learned his trade at John Hall's Rifle Works and then began working on a gun of his own. Sharps's design was clever, if disarmingly straightforward. It had a steel breech block held in a vertical channel, lowered and raised by a lever, thus exposing and closing the breech of the barrel. The Sharps used prefabricated paper cartridges, which were inserted into the gun's breech. The breech block was shaped so that when it was pushed up to close the breech of the barrel, its sharp edge sheared off the end of the cartridge, thus exposing the gunpowder charge. The gun used a standard percussion lock, although Sharps also patented a complicated, if superfluous, system for automatically dispensing percussion caps. Perhaps because of its simplicity, the Sharps's breech mechanism was exceptionally strong; however, like other early breech loaders, it leaked hot gasses when the powder exploded and it became hard to work as powder residue collected.[11] Nevertheless, the Sharps was probably was the best breech-loading rifle available, and its short-barreled carbine version was especially well-suited for mounted troops.

Christian Sharps had organized his company in 1851, but with no way to manufacture his guns in quantity, he asked Robbins & Lawrence to make 20,000 carbines and rifles for him. The parties had great plans: 5,000 carbines would come from Robbins & Lawrence's shops in Windsor, Vermont, and the rest of the guns from a new state-of-the-art factory Robbins & Lawrence would build for Sharps in Hartford. Already short of funds, Robbins & Lawrence had to borrow from Sharps's company to finance construction of the new plant, which ended up inextricably tying Sharps's fortunes to Robbins & Lawrence. In time, the two firms' finances became so exasperatingly intertwined that it was hard to see where Sharps left off and Robbins & Lawrence began.[12]

Richard Lawrence moved to Hartford to oversee completion of the new armory, and when the Machinery Committee came to visit, he showed them around the plant himself. The British were somewhat overwhelmed by "the beauty and efficiency of the machines." "This factory is only just established," the committee reported, "but it seemed to be conducted on the best manufacturing principles, machinery being applied to every part of the arm."[13] Learning that Robbins & Lawrence itself had made most of the machine tools, the committee quickly made its way north to Windsor.

Robbins & Lawrence was a collection of brick buildings perched on the hillside where Mill Brook tumbled down to the Connecticut River.* The firm was a focal point of the American gun industry; at one point or another, an amazing number of important designers, engineers, and machinists worked there. Robbins & Lawrence had been organized in 1844 when the US government, anticipating war with Mexico, put out a contract for 10,000 Model 1841 percussion rifles. An opportunistic Boston lumber dealer named Samuel Robbins joined forces with Richard Lawrence and they won the contract at $10.90 per rifle, deliverable in three years. The two bought land, built a factory, and began developing the tools they needed. Fortunately, Lawrence was one of the proverbial self-taught Yankee mechanical geniuses who so abounded in those times, and he bought or built the lathes, drills, rifling machinery, and milling machines Robbins & Lawrence needed. Largely thanks to this, the firm finished the contract early, won a follow-on contract for yet another 15,000 rifles, and turned a nice profit. After a disastrous foray into making railroad equipment, the firm hoped to recover its health by reentering the gun business.[14] Indeed, the reason Robbins & Lawrence sent its six M1841 rifles to the Great Exhibition was to drum up business in Europe.

Robbins & Lawrence was exactly what the British had been looking for. Finding that "the great number of milling tools that are required are of endless variety," the Machinery Committee ordered about one hundred milling machines for making lock plates, cutting screws, forming the nipple for the percussion cap, and making the trigger and butt plates. After

---

* The main building survives today as the home of the wonderful American Precision Museum, devoted, fittingly enough, to the history of American machine tools and technology.

this, the committee returned to Chicopee to place an equally large order with Ames for the fixtures, jigs, and gauges to go with the machinery it had just purchased in Windsor. With their work done, budget exhausted, and energy drained, the committee then headed home. Altogether, it had spent over $100,000.[15]

Britain's ready-made armory was shipped to Enfield the following year for installation in a newly built machine shop. The Royal Small Arms Factory was superintended by a British ordnance officer named W. M. H. Dixon, but Dixon relied upon a group of American armorers and machinists to make it work. His chief engineer was the Virginian James H. Burton, whom the Machinery Committee had met when visiting Ames in 1854. Burton had started his career at Harper's Ferry, where he rose to become a foreman at John Hall's machine shop, and then became the acting master armorer of the armory itself until he fell victim to Harper's Ferry's toxic politics. In addition to Burton, Dixon hired a raft of other Americans, including one Oramel Clark to oversee the new Blanchard lathes, a "Mr. Caulnin" to work with the forging shop, W. G. Chamberlain to supervise the barrel shop's milling machines, David Brown from Ames to work as a machinist, and a "Mr. Cadwell" to work in the tool room. Major Alfred Mordecai, visiting Enfield in March 1856, found the armory up and running with "the names of 'Ames,' of Chicopee, Massachusetts, and 'Robbins & Lawrence,' of Windsor, Vermont . . . to be read on most of the machines."[16]

TROUBLE

Robbins & Lawrence's business with Britain, unhappily, sowed the seeds of its demise. Although the inventors, machinists, and mechanics from Windsor went on to populate an entire industry, Robbins & Lawrence itself was gone within a few years.

The new shops at Enfield opened too late to help the British in the Crimean War. Fighting had started even before the Machinery Committee left for the United States, and as the war dragged on, Britain needed more P1853 muskets than the Birmingham trade could provide. Confident that Robbins & Lawrence could fill the gap, British purchasing agents ordered 25,000 guns in March 1855.[17] Unfortunately, the contract had tight deadlines and onerous penalty clauses.

Making a completely new gun required Robbins & Lawrence to invest in machinery and tooling, and the British agreed to advance $100,000 to help it along. Robbins & Lawrence could not turn a profit on a contract for just 25,000 muskets, but it took on the business anyway because of somewhat hollow promises of a large follow-on purchase. There was one problem after another, culminating in a drought in Pennsylvania that silenced the water wheels of the sawmills that were supposed to cut the walnut blanks for the gunstocks. This ended all of Robbins & Lawrence's hopes. The British rescinded the contract and demanded damages of $146,000. Robbins & Lawrence fell into the hands of the British government, which arranged to have it finish the contract and then sold off its assets.[18]

And this was not the only fatal arms contract with the British. About the same time as it ordered the P1853 muskets from Robbins & Lawrence, the Ordnance Board also decided to buy Sharps carbines for the British cavalry. In mid-1855, the board and Sharps signed contracts for 6,000 carbines at £5 apiece. Sharps subcontracted the work to Robbins & Lawrence, but the firm fell behind schedule, delivering only 2,900 carbines before it failed, thus saddling Sharps itself with penalty payments to the British. There were lawsuits. When the dust cleared, Robbins & Lawrence was gone, and the Sharps Rifle Manufacturing Company and the British began a decades-long fight over ownership of the Hartford armory. Richard Lawrence stayed on as Sharps's master armorer and plant superintendent to complete the work, and Christian Sharps left to start another firm. Sharps's assets were purchased in 1875 by a group led by the circus impresario P. T. Barnum, who moved its operations to Bridgeport.[19] (He happened to be the city's mayor.)

CHAPTER 5

The Minié Ball

THE URGENCY WITH WHICH THE COMMITTEE ON THE MACHINERY OF
the United States approached its work was driven by the fact that a revolution in small arms was underway at the same time as a major war was
brewing. The British Ordnance Board was in a hurry to reequip its infantry and, frustrated by the obdurate Birmingham trade, it decided to adopt
American methods. Understanding how all of this came about requires
a quick detour into the world of ballistics. (Readers leery of technical
matters may wish to jump ahead to chapter 6.)

SMOOTHBORE MUSKETS AND BENJAMIN ROBBINS
It was an accepted fact that smoothbore muskets had "almost incredible
inaccuracy." French General Guillaume Piobert calculated that only
one musket cartridge out of 10,000 reached the enemy. Surveying the
sorry history of musketry, British Lieutenant General Sir James Francis
Tennant noted in 1864 that, although the British fired 3.5 million cartridges (and 6,000 cannonballs) at the Battle of Salamanca in 1812, they
inflicted only 8,000 casualties. Similarly, during the Crimean War, the
French fired 25 million rounds but killed no more than 12,500; even a
more forgiving report from the London *Times* concluded that no better
than one bullet in 250 struck with lethal effect. During one engagement in their long-running war against the Xhosa in South Africa, the
British fired 80,000 shots but felled only 25 of the enemy. In its report
to US Secretary of War Jefferson Davis, the Delafield Commission of

1855–1856 concluded that "probably not one shot in a thousand rounds issued to the soldier ever does execution."[1]

This inaccuracy was, in a sense, inevitable: it happened because musket balls intentionally were kept undersized to make it easier to push them down the barrels of muzzle-loading guns. The gap between the musket ball and the musket barrel—called "windage"—allowed the ball to pass even when the barrel was caked with gunpowder residue. This, though, made smoothbore muskets inherently inaccurate. When a soldier fired his gun, the ball ricocheted from one side of the barrel to the other until it bounced off the edge of the gun's muzzle. Balls thus came out of the musket barrel spinning like a doctored baseball, going everywhere but straight. Years later, the American Chief of Ordnance wrote that "the smooth bore musket was not much more efficient as a weapon of accuracy and range than a piece of gas pipe closed at one end." This comported with military tactics of the time, where soldiers fought at ranges no greater than 150 yards. The thinking was that after several quick fusillades the enemy would be in shock and the battlefield so enveloped in gun smoke that there was little point in aiming anyway. Instead, the standard practice was to fire a few volleys, then mount a bayonet charge. As Russian General Alexander Suvarov put it: "The bullet is a fool, but the bayonet is a fine lad."[2]

Muskets' innate inaccuracy was further compounded by the fact that they fired large, heavy, and aerodynamically inefficient lead balls. But there was a reason for this, too. Musket bullets were spherical because cylindrical bullets—which were obviously more efficient aerodynamically than balls—were inherently unstable. After leaving the gun barrel, elongated projectiles began tumbling end-over-end, a problem known as "keyholing" because of the shape of the hole the bullets left in the paper or cloth targets ballisticians used in testing guns. No one really knew exactly why bullets tumbled, but the general thinking was that any projectile would have a tendency to revolve around its shortest axis. Unless there was some way of stabilizing them, elongated bullets would never work.[3] By default, muskets fired balls since balls, being spheres, had no "shortest" axis.

And physics dictated that musket balls should be heavy. Eighteenth-century scientists concluded from Newtonian physics that atmospheric resistance increased as a square to a projectile's velocity. Thus, if a gun-maker tried to double a musket ball's velocity, the forces impeding it would quadruple. But even this turned out to be an under-statement. In experiments he conducted in the 1740s, British mathematician Benjamin Robins found that the accepted formula stopped working when bullets approached a muzzle velocity of 1,100 feet per second. Instead, air resistance suddenly tripled, and even a five-fold increase in the powder charge increased a musket's range by only one-third. Robins astutely noted that the velocity of 1,100 feet per second also happened to be that of the speed of sound, but could not explain what caused the spike in atmospheric resistance.[4] (In fact, he had come upon the perplexing subject of transonic physics.) In any event, it obviously was pointless to try to shoot a cumbersome projectile like a musket ball at a speed—the "muzzle velocity"—much above 1,100 feet per second.

However, there were work-arounds. Even if the speed of sound were the practical ceiling on the muzzle velocity of a musket ball, it was still possible to increase the force of the ball—and thus its deadliness and range—by making it more massive. If a musket used both a larger musket ball and a heavy-enough powder charge, the ball could have sufficient kinetic energy to go a fair distance even if it left the gun's muzzle at sub-sonic speeds. This led gunsmiths to design muskets with barrel calibers—some as big as .80 inch—that are huge by today's standards. However, this still did nothing to improve the gun's accuracy.

RIFLING, RIFLES, AND RIFLEMEN

It had been long known that a projectile could be stabilized by making it spin on its longitudinal axis. Archaeologists have found evidence that the feathers—"fletches"—on arrows were angled long ago to induce spin, and there were crossbows that had spiral channels to make their quarrels rotate. This idea was adapted to firearms by Swiss and German gun-makers who began cutting twisting grooves into the barrels of sporting guns. It was these grooves—and the raised areas called "lands" left behind when the grooves were cut—that made the projectile rapidly spin and turned the gun into a rifle. (Indeed, the term *rifle* comes from the old French verb for scratching or grooving.) In the seventeenth century, German principalities began issuing rifles to their soldiers, and when German immigrants came to America they brought with them an appreciation of the rifled gun. Over time, the original German weapon was adapted to the needs of the frontier and evolved into the famous Pennsylvania and Kentucky rifles. American riflemen, British skirmishers, and Hessian *jäegers* all used rifled arms during the Revolutionary War, with the Colonists earning particular respect for their uncanny marksmanship.[5]

The problem with rifled firearms was that they were difficult to load. In order for a rifled barrel to work, the projectile must be seated firmly against the barrel's indented grooves and raised lands. Originally, loading a rifled musket was a cumbersome process of cramming the lead ball down the barrel and then distending it against the walls of the barrel by pounding it with a mallet and iron ramrod. The Germans and Swiss, having pioneered rifling, came up with a way to speed up the process a little. Benjamin Robins (who, it seems, also was something of an expert when it came to rifling) noted in 1742 that they wrapped the musket ball in a round piece of thin leather or cloth, greased on the bottom. The grease helped the ball slide down the barrel, the patch engaged the grooves and lands, and the patch and grease together helped clean out the barrel with each shot. Although American frontiersmen sometimes claimed credit for this invention, it seems instead that it was one that German immigrants brought over with them.[6]

The utility of the rifle as a weapon for light infantry had been known for years, and by the late eighteenth century, most armies had formations of riflemen to act as skirmishers. In the United States, the Militia Act of 1792 enjoined each militia battalion to have "at least one company of grenadiers, light infantry or riflemen," and as tensions with Britain mounted in the years leading up to the War of 1812, Congress authorized the creation of a special regiment of riflemen. As a result, paralleling the development of the musket for infantry use, there were also guns specifically known as "rifles," such as the British Baker rifle and the American Harper's Ferry M1803. The physics of rifles, though, were different than those of smoothbore muskets. By necessity, rifles had no windage, so their recoil was greater than a musket's. To offset this, they fired a lighter charge of powder, had a smaller caliber and lighter ball, and, usually, had a shorter barrel and heavier construction. In battle, rifles proved their worth, and there were obvious reasons why it would have made sense to issue them more broadly. However, even using greased patches and other expedients, loading a rifled gun still was too time-consuming for front-line soldiers. In 1805, for example, Napoleon banned their use by infantrymen.[7]

The solution to the problem was to invent a projectile that loaded quickly but fit snugly into the barrel's rifling. An answer came from an unexpected quarter. While stationed in South India, one Captain John Norton of the British Thirty-Fourth Regiment studied the blowguns used by natives. They, too, had a problem with sealing the gap between their darts and the walls of the blowgun tube, and they resourcefully solved it by putting a base of lotus pith on the bottom of their darts. When they blew into the tube, air pressure expanded the pith and sealed the gap. Borrowing the idea, Norton designed a "cylindro-conical" bullet in 1823 that had a hollow base, cylindrical body, and pointed nose. The force of the exploding gunpowder pressed the edges of the base into the grooves of the rifling, while the pointed nose increased range. In 1836, London gun-maker William Greener improved Norton's design by inserting a cone-shaped plug in the bullet's base.[8]

This invention not only made rifled guns practicable but also, in the bargain, opened the door for the use of elongated bullets and, thus, smaller barrel calibers. The British Board of Ordnance rejected Greener's bullet as too complicated, but the French saw the promise of the idea. After years of experimentation, they determined that Norton and Greener had been right all along. In 1851, French ordnance officers developed a bullet much like Greener's that had a sheet iron cup in its hollow base. Several ballisticians had a hand in the invention but one, Captain Claude-Etienne Minié, got most of the credit. The invention was soon copied all over the world, with Britain using the Pritchett ball, the United States the Burton ball, the Austrians a bullet designed by the Englishman James Wilkinson, the Russians a version of the Nessler ball, and the French using various designs, including Captain Minié's.* Still most people just called it the Minié ball.[9] The new bullets also helped reduce the fouling of the gun barrel. In the case of the Minié and Burton balls, circumferential grooves known as "cannelures" were set into the bullet's base in hopes of improving the round's ballistic qualities. It is debatable whether the cannelures did any good in this sense, but they were a useful place to put grease, wax, or another lubricant, which softened the caked soot, some of which was expelled with each shot. The British Pritchett ball was smooth-sided, but nonetheless greased with animal fat.†

ENFIELDS AND SPRINGFIELDS

The Minié ball made rifled muskets practicable as a weapon for line infantry. With the Crimean War looming, it was clear that Britain, France, Austria, Russia, and the other European powers would need to rearm. Indeed, even the reactionary Duke of Wellington—who had an almost-emotional devotion to the muzzle-loading Brown Bess—conceded that Britain had better adopt a rifled infantry arm.[10]

The question remained, though, just what this new arm should look like. Britain's first effort was an awkward .702-caliber arm designated

---

* The French already had committed to an earlier system known as the *carabin à tige* and, ironically, ended up behind the times. The *tige* was a design credited to French General Louis-Étienne de Thouvenin. Thouvenin installed a steel pillar or stem—a *"tige"*—at the bottom of the rifle's firing chamber. When a soldier rammed a skirted bullet into the chamber, it hit the *tige* and deformed to meet the rifling. *Tige* guns were adopted by the French army in 1846 and later copied by other countries. The system worked reasonably well, but gunpowder residue accumulated in the firing chamber, the narrow space around the *tige* was difficult to clean, and the *tige* itself sometimes corroded or bent. J. Benton, *Course of Instruction*, 310; A. Mordecai, "1856 Military Commission Report," 202–8; Great Britain, War Office, *Text Book*, 115; "Weapons of War," *Technical Educator*, 65–66.

† Although probably apocryphal, this was often said to have been a cause of the Indian Rebellion of 1857, sometimes called the Sepoy Mutiny. The British East India Company, a quasi-official British enterprise, maintained an army of well-trained native troops commonly known as sepoys. The company issued cartridges to the sepoys that were lubricated with either lard or tallow or both. This grease permeated the cartridge paper, which soldiers were instructed to tear open with their teeth in some circumstances. But lard came from pigs, which the Moslem sepoys believed were unclean, and tallow from cows, which the Hindu soldiers considered sacred. Faced with such sacrilege, the sepoys turned on their officers (C. H. B. Pridham, *Superiority of Fire: A Short History of Rifles and Machine Guns* [London, New York, and Melbourne: Hutchinson's Scientific & Technical Publications, 1945], 14n*; Great Britain, War Office, *Text Book*, 121). After this, the British resorted to beeswax.

as the Pattern 1851 rifle-musket. (Wellington insisted that it be called a "rifle-musket" to dispel any suggestion that infantry of the line were now mere riflemen.)[11] But this was simply a stopgap until the Ordnance Board had time to study the subject. There were any number of variables to test: the length of the barrel; the number, depth, and placement of the rifling grooves; which direction the rifling should twist and whether twist should be constant or "gain" to account for the acceleration of the bullet; the precise shape of the bullet; and, more than anything else, the caliber of the bullet and barrel and the size of the powder charge.

Viscount Henry Hardinge became Master General of the Ordnance in February 1852, and he quickly asked Britain's "most eminent Gunsmiths" to propose a new design to replace the P1851. Such admired names as Purdey, Westley Richards, Wilkinson, and Greener all made submissions, as did George Lovell, the Inspector of Small Arms at Enfield.[12] Extensive testing in mid-1852 demonstrated that Lovell's entry was the most promising, and a new prototype of his gun was made that added features from the other designs. With some more tinkering, a consensus was reached, which became the already-mentioned Pattern 1853 Enfield.

Including its bayonet, the P1853 weighed about nine and a half pounds. It had a thirty-nine-inch barrel rifled with three grooves of diminishing depth with one twist in seventy-eight inches. Its caliber was .577 and, at least initially, its bullet—the Pritchett ball—was .568 caliber and weighed 530 grains. The powder charge was 68 to 70 grains. The gun could be fired two to three times a minute and was capable of reasonably accurate fire up to 800 yards. This was, of course, a quantum leap over the capabilities of the smoothbore musket. Hardinge concluded that the P1853 was "the most deadly weapon ever invented."[13]

The United States did not begin testing Minié rifles until after the British were about done. In 1853 and 1854, Harper's Ferry commandant Benjamin Huger conducted a series of experiments with expanding bullets. He concluded that the Minié ball was preferable to the *tige*, that the bullet designed by Harper's Ferry's James Burton worked better than the Minié ball, and that musket calibers should be reduced. A year or so later, Lieutenant James G. Benton continued trials of different bullets and barrels at Harper's Ferry and Springfield. Benton ran barrels of .54, .60, and .69 caliber through their paces, and he compiled extensive tables detailing the deviation of different bullets fired from different guns under different conditions. Benton evidently also had a Britain Enfield P1853 musket (presumably the prototype recently given to the Ordnance Department by Colonel Burn), which he fired twenty-five times to determine the mean deviation of its Pritchett ball. But there was no testing of the Enfield besides this, nor did Benton (or Huger, for that matter) specifically test a .577- or .58-caliber musket barrel or ball.[14]

It is unclear whether the army's Ordnance Department paid much attention to Huger's or Benton's experiments. On June 26, 1855, possibly even before Benton had submitted his final report, the testing board recommended to Secretary of War Jefferson Davis that the army adopt an arm of .58 caliber having a forty-inch barrel rifled with three grooves of decreasing depth and one twist in six feet. On July 5, Davis endorsed the board's recommendation.

Strangely, even though the Ordnance Department had not rigorously tested it, the United States seems to have somewhat summarily adopted the British arm. The similarities between the Enfield P1853 and the Springfield Model 1855 were too close to miss. They were essentially the same caliber—.577 and .58 inch, respectively—and even this difference was somewhat illusory.[15] The Springfield's barrel was one inch longer than the Enfield's (forty versus thirty-nine inches) and their rifling systems were about the same. Both used three rifling grooves with a right-hand twist, with one twist in seventy-two inches for the Springfield and one in seventy-eight inches for the Enfield. Both had grooves of diminishing depth; the Enfield's began at .014 inch and ended at the muzzle with .004 inch, while the Springfield's went from .015 inch to .005 inch.[16] Although some enthusiastic Americans later claimed that the Enfield P1853 was a copy of the Springfield M1855, the opposite is true.[17] The two guns were siblings, but the Enfield was the firstborn.

"DANGEROUS SPACE"
However the United States Ordnance Department settled upon the M1855 Springfield, it did not make its decision with anything

approaching the British Ordnance Board's thoughtfulness. Ultimately this led to critical differences in how the two countries used and viewed the weapon.

For much of the nineteenth century, a central consideration in designing a rifle was its recoil. People were smaller then (the average Union soldier in the Civil War, for example, was said to weigh about 145 pounds), and repeated firing left a gunner shaken and bruised. Writing in 1858, Alfred Mordecai noted that "the men were in the habit of throwing away part of the powder, because they could not bear the recoil of the piece." Fear of recoil, in fact, was so pervasive that "a soldier grew to expect the gun's blow after a few shots and shrank back in anticipation of the impact," a reaction sufficiently common to be given a name—"flinching."[18]

This ended up determining how much powder should go into each charge and, since ballisticians had agreed that heavier bullets were better, the result was a massive round with a somewhat light powder charge and, therefore, a low muzzle velocity. Gravity required soldiers to fire these bullets in an arcing trajectory to reach distant targets. The ballistics of the Enfield P1853 and the Springfield M1855 were such that a bullet fired at a target 600 yards away would reach a height of 20 feet above the ground before it began to descend, and a round fired at a man 900 yards away would reach an apogee of 50 feet.[19]

A simple way of explaining these ballistics to the common soldier was to talk about the concept of a "dangerous space." The dangerous space was that segment in the bullet's flight where it flew at a height where it could strike an enemy soldier. Because of its parabolic trajectory, the rifle-musket's dangerous space was a short one. As the writer Brett Gibbons has observed, with perfect aim a bullet fired at an enemy estimated to be 600 yards away would graze the top of his head at 565 yards and hit his feet at 635 yards. The bullet would actually hit its target only in the interval between these two distances, making for a dangerous space of just 70 yards. At 900 yards, the dangerous space was only 30 feet, meaning that even a minor error in estimating distance would result in a missed shot. Interestingly, at such distances, the bullet descended 6 feet in its final 10 yards, coming down at an 11-degree angle. "At these ranges," Gibbons wrote, "the bullets were almost literally falling from the sky."[20]

Aiming the gun required a soldier to know exactly how far away his target was. The British thought it was possible to teach this to the average infantryman, and in 1853 they established a School of Musketry at Hythe, England, to create a body of instructors to do just that. Cribbed from the French, Hythe's course of instruction began with ballistics theory and ended with careful training and practice on the firing range. Contests and small prizes encouraged soldiers to excel in musketry and, with time, British troops became very good at it.[21]

Whether by accident or design, all of this led to a change in tactics. It remained difficult, of course, to hit an individual target at long range, but the British concluded that this might be irrelevant. Since infantry columns, cavalry formations, and artillery crews were concentrated to begin with, it was enough to aim deliberately at these large targets and take your chances. When fired in mass volleys, the sheer volume of fire was enough to decimate the enemy. It was perhaps this that celebrated Russian military engineer Eduard Totleben meant when he wrote that Russian artillery, in particular, suffered from "[a] perfect cloud of riflemen" in the Crimean War. Alfred Mordecai, writing about the Crimean War in 1858, remarked upon "the extraordinary means used by the besiegers and the besieged to protect their gunners from rifle shots, which could be fired with sufficient precision to enter an embrasure at 500 or 600 yards."[22]

CHAPTER 6

Breech Loaders, Needle-Guns, and "Patent Arms"

ONE OF THE STRANGER THINGS ABOUT THE DEVELOPMENT OF THE Enfield, Springfield, and other Minié rifles was that it intentionally ignored a much simpler alternative. This was the breech-loading rifle; that is, a rifle that loaded from the back of the barrel instead of the muzzle. Breech loaders were far from new. Many of the very earliest long arms had been breech-loading, and some form of breech-loading rifle already was in use in most places.[1]

The advantages of a breech loader were self-evident. Instead of having to push the bullet down the barrel, a soldier simply opened the breech and inserted a cartridge holding the powder and bullet. Sized to fit the barrel, the bullet immediately engaged the rifling without further complication. There was, of course, the overriding and stubborn issue of how to seal—or "obturate"—the breech to prevent hot gasses from escaping.[2] However, inventors already were at work on the problem, and anyone who was following patent applications could see that there was steady progress toward a solution.

Surprisingly, the bigger objection was that breech loaders were simply too efficient. Because they could be loaded and fired so quickly, breech-loading rifles surely would encourage soldiers to waste ammunition. The US Navy's John Dahlgren argued "masses of men can load and fire with the ordinary muzzle-loading muskets so much more rapidly than is consistent with good aim, as to render the practice a notorious and crying evil, which is frequently commented upon by the best military writers." Future general John Gibbon wrote that soldiers "fire too fast already, and that it is only adding to the evil to give them the means of firing four or five times as fast, by placing breech-loading guns in their hands." Foreign armies agreed. Russian General Nikolai Muraviev maintained that the breech-loading rifle would simply exacerbate soldiers' bad habits. The new guns "would do just the opposite of what was needed. . . . Troops having this weapon would cease to fight [hand-to-hand] and there would never be enough cartridges."[3]

This disdain for the breech loader was all the more remarkable because there was one country—Prussia—that already had issued breech-loading rifles to its infantry. This was the *Zundnadelgewehr*, or "needle-gun," a design credited to the German gunsmith Johann von Dreyse. One observer wrote that the bullet for Dreyse's gun was "peculiar in shape, being ogeval-shaped [*sic*] in front, and terminated in the rear by a hemisphere."[4] (Others noted simply that the bullet looked like an acorn.) The bullet rested in a papier-mâché sabot, which sat above the powder charge within a larger paper cartridge. The primer was put at the base of the sabot, so that ignition of the powder progressed backward, from the bottom of the sabot to the breech of the gun. The primer was ignited by a long needle-shaped firing pin—hence the name "needle-gun"—which penetrated the base of paper cartridge and reached the primer after having traveled through the length of the powder charge. The needle-gun had a bolt-action breech mechanism consisting of a steel cylinder that slid forward and back, and which closed the breech when the soldier pushed the bolt forward and twisted it clockwise until lugs on the bolt engaged with notches on the receiver.* Dreyse's gun could shoot about six times a minute.

Although the Prussians considered the Dreyse gun a military secret, it was not hard to get your hands on one, and both the British and the Americans tested it. No one was much impressed. The British thought that it was "too complicated and delicate" for service use and

---

* The mechanism was called a "bolt action" because it looked and worked on the principle of an ordinary door bolt. Capt. Mervin Drake, "On the Military Breechloaders of Prussia, France, and England," *Royal United Services Institution Journal* 15, no. 64 (1871): 439.

the Americans concluded that it "did not fire well."[5] Because the needle remained in position when the powder charge was ignited, it quickly corroded. Gas leakage also was a problem, since obturation depended upon the easily fouled metal-upon-metal seal between the gun's bolt mechanism and the breech. The needle-gun was something of a curiosity, ordnance officers concluded, obviously inferior to their new rifle-muskets. The *Zundnadelgewehr*'s effectiveness did not became apparent for another ten years, when Prussia unleashed it against Denmark in the Second Schleswig War.

"PATENT ARMS" AND SAMUEL COLT

Meanwhile, there were important things going on in the United States. Gunsmiths were experimenting with new types of guns far more capable than any seen before. Because these designs were often novel, gunsmiths took out patents on their discoveries, both to protect their invention and to stake out turf in the emerging land rush for the intellectual property rights surrounding revolvers, breech-loading guns, and repeating rifles. The weapons logically came to be known as "patent arms."

The new armorers were a different breed from the first generation of gun-makers—Whitney, North, Waters, Starr, and Pomeroy, to name a few—who had entered the gun business in response to the federal government's urging years before. This new group had little interest in musket-making. Freed of dependence upon the bureaucracy of the Ordnance Department, they explored new technologies. In this, they benefited from the fact that the barriers to entering the gun business were now lower. Many machine tools were now commercially available, while steam power allowed factory owners to move closer to major cities and a growing network of railroads simplified logistics.

Samuel Colt embodied, promoted, interfered with, and, for a time, defined this movement. He is credited with the development of the revolver, but it was his efforts to impede competition that probably stimulated innovation more than anything else.

Colt was born in Hartford, Connecticut, in 1814 and died there at forty-seven. Like any normal boy, he enjoyed blowing things up, and after one mishap Colt's father sent fifteen-year-old Samuel off to sea.

Tradition has it that while on shipboard to Calcutta, Colt was intrigued by the mechanics of the ship's capstan and came up with the idea of a handgun with several rotating barrels. He is said to have whittled one with his jackknife on the voyage home. Upon his return, Colt hired gunsmiths to make prototypes of his design, which evolved into a single-barrel gun with a rotating cylinder containing multiple rounds.[6]

Revolvers were an old idea. An "all-steel, 2-shot, revolving, wheel-lock, rifled pistol" was made in Italy in 1521, and there is a revolver in the collection of the Tower of London that was made around 1550. Mark Twain remarked in *Innocents Abroad* that in Paris he found "a revolving pistol several hundred years old which looked strangely like a modern Colt." In 1818, Artemus Wheeler of Boston obtained an American patent on his flintlock revolver, and his associate Elisha Collier obtained a British patent on a revolver using percussion caps in 1821.[7]

It is important to remember that Colt's revolver was a hybrid muzzle-loading and breech-loading weapon. The powder and bullets were loaded from the front into a circle of pocket-like firing chambers drilled into the face of a steel cylinder. At the back of the cylinder was a ring of nipples for percussion caps, each nipple vented to one of the firing chambers. Like other percussion weapons, Colt's revolver fired when the gun's hammer struck the percussion cap. With that, the bullet exited the cylinder, entered the breech of the barrel, and was on its way. Obturation remained an issue, but not a major one. Hot gasses did leak from where the front of the cylinder met the breech of the barrel, but they were an arm's length from the shooter's face and dissipated quickly anyway.

Colt's early models sold poorly, and he was out of business by 1842. But some of his guns were still in circulation, and the legendary Texas Ranger Jack Hayes found that repeating weapons like the Colt were an answer to the tactics used by the Comanche Indians. During the Mexican War, an equally famous Ranger, Captain Samuel Walker, concluded that revolvers were a useful sidearm, and he won approval from a skeptical Ordnance Department to order a thousand of them. Walker had some ideas on how Colt's revolver could be improved and, working with Colt, he developed the famous pistol known as the Colt Walker. Soon, there was an order for yet another thousand.[8]

For a while, Colt subcontracted manufacture of his guns to Thomas Warner, a well-known armorer who had leased Eli Whitney Jr.'s armory to make rifles for the government.[9] But with his business growing, Colt needed a factory of his own. After outgrowing two smaller plants, he began work on a huge complex on the Connecticut River floodplain south of Hartford. Completed in 1855, it consisted of three buildings tied together in a giant H. The largest building was 500 feet long, four stories high, and 60 feet wide. With its two companion structures, the entire plant had 230,000 square feet of floor space and 4,600 running feet of production capacity.[10] Colt christened the complex "Coltsville."

Scarred by earlier business failures, Samuel Colt entrusted his affairs mainly to family members or old friends. Colt's cousin Mathilda, fortunately, was married to Elisha K. Root, considered "one of the ablest mechanics New England has ever produced." Root was the paradigmatic native genius: born on a Massachusetts farm in 1808, he worked in a cotton mill, apprenticed at a machine shop, and then was hired by the Collins Axe Company. At Collins, Root reinvented the way axes were made: he replaced hand-forging with specially shaped rollers; sharpened axes with a shear instead of putting them to a grinding wheel; and invented a new way to temper axe heads. Colt lured Root away from Collins in 1849 with a large salary and free hand in designing and operating the new armory. Root's reputation was such that, by then, he already had turned down the job of master armorer at Springfield.[11]

Root's interest in streamlining production took full form in Hartford. Everything was mechanized: there were hundreds of machines to handle all stages of the manufacturing process. Root developed or improved a dizzying array of equipment, including the crank-driven drop hammer, a multi-spindle profiling machine, a double-turret lathe that allowed a machinist to work on both ends of a part simultaneously, a weight-driven vertical drill press, and a new type of rifling machine.[12] Perhaps more importantly, Root implemented a system akin to the modern production line, where parts flowed continuously through the many stages of manufacture to a final meeting in a fitting room, where Colt's guns and revolvers were assembled.*

For all of Elisha Root's innovations at Coltsville, what probably did as much for Colt as anything else was the amount of support he received, directly and indirectly, from the federal government. Indeed, without it, Colt would not have gotten off the ground. One of his first sales, early on, were fifty revolving rifles he sold to the army in 1838 at the somewhat shocking price of $125 and, as mentioned, he was able to reenter the gun business only after the Army Ordnance Department agreed to order 2,000 of his revolvers.[13]

But more than anything else, Colt's success was due to the amazing breadth of the United States patent he received on February 25, 1836. It gave him exclusive control of such fundamental things as placing percussion caps at the end of the cylinder, the idea of holding the cylinder in place with an arbor anchored to a projection under the barrel, and even "the principle of locking and turning the cylinder." It was nearly impossible for competing revolver-makers to circumvent these claims, a point proven when Colt won an epic patent lawsuit in 1851 against the competing Massachusetts Arms Company. Colt's position was further strengthened in 1849, when the government agreed to extend his patent to 1857.[14]

Colt's patent monopoly ended up having wide-ranging effects. Because no one else could make, use, or sell a single-barrel gun with a revolving multiple-chambered cylinder, the designs of repeating arms took a different direction. Although the convoluted story is too long to be told here, one effort to create a pistol circumventing Colt's patent ended up involving such famed gun designers as Horace Smith, Daniel Wesson,

---

* One thing Root and Colt did not try for or achieve, though, was interchangeability. One reason for this was that revolvers were more intricate than muskets, with many small parts that had to precisely fit together. Largely because of tool wear, the machinery of the time lacked the ability to work such parts to a consistent tolerance, and any attempt to constantly replace and correct tools would have been uneconomical. Instead, the Colt system produced parts that were "uniform"; that is, close enough in shape that they could be hand-filed to their final dimensions and selectively fit. In fact, well into the twentieth century, Colt and other revolver makers continued to rely upon hand-fitting in assembling their guns. R. Howard, "Interchangeable Parts Reexamined," 637 and n. 8, 642–44, 648; D. Hounshell, *American System*, 48; N. Rosenberg, *American System*, 47; J. Rasenberger, *Revolver*, 331.

and Benjamin Tyler Henry and ultimately produced what we now call the Winchester rifle. Another was the notion of bypassing Colt's monopoly on guns with revolving cylinders with a handgun that had a revolving bundle of barrels—the so-called "pepper box" pistol.

JOHN FLOYD

Colt also resorted to outright bribery. Perhaps the worst case was Colt's subornation of Secretary of War John Floyd, who ran the War Department from March 1857 to December 1860. Floyd was notoriously crooked; as historian James McPherson put it, Floyd "presented the biggest target to graft hunters" even in the dismally corrupt administration of President James Buchanan. The opportunity to leverage Floyd's dishonesty was not lost on Samuel Colt. Working through intermediaries, Colt arranged to make large loans to Floyd in return for lucrative orders from the War Department. It was money well spent: in return for bribes measured in tens of thousands of dollars, Colt received $310,816.79 in War Department business in Floyd's first eighteen months on the job alone. In fact, so beholden was Floyd to Colt that when Colt mounted a vigorous lobbying effort in 1858 to resurrect his now-expired revolver patent, Floyd energetically supported the proposal, even though its direct effect would have been to materially increase the price his department paid for revolvers. This was in keeping with Floyd's outspoken advocacy of breech-loading guns, which years later garnered him praise for his foresight. In truth, Colt had high hopes for his revolving rifle and Floyd's promotion of breech loaders now seems less a matter of Floyd's perspicacity than the fact he was taking money from Colt. So exasperated was Congress at Floyd's venality that it passed a law in June 1860 prohibiting the government from purchasing patent arms of any type, a measure it repealed only after Floyd had left office.[15]

SMITH, WESSON, AND SMITH & WESSON

For a while, it looked like no one ever would have a chance in the revolver business. Samuel Colt's patent foreclosed anyone else from making single-barrel revolving arms. Even worse, Colt was known to have enormous influence in Washington—he was not above offering cash to congressmen and senators, and it was not beneath them to accept it—and it was feared that Colt would bribe his way to a second extension when the time came. Fortunately for everybody, Colt's lobbying met serious headwinds, and soon it became apparent that his patent would indeed expire as scheduled on February 25, 1857.[16] With the end of Colt's stranglehold in sight, gunsmiths began working on new revolver designs that otherwise would have been a waste of time.

The famous pair of Horace Smith and Daniel Wesson were two of these. Both grew up in the gun business. Smith's father had worked at the Springfield Armory, and Smith started there when he was sixteen. After eighteen years at Springfield and a brief stint at the Whitney factory, Smith opened his own shop in Norwich, Connecticut. Daniel Wesson was seventeen years younger than Smith. He was born on a Massachusetts farm and then sent off to apprentice for his older brother Edwin, a respected maker of target and sporting rifles. Smith and Wesson probably met around 1851 at the Robbins & Lawrence plant in Vermont. Robbins & Lawrence had taken a contract to manufacture the Jennings repeating rifle, and Smith was sent there to tinker with the gun's design and oversee its production. Similarly, Robbins & Lawrence also had a contract to make a pepper-box pistol for a man named George Leonard, and Leonard hired Wesson to go to Windsor as an inspector of the pistols. Soon, the men formed the first of their several partnerships. For a while, they concentrated on improving the Jennings breech system, a frustrating effort that ended when they sold out to a handful of investors, one of whom was the forceful New Haven clothing manufacturer Oliver F. Winchester. At that, Smith and Wesson dissolved their partnership and each returned to Springfield.[17]

Meanwhile, another gunsmith named Rollin White was at work. White is seen as something of a hapless figure, but in fact was a gifted inventor himself. He had a number of patents to his credit and seems to have worked, if briefly, for Richard Lawrence at the Sharps works in Hartford. In 1855, White patented an improvement to the Sharps gunlock by which the lever that closed the breech also automatically cocked the gun's hammer, and some say that he invented (but did not patent) the Sharps "knife edge" breech block. One way or the other, White became familiar with the paper cartridges Sharps used, which were inserted as a single piece into the breech of Sharps's rifle. White seems to have started thinking whether cartridges like these could be used in a revolver.[18]

White's breakthrough happened when he was working for his older brother, who was an inside contractor at Colt. Using two cast-off revolver cylinders, White machined away the closed end of each and then welded the two halves into a single cylinder. Unlike the original Colt cylinders, the firing chambers of White's new cylinder were now bored completely through; this meant that they could be loaded from the rear of the cylinder instead of the front. White got a patent on April 3, 1855, the main claim being the invention of "[e]xtending the chambers . . . of the rotating cylinder . . . right through the rear of the said cylinder for the purpose of enabling the said chambers to be charged at the rear." At the time, no one—White included—fully grasped the monumental implications of the concept. But as events would soon prove, White now controlled an idea almost as valuable as the revolver itself.[19]

In the course of their work on the abortive Jennings rifle, Horace Smith and Daniel Wesson had come up with a simple metallic cartridge, which they patented on August 8, 1854. Two years later, Wesson made a wooden model of a revolver with bored-through chambers that could use his cartridge. After running a patent search, Wesson was chagrined to find that Rollin White already owned rights to the idea. But White was willing to license these, and so on November 17, Wesson and Smith—now reunited—signed an agreement giving them the exclusive rights to White's invention. As events would prove, this became a windfall for Smith and Wesson and a disappointment for White. In addition to an up-front payment of $500, White was promised a royalty of 25 cents for every pistol sold during the life of the patent. Unwisely, he also agreed to shoulder the expense of defending his patent against infringers. He spent years in court.[20]

Contract in hand, Smith and Wesson opened for business in Springfield in April 1857. Things were slow for a while: Rollin White received only $1 of royalties in 1857. Now, though, the tables were turned. With the advent of metallic cartridges around the corner, Smith & Wesson now had a patent monopoly of their own on cartridge revolvers that Colt could only envy. In fact, when Colt offered to buy White's patent rights in April 1866—when the patent had but three more years to run—Smith & Wesson asked $500,000 for them.[21]

BREECH-LOADING RIFLES

As pivotal as repeating rifles and revolvers were, there was even more inventiveness when it came to breech-loading rifles. Between 1855 and 1860, new designs were patented by Benjamin Joslyn, Edward Maynard, William Montgomery Storm, George Morse, Ebenezer Starr, Edward Lindner, Joseph Rider, and Christian Spencer, just to name a few. The profusion of patent arms during the 1850s was such that it would be impossible to give proper treatment to them all. Most, though, did not survive the Darwinian battle for survival in the coming years, and they are remembered now only by historians and gun collectors.

A case in point is the rifle patented in 1856 by Ambrose Burnside, who was then a major general in the Rhode Island militia. Burnside's gun, like Colt's revolver, was part muzzle loader and part breech loader. It had an unusual metallic cartridge that was shaped like a truncated cone, broadest at the top where the bullet was seated and then tapering away to a narrow flat at the bottom. The rifle's design was simple. The breech of the Burnside was a block of steel with a pocket drilled into it, thus creating a closed-end firing chamber that abutted the rear of the barrel. The block was hinged at the rear so that when a lever was pulled down, the front of the block popped up. The soldier dropped the cone-shaped metallic cartridge bottom-first into the open mouth of the firing chamber, then lifted the lever to snap the breech closed. An exterior hammer and percussion cap ignited the cartridge; as with the Colt revolver, the bullet exited the front of the firing chamber, went into the rear of the barrel, and kept going. A movable device Burnside called a "cone-seat" helped push the spent cartridge out of the firing chamber during reloading, a process simplified by the cartridge's tapered shape.[22]

In August 1854—evidently in response to heavy lobbying by Colt or Sharps—Congress appropriated $90,000 "for the purchase of the best breech loading rifles in the opinion of the Secretary of War . . . after a fair practical test thereof." In the next few years, several ordnance boards tried Burnside's gun and gave it favorable reviews. Burnside thought a profitable contract would be forthcoming, and he borrowed to complete and equip his armory. From here accounts differ. Secretary of War Floyd and his Chief of Ordnance seemed to have gotten cold feet about ordering breech loaders, and decided against placing an order for Burnside's or anyone else's. In Burnside's telling, things were much darker. Floyd let it be known that a kickback of some sort would be needed before a contract would be awarded and, according to Burnside, sent someone to demand a $5,000 bribe, which Burnside refused to pay.[23]

Whatever the truth, Burnside was a ruined man; his creditors took control of his company and he was forced to sell his uniform, epaulettes, and sword to raise enough money to support his wife while he struck westward in search of work. Fortunately, one of Burnside's friends from West Point days, George McClellan, had just resigned his army commission to take the job of chief engineer and vice president of the recently organized Illinois Central Railroad. McClellan gave Burnside a job at the Illinois Central to put him back on his feet. While in Illinois, McClellan (and, presumably, Burnside) came to know the railroad's lawyer, the up-and-coming Abraham Lincoln.[24] A few years later, Lincoln appointed McClellan and, later, Burnside to command the Army of the Potomac, a position where neither succeeded.

Burnside had no further involvement with his eponymous armory. Ironically, the merits of his gun were recognized during the Civil War, when the Ordnance Department ordered thousands of Burnside carbines for the use of the Union cavalry. Burnside, though, received nothing for the use of his invention.

ARMY ORDNANCE

This profusion of new ideas—metallic cartridges, repeating arms, breech-loading rifles—did little to shake ordnance officers' confidence in the rifle-muskets. Pleased with their guns' effectiveness in Crimea and in suppressing various colonial revolts, the British instead focused on improving their tactics and the P1853's ballistics. Austria was manufacturing its rifle-musket, the Lorenz, as fast as it could, and, although still using *tige* rifles, France was as committed to the concept as anyone. Even in America, the hotbed of new gun designs, there was remarkable self-satisfaction with the rifle-musket. Colonel James Ripley spoke for many when he proclaimed in June 1861 that "the U.S. muskets as now made have no superior arms in the world."[25]

CHAPTER 7

John Brown, Harper's Ferry, and the Beginning of War

To some, the opening salvo of the Civil War occurred on October 16, 1859, when a party of twenty-two would-be insurrectionists attacked the United States Armory at Harper's Ferry. Led by the abolitionist John Brown, the group's plan was to seize the guns stored there, distribute them to enslaved Blacks, and ignite a rebellion against the institution of slavery. Brown's raid failed, but it threw kerosene on the smoldering fire of political and sectional differences. Indeed, when Brown was hanged at Charles Town on December 2, Thomas J. ("Stonewall") Jackson, John Wilkes Booth, and the militant secessionist Edmund Ruffin—said to have fired the first shot against Fort Sumter on April 12, 1861—came to watch his execution.

There were layers of symbolism and irony in John Brown's raid. He knew quite a bit about guns and about the federal armories. He had lived in Springfield from 1846 to 1849, operating a wool business while his anger brewed. He then became an enthusiastic combatant in the venomous fighting on the Missouri-Kansas border generally known as Bleeding Kansas, armed with a custom-made Sharps rifle. The year before his raid on Harper's Ferry, Brown had even designed a revolver, and he somehow prevailed upon the armorers at Springfield to make and test a prototype of it for him.[1]

But it was Harper's Ferry that Brown chose to attack. After killing an unarmed free Black man and taking various hostages (including at least four armory employees), Brown and his men were cornered in the armory's firehouse by local militiamen. Immediately, Secretary of War Floyd dispatched a contingent of marines—under the command of then-colonel Robert E. Lee—to Harper's Ferry to suppress the raid and capture Brown. The emissary Lee sent to demand Brown's surrender was a cavalry officer on leave from duty in the Kansas Territory named J. E. B. Stuart who, by chance, recognized Brown from previous acquaintance in Kansas.[2]

NORTH AND SOUTH

The contrast between the Springfield and Harper's Ferry armories was, in miniature, a reflection of differences between the two halves of the country. The Springfield Armory was on a gently sloping plain near a prosperous town in an urbanizing region whose culture prized education, self-reliance, and inventiveness. Harper's Ferry was sandwiched in a tight gorge, prone to flooding and disease, in a slave state controlled by an insular rural aristocracy. With time, Springfield became an incubator of technology while, as Merritt Roe Smith has written, Harper's Ferry, "lodged 'among the rocks and mountains' of an agrarian hinterland," was dominated by a handful of local families who saw the armory "not as an efficient producer of military ordnance but as a convenient pork barrel of jobs, contracts, and political patronage for those who inhabited the inner reaches of the Potomac Valley."[3]

Sentimentally viewing Harper's Ferry as the "Mother Arsenal," a Southern-dominated Congress consistently appropriated more money to Harper's Ferry than to Springfield. The disparity of funding, though, was counterproductive. With less funding, Springfield was forced to become more efficient and innovative, while Harper's Ferry was slow to embrace machine tools and slower yet to require of its workers the punctuality and sobriety required of an industrial organization. In fact, when a new superintendent was appointed in 1829 to instill discipline into the Harper's Ferry workforce, he was assassinated by a disgruntled former workman. Subsequent efforts to restore order had mixed success. In 1841, Colonel Henry Craig started to modernize the plant and impose tighter work rules—albeit his workers went on strike and even complained to President John Tyler that Craig's regulations treated them as "mere machines of labor." Helped by generous congressional appropriations, Craig's successor, Major James Symington, modernized, expanded, and essentially rebuilt Harper's Ferry between 1845 and 1855. But this progress stopped in August 1854, when Congress bowed to politically motivated complaints from armory workers and removed both Springfield and Harper's Ferry from military management. With Symington gone, Harper's Ferry relapsed into its old habits. Things declined so badly that, by 1860, the parts of the muskets made at Harper's Ferry no longer interchanged with those made at Springfield, violating one of the Ordnance Department's founding premises.[4]

Virginia seceded on April 17, 1861, and immediately sent its militia to seize Harper's Ferry's buildings, machinery, tools, stored arms, and unfinished guns. Unable to defend the armory, a detachment of federal recruits led by Lieutenant Roger Jones burned it the next day. The fire destroyed 15,000 arms then in storage and damaged some of the machinery before Southern-sympathizing townspeople suppressed the flames. Saved from the fire, two complete sets of gun-making machinery, countless tools, and tons of raw materials were sent to equip the armory Virginia was building in Richmond. The Ordnance Department in Washington was undoubtedly chagrined at the loss of Harper's Ferry, but one suspects there was a sigh of relief that finally it was gone. There was no serious effort to rebuild it. After the war, Congress ordered that the "lands, tenements, and water privileges" of the Harper's Ferry Armory be auctioned off, and even authorized the Secretary of War to extend credit to the high bidder.[5]

JOHN B. FLOYD AND TRANSFERS OF ARMS

It was oddly fitting that the Secretary of War at the time of Brown's raid was John Floyd. Floyd, like his father before him, had been governor of Virginia, and the commonwealth had longstanding fears of slave revolts. In June 1788, Patrick Henry raised the specter of "an insurrection of slaves" as a reason to reject the proposed US Constitution, which—he maintained—would limit Virginia's ability to call out its militia. Partly to assure that this militia would be suitably armed, Virginia established its own factory in 1798 to produce guns, swords, and bayonets, only to have a literate, enslaved blacksmith named Gabriel Prosser plan a revolt in 1800 whose objectives included seizing the arsenal, occupying the state capitol, and taking then-governor James Monroe hostage. Twelve years later, the elder John Floyd was one of the county magistrates charged with interviewing a slave, now known only as Tom, who had killed his master, learning in the process that there were perhaps twenty or thirty other slaves in the county thinking of doing the same thing. The senior Floyd was elected Virginia's governor in 1830 and happened to be in office in August 1831 when the preacher Nat Turner mounted yet another slave rebellion that killed about sixty whites before it was suppressed by the local militia and detachments of sailors.[6] And now the younger Floyd learned that an overwrought abolitionist, hoping to start yet another insurrection, had attacked his armory.

Although the reaction to John Brown's raid was surprisingly measured elsewhere in the South, in Virginia it verged on hysteria. On December 6, 1859, the Virginia House of Delegates formed a committee to consider "the removal or enslavement of the free negroes of the commonwealth." On January 10, 1860, the Virginia General Assembly took up a bill to appropriate money for the purchase and manufacture of arms and munitions, and it resolved the next day to explore the expediency of appointing commissioners "to visit all the slaveholding states, to urge the establishment of a joint armory for the manufacture to arms and munitions of war." Later that month, the legislature appropriated funds to reopen the state Manufactory of Arms, which became known as the Richmond Armory.[7]

Treachery?

A few weeks after Brown's raid, Floyd ordered Colonel Craig—who was now the Chief of Ordnance—to tabulate just how many muskets and rifles the federal government had. Craig reported that there were 48,862 rifles and 561,400 muskets, but that 90 percent of the muskets were smoothbore guns and only about 5 percent were the new .58 caliber. About 190,000 of the guns, moreover, had been condemned a few years back as obsolete. Almost all of the weapons were stored in arsenals in the

North or West. Even including the guns kept at Harper's Ferry, there were less than 50,000 guns in the War Department's southern facilities.[8]

John Floyd's motives during the next year have long been debated. Superficially Floyd was opposed to his home state's secession, but he certainly sympathized with the South. For whatever reasons, on December 30, 1859, he ordered 115,000 muskets and rifles removed from Massachusetts and New York and shipped to War Department arsenals in Georgia, South Carolina, North Carolina, Alabama, and Louisiana. As the 1860 presidential election drew near, Southern states began asking for arms and Floyd complied. On November 1, 1860, the adjutant-general of the Virginia Militia asked the War Department to send Virginia the quota of arms due its militia for 1861. Two days later, Floyd agreed to sell Virginia 5,000 percussion muskets for $2.50 apiece. In December, Floyd directed that 5,000 altered percussion muskets be sold to Louisiana, again at the going price of $2.50.[9]

Floyd also authorized the outright sale of large numbers of War Department arms to private dealers. On November 22, he accepted a proposal from one A. A. Belknap to purchase, at good prices, "100,000 muskets, and as many more, up to the maximum number, as the service will spare." On November 24, Floyd granted the proposal of the Southern banker and cotton magnate Gazaway Bugg Lamar to buy 10,000 altered percussion muskets from federal arsenals at $2.50 each. Later in the month, Virginia Master Armorer Salmon Adams asked Floyd for permission to copy the machinery, fixtures, and tools from Springfield in order to expedite production of weapons at the newly reopened Richmond Armory. Adams was not a subtle man: "I desire to get all the assistance we can from the national armories before our much-honored and esteemed Secretary of War vacates his office, for I have no hopes of any assistance after a Black Republican takes possession of the War Department." Floyd granted the request. Similarly, Floyd acceded to a December 6 entreaty from the Virginia Adjutant-General to have the Washington Arsenal make "the implements and machinery for manufacturing the Bormann fuse for the State" and to an inquiry from Georgia for advice on the best projectile to use in its rifled cannon and optimum weight and bore of field artillery.[10] Clearly, the South was arming itself.

Growing alarm turned into mob action on December 22, when news leaked that Floyd had ordered the Ordnance Department's Allegheny Arsenal in Pittsburgh to send forty-six large coastal defense cannon to Mississippi and another seventy-eight large guns to Galveston. A near-riot followed, with a company of local Pennsylvania militia threatening to attack the steamer that was standing by to receive the cannon. On Christmas Day, civic leaders implored President Buchanan to counter-mand Floyd's order, a request Buchanan duly forwarded on to Floyd.[11]

By now, though, Floyd was on thin ice. Word of the War Depart-ment's arms sales to Southern states had gotten out, and on December 21, Massachusetts Senator Henry Wilson demanded an accounting. Even worse, a few days later Floyd was implicated in a scandal involving the theft of securities the government held in trust for Indian tribes and then was accused of misuse of War Department funds. Upon learning this, President Buchanan purportedly asked for Floyd's resignation but he preemptively quit, ostensibly in protest against Buchanan's refusal to order the army to evacuate Fort Sumter. Postmaster General Joseph Holt temporarily replaced Floyd and countermanded his unfulfilled orders.[12]

After the Civil War broke out, the North found itself desperately short of arms, and Floyd's transfers and sales of weapons were seen as treason. In fact, none of the guns Floyd ordered sold or transferred were first-class weapons—many were obsolete, if not already condemned, and most were unrifled muskets—and the arms that left Northern armories often were sent to places they genuinely were needed near the nation's frontiers or were put in the depots long maintained for the use of state militias. The fact remained, however, that the North needed these guns and the South now had them. In his *Memoirs*, Ulysses Grant summed up the general feeling: "Floyd, the Secretary of War, scattered the army so that much of it could be captured when hostilities should commence, and distributed the cannon and small arms from Northern arsenals through-out the South so as to be on hand when treason wanted them." Although Floyd had left the cabinet by the end of 1860, "the harm had already been done. The stable door was locked after the horse had been stolen."[13]

If not all of Floyd's decisions were treacherous, any nuanced judgments about them were overtaken by wartime passions, and it did not help matters that Floyd soon became a brigadier general in the Rebel army. But Floyd's misfortunes continued. He was sent west to take command of the vital Fort Donelson on the Cumberland River where his opponent, unfortunately for Floyd, happened to be Ulysses S. Grant. Poor generalship led to the loss of the fort and its 12,000-man garrison on February 16, 1862, but not before Floyd had shucked off his command and, seizing all available vessels, fled to safety with much of his own Virginia brigade. To the furor of the Confederate Congress, Floyd's haste stranded Confederate soldiers on the riverbank even though there had been room in the boats.[14] Jefferson Davis stripped Floyd of command and he died in August 1863, reviled by the North as a traitor and despised by the South as a coward.

Years later, Congress directed the Secretary of War to prepare a compilation of the surviving Civil War reports, orders, documents, letters, and other papers, from the Union and Confederate sides alike. The project was assigned to an exceptionally talented officer named Robert Nicholson Scott, and it resulted in the compilation titled *The War of the Rebellion*. The monumental work took a quarter century to complete and ultimately ran to 128 volumes and tens of thousands of documents. Tellingly, the first one of its 125,000 pages was Colonel Henry Craig's November 12, 1859, report to John Floyd, listing the numbers and types of guns held in Northern armories and arsenals, a menu perhaps of the weapons for Floyd to send south. So far as the official record went, this was where the rebellion started.[15]

CHAPTER 8

New Armies

ABRAHAM LINCOLN WAS INAUGURATED MARCH 4, 1861. THE POLITICS
of awarding cabinet positions were difficult, and Lincoln reluctantly
settled leadership of the War Department on the famously unethical
Pennsylvania politician Simon Cameron. It was a controversial appointment; even Lincoln privately admitted that Cameron's "very name stinks
in the nostrils of the people for his corruption." Cameron turned out
to be a monumentally incompetent manager, but he was no fool. After
the attack on Fort Sumter drove home the fact that the country was at
war, Cameron took steps to shake up the torpid War Department. On
April 22, he startled his staff by ordering the department to stay open
every afternoon until the astonishing hour of five o'clock. That same day,
unhappy to learn that his slow-moving Chief of Ordnance, Henry Craig,
had left the Ordnance Bureau in the care of a junior officer on the pretext
of a minor illness, Cameron forced Craig into retirement on the pretext
that Craig's health was failing.

His replacement was Lieutenant Colonel James W. Ripley, the same
officer who had generously shown Britain's Committee on Machinery
around the Springfield Armory seven years before.[1] Born in Connecticut
in 1794, Ripley had graduated from West Point in 1814 and worked
his through the ranks. His career break came in 1841, when he was
appointed Springfield's superintendent. Ripley commanded the armory
for fourteen years, and it was during his tenure that it finally succeeded
in mass-producing muskets with interchangeable parts.[2] Ripley knew
every machinist, gun designer, and entrepreneur worth knowing in the

arms business and, by the time he stepped down at Springfield, he knew as much about manufacturing firearms as any man alive.

Ripley did things by the book. The armory he saw when he arrived at Springfield was a disorganized place largely run by its workmen. Ripley summarily ended this indiscipline, banning newspapers, tobacco, alcohol, and even anything he considered idle chatter. Finding the armory's expenses excessive, he cut wages and, when workers protested, he closed the armory for retooling and rehired only those workmen pliant enough to be managed. He purchased land to expand the armory, replaced dilapidated buildings, landscaped the armory grounds, and enclosed the facility with the iron fence still evident today. Moving forward, he installed steam engines to free the armory from its overdependence upon waterpower, added machinery, reduced the size of the workforce, and divided the gun-making process into ever-smaller increments. His reforms cut the cost of a musket from $22 or so to about $17 and increased Springfield's annual production from 15,000 to as many as 25,000 muskets. As a biographer later wrote, "Springfield Armory is truly Ripley's monument."[3]

Ripley later became a scapegoat for many of the North's discontents, but in fact he deserves credit for the disaster he averted after he took over the Ordnance Department. The department was historically understaffed, and never more so than now. It had only forty-one officers in 1861, some of whom soon left for field commands or defected to the Confederacy.* This number barely grew in the next two years and, even at the peak of the war, the department numbered but 64 officers and

---

* The greatest loss was Major Alfred Mordecai. Mordecai stood out in many ways, not the least being that he came from an Orthodox Jewish family from North Carolina, entered West Point at fifteen, and graduated first in his class in 1823. Mordecai taught at the academy for two years after his graduation, served in the Corps of Engineers, and joined the Ordnance Corps in 1832. He became the country's foremost expert in ballistics, if not one of its leading engineers. He was given a series of special assignments, perhaps the best known being his appointment in 1855 to the commission headed by Major Richard Delafield to travel through Europe to study the lessons of the Crimean War, which he summarized in an influential report on the state of European weaponry published in 1860. (The third member of the commission was then-captain George McClellan.) Mordecai was widely admired for his intelligence, cultivation, and kindness. To this should be added Mordecai's sense of honor: when the Civil War began, both sides offered him commands but, feeling "he could not draw his sword against the companions of his boyhood, nor would honor and duty permit rebellion against the flag of his country," Mordecai resigned his commission and left the army altogether. G. Cullum, "Alfred Mordecai," *Biographical Register*, vol. 1, 299, 301; James A. Padgett, "The Life of Alfred Mordecai," *North Carolina Historical Review* 22, no. 1 (January 1945): 60–61, 105.

600 enlisted men. The small cadre of officers was expected to manage the Springfield Armory and the department's many depots and arsenals; supervise the production, inspection, distribution, and repair of cannon, equipage, small arms, and accoutrements; test, develop, and improve new weapons; manufacture or buy everything from percussion caps and musket cartridges to shells for siege mortars; and acquire and inspect pistols, sabers, lances, swords, and other weapons that the government did not itself produce.[4] For most of the Civil War, the Ordnance Department was stretched to its breaking point.

THE DEMANDS OF WAR

At the beginning of 1861, the Ordnance Department reported that it had on hand 480,687 rifles and muskets, before deducting the 56,362 that were stored in the department's southern arsenals. Most of the muskets and rifles were the outdated .69 and .54 calibers, respectively, and almost 200,000 of the muskets were previously condemned smoothbore guns. Of the "latest improved arms" of .58 caliber, there were only 22,827 muskets and 12,508 rifles. Fortunately for the Union, the new M1855 rifle-muskets mostly were stored in Springfield; unfortunately, almost all of the M1855 rifles were at Harper's Ferry, where they would soon be destroyed by Lieutenant Jones's troops or captured by the South.[5]

By statute, the authorized strength of the regular army was slightly over 18,000, although the actual number in service was lower. These soldiers were well-equipped, but there were only about 11,000 in active service. The balance of the soldiers the Union needed would have to come from state militias and volunteers. Two days after Fort Sumter fell, Lincoln invoked his statutory authority to call out 75,000 militiamen, each limited by a 1795 law to three months' service. In fact, more than this volunteered, but still it was not enough. When it became clear that the South, too, was raising troops, Lincoln issued a proclamation on May 3 increasing the size of the regular army by 22,714 officers and men and calling into service another 42,034 volunteers to serve for a three-year term. This time, Lincoln did not have a leg to stand on legally, but Congress did not seem to mind and, as the reformist Emory Upton later wrote, "what else could be done?" By June 30, 1861, army returns reported that it had almost 130,000 officers and men present for duty, and probably more. The next day, Simon Cameron wrote to Lincoln that the total force under his command was 310,000, including 80,000 or so volunteers whose three-month term would soon expire.[6]

The fact that the math did not add up was indicative of the War Department's disorganization. In any event, everyone seemed to think that there now were enough men and muskets. On June 8, Ripley had reported to Cameron that "[w]e have supplies of all [arms and equipment] to meet immediate exigencies, except of rifled muskets, and our supply of this arm, smooth-bored, of good and serviceable quality, will for the present meet this deficiency." On July 5, Cameron politely declined an offer of assistance from a group of sympathizers in Geneva, writing, "We have already an army composed of more than 300,000 men, a number greater than we need for the actual crisis."[7]

This certitude came crashing down on July 21, when the half-formed Union army—prematurely thrown into battle because of the impending discharge of the "three-month men"—was routed by an equally jumbled Confederate force at Bull Run. Almost overnight, Congress acceded to Lincoln's request to accept another 500,000 volunteers into service and enacted the necessary enabling legislation. The next week, it increased the size of the regular army by establishing nine regiments of infantry and one each of cavalry and artillery. These soldiers, of course, had to be armed, and on July 31, Congress appropriated $10 million for the purpose.[8] The underlying issue was how an understaffed, overwhelmed Ordnance Department would manage.

As Cameron and Ripley sorted out their problems, they settled upon a multiprong strategy. Right away, the department would buy whatever was available on the domestic market. Meanwhile, Springfield would be expanded as rapidly as possible to mass-produce the improved Model 1860 Springfield .58-caliber rifle-musket. Supplementing Springfield's production, the department would contract with private firms to make muskets, interchangeable with those coming from Springfield. While all this was going on, the government would send someone to Europe to buy arms there.[9] As it turned out, each of these efforts would have lasting consequences.

CHAPTER 9

The North, the South, and the English

NEITHER SIDE WAS PREPARED FOR WAR, AND NOBODY FORESAW ITS colossal scope. The South had no functioning armory worth mentioning. The North was better off, with the federal armory in Springfield and a few state-of-the-art arms plants elsewhere. Yet when the war started in April 1861, even these factories were inadequate for the volume of arms the Union needed.

For both sides the obvious—and only—place to go was Britain and continental Europe. But they approached the matter with fundamental differences. The North had a large industrial base which, once tooled, would produce an immense quantity of war matériel. The South, by contrast, was an agrarian economy and unlikely to become self-sufficient in weapons production. Thus, foreign purchases were a stopgap for the Union and a lifeline for the South. The War Department in Washington believed, optimistically, that there would be no need to import arms after 1862, while the War Department in Richmond knew it would depend upon European weapons as long as the war lasted.

Pervading everything was the fact that England would be the largest exporter of weapons and the English were almost unabashedly pro-Southern. Despite the fact that the United States had longstanding diplomatic ties to the United Kingdom, on May 13, 1861, Queen Victoria issued a proclamation announcing that Britain would remain formally neutral in the Civil War, thus tacitly recognizing the Confederates' right to make war on the United States. The perceptive American scholar Henry Adams arrived in London about then with his father, Charles

Francis Adams, who was the newly appointed American Minister to the United Kingdom. (Henry was his father's private secretary.) Henry Adams found that "no one in England—literally no one—doubted that Jefferson Davis had made or would make a nation, and nearly all were glad of it." No longer a struggling young nation, the United States was now a serious economic competitor, and British Prime Minister Palmerston privately welcomed secession of the Southern states as a fortunate "diminution of a dangerous power." "Every one waited to see Lincoln and his hirelings disappear in one vast *débâcle*. All conceived that the Washington Government would soon crumble."[1]

After the diplomatic incident known as the *Trent* affair, the Queen issued a proclamation on November 29, 1861, banning the export of gunpowder and saltpeter and, five days later, another one stopping exports of arms, ammunition, and military stores. British authorities considered the proclamations meaningless, and they did little to stop exports of armaments to the South. The two proclamations were vacated on February 7, 1862, having been replaced by a new one purporting to bar belligerent warships from using British ports and denying the use of British waters to warships or privateers for "the purpose of obtaining any facilities of warlike equipment." This had no more teeth than its predecessors.[2]

England's textile mills depended on cheap Southern cotton and, despite their lofty condemnations of slavery, the British had gotten rich off of it. And, besides, there were fortunes to be made selling ships, cannon, guns, and war matériel to the Confederates. When the South successfully floated a $15 million issue of cotton-backed bonds through Emile Erlanger & Company of Paris in March 1863, investors included two privy councilors, the private secretary to Prime Minister Palmerston, the editor of the *Times* of London, the son of a Lord Chancellor, eight members of Parliament, and, evidently, future prime minister William H. Gladstone.[3] Clearly, the English ruling class was betting on the South.

CALEB HUSE

The South got off to a quick start. Even before Fort Sumter, the Confederate government's new Chief of Ordnance, Josiah Gorgas, ordered agents overseas to procure weapons and military supplies. Among the

South's buyers was an artillery officer named Caleb Huse who, like Gorgas himself, was Northern-born and West Point–educated. On April 15, Captain Huse was instructed to sail for Europe without delay to purchase everything he could. After making his way surreptitiously to New York, Huse arrived in England in May 1861, where he soon was joined by a second officer, Edward Clifford Anderson.[4]

For the next two years, Huse and Anderson competed with Northern agents to buy as many serviceable arms as possible. P1853 Enfields were the prized guns, but not all "Enfields" were created equal. The ones made at the Royal Small Arms Factory at Enfield were machine-made and interchangeable but, of course, not for sale. There was a private firm called the London Armoury Company that made P1853s of equal quality using American machinery and methods but, for now, its capacity was spoken for by the British government. The Birmingham gun trade had the capacity to manufacture enormous numbers of first-class Enfields, although these still were made artisanally. On the European continent, Liege, Belgium, was the largest center of private gun production and its armorers, still using hand methods, were capable of producing almost any form of firearm, including Enfield knock-offs. The state of Saxony used a gun called a "Dresden rifle," some of which still used the *tige* system, but had the same caliber as the Enfield's. The Hapsburg Empire relied upon the Lorenz .55-caliber rifled musket that sometimes was referred to as the "Austrian Enfield." Sturdy if somewhat rough-looking, the Lorenz could be reamed and re-rifled to take the standard .58 Burton round.[5]

In the beginning, one of the greatest constraints on Huse's mission was a shortage of funds. After a while, though, the South was able to cobble together a system where the Confederate government bought cotton from planters with Confederate dollars and used the cotton as security for loans abroad. As money became more available, Huse began buying enormous numbers of weapons and other goods. In October 1861, the US Consul in London wrote that the South had thousands of Enfields ready for shipment and had "all the armories here at work for them."[6]

In his accounting for purchases in 1862 alone, Huse wrote that he had acquired 131,129 arms, including 70,980 long Enfield rifles, 9,715 short Enfields, 27,000 Austrian rifles, 21,040 British muskets, and

2,020 Brunswick rifles, along with various appurtenances. In addition, Huse exported 129 cannon, along with shells, fuses, carriages, and spare parts, and almost a half-million pounds of gunpowder, over four million cartridges, fifty tons of saltpeter, and ten million percussion caps. After the Confederacy's finances were bolstered by the Erlanger cotton loans in early 1863, Huse signed a contract to take the Amoury Company's entire output. By the end of the war, the Armoury Company had sold Huse between 50,000 and 70,000 first-class Enfields.[7]

THE NORTH

The Union first thought that its inventory of arms on hand, those available in the domestic market, and Springfield's production would meet its needs. This confidence slowly vanished, however. The domestic market, in particular, did not yield much. By year-end 1861, the Ordnance Department had scared up a mishmash of 10,000 sporting guns, outdated smoothbore muskets, obsolete Hall's breech loaders, and old .54-caliber rifles. Even then, the North did not have much enthusiasm for buying guns abroad. When James Ripley recommended in late April 1861 that the department send West Point graduate Daniel Tyler to Europe to buy 100,000 rifles and dozens of rifled cannon, Simon Cameron dismissed the idea and General Winfield Scott thought it was needlessly ambitious. What efforts there were came from individual states that sent agents to negotiate contracts with British armories directly, or Union diplomats who looked around for arms to buy on their own initiative.[8]

But panic set in after Bull Run. However meager the supply of arms in Europe, the North had no choice but to send someone across the Atlantic to do what they could. The man chosen was a fifty-year-old New Yorker named George Lee Schuyler. It would have been impossible to find a man more patrician. He was the grandson of Revolutionary War General Philip Schuyler, heir to great family wealth, and a successful businessman besides. Alexander Hamilton's wife had been a Schuyler, and George himself had married one of Hamilton's granddaughters and, when she died, her sister. His best friend was his cousin—also named Alexander Hamilton—and another cousin, Schuyler Hamilton, was General Winfield Scott's military secretary. Schuyler was a well-known yachtsman (he was one of the original owners of the *America*) and a founder of the New York Yacht Club.[9] Despite his age, he had rallied to the Union cause after the attack on Fort Sumter and had been commissioned a colonel in the New York militia.

Schuyler was duly appointed in late July and sent on his way to England. His mission, though, was snakebitten from the start. The arms inspector the Ordnance Department sent to assist him fell ill and, of course, the easy pickings were gone. Writing from London in mid-August, Schuyler informed Cameron that "no rifled muskets of the Enfield pattern can be procured in England." Worse, "all the private establishments in Birmingham and London are now working for the States of Ohio, Connecticut, and Massachusetts, except for the London Armoury Company, whose manufacture is supposed to go to the rebels." Schuyler was remitted to scavenging for arms. "The market, both here and on the Continent," he lamented, "is flooded with rejected arms of all descriptions."[10]

Schuyler also was bedeviled by Britain's favoritism of the South. Caleb Huse, for instance, boasted of an incident where British authorities helped him evade restrictions on sending a shipload of supplies to Charleston by hinting that he should say they were destined for Australia and put a British captain in nominal command of the vessel he had chartered. But Schuyler's worst nemesis was his own country. Unable to resist the temptation to meddle, various government officers began, in essence, competing with him.[11]

The biggest offender was Simon Cameron himself. On September 4, 1861, for example, a New York cutlery importer named Herman Boker & Co. wrote Cameron to say it controlled over 100,000 rifled muskets "new and in good condition" available for only $18 each. Cameron did not bother to tell Schuyler (or Ripley, for that matter) about the offer, but instead went directly to President Lincoln, who endorsed his approval with the self-serving lawyerly admonition to carry this through "carefully, cautiously, and expeditiously" and to "[a]void conflicts and interference." It turned out, unsurprisingly, that Boker had neither the number nor types of arms it had promised. When Captain Silas Crispin, the Ordnance Department's New York purchasing officer, examined the

61,485 rifled weapons Boker shipped over in early February 1862, he found they were largely worthless.[12] Similarly, in 1861 and early 1862, the War Department made deals directly with well over a dozen arms brokers who were often competing with Schuyler, and each other, for the same pool of available arms. Meanwhile, the American Minister to Belgium, Henry Sanford, had embarked on an arms-buying program of his own. Given a $1 million credit by the US Treasury Department, Sanford bought approximately 56,000 Belgian-made guns, most of which turned out to be either smoothbore muskets or poorly made rifles.[13]

Not surprisingly, this disorganization doomed the effort. "[M]embers of the same national family bid directly against each other," Joseph Holt later wrote. The "government itself employed, directly or indirectly, numerous agents not acting in unison, and often becoming, therefore, competitors of each other." "[T]he practical result," Holt continued, was that "tens of thousands of the refuse arms of Europe are at this moment in our arsenals, and thousands more still to arrive, not one of which will outlast a single campaign, while most of them will never be issued at all, being entirely unfit to be placed in the hands of civilized troops."[14]

Failure, as the saying goes, is an orphan, and official Washington heaped blame on Schuyler. Cameron and Scott were relentless in criticizing Schuyler, and even Ripley accused him of extravagance and incompetence. In fact, Schuyler had done a remarkably good job. He ultimately was able to ship 15,000 Enfield rifles, with bayonets, to New York at the reasonable price of $18.45 each. And Schuyler had some luck on the continent. The Hapsburg Empire, looking to get rid of its aging Lorenz rifles, sold him over 70,000. Many were *tige* weapons, prone to fouling and difficult to clean, but they were rugged and reliable. Elsewhere, Schuyler also found over 27,000 so-called Dresden rifles. These were, again, mostly *tiges*, but at .577 they were the same caliber as the Enfield. In all, Schuyler sent back nearly 127,000 shoulder arms, as well as 10,000 excellent Lefaucheaux revolvers. He later was denounced for buying worthless weapons, but in fact only 10,000 of the guns he bought were unrifled.[15]

However, as an outsider, Schuyler was a convenient scapegoat for the dysfunction of Cameron's War Department. Whether it was the War

Department's unhappiness with the quality of the arms it was receiving or the Ordnance Department's misguided optimism about its own abilities, the Union stopped giving orders for foreign guns in December. Ripley, who resented the involvement of any private party in the Ordnance Department's work, churlishly denied Schuyler compensation commensurate with his military rank, insisting instead that he was simply one of the department's civilian employees, entitled only to a modest per diem for his efforts. Understandably, Schuyler was offended by this treatment, and in his later years seems to have little mention of his service to the Union or his mission to Europe. He returned to New York on the RMS *America* in mid-December, arriving home on Christmas Eve. On the ship's manifest, he gave his occupation simply as "Gentleman."[16]

MARCELLUS HARTLEY

The Union's decision to stop ordering arms from Europe was short-lived. In June 1862, Ripley warned the new Secretary of War, Edwin Stanton, that deliveries of muskets from Springfield and private armories "are not certain and cannot be relied upon." With bureaucratic caution, Ripley went on to suggest that it would be prudent to take measures to increase the supply of arms "to meet any emergency that may arise." This was as close as Ripley could come to admitting that the Union needed to return to Europe to buy weapons. But he did have a candidate in mind, a shrewd New York gun dealer named Marcellus Hartley. After others seconded Hartley's name, Stanton offered him the job. To make sure Hartley had the latitude and authority he needed to succeed, Lincoln made him a brigadier general and the Treasury Department opened a large line of credit for him with Baring Brothers.[17]

Marcellus Hartley had been born in 1827 to a prominent New York family. After working in his father's business, he went to work in the gun department of Francis Tomes & Sons, a firm that dealt in "fancy hardware." By the time he was in his late twenties he was ready to start his own firm, and he went into partnership with two others to form Schuyler, Hartley & Graham (SHG), dealers in luxury items and sporting goods. When the Civil War broke out, SHG jumped into the military gun market.[18]

Hartley sailed to England in July 1862. Despite his military rank and official status, he chose to stay in the background and work through his old firm and other agents. Hartley avoided hiring local clerical help in England because he suspected that gun-makers—he called them "a slippery set"—would sneak a spy into his operations. Instead, he brought over from America his younger brother Isaac (who also happened to be an Episcopal priest) and an SHG employee named Henry Tomes.[19]

As a seasoned businessman, Hartley's instinct was to eliminate the middleman, and so he ignored the countless English and European gun speculators and instead focused his attention on the gun manufacturers themselves. Hartley had no illusions about the ethics of the gun business: he knew gun-makers would try to sell him defective arms, back out of contracts, spread false rumors, and ignore delivery dates if it suited them. In Birmingham, his biggest problem was that the gun-makers had created a cartel—the Birmingham Small Arms Company (BSA)—to give them leverage to fix prices and control the supply of guns. When supplies were tight in late 1861, BSA had demanded unheard-of prices for Enfields, and it still asked too much. Hartley knew that cartels were inherently unstable, though, and so he began to chip away at BSA by buying what he could from gunsmiths who were willing to sell outside of the cartel. The strategy worked. After just a few weeks in England, Hartley wrote Assistant Secretary of War Peter Watson that "[e]verything thus far has worked splendidly."[20]

Hartley's efforts, the blockade, and the Union's buying power combined to erode BSA's position. In November 1862, BSA agreed to sell the War Department 100,000 Enfields at the reasonable price of $16, deliverable at a rate of 7,000 guns a week. This satisfied the North's needs and, of equal importance, preempted Birmingham as a source of guns to the South until mid-1863. Meanwhile, Hartley worked to impede the Confederate agents wherever he could. He began a public relations campaign of sorts, reprinting the speeches of the British liberal John Bright excoriating slavery, and he also provided intelligence to the Union navy about the names and sailing dates of vessels bound for Nassau with Confederate arms. In one well-known incident, Hartley got wind of a large Confederate order for muskets and combed the continent for details.

After learning that the order was being given to the gun-makers in Liege, he promptly traveled there and offered slightly more for the guns. To Hartley's delight, the "unscrupulous manufacturers" quickly agreed and sold him the guns instead.[21]

Hartley stayed in Europe until the end of the year, acquiring over 200,000 arms, half of them Enfields. In his final accounting to Assistant Secretary of War Watson, he disclosed that he had spent about £490,00 buying weapons and supplies in Britain and Europe. Hartley was a conservative spender and a meticulous bookkeeper. In his letter to Watson, he noted that he had an unused credit of £90,000 that would be coming back to the Union treasury, as well as £288 from a banking error he had discovered in his favor.[22]

A decade later, a commission was appointed to handle damages claims American ship owners made against Britain for violating neutrality during the Civil War by building and equipping Confederate commerce raiders. One of Britain's defenses to the claims was that it—and other European powers—had sent far more weapons and war supplies to the North than to the South. According to the British statistics, between 1861 and 1865 the Union had imported over 520,000 muskets and rifles from England alone, not to mention cannon, swords, bayonets, unfinished rifle barrels, saltpeter, percussion caps, ammunition, boots, blankets, and countless other items. And this, of course, is simply the list of the goods that went North. The British did not disclose how much they had shipped to the Confederacy and, after the war, English gun-makers destroyed their records to make sure no one would ever find out.[23]

British exports, of course, were only part of the picture. Altogether, the Union purchased 436,326 Enfields and imported over 650,000 other foreign muskets and rifles during the war. The South bought at least 500,000 guns from England, and enormous numbers beyond that from Belgium, Austria, and Germany. The overall numbers imported by the Confederates is unknown, but the Rebels were never short of weapons, gunpowder, or ammunition. Later in the war, there were reports in the South of "guns being so plentiful that they were allowed to go rusty in open-air dumps."[24]

CHAPTER 10

Tooling Up

A CORNERSTONE OF UNION STRATEGY WAS TO HARNESS THE NORTH'S large industrial base to the war effort. Yet this grated on the Chief of Ordnance. James Ripley had an abiding faith in the Ordnance Department's ability to supply the army from Springfield alone. Experience, he said, showed that arms from private firms cost more than, and were not as good as, the guns the government made itself.[1]

At first, Ripley thought the Union's shortage of arms was a short-term problem that would take care of itself once Springfield's production ramped up. But meanwhile something had to be done to reassure worried field officers, mollify anxious state governors, and appease the profiteers clamoring for government contracts. Ripley knew that few people had any idea just how difficult it was to make a gun, and he knew equally well that most entrepreneurs who entered the arms business would fail. Mass production of arms was capital-intensive and depended upon having the right people and tools. Those clamoring for government contracts, Ripley wrote, almost surely lacked the "requisite machinery, tools, and fixtures for making such arms, and but few who can prepare them in less than one year's time." Still, something had to be done, and Ripley came up with a deceptively straightforward approach. The government would issue four contracts, each for 25,000 Springfield muskets, with a stringent delivery schedule enforced by the threat of forfeiture of the contract.[2] As an inducement to bidders, the government would offer them a "liberal profit" over the $12 it should cost to make the arm. Contractors who met

69

this schedule would not only make money, but also be in the running for future contracts.

The one private armory Ripley had a grudging respect for was Colt, and on July 5, 1861, he awarded it the first contract for 25,000 guns at $20 a stand.[3] On July 11 and 13, Ripley gave identical contracts to Lamson, Goodnow & Yale, Alfred Jenks & Son, and Providence Tool Company. The standard-form contract required the contractors to begin delivering guns within six months, to supply 10,000 within twelve, and to ship the remainder at the rate of 2,000 each month. But Ripley well knew that none of the contractors—with the possible exception of Colt (who had presciently sent an agent to England to buy machinery for rolling musket barrels within ten days of the attack on Fort Sumter)—could live up to that schedule.[4] The Ordnance Department, then, could walk away from the deal at will, freeing the government of any liability and sticking the contractors with factories full of idle machinery and piles of half-finished muskets.

Ripley's self-satisfaction did not last long. After Congress complied with Lincoln's request for 500,000 volunteers on July 22, Simon Cameron directed Ripley to award musket contracts to anyone willing to sign one. On July 26, 1861, Ripley ordered 10,000 .58-caliber Minié rifles from John Ponder of Philadelphia at $18.50 apiece. On July 30, Ripley contracted with E. Remington & Sons to make 10,000 1855 Harper's Ferry rifles at $20, and three days later accepted the proposal of New York's Sarson & Roberts to manufacture 25,000 Springfields at $18.50. On August 31, 1861, Ripley was told to award a 20,000-gun contract to R. H. Gallagher of New York at $20.[5]

And then things picked up. Early in October, the Ordnance Department doubled its orders with Jenks and Lamson and agreed to buy another 20,000 muskets each from R. H. Gallagher of New York and Casper Schubarth of Providence. A month later, three new entrants into the gun business—W. W. Welch, Union Arms, and John Rice—got orders for 79,000 muskets, while the two Rhode Island armories—Providence Tool and Schubarth—had their contracts increased by a total of 55,000 guns. Secretary of War Cameron demanded that still more contracts be issued and, within a few weeks, the department ordered another

580,000 muskets. By the end of 1861, the Ordnance Department had arrangements with twenty-two companies to supply 854,000 Springfield muskets at the staggering price of $46,144,665. As if that were not enough, the department handed out contracts for 185,000 more Springfields in the first ten days of 1862.[6]

PROVIDENCE TOOL COMPANY AND JOHN B. ANTHONY

Many of the companies that won arms contracts gave up, but some stayed with it and became the foundation of the post–Civil War American arms industry. E. Remington & Sons, Providence Tool, the New Haven Arms Company (later renamed Winchester Repeating Arms Company), and other firms that previously had been peripheral to the arms industry were now important parts of it. Similarly, the war kept alive many of the firms that made patent arms—Sharps, Burnside, Joslyn, Merrill, Spencer, Smith & Wesson, and Massachusetts Arms are a few—and spawned others. Particularly in the impending race to adopt breech-loading arms, these firms were critical to the industry's future. Thanks to a lawsuit about a sales commission, we happen to know a remarkable amount of detail about how one of these companies—Providence Tool—fared.

Overlooked today, Fall River, Massachusetts, was one of the country's leading textile manufacturing centers in the nineteenth century. The town is located about twenty miles north of Newport, Rhode Island, on granite bluffs overlooking the tidal estuary known as Mount Hope Bay. The town was built around a small stream called the Quequechan River, whose eight waterfalls tumbled down the bluffs into the bay. Fed by two large, spring-fed ponds, the Quequechan never ran dry, giving Fall River a unique combination of reliable, year-around waterpower and easy communication by sea.

In the first half of the nineteenth century, entrepreneurs with names like Anthony, Borden, Durfee, and Brayton acquired waterpower privileges on the Quequechan and went into in the textile business. One of them, Richard Borden, got rich and, looking beyond Fall River, began to invest in the burgeoning manufacturing sector in nearby Providence. In 1853, Borden took control of the Providence Tool Company which, despite its name, mainly produced prosaic items like nuts and washers.

He soon installed his nephew, John Brayton Anthony, as the company's treasurer. Born in Fall River in 1829, Anthony was a Borden on his mother's side, an Anthony on his father's, and through the Bordens connected to the Braytons and Durfees. He entered the business world at seventeen as a clerk, and at the time Borden made him Providence Tool's treasurer, John Anthony was barely twenty-four.[7]

The outbreak of war in 1861 cut off supplies of cotton and almost wrecked Rhode Island's textile-based economy. With little work in its regular line of business, Providence Tool began looking for new opportunities. In the spring of 1861, George Foster of the neighboring Burnside Rifle Company came to see Anthony about a contract to make "Birmingham" muskets for the Austrian government. Anthony was not particularly interested, especially since Foster estimated that the cost of tools and machinery would be $42,000. Anthony also was troubled by the fact that Foster came with a man named Samuel Norris. Because of Norris's reputation as a somewhat shady character, Anthony declined "having anything to do with any part or lot which Mr. Norris might have in the matter." But the situation was desperate, so when Norris dropped by a month later to see if Providence Tool might want a government contract to manufacture Springfield muskets, Anthony overcame his misgivings. Norris suggested that Providence Tool might be able to get a contract to manufacture 50,000 muskets for the Union at $15 each or 25,000 at $17.[8]

Norris lobbied in Washington for war contracts for himself and anyone else who would pay him. On July 13, 1861, the War Department offered Providence Tool a contract for 25,000 Springfield muskets for $20 a stand. Providence Tool agonized about accepting the contract. Knowing virtually nothing about the arms-making business, Anthony and a few of Providence Tool's directors visited the Springfield Armory, Colt, and Sharps. Sharps superintendent Richard Lawrence introduced the group to his top mechanic, Frederick Howe. Howe, as it turned out, knew volumes about the gun trade: he had been the superintendent at Robbins & Lawrence when it filled the British government's orders for machine tools and Enfield muskets in the 1850s. Howe estimated that the capital investment needed for a Springfield musket contract would be $150,000, not including buildings, shafting, a steam engine, and other incidentals. Howe also guessed that it would cost Providence Tool $12 to make a musket, and that it would be at least a year before any would be ready.[9]

A more daunting requirement was the fact that the muskets must be fully interchangeable with those made at Springfield. For this, Providence Tool would need to base its tooling upon a standardized "pattern" gun from the Ordnance Department or, at least, a full set of the necessary gauges. Yet when the company's officers visited the Springfield Armory, they were told that the armory could not give them a pattern gun to work from, nor spare even a set of gauges. On July 20, Anthony went to Washington to see General Ripley, who flatly told him the same thing.[10]

Ripley nevertheless "desired that we go on, however, with the work and drive it as rapidly as possible, the government being in great need of arms," Anthony remembered. "This was the Monday morning following the battle of Bull Run, and the whole city was in disturbance." In the end, Providence Tool agreed to the contract with many misgivings and some patriotic fervor. Colonel Borden overcame his reservations because there "seemed to be a great call for arms" and he thought Providence Tool could be made whole. Philip Borden testified that Providence Tool accepted the contract because it believed that, after the disaster at Bull Run, the War Department probably would issue further contracts. Former director Edward Pearce was "very doubtful about the adventure, but that so much had been said about it that I thought we had better sign the contract and take the risk of it." One of Providence Tool's founders, Rufus Waterman, testified, "We thought at that time that arms would be wanted on account of the reverses that had happened, and we thought that it would employ a great many men in Providence." Anthony signed the contract on July 24.[11]

If Providence Tool's directors learned anything from their visits to other armories, it was that they would need to hire exceptional talent to have any hope of success. Fortunately, Frederick Howe was looking for a job. Howe was described as "a smooth-faced, well-dressed man, with a restless inventive mind . . . when he finished anything it was thoroughly done." Of the many impressive men who passed through Robbins & Lawrence, Howe probably was the most talented. The son of a Massachusetts blacksmith, he made his way to Robbins & Lawrence as a young man and quickly became factory superintendent, developing a remarkable array of machine tools in the process. Having already manufactured Enfield muskets, Howe was a perfect fit for Providence Tool, and Anthony hired him immediately at a salary of $5,000 and, possibly, a share of the company.[12]

Tooling up for production was an enormous challenge. There were few skilled workers, and the government warned Anthony that it would terminate the contract if he tried to hire away anyone from the Springfield Armory. Such basic machine tools as lathes, milling machines, drill presses, and rifling machines were hard to find, and Howe had to rebuild many of the machines once they did arrive. Tired of waiting, Howe ended up making many of Providence Tool's machine tools himself.[13]

As a new entrant into the gun business, though, Providence Tool had the luxury of adopting the latest technology. The most crucial and costly part of the musket was the barrel, and Anthony and Howe took the calculated risk that the company should invest in the English method of making barrels by using large iron rollers instead of welding them with trip-hammers.[14] This was easier said than done, however, and Providence Tool had difficulty obtaining the machinery and training workmen in how to use it. Howe ordered barrel rolls from Worcester, Massachusetts, but he had to send them back three times before they worked and ruined 2,000 expensive iron skelps in the process.[15]

Shortages and price-gouging were endemic. Providence Tool had to pay a premium for machinery and any skilled workmen it could find. There was not enough iron to make barrels because the Ordnance Department had exhausted the entire supply of the high-quality English "Marshall" iron the rolling process required. And then, of course, there was the underlying challenge of actually manufacturing guns. Howe estimated that there were 535 or 540 different operations in making a musket and no end of the specialized cutters, fixtures, and jigs needed on the factory floor. There was no way to buy these; as Howe remembered, "We had to make tools to make tools with."[16]

But the most serious problem was the Ordnance Department's inability to provide Providence Tool Company with a pattern musket or set of gauges. The pattern arm was indispensable because, in essence, it embodied the contract's specifications. It was the basis for the dozens of gauges armory practice required. Beyond that, it was routinely disassembled so that its parts could be used to help toolmakers sink the dies necessary for forging, design the "formers" used by recessing and profiling machines, and fashion the jigs for precision drilling and filing. As things wore out, it was the pattern gun that was the template for recalibrating gauges and sharpening cutters. Proceeding without a pattern gun was a risky, if not rash, decision. But with no pattern guns to spare, all Ripley could offer was the poor alternative of letting Howe copy Springfield's gauges whenever they were not otherwise in use. Providence Tool rented a room near the armory and set a half-dozen men to work at the painstaking task. As late as July 1862, Providence Tool had not completed the process of making its gauges, and it did not deliver its first musket to the government until late that year.[17]

This, of course, was precisely the trap Ripley had laid for the contractors. Ripley was unbending. He took the position that the private firms had breached their contracts and that the government would accept from them only the arms promised for the future, and not those overdue from the past. In the case of Providence Tool, this meant that it would deliver only about 13,000 under the first contract, instead of the 25,000 contracted for. By July 1862, the company had spent $107,500 for machinery and tools alone, and Anthony expected that number eventually would reach $200,000. These higher expenses and the partial forfeiture of its contract meant that Providence Tool's per-unit cost was now about $18. Anthony calculated that at these levels, his company would lose $145,000 on its contract.[18]

The only way to salvage things was to get a second contract with the Ordnance Department. At this stage, Providence Tool's problems escalated. Other firms were in the same boat, and the decision would be made personally by Secretary of War Cameron. This made Anthony especially reliant upon the influence of Rhode Island's congressional delegation, including its disgracefully corrupt senior senator, James F. Simmons. Even before Providence Tool had accepted the first arms contract, Simmons let it be known that he needed money to outfit an expedition he was organizing to buy cotton in North Carolina and expected a commission of 20 cents per musket on the contract. Anthony tried to sidestep Simmons's demand, until it became apparent that Simmons was in a position to assist—or, worse, block—Providence Tool's efforts to win a second contract. Anthony relented and "loaned" Simmons the $5,000. When examined about the payment, Anthony explained:

> I thought he was in a tight place, and I know I was. . . . I knew perfectly well, from what had transpired, that it was of the greatest importance that Mr. Cameron would not retain his position long, and I was afraid Mr. Simmons would not succeed as well with his successor as he would with Mr. Cameron; therefore, between the two evils I thought I chose the least.

As it turned out, Simmons had little influence on the contract award. Memorably, Cameron was quoted as saying that he selected contractors based on a state's contribution to the war effort: "I am in favor of sending the money where the men come from." News of Simmons's demands for bribes became a national scandal, however, and he resigned to avoid expulsion from the Senate.[19]

But that was not the end of Anthony's headaches. In October 1861, Samuel Norris sued, claiming that he, too, was owed a rich commission—as high as $3 per musket—for his role (such as it was) in getting rifle contracts for Providence Tool. The case was tried to a jury over the course of two weeks in July 1862. Anthony conceded that he had promised Norris some commission, but one far lower than Norris now demanded. Providence Tool's argument was that Norris's demand for a $3-per-musket commission was not credible because the company was making less than $3 per musket anyway. As proof, its lawyers offered extensive evidence of the cost of manufacturing guns and, within that, the impracticality of saving money by subcontracting parts of the musket.

The list of witnesses was impressive. There was a succession of prominent Rhode Island capitalists, and General Ripley, former Secretary of War Cameron, and even the corrupt Senator Simmons gave depositions. The witnesses called to testify about the technical side of musket-making were equally renowned. Besides Frederick Howe, they included Thomas Warner; Barton Jenks of the Philadelphia gun-making firm A. Jenks & Son; the government's principal inspector of contract muskets; and a wide variety of men who worked in armories, inspected guns, or manufactured gun-making machinery.[20] A wealth of detail emerged about wages, prices of machinery and tooling, productivity, government inspection practices, nineteenth-century accounting methods, manufacturing tolerances, and the fine points of gun-making. Few of the witnesses had any perceptible bias, and each testified under oath and was cross-examined at some length.

In the end, the jury returned a verdict in Norris's favor of $13,500. Providence Tool appealed to the Supreme Court, where it was decided as *Tool Company v. Norris* in 1864.[21] The Holt Commission by then had exposed cases of war profiteering by "middle men," and public opinion had turned against anyone suspected of taking advantage of the Union's needs. The Supreme Court overturned Norris's judgment, holding that contracts to pay compensation for "control[ling] the business operations of the Government" were void because they violated public policy.[22] Norris, then, was to get nothing.

Providence Tool finally hit its stride in 1863, when it began to deliver muskets at a rate of 500 a week. The company's gamble on barrel-rolling, in particular, paid off. By mid-1862, Providence Tool was operating its barrel rolls around the clock, and it made enough barrels to sell some to other gun-makers. Beyond efficiency, barrel-rolling also resulted in stronger barrels. Ordnance Department regulations called for barrels to be tested, or "proved," by firing them twice with an overloaded powder charge. Barrels made with traditional welding methods sometimes failed at a rate as high as 10 percent, but Providence Tool found that only about one barrel in a thousand breached.[23]

Providence Tool did indeed get a second contract for 25,000 on November 26, 1861, and then a third on May 1, 1864, for 32,000. It became one of the most efficient armories in the country, reaching production of 1,000 muskets a week. Providence Tool's methods so impressed *Scientific American* that it ran a series of articles about the company in late 1863. The magazine reported that, thanks to Howe, Providence Tool was using machine tools so sophisticated that they were considered trade secrets. This included an "entirely self-acting" rifling machine with an advanced lubrication system that grooved in two barrels at once, and a semiautomatic tapping machine that cut threads into the breeches of six barrels at a time. In the process, Howe also improved or conceived of other machine tools, including the turret lathe and the superbly adaptive universal milling machine.[24]

Providence Tool delivered 27,000 muskets to the War Department in 1863, 30,000 in 1864, and 13,000 in 1865. Altogether, it had shipped 70,000 Springfields before the order went out on April 28, 1865, instructing the Chief of Ordnance to "stop all purchases of arms, ammunition, and materials therefor, and reduce the manufacturing of arms . . . as rapidly as can be done." This stuck the company with 9,000 Springfields no one wanted, which Anthony later disposed of as best he could.[25]

Despite Anthony's earlier worries, the gun business turned out well. Providence Tool's gun sales totaled over $1.435 million, and it turned enough profit to declare $144,000 in dividends to its shareholders in the last two years of the war. In 1864 (wartime tax returns were public documents) John Anthony reported a handsome income of $20,000, not much less than Abraham Lincoln's $25,000.[26]

Holt Commission

Lincoln dismissed Simon Cameron from the War Department in January 1862 as much for his ham-handed political meddling as for his administrative ineptitude. His successor, Edwin Stanton, immediately took steps to resolve the procurement mess Cameron had created. For this, he turned to a seasoned Washington insider, the lawyer Joseph Holt. Holt had much to untangle: Cameron had awarded too many contracts for small arms, given contracts to firms that had no reasonable chance of performing them, agreed to import huge quantities of unserviceable arms, and overpaid for just about everything. For months, Holt plowed through what he could find of Cameron's shambolic purchasing system.

Troubling Stanton was the fact that Cameron had ordered 1,164,000 rifle-muskets for the coming year when the War Department needed no more than 500,000. Many contractors, ignorant of the gun business, were far behind in their deliveries. Yet some had proceeded in good faith and had invested enormous amounts in constructing munitions plants; down the road, the country might well need them. Holt devised a simple legal theory that elegantly fixed the problem: Cameron's entire procurement program had been illegal. Under laws reaching back to 1809, the government could purchase supplies only by competitive bidding, and the War Department's arbitrary handing out of contracts came nowhere close to meeting this requirement. Although there was an exception in cases of emergency, this authorized the government only to buy supplies readily available on the open market; obviously contracts for future deliveries of yet-to-be-made muskets did not qualify. Since almost all of Cameron's contracts violated the 1809 law, the government was free to walk away from all of them.[27]

"The habitual disregard of this law by the War Department," Holt continued, "has been attended by the evil of exorbitant prices." Colt, for example, was selling its Navy revolvers to the government at $22, when it cost but $9 to make them and Colt had recently charged the English government only $12.50. Another result of Cameron's practices was "to call into existence a class of speculators known as 'middle men,' all of whose profits are unwarrantable abstractions from the public treasury."[28] Thus, the government was paying the wrong people too much for arms it did not need and would not get on time.

Armed with this legal power, the Holt Commission proceeded to renegotiate Cameron's contracts. Generally, its approach was to declare forfeit any undelivered arms, but allow the contractor to perform the balance of the contract; extend delivery schedules in return for reduced prices; and, in egregious cases, require the contractor to post a performance bond. Faced with this, many would-be suppliers folded their tents and disappeared. Other times, especially when the contractor had built a state-of-the-art factory and, as Ripley had written a year before, "had prove[d] themselves worthy," Holt was remarkably lenient.[29]

Holt's work had enormous implications. In the end, the government was on the hook for only 643,439 of the muskets Cameron had ordered.[30] Perhaps equally important, it winnowed down the arms industry, reduced competition for resources, and kept the most promising firms in business.

SPRINGFIELD ARMORY

Despite the efforts of the private sector, James Ripley still put his money on Springfield. Even before hostilities began, the armory had tripled its output from a baseline of 800 muskets a month in January 1861 to 2,500 by June. One irritant to Ripley was the fact that the armory had been headed by a civilian since Congress placed management of the national armories under civilian leadership in 1854. In August 1861, Ripley had Congress return control to his department, and he appointed Captain Alexander B. Dyer as Springfield's new manager.[31]

On a crash basis, Dyer enlarged the armory's grounds, expanded its physical plant, and reorganized its operations. By the time he was done, Springfield covered seventy-two acres and was indisputably the largest weapons plant on earth. Dyer increased its workforce from 227 employees to 1,309 in 1862, 2,203 in 1863, and 2,467 in 1864, working double shifts six days a week. Expanding upon existing production methods, Dyer subdivided work into ever-narrower steps: from 113 different occupations in 1860, Springfield had 390 in 1865. Dyer, of course, had the benefit of a nearly unlimited budget and first call on machinery, men, and raw materials and could staff the armory's middle ranks with military men. But his success was mostly due to his relentless management. Despite the grime, soot, and noise produced by its furnaces, forges, grinding wheels, and machinery—and the inherent dangers in proving hundreds of gun barrels daily—the Springfield Armory was remarkably clean and industrial accidents were few.[32] And Springfield did more than manufacture muskets. It was, simultaneously, responsible for the ongoing improvement of the Springfield rifle-musket, assisting almost three-dozen private arms contractors in tooling up for their own production, and once the contractors were underway, providing them with government inspectors.[33]

James Ripley could look with satisfaction at his department's success in growing the Union's weapons output. Almost from a standing start, the North's arms-producing capacity was astonishing. By 1864, Springfield was capable of producing 300,000 rifle-muskets a year, while the private sector was good for another 250,000 rifle-muskets, 100,000 carbines, and 300,000 pistols. At year-end, the Ordnance Department's arsenals held 650,000 Springfields and another 100,000 Enfields, and this was on top of the hundreds of thousands of guns in the hands of troops. Springfield began cutting production in late 1864 because the Union had more new muskets on hand than it would ever use. Indeed, the North "could sometimes afford to use captured rifles to corduroy its roads." As the war entered its last months, Confederate Chief of Ordnance Josiah Gorgas guessed that the North was making 5,000 arms a day, while the South averaged fewer than 100.[34]

CHAPTER 11

The Breech Loader Prevails

By mid-1863, both sides had largely overcome their deficits of arms. The Union had made or purchased 2,057,511 muskets and carbines, issued 1,649,694 to troops, and held another 849,326 in storage. The Confederates seemed equally well equipped. When Confederate General John Pemberton surrendered to Ulysses Grant at Vicksburg on July 4, his 31,600 men handed over 60,000 muskets. "The enemy had generally new arms which had run the blockade," Grant later wrote, much better than the amalgam of Belgian muskets and converted flintlocks his Army of the Tennessee carried. Grant allowed his officers to place their hodge-podge of muskets in the stack of captured arms and replace them with ones taken from Pemberton.[1]

The North and South, it seemed, now were ready to fight a modern war at the long ranges their rifled guns were meant for. This had been the expectation. The American military studied European weapons and tactics closely, and reports had filtered back of Britain's devastating use of the still-crude Pattern 1851 in the Crimean battles of Alma, Balaclava, and Inkerman, often at ranges of several hundred yards. More recently, in the Indian Rebellion of 1857, outnumbered soldiers of the British army and East India Company prevailed against an army of mutinous sepoys in part because of their effective use of their new P1853 Enfield at long range.[2]

At least on paper, these lessons had not been lost on American theorists. In October 1857, Captain Henry Heth was ordered to draw up a riflery manual for training US infantrymen. Heth produced *A*

System of Target Practice, which he admitted was mostly a translation of a recently published French instruction manual. It still was good enough: it remained the army's official musketry manual for twenty years. Heth's *System* was supplemented, if unofficially, in 1859 when another infantry officer, Lieutenant Cadmus Wilcox, published *An Elementary Treatise on Rifles and Rifle Practice*. Wilcox went into the subject in greater technical depth than Heth and emphasized the notions of "dangerous space," high trajectories, and accurate estimations of distance. A soldier "will no longer fire by hazard, but will use his elevating sight." And Wilcox went on to predict that the rifle would transform warfare altogether. "Formerly the position of the enemy could be approached to within 300 yards without experiencing much loss from the fire of his infantry," he wrote. "Now this fire is destructive at 1000 or 1200 yards," Wilcox continued, "and well directed at 600 yards, becomes irresistible." The next year, Captain John Gibbon published his *Artillerist's Manual*. There, Gibbon asserted, "A *cool, well-directed* fire from a body of men armed with the new rifle or rifle musket is sufficient to stop the advance of almost any kind of troops."[3]

But this did not happen. The Civil War was not fought at great distances; instead, soldiers often fought at point-blank range. Analyzing battles in the western theater, the late British military authority Paddy Griffith found that the separation between forces there averaged almost exactly 100 yards. Distances were greater in the east, but even then the average at Cold Harbor and Petersburg was only 186 yards. Historian Earl Hess analyzed dozens of Civil War engagements beginning with Shiloh in April 1862 and ending with Bentonville in March 1865. The majority were fought at ranges under 100 yards, he concluded, and only a few above 200. At Antietam, the shortest range Hess found was 30 yards and the longest 165. At Gettysburg, the ranges were 75 to 200 yards, at Chickamauga 50 to 200, and at Franklin 30 paces to 400 yards. The overall average, he concluded, was just 94 yards.[4]

And Civil War soldiers wasted just as much ammunition as their predecessors. Union Brigadier General John Geary, commanding troops defending Culp's Hill at Gettysburg on July 3, 1863, estimated that his men fired 277,000 rounds against Confederate losses of 1,200 killed and 4,800 wounded, a hit rate of about 3 percent. Overall, Union troops at Gettysburg were issued 5,400,000 rounds and inflicted under 25,000 casualties. Even assuming that only half of the ammunition issued was ever fired, this leads to a casualty rate under 1 percent.[5] The numbers are comparable on the Confederate side. The Confederate Ordnance Department estimated that each of Lee's 75,000 troops at Gettysburg fired about 25 or 26 shots, inflicting 23,000 Union casualties, for a rate of 1.2 percent, and even this assumes that Confederate artillery did not kill or wound a single Northern soldier.[6]

Some of the subsequent disagreements about equipping soldiers with breech-loading arms—at least in the North—comes from this divergence between what the Springfield was capable of and how it actually was used. The main reason for the disparity was that effective use of the rifle-musket required careful training. The French and British, for instance, taught their soldiers the theory behind the weapon, the fundamental need to accurately gauge distances, and the effectiveness of massed volleys of concentrated fire. In the Civil War, neither side made much of an effort. Writing twenty years later, the Chief of Ordnance blamed this inefficiency on the army's failure to provide its soldiers with target practice, as the British had done so successfully in the 1850s. "Prior to the outbreak of the rebellion in 1861, little or nothing had been done in the army towards systematic instruction in rifle practice," he declared. To officers accustomed to the inaccuracy of the smoothbore musket, "the capabilities of the new rifle, as to range and accuracy, was [sic] entirely beyond comprehension."[7]

Whatever the cause, the rifle-musket in the hands of the Civil War soldier did not become the transformative weapon it promised to be. Untrained in the use of their arm at distance, soldiers aimed more or less directly ahead. Because of its heavy bullet and low muzzle velocity, the Springfield's dangerous space at zero elevation was no farther than 200 yards, which may explain why so many Civil War battles were fought within that range. In fact, some experienced observers even suggested that the smoothbore musket might be the better weapon after all. Reporting on the Battle of Fort Donelson in early 1862, Confederate Colonel William Baldwin remarked upon "the efficiency of the smooth-bore musket and ball and buck-shot cartridges" whose "rapid loading and firing proves immensely destructive." Later that year, "[s]o effective was buckshot at short ranges that one New Jersey regiment at Antietam tore apart their buck and ball cartridges to add more buckshot to each charge which they fired." In February 1863, Union Colonel George L. Willard published an essay questioning the efficiency of rifled arms over smooth-bored ones. This agreed with an analysis by anonymous French statisticians in 1861 that concluded that there was little difference in the lethality of rifled versus smoothbore muskets. The confusion of the battlefield made it difficult to aim with any precision, and the fouling of barrels often prevented the bullets from taking the grooves of the rifling anyway.[8]

All of this, of course, was anathema to the ordnance officers who had so carefully studied, tested, and compared Minié rifles the decade before. They were sure that the Springfield was a deadly weapon in the right hands, and the British had shown that organized volley fire from rifle-muskets was devastating. Nevertheless, on the Civil War battlefields, the Springfield's capabilities were rarely tested. All three officers whose prewar monographs about the rifle-musket are mentioned above—John Gibbon, Henry Heth, and Cadmus Wilcox—were generals in the Civil War, and all three happened to be on the field at Gettysburg (Gibbon with the Union, Heth and Wilcox with the Confederacy). There were several points in that struggle where the rifle-musket's range and capabilities might have made a difference to one side or the other, but it did not happen.

BREECH LOADERS

In the chaotic months following the attack on Fort Sumter, the Ordnance Department was besieged by gun-makers, politicians, aspiring war profiteers, and countless interlopers with war-winning ideas or fanciful contraptions. The worst may have been inventors with a breech loader to sell. (One ordnance officer complained in 1857 that the Chief of Ordnance was presented with two new breech loader designs every week.) Compounding this was the meddling of high-ranking officials, not the least of whom were Secretary of War Simon Cameron and even President Lincoln himself. Chief of Ordnance James Ripley did what he could to fend them off. "A great evil now specially prevalent in regard to arms for the military service," he wrote on June 11, 1861, "is the vast variety of the new inventions, each having, of course, its advocates." "This evil can only be stopped by positively refusing to answer any requisitions for or propositions to sell new and untried arms, and steadily adhering to the rule of uniformity of arms for all troops of the same kind, such as cavalry, artillery, and infantry."[9] Adding new models of guns was a recipe for confusion, especially given the jumble of imported weapons the Union already had to deal with. This exposed the greatest of the Ordnance Department's fears: a profusion of different weapons, each demanding unique ammunition. Cartridges were expensive, heavy, fragile, and difficult to transport. Every new arm magnified the department's ammunition problems geometrically.

Breech-loading arms had been around for years. The army issued breech-loading Hall's rifles and carbines to troops in the 1820s, and it had periodically looked into them since. An ordnance board had held firing trials of breech loaders in the fall of 1857, and the next year Congress appropriated $25,000 for breech-loading carbines and another $25,000 to convert "old arms so as to make them breech-loading arms" upon a not-yet-decided design. However impure may have been his motives, even Secretary of War John Floyd extolled the advantages of breech loaders in his annual reports to Congress in 1859 and 1860.[10]

But so far as ordnance officers were concerned, this debate was already over. Breech loaders had been studied, tested, and rejected: they leaked gas at the breech, were complicated and expensive, and usually required special ammunition. By contrast, the Springfield was accurate, powerful, reliable, and simple to use. It had a light recoil and did not use much powder. The heavy Burton ball could penetrate eleven one-inch white pine boards at 200 yards and bring down a man on horseback at 600. To be sure, loading was cumbersome, but the Springfield still was capable of two or three shots a minute, as fast as a soldier's supply of cartridges would last anyway. Thanks to decades of painstaking work, all Springfields had interchangeable parts and, with equal credit to Yankee ingenuity, they could be made cheaply and in remarkable volumes.[11]

But there was one area where breech loaders were tolerated. Army doctrine was that dragoons—a variety of mounted infantry—should carry breech-loading carbines because of the impracticality of using a muzzle loader on horseback. Early in the war, Ripley began placing orders for them. On June 29 he asked the Sharps Rifle Company to ship 3,000 carbines *"in the shortest time possible"* (the italics were Ripley's) and he purchased another 3,000 the next week. This became an open order. Sharps began delivering guns in September and thereafter kept producing them at a rate of about 500 each week until, by June 1865, it had sold the War Department 80,512 carbines and rifles.[12]

In testing before the war, the Burnside breech loader also had performed well, and in mid-July Ripley asked the Burnside Rifle Company for 800 of its carbines. Ripley quickly learned that the company was being reorganized, was still building its factory, and could not ship anything for months. But he let the order stand anyway and, in fits and starts, Burnside began delivering its carbines in October. Apparently thinking that he had done all that he could for now, Ripley turned his attention to other things.[13]

Lobby Leeches and Treasury Thieves

But Ripley underestimated the persistence of gun-makers, the influence of lobbyists, and the near-panic in Washington following Bull Run. Within weeks, he was facing pressure to buy arms of any kind, including breech loaders that were unproven, impractical, and, sometimes, almost nonexistent. As often as not, gun companies bypassed Ripley altogether, taking their proposals directly to Secretary of War Cameron or Assistant Secretary Thomas Scott. This set up a veritable fight to the finish between Ripley and what a Ripley biographer called "the whole crew of lobby leeches, treasury thieves, sham inventors, and charlatan contractors."[14]

One of the first was a proposal in mid-July from Isaac Hartshorn, a Rhode Island rubber magnate who now ran the Burnside Rifle Company. Hartshorn proposed to sell the government nearly a million dollars' worth of breech-loading muskets and carbines. Ripley pointed out to Secretary Cameron that this was pointless, since only days before the company's treasurer had admitted he could make only about 600 guns per month and would not be in full production until January 1862. About the same time, Baltimore gun merchant Thomas Poultney offered to make 25,000 Smith's breech-loading carbines for the government. The Smith's design was fairly conventional as breech loaders went (it broke in the middle like a shotgun) but, unusually, it used a patented cartridge made of rubber. On August 17, 1861, Ripley rejected Poultney's proposal on the grounds that the Smith had never been tested, was expensive, and required the special cartridge. More fundamentally, it simply was not needed, since Ripley already had ordered 17,000 carbines, more than enough for now.[15]

Cameron's notoriously chaotic War Department ignored Ripley's advice. (In fact, Assistant Secretary Scott admitted that he had misplaced the relevant papers.) "The Secretary is desirous to employ all of the eastern establishments on guns," Scott wrote Ripley, directing him to buy the Burnside and Smith guns. "Set the parties to work at once." Hartshorn accordingly got an order for 7,500 Burnside carbines at his asking price of $35, with the entire lot to be delivered by June. Similarly, Ripley ordered 10,000 Smiths with deliveries to be done within the year. Predictably, neither company came anywhere close to meeting its schedule.[16]

This pattern repeated itself until Cameron was forced out of the War Department in January 1862. On September 13, Scott instructed Ripley to buy 5,000 Gallagher carbines and 200,000 of their special cartridges, noting that the sample was "highly approved" and the price attractive. Scott told Ripley on October 24 to buy 600 .54-caliber Merrill carbines, with 60,000 cartridges and 80,000 percussion caps. On November 6, Cameron approved a proposal from a Washington agent to sell the government 400 Linder's carbines and 40,000 cartridges specifically for a single regiment. Two weeks later, it was 10,000 Starr's carbines, after that 10,000 Gibbs, then 1,140 Cosmopolitans, and on Christmas Eve 5,000 more Merrills.[17]

Ripley was right in predicting that these firms would not deliver on time. Of the almost 50,000 carbines Cameron instructed Ripley to purchase in 1861, only about 11,400 had shown up by the following June and some of the contractors—Starr, Gibbs, Merrill, and Cosmopolitan—still had shipped no guns at all. Most persevered, however, and by the war's end the laggards had delivered about 160,000 carbines and other gun-makers—chiefly Sharps and Spencer—had added 222,374 more.

After the war was over, the Ordnance Department calculated that the Union army had used nineteen different American-made breech-loading carbines and eight patterns of breech-loading rifles.[18]

HIRAM BERDAN AND THE SHARPSHOOTERS

Ripley undoubtedly had hoped that carbines would be all that he had to worry about when it came to breech loaders. After all, he had an enormous, and growing, army to equip; an overburdened department; and a job that could only be done with discipline, uniformity, and strict organization. However, no one had imagined a war of this magnitude or scope, and the country's decentralized politics resulted in an entropy that Ripley could not overcome. As the months wore on, demands for breech-loading arms only grew.

As good a place to start as any is the organization of special sharpshooter units in 1861. Early in the war, many were captivated by the thought of special regiments of "sharpshooters." These men, culled from the ranks of the North's crack shots, would harass the Rebels and systematically eliminate their officers.[19] Surely, this could solve everything.

In the North, a promoter of the idea was a thirty-seven-year-old engineer named Hiram Berdan, who happened to be one of the finest rifle shots in the country. Berdan had more than his share of admirers and detractors, and both sides had plenty of evidence. He was a prodigious inventor, albeit chronically accused of stealing ideas from other people. As a young man, Berdan patented a threshing machine, a machine for processing gold ore, a collapsible lifeboat, an inkstand of some sort, and an apparatus for laying undersea cables. He achieved some fame in the late 1850s when he established automated "mechanical bakeries" in five cities to mass-produce bread. Opposition from local bakers impeded Berdan's progress in some places, and his baking plant in Brooklyn was destroyed by fire—possibly arson—right after it opened. Berdan's baking plants in Chicago and Baltimore did better, and he even traveled to Paris in hopes of selling his idea there.[20]

Berdan was one of the countless men aspiring to become a high-ranking officer in the Union army. The regular army, fractured and tradition-bound, had no place for the likes of him, but after Congress authorized the raising of volunteer units, anyone who won official approval to assemble a regiment of volunteers might wake up one day and find himself a colonel. Using his wealth and political connections, Berdan petitioned President Lincoln, Secretary of War Cameron, and anyone else he could find for authorization to form regiments of such sharpshooters. The idea was approved by General Winfield Scott in June 1861.[21]

Berdan's conception of the sharpshooters changed over time, but the essential idea was that a select corps of champion marksmen, armed with their personal target rifles and dressed like hunters, would prowl the margins of the battlefield, picking off targets of opportunity. Reality soon intervened: target rifles were clumsy, the uniforms were too fancy, and there already were well-defined doctrines for deploying skirmishers in advance of the line of battle. Before long, Berdan concluded that sharpshooter tactics required a breech-loading rifle, mainly because the stealthy methods he envisioned required a level of concealment inconsistent with the complications of using a muzzle loader. He looked at both the Sharps rifle and the Colt revolving rifle, evidently preferring the former but willing to take the latter. This involved Berdan in an unpleasant battle with the Ordnance Department, which had its hands full with more pressing matters. Ripley had no quarrel with the Sharps gun, but they were scarce and the army had decided that Sharps's limited production should be directed to making carbines for the cavalry. Colt's revolving rifle was less of a problem, since the Ordnance Department did not like it anyway.[22]

After an intense lobbying effort—which included the intervention of President Lincoln—the Ordnance Department ordered 2,000 Sharps rifles (and 1,000 of the less-desirable Colts) for the sharpshooters in early 1862. Delivery of the Sharps was delayed, and yet another bureaucratic fight ensued when it turned out that Berdan had told the Sharps factory to make unauthorized modifications to the Sharps gun, which the Ordnance Department refused to pay for. However, Berdan's men were pleased with the Sharps when they finally got it.[23] The sharpshooters' use of the Sharps caused many to conclude that the word *sharpshooter* came from this connection with the Sharps rifle, but this is certainly wrong.

The term was in use before Berdan organized his regiments, and Berdan himself used it before his regiments got their Sharps rifles.[24]

Although Berdan's idea was met with great public enthusiasm, his men never quite fit into the North's command structure. Often, they were used as skirmishers, where they fought gallantly and effectively, but suffered such heavy casualties that the sharpshooter companies were decimated by 1863 and broken up in early 1865. Berdan himself, accused of cowardice and malfeasance, left the army because of a claimed medical condition in January 1864 and immediately turned his inventive talents to the arms business.[25]

Nevertheless, the sharpshooters' success with breech loaders was the proof of concept. Besides their better rate of fire, breech loaders allowed soldiers to remain prone or under cover while reloading, protecting them from at least some of the dangers of the battlefield. Gun companies, sensing an opportunity, dispatched salesmen to Union camps, talking up the merits of breech loaders and even selling their rifles to individual soldiers who could afford one.[26]

REPEATING RIFLES

A more difficult subject for Ripley to shunt aside were the intriguing possibilities of repeating rifles. Reaching back to the popularization of the Colt revolver in the 1840s, the advantages of repeaters were easily understood. There were three main repeating rifle designs to choose from during the war.[27] In the end, only one—the Spencer—was ordered or used in significant numbers.

The most curious was the Colt revolving rifle, a generally enlarged version of Colt's famous handguns. The Ordnance Department was wary of it for several reasons. It was expensive ($42 to $45), heavy, "unreliable, prone to get out of order, and even dangerous to the user." It leaked gas at the junction of the cylinder and the barrel and, if the two were misaligned, might spew sharp lead shavings as its bullets left the cylinder and entered the breech of the barrel. More worrisome was the possibility of "chain fire" where the firing of one chamber spread to its neighbors, disastrously igniting all of the ammunition in the cylinder. Although the Ordnance Department sporadically contracted for the Colt revolving rifle when it was pressured to do so, the number it bought (4,612) was small compared to other arms, and it stopped giving Colt orders for them after January 1863.[28]

A second repeater that failed to get much traction was Oliver Winchester's Henry rifle. The Henry was a handsome gun of ingenious design, simple operation, and impressive speed. However, it had a light round, short range, awkward length, and intricate workings. And even if the Ordnance Department had wanted to arm troops with the Henry, Winchester's New Haven Arms Company had difficulty making them in quantity; at best, he could manufacture only 300 a month. Nevertheless, Winchester did his best to interest soldiers in his fast-firing gun. He dispatched salesmen to Union camps and disseminated sensational accounts of its devastating effectiveness.[29] The Ordnance Department did not order very many Henrys (1,731), and only half of these came before the war ended.[30]

The one successful repeater was the Spencer, which was produced as both a carbine and an infantry rifle. It was the invention of Christopher Miner Spencer, who thought it up while working at Colt in the mid-1850s. Spencer got a patent for his gun in March 1860.[31]

A selling point of the Spencer was its strength and simplicity. It had a magazine of seven brass rim-fire metallic cartridges, kept nose-to-tail in a spring-loaded tube in the gun's buttstock. It was a rolling-block gun, so called because its breech block was, in essence, a lever-operated steel disk that pivoted forward and backward. When the lever was dropped, the breech block rolled away from the end of the barrel, and when the lever was raised, the block rolled forward. There was a large slot cut into the top of the breech block, and anchored inside of this slot was a block of steel that Spencer called the "bolt." The bolt was linked to the lever, so when the lever was lowered, the bolt was pulled down, and when the lever was raised, the bolt was pushed up. (Later, springs were added to improve the bolt's operation.) The shape and working of the breech block closed off the magazine until the breech block was rolled all of the way back; with that, the face of the magazine was unobstructed and the magazine's spring pushed a cartridge into a flat at the top of the breech block. When the soldier lifted the lever, the breech block rolled forward and the bolt popped up immediately behind the cartridge. As the breech block completed its forward rotation, the bolt shoved the cartridge into the breech and locked everything in place. The Spencer was fired with a manually cocked external hammer. After firing, the soldier dropped the lever, the breech block rolled back, an extractor pulled the spent cartridge shell out of the barrel, and, as mentioned, a new cartridge came out of the magazine.

Spencer had, for a time, worked in a Connecticut silk mill, where his inventiveness impressed the owners—brothers named Cheney—who became his backers when the time came to commercialize the new rifle. After buying Spencer's patent rights, the Cheneys joined forces with a Boston financier named Warren Fisher to form the Spencer Repeating Rifle Company. Despite its imposing name, the company had no facilities to make guns, and so it leased space at a Boston piano factory, raised a half-million dollars, and set to work building an armory. Fortunately for everybody, Christopher Spencer was one of the great engineers of the era; he became the armory's superintendent and shouldered the task of equipping the armory and overseeing production.[32]

The Cheneys had ties to Connecticut politician Gideon Welles, who became Secretary of the Navy in March 1861. Obligingly, he agreed to test Spencer's repeater at the Washington Navy Yard. The more the navy tested the Spencer, the more they liked it, and soon there was an order for 1,000 guns. Hearing of this, the army began tests of its own, with similar results. Before long, Ripley was asked to give his opinion on both the Spencer and the Henry.[33] Predictably, Ripley disliked both. They needed special ammunition, weighed too much, cost a lot, and were not discernibly better than other breech loaders. Already, Ripley wrote, he now had 73,000 breech-loading guns on order, and there was no need to add a new one to the mix of weapons. It would be just another case of "the multiplication of arms and ammunition of different kinds and patterns, and working on different principles."[34]

But Ripley would lose this battle, too. On December 18, Fisher offered to provide 10,000 Spencer rifles at $40 each, deliverable within twelve months. A week later, an undoubtedly chagrined Ripley agreed to give Fisher a contract on these terms. As Ripley probably suspected, this was an unrealistic delivery schedule, and Fisher quickly fell far behind. Meanwhile, Fisher disclosed that he and his partners, having invested enormous sums in outfitting their plant, were having problems "perfecting the machinery." The entire muddle landed in the Holt Commission's lap, which ultimately declared undelivered guns forfeit and cut the contract to 7,500 guns deliverable at a rate of 1,000 guns per month beginning July 1862. Fisher missed even this deadline by a year.[35]

In the ordinary course of things, this would have been the end of it. By mid-1863, though, Spencer's armory was up and running, capable of making 2,500 guns each week. Looking for business, Spencer began visiting Union camps to show off his rifle. He hit pay dirt during a February 1863 trip to General William Rosecrans's Army of the Cumberland. A lieutenant colonel named John Wilder had persuaded Rosecrans to grant permission to form a brigade of mounted infantry to confront Confederate cavalry, protect supply lines, and exploit the fluidity of the western theater of war. Impressed by the Spencer's firepower, Wilder personally placed an order for 2,000, possibly financed by a loan from his hometown bank back in Indiana. The guns began arriving in May, about the same time Spencer was wrapping up its first contract with the federal government.[36]

Spencer was an indefatigable salesman, and he had yet another lucky break on August 18, when he somehow got a personal audience with Abraham Lincoln. Spencer later recounted:

> After a brief introduction, I took the rifle from its cloth case and handed it to him. Examining it carefully, Mr. Lincoln requested me to take it apart "and show me the inwardness of the thing." The separate parts were soon lain on the table before him. It was the simplicity of the gun which appealed to President Lincoln, and he was greatly impressed with the fact that all that was needed to take it apart was a screw driver. With this implement, he bared the vitals of the gun and replaced them so that the gun was ready to shoot in a few minutes.

Lincoln asked Spencer to return the following afternoon. Then, with his son Robert in tow, he led Spencer and Navy Department clerk Charles

Middleton to the spot where the Washington Monument now stands. (Lincoln sent Robert to ask Edwin Stanton to join them, but Stanton replied that he was too busy.) The target was a board six inches wide and three feet high, with a two-inch black spot on each end. Firing from forty yards away, Lincoln hit the bull's-eye with his second shot and placed the remaining five in a close circle.[37]

In the telling, this meeting between Lincoln and Spencer humbled the obdurate Ordnance Department, vindicated breech loaders, vanquished Ripley, and opened the path to modernization. The truth, though, is less dramatic. In fact, over a month before Lincoln and Spencer's target shooting, Ripley inked a contract with Warren Fisher for 11,000 more carbines. Although Ripley probably still harbored doubts about repeaters, the fact that he handed out this contract so soon after Spencer finished its first one suggests that the Ordnance Department already had made up its mind. Ripley would soon retire, but his successor, George Ramsey, freely gave out more orders for the Spencer. By then the Burnside Arms Company was licensed to make Spencers, too, and on September 30 Ramsey gave Burnside a contract for 12,500 carbines. On December 24, Ramsey offered Fisher a further contract for 34,500 carbines. As if there were any doubt, the following spring Ramsey agreed to take as many carbines as the Spencer and Burnside armories could make. When the dust settled, the department had purchased 94,196 Spencer carbines, 12,471 Spencer rifles, and over 58 million rounds of Spencer ammunition.[38]

OBTURATION, SOLVED

The reason for the large, and increasing, orders of breech loaders was that they had become practical because the nagging problem of obturation had been solved. Breech loaders had been dogged from the beginning by the problem of the superheated gas that escaped from the joint of the breech block and the breech itself. There had been any number of attempts to solve this, from needle-guns to rubber seals to pop-up firing chambers, but none worked very well. However, by the late 1850s it was apparent that the solution would be the metal-cased cartridge.

Drawn from a ductile metal like copper or brass, the cartridge case was, in essence, a tube closed at one end. The metallic case expanded to meet the walls of the firing chamber when the gunpowder exploded, creating a strong, tight seal. After the bullet exited the barrel, the pressure abated and case sprung back to its original shape, which allowed the spent cartridge to be pulled out of the end of the gun barrel. It was a simple and effective fix to a problem that had defied all other solutions. But one challenge remained; namely, how to mass-produce metal cartridge cases to the tolerances breech loaders required. Fortunately, a large copper and brass industry had developed years earlier in west-central Connecticut, and by the mid-nineteenth century firms in Waterbury and other Naugatuck Valley towns had developed an array of machinery for rolling, punching, and drawing copper and brass.[39] A private cartridge industry had emerged in New England and, as the war went on, it was able to supply more and more metallic cartridges for the army's needs.

And this changed everything. The polymath Clarence Dutton was exaggerating a little when he wrote in 1896 that the metallic cartridge was "the greatest military invention since the discovery of gunpowder." But it was true that the breech loader would have continued to struggle without the metallic cartridge; it was the ammunition that made the gun. "Before the metallic cartridge was perfected, breech-loading arms were all of varying degrees of badness; afterwards they were all of varying degrees of goodness," Dutton wrote. Or, as a British ordnance expert put it, "select a good cartridge and the difficulty of finding a good rifle is more than half solved." This, then, heralded the second great revolution in small arms in the nineteenth century. The metallic cartridge opened the door to the practical breech-loading rifle.[40]

THE BREECH LOADER TRIUMPHS

The Ordnance Department was reluctant to let go of the Springfield. The armory was now in full production, spitting them out at an amazing rate and finally enabling the department to put away foreign weapons and realize its mandate for the "uniformity of manufactures of all arms." Abandoning the rifle-musket for the breech loader meant tossing aside all of this progress and retooling everything. And this was, at bottom, the institutional problem: the War Department was simultaneously the nation's largest user of firearms and its largest manufacturer of them. Change of any sort would cascade upward to the narrowly specialized machine tools, jigs, fixtures, cutters, and gauges upon which mass production depended. Like the precisely made Springfield musket itself, the armory was, in essence, a machine that worked only when all of its parts fit neatly together. Changing one meant changing the rest.[41]

Misused as it was in the war, though, the rifle-musket's shortcomings eclipsed its advantages: it had all of the bother of a muzzle loader, but did not seem that much better than the smoothbore muskets it had replaced. However imperfect the breech loaders might be, they were still enough of an improvement to justify change. The army just needed an excuse, and soon there were three.

The first was the somewhat shocking realization that the Springfield was not as soldier-proof as expected. After Gettysburg, Ordnance Department detachments scavenged the battlefield for discarded guns and sent them back for reconditioning. To their surprise,

> [o]f the twenty-seven thousand five hundred and seventy-four muskets collected after the battle, it was found that twenty-four thousand were loaded: twelve thousand contained each two loads, and six thousand (over twenty percent), were charged with from *three* to *ten loads* each.
>
> One musket had in it *twenty-three loads*, each charge being put down in regular order. Oftentimes, the cartridge was loaded without being first broken, and in many instances it was inserted, the ball down first.

We can debate the fine points of this, but the overall message was clear. In the confusion and terror of battle, the complicated routine of handling a muzzle loader was beyond what many soldiers could manage. In an evident dig at the army, Navy Secretary Gideon Wells wondered the following year how venerated military experts could have missed "this inherent and certainly mortifying defect," and cited it as further evidence of the need for the navy, at least, to abandon muzzle loaders. It became hard to defend muzzle loaders; however frightened a soldier might be, it was almost impossible to misload a breech loader.[42]

The second was firepower. Breech loaders were undeniably deadly. Speaking after the war, a Confederate soldier who faced the sharpshooters at Petersburg remembered how dangerous the Sharps was. Slightly larger than the caliber of the barrel, the Sharps's bullets were "forced" through the barrel and traveled at supersonic speeds. "[I]f it was a breech-loader, the bullet got to you before the report . . . you can just bet your boots that we were mighty careful how we got in their way." With its higher muzzle velocity, the Sharps had a flatter trajectory and better accuracy than a Springfield; there were instances of Rebel soldiers being killed by Sharps-armed snipers a half mile away. And the rate of fire was lethal, too. In the close-quarter fight at the cornfield at Antietam, the 2nd US Sharpshooters were thought to have inflicted at least 225 Confederate casualties, if at a high cost to themselves. In his exhaustive treatise on Civil War regimental losses, Lieutenant Colonel William Fox concluded that Berdan's sharpshooters "undoubtedly killed more men than another other regiment in the army." Similarly, the Union decision to arm mounted troops with breech loaders had led to new tactics exploiting this firepower. Colonel John Wilder's "Lightning Brigade" had well-publicized successes in the western theater, particularly in its daring seizure of Hoover's Gap in June 1863 and in resisting Confederate advances that September in the Battle of Chickamauga. Wilder himself wrote in January 1864 that he "could enumerate at least thirty fights in which the 'Spencer Rifle' has triumphed over other arms in such apparently overwhelming numbers as to appear almost incredible." Although some of these testimonials must be taken with a grain of salt, there were many accounts of small numbers of Northern troops overwhelming Southern troops with their firepower and of Confederate officers thinking they faced a regiment of men when in fact it might be only a company.[43]

Finally, the breech loader replaced the rifle-musket because soldiers demanded it. "From the first day that soldiers saw the new breech-loading and repeating arms, they would do anything to get one of them," the late historian Carl Davis wrote. "They lied to their commanders, the Ordnance Bureau, the Secretary of War and even to the President to get them. Men who were normally honest would steal one at the first oppor-tunity."[44] Soldiers felt safer with breech loaders and repeaters, and it was pointless to continue debating the point.

And one of the main objections to breech loaders and repeating rifles—the waste of ammunition—sort of went away on its own. In 1865, ordnance officer Theodore Laidley thoughtfully acknowledged that "there is a vast deal of ammunition thrown away uselessly," but he went on to ask:

> But why lay such special stress on this waste of ammunition? In war, of what is there not a great waste? A waste of men, of arms, of ammu-nition, of supplies of all kinds; so that it may be properly designated as in itself a great waste.
>
> Increase the accuracy of fire to its utmost possible extent, but let it not be pretended that it is not desirable to deliver a greater number of shots in a given time than the enemy.

Rifle fire did not have to inflict wounds to do its job: it intimidated the enemy, formed the battlefield, and was effective precisely because of its volume. "This is one of the fallacies that belong to the past," Laidley wrote. Firepower was an end in itself.[45]

AFTERMATH

Edwin Stanton forced James Ripley into retirement in mid-September 1863, ostensibly because of his age. If overdue, it also was irrelevant. By now, the federal government was buying as many Joslyn, Maynard, Merrill, Sharps, Smith, Spencer, Gallagher, and Warner breech loaders—not to mention untold numbers of revolvers—as it could get. From the standpoint of small arms, the war was becoming increasingly one-sided. The South did not have the ability to manufacture breech loaders, nor effectively used captured ones because of ammunition shortages. And although Britain, France, and other countries were experimenting with breech loaders, they had none to export.[46]

When it came, the triumph of the breech loader was anticlimactic. On December 5, 1864, Dyer announced it in a brief memorandum to

Secretary of War Stanton: "The experience of the war has shown that breech-loading arms are greatly superior to muzzle loaders for infantry as well as for cavalry, and that measures should immediately be taken to substitute a suitable breech-loading musket in place of the rifle musket."[47] Boards were to be convened and trials conducted, and the Ordnance Department would proceed down the long path to choosing a new infantry arm and retooling the Springfield Armory to make it.

Lee surrendered four months later, and soon the order went out to stop wartime activities. The Ordnance Department terminated its contracts with those private armories that were still making Springfields, usually agreeing to take some of the work in progress but nevertheless leaving the companies with thousands of unwanted, obsolete guns. By then, the government had in storage almost a million serviceable Springfields and a half-million foreign and captured arms.[48]

It took the Ordnance Department some time to tabulate exactly how many guns it had made or bought during the war years, and so it was not until October 1866 that it had a final tally. The numbers were somewhat amazing. Between January 1, 1861, and June 30, 1866, the department had made 801,997 Springfields and bought another 670,617. In addition, it had purchased 436,326 Enfields and over 735,000 other foreign muskets and rifles. The department also had ordered more than 400,000 breech-loading rifles and carbines, although many were not delivered until after the war was over. The numbers reflected the somewhat haphazard methods the Union had used to assemble this arsenal. During the war, the North had used "79 different models of rifles and muskets, 23 different models of carbines, and 19 models of pistols and revolvers."[49]

CHAPTER 12

Center-Fire

In 1866, a fifty-three-year-old job-seeker stopped at the door of a sporting goods store at 19 Maiden Lane in downtown Manhattan. Turned away, he headed back to the train station. When the store's owner learned of it, he ordered a runner to chase down the man and, when that failed, sent a telegram imploring him to return. The man at the door was none other than Alfred C. Hobbs, the locksmith who had so upended Victorian self-satisfaction at the Great Exhibition fifteen years earlier. He was now back in the United States, managing the sewing machine factory his friend Elias Howe had built in Bridgeport. Howe's meddling had come to annoy Hobbs, and he wondered if there might be an opportunity in the large new plant going up a mile away on Barnum Avenue.[1]

Nineteen Maiden Lane was the storefront of Schuyler, Hartley & Graham (SH&G). Ostensibly a dealer in fine goods and firearms, SH&G in fact was one of the largest arms dealers in the world. It was the realm of Marcellus Hartley, the man Abraham Lincoln and Edwin Stanton had sent to England in 1862 when the Union so desperately needed arms. Hartley superintended his domain from a desk on the mezzanine level at the back of the store behind displays of firearms, fine cutlery, military ornamentation, and ceremonial Masonic paraphernalia. But appearances could deceive: Marcellus Hartley was rich and powerful, and SH&G was the cortex of the American arms industry. Hartley was entering the ammunition business, and Alfred C. Hobbs was just the man he needed.

New Guns, New Businesses

As the North's strangulation of the South took hold, Hartley knew his trade was about to change. Between the threat of peace and the advent of breech loaders, gun-making was becoming unpredictable. Astutely, Hartley saw that the future lay in the copper and brass cartridges the breech loaders consumed at prodigious rates. As always, there were challenges. Metallic cartridges were complex mechanical and chemical marvels that had to be made to exact tolerances, endure enormous pressures, survive harsh field conditions, last indefinitely, cost little, and never fail. This was a field ripe for mechanization once the necessary machinery was perfected, and any entrepreneur who assembled a strong patent estate might have much of the market to himself. Hartley guessed as well that any foreign country unable to make its own guns also would be unable to manufacture its own ammunition, so there was a big export market in the offing.[2]

Hartley also knew that he did not have to start from scratch. With its near-obsession with ammunition, the Ordnance Department was ahead of the curve in designing metallic cartridges and the machinery needed to mass-produce them. As early as August 1864, it had directed the commandant of Philadelphia's Frankford Arsenal to increase its annual capacity to 450 million metal cartridge cases. Frankford began developing machinery for drawing metallic cases and refining techniques for working copper and brass, all the while improving the designs of military ammunition. "Though the gun design field was nearly pre-empted by civilians," ordnance authority Berkely Lewis observed, "the opposite was true in cartridges. Frankford Arsenal led the world in design and production of small arms ammunition."[3] And, since the government seldom bothered to protect its intellectual property, these inventions were there for the taking. In effect, this new industry would be massively subsidized by the federal government.

During the Civil War, a cartridge industry had developed in tandem with the arrival of the breech loader. Firms in Connecticut and Massachusetts entered the business and, by the time the war ended, the Ordnance Department had bought over 100 million metallic cartridges from them. With the conflict over, cartridge companies could be scooped up cheaply. In August 1864, Hartley bought Crittenden & Tibbals of South Coventry, Connecticut, and in late 1865 took over Springfield's C. D. Leet & Co. A sensible place to headquarter an ammunition company was Bridgeport, Connecticut. It had a good harbor and, perhaps more critically, a direct rail connection to Waterbury, the source of the precisely rolled, high-quality sheet copper and brass needed to draw cartridge cases. Hartley bought a tract of land from P. T. Barnum in September 1865 and christened his new enterprise the Union Metallic Cartridge Company (UMC).[4]

Mass-producing metallic ammunition was a complicated process. It began with drawing the cartridge case and continued until the cartridge had its powder, primer, lubrication, and bullet. The first steps in fabricating the case were punching a circular blank from a sheet of copper or brass, then forming the blank into a small cup. The cup was then dropped into a press where a steel punch squeezed it through a circular die, stretching the metal into a tube of precise dimensions, closed at the bottom and open at the top.[5] It was then trimmed of excess metal and "headed," that is, given its bottom rim, by a machine that compressed the base of the shell until a lip, or flange, extended beyond the tube's perimeter. (Confusingly, the bottom of the cartridge case was known as the "head.") Repeatedly, unfinished cases were gauged for accuracy and annealed to maintain the metal's ductility.

Only machinery could do this work, and considerations of cost and safety—it was dangerous business—meant that every step of the process must be mechanized. That was where Alfred Hobbs fit in, and Hartley immediately hired him to run UMC's plant. Hobbs went to work with his usual energy and, over the years, improved the company's cartridge designs and took out patents on a percussion cap, cartridge primers, and machines for loading cartridges and punching cartridge heads. By 1867, he had over 1,000 employees working there and, before much longer, was producing 400,000 cartridges a day.[6]

RIM-FIRE AND CENTER-FIRE

The immediate challenge facing Hartley and others was to find a way to make a more powerful round of ammunition. The underlying problem was figuring out where to put the fulminate necessary to set off the powder charge.

Fulminate, as discussed in chapter 2, was the combustible substance used in percussion caps to start the ignition process. As unstable as it was, fulminate still needed to be sharply crushed between two hard surfaces before it would explode reliably. By the late 1850s, it became apparent that one approach would be to pack the fulminate inside the hollow flange at the head of the cartridge case. When the gun's hammer or firing pin struck the flange, it smashed the bottom of the flange against the top, thus igniting the fulminate. (For obvious reasons, this became known as a "rim-fire" cartridge.) By 1860, various inventors—Horace Smith, Daniel Wesson, Christian Sharps, and Benjamin Tyler Henry among them—patented improvements on the idea, and during the Civil War, the rim-fire cartridge became the standard all-metal round for breech loaders.[7]

But there was an inherent problem with rim-fire cartridges. They worked only if the metal in the flange was thin enough and soft enough to be smashed, so they were made of copper and drawn to be thin at the head. This intentional weakness substantially limited how much gunpowder the case could take. The Henry rifle's rim-fire cartridge had a bullet and powder charge less than half that of the Springfield, and even the more robust Spencer had only three-quarters of the Springfield's force.[8] The rifles carried by the line infantry (by now, the term "rifle-musket" had been abandoned) required heavier charges.

The evident solution was to make the cartridge head stronger and somehow put the primer in the center. The idea was not new. Swiss gunsmith Johannes Pauly had received French and British patents decades earlier on a breech-loading gun that used a center-fire cartridge, and in 1858 Louisiana plantation owner George Morse had patented two versions of a metallic cartridge with a percussion cap in its base. Before these plans could become reality, though, a series of technical problems needed to be solved. Drawing brass or thick copper shells required presses capable of applying 60,000 pounds of pressure, and such machines existed only on the drawing board.[9] There also was doubt as to how the priming system should work: Should it be an integral part of the cartridge head, or would it be better to have a separate primer cap inserted into an opening in the head? What was the best way to crush the fulminate and, once ignited, to convey the flame to the cartridge's powder charge? And, since cartridge cases were expensive, would it be possible to somehow invent a priming system where the empty case could be reused?

THE BERDAN PRIMER

Several center-fire priming systems were developed in the 1860s, but the most successful was one credited to Hiram Berdan. Berdan received a patent on his system in March 1866, and a follow-on patent in September 1868.[10] His approach was to punch a small hole in the center of the head of the cartridge shell and to insert a tight-fitting cup into the hole. The bottom of the cup was open; the top had a small anvil-like protrusion Berdan called the "teat." A "shallow pellet-like cap" of primer was inserted into the bottom of the cup, then covered with varnish to keep it in place and protect it from the elements. When the trigger was pulled, the hammer or firing pin crushed the fulminate against the anvil, and the flame of ignition passed through vents in the top of the cup onto the cartridge's powder charge. Berdan claimed many advantages from this design, including the thought that the explosion of the fulminate would expand the cap sufficiently to prevent leakage of gas, the belief that the cup's design would prevent the accidental detonation of the cartridge, and the fact that cartridges would be safer to manufacture.

Berdan was troubled throughout his life by questions about his personal character, and his checkered history suggests that he was something of a sociopath. There are numerous stories of his dishonesty, and he had a well-known propensity to claim inventorship of things that he did not invent. Later, when Berdan began patenting breech-loading rifles, at least two courts questioned the originality of his ideas.[11] His claims about his center-fire cartridge raised eyebrows, too. Berdan's 1868 cartridge patent dropped the idea of putting a hole in the head of the cartridge in favor of making the cartridge out of a single piece of metal so that "the anvil is of the same continuous piece of metal as that of which the case is made." However, in an engineering study prepared in 1873 about the experiments conducted at the army's Frankford Arsenal, Major Thomas

Treadwell wrote that Berdan's cartridge actually had been invented by the Ordnance Department's Stephen Benét. Since the department's facilities were, as a general matter, open to the public, anyone was free to study, copy, and even expropriate inventions made there. According to Treadwell, this is what happened. While Benét was experimenting with different cartridge designs in early 1866, Berdan had come "to the Arsenal and obtained the necessary information, taking with him samples & sizes of tools and afterwards applying it to his cartridges, which previously had a separate cup inserted at the head."[12]

Fairly or not, Berdan got a patent on the design and was greatly enriched when Hartley's Union Metallic Cartridge licensed rights to it. UMC made the Berdan cartridge by the billions, and entire wars were fought where both sides used it. Even today, a form of the Berdan primer is found in many cartridges.

CHAPTER 13

Trapdoors, Snuff Boxes, Rolling Blocks, and Peabodys

A SILVER LINING TO THE WAR DEPARTMENT'S CHAOTIC PROCUREMENT system was that it had encouraged a profusion of gun designs. The Union's appetite for breech-loading carbines seemed boundless, and government money was excellent fertilizer. Between 1860 and 1871, the US Patent Office issued over 550 patents on breech-loading mechanisms; so busy were inventors that it was not uncommon for the Patent Office to grant several breech loader patents on a single day. On Tuesday, November 24, 1864, for example, the Patent Office awarded patents for breech-loading firearms to Robert Hughes, Robert Wilson, and Joseph Rider and on June 11, 1867, did the same for Benjamin Roberts, Robert Stevens, and Isaac Milbank. Unsurprisingly, this made for a crowded field, and there was constant friction at the boundaries of different patent claims. In his annual report to Congress in 1867, Secretary of War Ulysses S. Grant complained that intellectual property claims were complicating efforts to convert Springfield muskets into breech loaders: "Several parties, in some instances, claim to hold patents for the same thing; and every improvement, it is believed, is claimed by more than one inventor."[1] Patent rights became a prime consideration in designing new weapons, and at times the country's most violent showdowns were between patent lawyers, not gunslingers.

There are hundreds of excellent books about the early years of breech-loading rifles, and it is beyond our scope here to do more than touch upon the subject. Almost all breech-loading guns, though, had a few things in common: a breech block that moved to permit loading and locked to secure the cartridge in the breech; a specially shaped hammer or firing pin to detonate the primer; a method to pull the spent shell out of the breech; and, sometimes, another device to eject the empty shell out of the gun altogether. There were many ways to realize these goals, and it is fair to say that every imaginable design was tried. Guns had breech blocks that lifted up, fell down, rolled back, swung sideways, pivoted forward, rolled left, turned right, pulled backward, or slid forward and were hinged in front, in back, on top, on bottom, on the left, on the right, or not at all. In some cases, it was the barrel that moved, either by "breaking" on a hinge at the breech, sliding sideways, moving forward, or even twisting around to expose the breech end of the barrel. Devices for extracting and ejecting spent shells were equally varied, using springs, claws, hooks, fingers, knuckles, projections, levers, flippers, gravity, or simple geometry.[2] For a while, most designs continued to have an external hammer to ignite the primer, but ultimately internal spring-driven firing pins replaced hammers.

Trapdoors and Snuff Boxes

The development of the center-fire cartridge meant that breech loaders now had the power to take their place on the line of infantry. The first order of business, though, was to find a way to convert the mountains of muzzle-loading rifles to breech loaders. In fact, as a way of forcing the Ordnance Department to recycle its countless Springfield muskets, Congress in 1868 temporarily prohibited the department from paying for any new small arms at all.[3]

Because the whole point of conversions was to save money, the breech systems for conversions tended to be simple; the most common conversions were designs where the breech block was lifted up or flipped over. The process of conversion was relatively easy. Usually, it involved milling away the top half of the last few inches of the barrel, welding or brazing new fittings at the breech, and installing a prefabricated breech mechanism.[4] Everything else—the stock, barrel, hammer, sights, and fittings—was reused. It cost about five or six dollars to convert a musket this way, although the price could go up if an armory decided to reduce the caliber of the barrel.[5]

There were two principal conversion systems. In the United States, Springfield master armorer Erskine Allin came up with a design called the "trapdoor" because of the way the breech opened and closed.[6] The Allin design, which later became the basis of the Springfield Models 1868 and 1873, had a stout breech block that was hinged in the front and lifted up and forward by hand to expose the breech and then dropped down to close it. The firing pin ran through a channel in the breech block and was driven by the external hammer. The trapdoor was well-liked despite its awkward looks, and the hinge of its block readily accommodated a spring-loaded device to expel the spent cartridge shell. Besides the United States, the Austrian government also adopted a trapdoor-like mechanism for its conversion system, the Wänzl.

Britain, France, Russia, and other countries adopted a design called a *tabatière* because of its resemblance to a French snuff box. Instead of flipping up and forward, the *tabatière's* breech block was hinged on the side (the Russian M1867 Krnka on the left; the French *tabatière* and the British Snider-Enfield on the right). Loading the gun was a matter of lifting the breech block up and over, pushing in the cartridge, and rolling the breech block back into place. Firing was, again, a matter of cocking the external hammer and pulling the trigger. Extracting the spent shell required the soldier to pluck it out with his fingers, although the process was helped along in the French and British guns by a feature that let the opened breech block slide backward on a rod, pulling the empty shell along with it.[7]

Although these systems were intended only as stopgaps, some were successful enough that they survived as main line infantry weapons. Allin's system became the basis of the Springfield Model 1873 which, as improved, remained so popular with troops that the Ordnance Department had difficulty persuading them to adopt newer patterns. In Britain, ordnance authorities found that the Snider was "simple, durable, economical, [and] capable of a rapidity of fire from twelve to eighteen shots per minute" in capable hands.[8]

Because the economics were so compelling, there was a big market for converted muskets. In 1866, Remington took advantage of the opportunity and sold Spain 10,000 surplus muskets converted to Remington's rolling-block system, while Colt agreed to supply 17,100 Snider conversions to Egypt. Turkey was by far the biggest buyer, purchasing 114,000 Enfield and 225,000 Springfield rifles from the US government in mid-1869 and early 1870 at prices ranging from $4 to $7, again for conversion to the Snider system. In early 1867, the Ordnance Department found that even Germany was interested in buying converted Springfields.[9]

THE NEXT GENERATION

The trapdoor and *tabatière* systems, though, were crude compared to newer designs. These were guns that had started out as breech loaders. They were simpler, quicker firing, and had better ways to extract spent shells. Perhaps more importantly, they had different, and much improved, ballistics.

No matter where they were from, ordnance officers seemed to compulsively test new gun designs, and never was this more true than when breech loaders came onto the scene. There was a regimen of sorts for doing this. Different barrels were tried with different breech mechanisms and with different bullets and powder charges under different conditions. Prototypes were fired hundreds of times to test their robustness and expose their flaws. Using the statistical methods of the day, ordnance experts fired test guns at large paper or cloth targets set at various distances, and then measured the horizontal and vertical deviation of each round to determine the relative accuracy of each type of gun, bullet, or cartridge. There were other trials, too. Rifles were immersed in salt water, smeared with dirt, rolled in sand, dropped from ladders, overcharged, tested with defective cartridges, and subjected to any other form of abuse an imaginative officer might contrive. Other variables were carefully checked, too, and none more carefully than those having to do with ballistics. Ordnance boards experimented with various calibers, rifling schemes, bullet shapes, bullet weights, and gunpowder charges and scrutinized even the tiniest differences. Ordinarily they compiled their findings and recommendations in a report that navigated its way through military bureaucracy and political intrigue.

REMINGTONS AND PEABODYS

The rifle adopted in the greatest numbers was the Remington rolling-block rifle, so called because its breech block rolled forward and backward on a rivet anchored to the sides of the gun's frame. Rolling-block guns had been around for a while. In 1858, for example, a New Yorker named Thomas Lee had patented a rolling-block design, and there probably were earlier examples, too. The challenge to rolling-block designs was how to lock the breech block in place when the gun was fired. In the early 1860s, Remington employee Leonard Geiger came up with the idea of having the hammer itself provide this bracing. Geiger's design, subsequently improved by Ohio gunsmith Joseph Rider, consisted of two interlocking pieces, one of which was the breech block and the other the gun's hammer, which itself rolled forward and back directly behind the breech block. To expose the barrel and load the gun, a soldier used his thumb first to roll back the hammer and then pull back the breech block. After loading the gun, the soldier snapped the breech block back into place. When the gun was fired, the shoulders of the hammer pivoted "in, under, and against the breech-block, and lock[ed] it there."[10] To remove the spent shell, the soldier reversed the loading process; an extractor mechanism activated by the rotation of the breech block ejected the spent shell from the breech.

The rolling block had advantages over the trapdoor or *tabatière* designs. Loading the gun required the soldier only to cock the hammer, pull back on the thumbpiece of the rolling block, and insert the cartridge, an operation he could do without obstructing his view of the target. By design, the gun could not be fired until the rolling block was closed, which was a useful safety feature for untrained soldiers. Unlike the heavy breech block of a trapdoor rifle, the rolling block was easily opened and closed. The design, obviously, was not perfect. But the Remington rolling block was the simplest and, for quite a while, the most successful single-shot rifle around.

After the Remington, the second-most-common design in those years was the mechanism patented by Boston's Henry O. Peabody in 1862. The Peabody was a lever-operated gun with a "falling" breech block that was hinged at the rear. When a lever (which doubled as a trigger guard) was pulled down, a linkage lowered the front end of the breech block to expose the breech for loading; retracting the lever raised the block back up to its locked position. The spent shell was extracted in the reloading process by the fingers of an elbow-shaped rocker moved by the action of the lever. The Providence Tool Company bought patent rights from Peabody in October 1864 and produced Peabodys by the thousands in the 1860s.[11] More importantly, the Peabody action was copied abroad; among others, Britain's famous Martini-Henry rifle was based on the Peabody.

Finally, the rifle designed by Horace Smith, Daniel Wesson, and Benjamin Tyler Henry—by now, known as the Winchester—became the most commonly used repeating rifle. It was steadily improved over the years to take a heavier round, although experience showed that even with a relatively light bullet it was effective in close-range encounters. Yet another reason was that Oliver Winchester's Repeating Arms Company steadily devoured its competitors. In 1869, Winchester acquired the American Repeating Rifle Co. (which made the Fogerty rifle) and in 1870 the Spencer Repeating Rifle Co. In 1874, Winchester took over the Adirondack Arms Co., maker of the Robinson repeating rifle, and finally, in 1888, he bought the venerable Whitney Arms Co. (which had repeating rifles of its own) and moved its machinery down the road to his plant in New Haven.[12]

BALLISTICS

Nothing was tested more intently than the ballistics of these new rifles. If nothing else, everyone agreed that smaller calibers were better than larger ones. Thus, when the French adopted the Chassepot rifle in 1866, they decided upon a bore of eleven millimeters, or .433. After fifty-five days of trials that same year, a US ordnance board recommended a caliber of .45, although for practical reasons—there were now countless leftover .50-caliber weapons in the nation's depots—the War Department adopted the larger caliber instead. At the end of equally extensive tests, the British Select Committee on Breech-Loading Arms also concluded that .45 was the optimum caliber. When Remington began mass-producing military arms for a number of foreign buyers in 1867, it made them with calibers ranging from .43 for Spain and Egypt to .48 for Denmark and Sweden. Later, the Russian army specified a 10.75-millimeter barrel (slightly over .42 inch) for the guns they ordered from Colt in 1869.[13]

With smaller caliber came a concomitant reduction of mass. Minié balls usually weighed somewhere in the neighborhood of 500 grains, but the newer bullets typically were no more than 400. (An exception was the British Martini-Henry, which continued to use a heavy [480-grain] bullet.) But powder charges, if anything, increased. While the Springfield, Enfield, and other rifle-muskets used between 60 and 70 grains of powder, powder charges for the new breech loaders were about 10 to 20 percent higher.[14]

Because ammunition was loaded from the breech, bullets now were slightly larger than the caliber of the barrel to assure a tight fit with the rifling.[15] Coupled with better ballistics and higher powder charges, this meant that the breech loader's bullets slugged better into the rifling and could even overcome the supersonic limits that Benjamin Robins had noticed 125 years earlier. The Chassepot, Martini-Henry, Remington, and other weapons had muzzle velocities of about 1,350 feet per second and some, like the Berdan rifle, reached almost 1,450.[16] Collectively, these improvements—smaller calibers, heavier powder charges, and center-fire cartridges—were a classic example of changes in degree becoming changes in kind. The breech-loading rifle had become much more than a rifled musket that loaded at the breech.

CHAPTER 14

Venturing Abroad

THE CIVIL WAR'S END BROUGHT JUBILATION IN THE NORTH, BUT arms-makers probably celebrated it less than most. There were few domestic customers and, tooled for war, the industry's immense works were uneconomical at low production rates. The War Department countermanded the undelivered portions of outstanding arms contracts, saddling gun companies with large inventories of unwanted weapons. Surplus rifles were another problem. The government began emptying its depots of unneeded guns, dumping them at distress prices. And not all were old muzzle loaders. The Sharps Rifle Manufacturing Company, for example, found that the Ordnance Department was selling off surplus Sharps carbines and rifles for as little as $5, a fraction of what Sharps was asking for new ones.[1]

After Appomattox, some arms firms left the business almost as quickly as they had entered it; even successful contractors like Amoskeag Manufacturing, A. H. Jenks & Son, Lamson Goodnow & Yale, and J. D. Mowry decided to do other things. Others struggled because there were simply too many guns around or because the new metallic cartridges had made their designs obsolete. Before long, most of the breech-loading carbine systems used in the Civil War—Burnside, Cosmopolitan, Gallagher, Gibbs, Lindner, Merrill, Smith, Starr, Warner, Wesson, and so on—were gone. Colt's William Franklin worried in May 1865 that "the arms trade will not be large again for a long time."[2]

Yet Franklin spoke too soon. Barely a year later, every army in the world was looking to rearm itself with new breech-loading rifles. The impetus for this was not the American Civil War, which remained for most European armies a confusing military sideshow. Instead, it was Prussia's crushing defeat of Austria in the aptly named Seven Weeks War of 1866.[3] However outdated the Prussian needle-gun may have been by then, it easily outmatched Austria's muzzle-loading Lorenzes, even if some grumbled that this was just a handy excuse offered by Austrian generals to hide their shocking incompetence. Wherever the truth lay, France was nervous about Prussia's growing strength, the Austro-Hungarian Empire was fading, Russia was nursing grudges from the Crimean War, the Ottoman Empire was falling apart, and Britain was worried about the strategic implications of the almost-finished Suez Canal. A new and potentially decisive weapon had shown up just as the European balance of power was changing.

Those who stayed in the arms business were risk-takers, although for a while it was unclear just what risks they were taking. The mid-1860s was a period of technological ambiguity. The United States and virtually every other country conducted trials of different breech loader designs, but all too often concluded only that they needed to do even more testing. Although the all-metal cartridge seemed like an obvious solution to the problem of obturation, drawing cartridge cases was tricky and, at least in Europe, copper was pricey. (The United States had ample amounts from the recently opened Lake Superior mines.) Center-fire priming systems were still unperfected and, for a while, gun-makers still promoted rim-fire systems.[4]

Yet it soon became apparent that the American lead in breech loader design was so overwhelming that most places, for now, would have to import their guns and technology from the United States. In April 1867, the Exposition Universelle opened in Paris, the latest in the series of Europe's periodic industrial fairs and expositions. Colt, Remington, Providence Tool, Smith & Wesson, Spencer, and even the Gatling Gun Company were all there. Impressed by this tour de force, the judges awarded a gold medal to the entire "Arms Manufacturing Industry of the United States," diplomatically writing that they had found it "so difficult to decide upon the relative merits of the portable fire-arms exhibited in the American section, and their superiority was recognized as so indisputable." Beyond that, silver medals were awarded individually to Colt, Gatling, Providence Tool, Remington, Smith & Wesson, Spencer, and Vermont's Windsor Manufacturing Co. "[A]ll the civilized nations of the earth must be re-armed," John Anthony observed, and until the rest of the world could catch up, the field was open to the Americans.[5]

AGENTS AND INDUCEMENTS

Americans soon found, though, that selling arms abroad was not as simple as showing up at the palace door with a box of breech loaders and a case of metallic cartridges. You had to understand each country's domestic politics, know different military cultures and doctrines, and keep a wary eye on the competition. The men at the center of America's arms industry—the Remington brothers, William Franklin, Marcellus Hartley, Oliver F. Winchester, and John Anthony—were often in Europe to keep abreast of things. But with their hands full at home, they also hired agents to promote their rifles and close deals.

The best known was Samuel Norris, the man who unsuccessfully sued Providence Tool in 1862. Ambitious to a fault, Norris entered the arms business on his own in 1862, assembling guns from parts he sourced from different New England workshops. Seeing the promise of Remington's rolling block, he licensed the design during the Civil War and contracted with the Savage Arms Company to make 5,000 "split breech" Remington carbines for the War Department. Building on his Remington relationship, he moved to England in 1865 as the Remingtons' European agent. He seemed to be everywhere; as a short biography said about him, "Wherever there were wars or rumors of wars, Colonel Norris . . . would be on hand." In addition to Norris, the Remington brothers also relied upon Colonel Watson C. Squire, a lawyer and Civil War veteran who was pulled into the arms business after he married Philo Remington's daughter.[6] And presiding over it all was Samuel Remington himself, who moved to Europe in 1867 and, in a sense, personified the entire industry.

Besides his frequent personal visits, Oliver Winchester relied upon his Yale-educated son-in-law, Thomas˘ Gray Bennett, and even hired former Confederate purchasing agent Caleb Huse. Another was a colorful Irishman who went by the pseudonym of Thomas Emmett Addis, a natural salesman who began as a worker on Winchester's factory floor and became one of its most successful agents.[7] Providence Tool used the New Yorker Marshall Benton as well as a network of commission agents. Colt was represented in Europe by Frederick August Kunow Waldman von Oppen, a Prussian-born aristocrat who was married to a woman who may have been the mother of Samuel Colt's illegitimate son or, for a single day, the wife of Colt's soon-to-be-executed brother John, or both. Others in the gun business—Hiram Berdan and Richard Gatling to name two—represented themselves, sometimes relocating to Europe for years at a time. At one point or another, almost everyone engaged Marcellus Hartley's firm. Many of these agents were not especially punctilious about conflicts of interest, sometimes even competing with their own clients. The French-Canadian salesman William Saint Laurent at various times worked for Samuel Remington, Marcellus Hartley, Providence Tool, Colt, and any number of British and European clients, and opportunistically made personal deals on the side.[8] Similarly, even while he was Remington's chief salesman in Europe, Samuel Norris bought the rights to the Mauser rifle for himself.

Whoever handled it, foreign arms sales involved a minuet among the Americans, their foreign sales agents, European military authorities, politicians of every stripe, local business partners, and all manner of lobbyists, influencers, and hangers-on. Every government and gun-maker hotly denied that anything so base as bribes was involved, yet government officials routinely asked for "commissions" and arms-makers routinely obliged them. Then, as now, the trick was to get money off company books and into the hands of a third party who could arrange the bribe. Usually, this was done by paying the agent an overly generous fee that gave him the wherewithal to pay off corrupt officials. Sometimes details emerged. A lawsuit between Samuel Norris and Remington revealed that Norris was paid a 10 percent commission on orders from "any European countries, or any associations . . . contracting for European powers." The Turkish consul in New York had a similar agreement—in writing—with Oliver Winchester for a commission of 10 percent on all sales of arms, guns, and ammunition to the Ottoman Turks. In a proposal to sell Berdan II rifles to the Russians in December 1869, Colt promised Hiram Berdan everything above 20 shillings for any breech mechanisms Russia bought. This last provision would have given Berdan a jaw-dropping 33 percent commission, since he was proposing to sell the breech mechanisms for 30 shillings apiece. It would have made sense for Colt to cut its prices to get the contract, but a panicked Berdan warned Colt against it: without a high price Berdan would not get a high commission, and he needed the high commission because he was kicking some of it back. On October 5, 1870, he sent a "Confidential" note: "There are many things about this matter which I ought not to communicate," Berdan wrote William Franklin, "but believe me when I say I am almost certain you will receive the order." He urged Franklin to keep his prices "as liberal as possible for I receive less than one-half." Even John Anthony, who had suffered extortion at the hands of Senator James Simmons a few years prior, agreed to a generous 10 percent agency fee by the time Turkey began looking for guns in 1872.[9] So endemic were these practices that both of the seminal commercial bribery cases decided by the US Supreme Court in the nineteenth century involved the American gun business.[10]

One of the more reputable representatives, Winchester's Thomas Bennett, bemoaned the company he was forced to keep. He referred to Gatling gun salesman Lewis Wells Broadwell—whom he actually liked—as being "of that class of gun men, Americans who came out to skim these ignorant European nations." Less bearable was "this wretch" Berdan who, in Bennett's view, had perpetrated any number of swindles, and had even been convicted in absentia in Russia for defrauding his creditors. "A miserable business is it not?" Bennett complained to his wife in 1879.[11]

THE FIRST ORDERS

For a while, sales were small and close to home. Canada may have been the first country to buy American breech loaders. The North had enlisted large numbers of Irish immigrants into the Union army, and after the war some number of these veterans turned their attention to the cause of Irish independence. They organized a secret society called the Fenian Brotherhood and began mounting raids on Canada from United States soil as a way of applying pressure on Britain to withdraw from Ireland. There were never enough Fenians to seriously threaten Canada, but the Canadians were worried enough to buy better rifles. The Peabody had performed well in trials in August 1866, and the next month Canada signed a contract for 5,000 of them (later cut to 3,000) at $25. There is evidence that some of the Fenians were armed with Roberts breech-loading rifles which, as it happened, also were made by Providence Tool under contract. That same year, Winchester sold 1,000 rifles to France, which evidently went to Mexico to arm the French forces Napoleon III had sent there to support the abortive rule of Maximillian I.[12]

REMINGTON

Soon there were more substantial orders, most of which went to Remington. The first were in Scandinavia. Denmark, having lost the Second Schleswig War to Prussia in 1864, was intent on modernizing its army. In February 1867, the Danes held gun trials in Copenhagen, and soon they sent a commission to the United States to examine American armories. The Danish officers initially favored the Peabody, telling John Anthony his gun was "the best single shot breech-loader with which copper cartridges are used." However, clued in by Denmark's Minister of War, Samuel Norris followed the commission to America and succeeded in persuading them to choose the Remington instead. A disappointed Anthony hinted that some dubious influence had come into play. "Kissing goes by favor," he cryptically wrote.[13] Norris, still smarting from losing his lawsuit against Providence Tool, must have delighted in his success.

One hundred fifty years later, it is difficult to find precise numbers for Remington's gun sales However, the best guess is that Denmark's first order was 30,000 rolling blocks, followed by a second order for 12,500, the guns being a mixture of rifles and carbines.[14] Denmark, like other countries Remington sold to, also ordered gun-making machinery and licensed the right to produce rolling blocks domestically. About the same time, Norway also put in an order for some number of Remingtons, and then Samuel Norris's brother John closed a deal with Sweden for at least 10,000 guns and 20,000 rolling-block mechanisms, plus machinery and rights to make the guns themselves.[15]

But there were setbacks, too. After losing its war against Prussia, Austria took steps in mid-1866 to adopt a new infantry arm. A commission held the customary trials of competing designs, finally settling upon the Remington rolling block. In keeping with imperial tradition, a ceremony was arranged for Emperor Franz Joseph I to receive the commission's report and inspect the weapons it recommended. Samuel Norris stood by, and Samuel Remington traveled to Vienna to attend the formalities. Arriving with a retinue of seventy magnificently uniformed officers, Franz Joseph formally accepted the report and then asked to fire the Remington rifle. He was handed the gun, given a cartridge, and shown how to load it. Taking aim, the Emperor squeezed the trigger—and nothing happened. The problem was not the gun, though. Instead, the Austrians had insisted upon using a locally manufactured rim-fire cartridge whose fulminate was defective. Nevertheless, the embarrassing moment doomed the rolling block's chances in Austria, and tainted the arm's reputation elsewhere after Remington's competitors distorted the minor mishap into tales of an accident that nearly cost Franz Joseph his very life.[16]

PROVIDENCE TOOL

About the same time, Providence Tool landed a contract from Switzerland, if in a roundabout way. The Swiss held trials in late 1866, and the testing board recommended the Winchester rifle. Despite reports that a massive contract was in the wings, the Swiss army rejected the board's recommendation. After further trials, the Swiss then chose the rolling block and offered Remington a contract for possibly 100,000 rifles. By now, though, Remington had landed its large order from Denmark. It could not commit to the Swiss's delivery schedule, and Remington's competitors—with guns of their own to sell—would not agree to make rolling blocks on subcontract. With that, Switzerland decided to adopt the home-grown Vetterli, a bolt-action repeating rifle that borrowed various elements of the Winchester. However, to meet its immediate needs, Switzerland ordered 15,000 Peabodys, chambered for Switzerland's soon-to-be outdated .41-caliber rim-fire cartridge.[17]

More complicated were the orders the Principality of Roumania placed in 1868. Roumania was a union of the Balkan territories of Moldavia and Wallachia, but itself in an uneasy vassalage to Ottoman Turkey. With a barely concealed ambition for independence, Roumania began studying American breech loaders and was impressed by favorable reports the Peabody received after the US Ordnance Department tested it in 1865. Somewhat surreptitiously, the Roumanian authorities began negotiating to buy Peabodys, first signing an order for 15,000 of the .41-caliber Swiss model in April 1868 and then a follow-on contract for 10,000 guns chambered to take the more powerful .45 Berdan center-fire cartridge. To avoid Turkish suspicion, the guns were transshipped through Hamburg, and they were all safely in Roumanian storehouses by the end of 1869.[18]

Providence Tool also won two other contracts in 1868. The larger one was from Spain for 12,500 Peabodys destined for Cuba, where an independence movement had mounted an insurrection months before. These Peabodys became known as the Spanish Model because they had the same .433 caliber as the rolling blocks Remington was selling to Madrid. Providence Tool also signed a contract that year to supply Mexico with 8,500 of the same Spanish Model Peabodys.[19]

FRANCE

One of the more intriguing, yet perplexing, opportunities was France. In 1866 and 1867, France was still considered the foremost land power in Europe and a leader in military science. After Prussia's destruction of the Austrian army at Sadowa on July 3, 1866, French Emperor Napoleon III ordered the immediate adoption of a breech-loading rifle. His army chose the arm devised by Antoine Alphonse Chassepot of the artillery works at Saint-Thomas-d'Aquin. Like Prussia's Dreyse, the Chassepot was a bolt-action gun with a needlelike firing pin, but it had a reduced .433 caliber against the Dreyse's .61 and fired a 386-grain bullet with an 86.4-grain powder charge. This gave the Chassepot a muzzle velocity over 1,350 feet per second, an extreme range of 1,800 yards, and a rate of fire of at least a dozen times a minute.[20]

Instead of the Dreyse's easily fouled metal-on-metal seal, the Chassepot used a segmented rubber ring—the *tête mobile*—to obturate the breech. The ring eroded with use, but it worked reasonably well and was readily replaced in the field. The Chassepot's principal weakness was its cartridge. Because the French ran into problems manufacturing metallic cartridges, they resorted instead to paper ones. In theory, the exploding gunpowder would completely consume the paper, avoiding the annoyance of extracting a metallic cartridge case. In practice, though, pieces of the paper cartridge survived ignition and were sometimes found still smoldering in the breech.[21]

Samuel Remington did what he could to interest the French in the rolling block, but they stuck to the Chassepot from a mixture of nationalism and, possibly, a conviction that paper cartridges made more sense for them than metallic ones. For a while, there was hope that the French might have some Chassepots made in the United States, and in April 1867 a group of French officers came over to look into it. Providence Tool evidently was approached—its archives contain an exquisite engineering diagram of the Chassepot—and the French asked Colt about producing 100,000 Chassepots. After studying the matter, Colt offered an estimate of $1,875,000 for 100,000 rifles but nothing came of it. One American gun the French did order was the breech loader invented by Civil War General Benjamin Roberts. The Roberts used a simple lever to drop and raise the breech block, a design that lent itself to musket conversions. The French ordered 30,000 of them from the Roberts Breech-Loading Arms Company which, despite appearances, had no factory. Roberts subcontracted the order to Providence Tool. After Providence Tool fell behind schedule, the French cancelled the contract, but Roberts was eventually able to sell some number of the guns to Brazil and other buyers.[22]

Some markets were harder to access than others, and parallel to the efforts of Remington, Providence Tool, and others there was a thriving market in surplus arms from the Ordnance Department and for new guns made by smaller firms. These arms, too, were sold through agents and brokers, the largest of which was Marcellus Hartley's Schuyler, Hartley & Graham. Speaking to a Senate committee in 1872, Hartley guessed that his firm had sold between 200,000 and 300,000 arms to foreign governments just between 1865 and 1870, and perhaps another 50,000 since. "There is a trade more or less all over the world," Hartley mused. "There is always fighting somewhere or other."[23]

MACHINERY FOR SALE

And it was not just guns Americans were selling overseas. Most large armories and ammunition firms—Colt, Winchester, Remington, Providence Tool, and Union Metallic Cartridge stand out—also sold machinery either as a sideline business or as a concession to close a deal. There was, to be sure, a measure of myopia in this: foreign countries that bought gun-making machinery from the United States would, sooner or later, stop buying American guns. But there was money to be made and probably no way to stop it. Thus, a large business developed in selling specialized equipment to foreign countries. Sometimes, it was entire factories.

One particular success was the Hartford company founded by two former Colt machinists, Francis A. Pratt and Amos Whitney. The two got into the business of selling gun machinery during the Civil War, and soon had their hands full. According to somewhat fragmentary records, it seems that Pratt & Whitney was so busy in 1867 that it turned down an order from Austria for machine tools to manufacture the Werndl rifle and sent the business over to Colt. But the firm's biggest foreign customer was Prussia. In the early 1870s, Prussia rushed to replace the obsolescent *Zundnadelgewehr* with the new, state-of-the-art Mauser rifle. Perhaps hearing of this, Francis Pratt made a trip to inspect the Prussian state armories in 1872 and returned with $350,000 in orders for machinery. The next year, Prussia contracted to buy an additional $1.5 million worth of machinery from his firm. It took Pratt & Whitney two years to complete the orders. The machine tools were eventually installed at the Prussian state armories at Spandau, Erfurt, and Danzig and raised their annual capacity to 200,000 rifles. Probably as part of the same requisition, another Hartford company, Billings & Spencer—started in 1869 by forging expert Charles Billings and the famous gun designer Christopher Miner Spencer—sold Prussia forty-two tons of finished dies for forging gun parts.[24]

Foreign machinery orders continued for years. Remington often sold gun machinery as part of its foreign gun sales, and it equipped countries as far-flung as Norway and Egypt. In addition to importing a factory full of the machinery Colt had used to produce its Berdan I rifles, Russia also imported rifling machines, Blanchard lathes, and universal milling machines from the United States after it began manufacturing the Berdan II. And sales extended beyond tools for making guns. Spain and Turkey bought cartridge-making machinery from Winchester, and Union Metallic Cartridge maintained a healthy flow of machinery sales as well.[25] Often, foreign buyers imported American workers, too, and it was not rare to learn that a machinist from Massachusetts or Connecticut was at work in a distant arms plant.

As the 1860s drew to a close, the experiment of selling abroad had turned out well. The rise of the American gun-makers was such that in 1869 one French wag said he was preparing a pamphlet titled *Invasion of Europe by the Arms of the United States*. Birmingham gun-makers found their trade so depressed that they petitioned the British government in April that year to close down the Enfield armory to preserve their business. The major European powers, to be sure, would become self-sufficient sooner or later, but it was a global market now, and it seemed that there always would be a need for American weapon exports.[26]

CHAPTER 15

England

American dominance in small-arms design and manufacture undoubtedly troubled other nations, and none more than the United Kingdom. Britain prided itself as the foremost industrialized nation in the world. With strategic needs of their own, the British could not afford to be left behind by the United States, and they intended to give the Americans a run for their money. Sooner or later, the English seemed to think, they would reestablish the lead they had once enjoyed. In the meantime, though, they would have to borrow American technology, improving upon it as they went. The two breech-loading arms Britain adopted in the 1860s were both American in one way or another.

THE SNIDER
The conversion system the British chose was the *tabatière* design invented by the American Jacob Snider. The Snider's breech block lifted up and to the right for loading and then flipped back down to lock the breech. In sheer numbers and breadth of usage, the Snider was easily the most successful of the several systems for converting muzzle loaders, and it held its own against many of the newer breech loader patterns. However, Jacob Snider himself benefited very little from his invention. There are few more disgraceful stories in the complicated history of the arms business than that of Britain's treatment of him.

Born in Georgia in 1811, Snider moved to Philadelphia at a young age, married, and for a time prospered as a wine merchant. A religious and charitable man of unimpeachable character, he was among the founders of the Pennsylvania Institution for the Blind, and he developed a method of printing books with embossed type that enabled the sight-impaired to read. Using this process, Snider published in 1833 the Gospel of Mark for the blind. He was an expert on French wine, spoke French fluently, and, by one account, "a naturalist, and stuffed birds."[1]

Snider's business failed in the late 1850s and, after paying off what claims he could, he left his family in Pennsylvania and moved to Europe in hopes of restoring his fortunes. He began promoting a breech mechanism he had designed, which Britain tested successfully in 1860 and then shelved. The triumph of Prussia's needle-gun in its 1864 war with Denmark, though, prompted the British army to think about ways of converting its inventory of P1853 Enfields to breech loaders, and so in August 1864 the War Secretary published a notice inviting gun-makers to come forward with suggestions. As an inducement, the War Office offered a £5,000 reward to the successful applicant.[2]

After exhaustive testing, retesting, consideration, and reconsideration, the Ordnance Select Committee settled upon Snider's system in May 1866. Snider had a British patent, and he justifiably expected financial rewards from his invention. However, the British War Office—advised by a pettifogging lawyer and supercilious bureaucrat named Charles Clode—cheated him out of it in a succession of steps of monumental cynicism. First, it pointed out that under the authority of the case of *Feather v. The Queen*, it was not legally possible for Queen Victoria to do anything wrong, which also meant that no underling of the Queen could do anything wrong either, since that would be—well—wrong. Thus, Snider could not sue the British government for infringement of his patent. Second, it appeared that there were other inventors who impugned Snider's patent, and so maybe the patent was no good anyway. Third, even though the War Secretary had promised a reward of £5,000 to the successful entrant, Snider was not entitled to it since there was always the possibility that his gun might not, in the end, actually be a success. Instead, the government offered Snider a payment of £1,000 in August 1866 for his "personal services," all of which went to pay Snider's creditors. But this was too late, as well as too little: Snider had already suffered a stroke, and he was dead within months.[3]

The British government's behavior, of course, was a shameful miscarriage. Far from being proved a failure, Snider's breech mechanism was a resounding success. The British converted their entire stock of P1853s to the Snider system, then went on to adapt other muzzle loaders and, after that, began making new Sniders. By 1880, Britain had 700,000 Snider-Enfields on hand, and some of Britain's most famous victories in its colonial wars were with them. But other than the token £1,000, Snider profited not at all from his invention. As his friend and biographer wrote, "He died penniless, and in debt. He trusted to England's honor, and it failed him."[4]

THE BOXER CARTRIDGE

Since it began life as a conversion, the Snider-Enfield was as much Enfield as it was Snider. The P1853 Enfield barrel caliber was .577 and, after some modifications in 1859, it fired a .550-caliber cylindro-conical bullet weighing 530 grains, propelled by 68.8 grains of powder. Ballistics tests and calculations determined that the Snider-Enfield round should have a .573 bullet weighing 480 grains and use a powder charge of 70 grains. The Snider-Enfield bullet had about the same external dimensions and general shape as the P1853's 530-grain Minié ball, but weighed less. The cartridge's designer, Colonel Edward Mounier Boxer, the superintendent of the Royal Laboratory at Woolwich, accomplished this by putting a cavity in the nose of the bullet, which allowed him to preserve the bullet's length with a lower mass. Subsequent tests showed that the Snider rounds had better ballistics than the P1853 and also were more deadly because of the bullet's hollow head.[5]

As with other breech loaders, it was the cartridge that obturated the breech. In the Snider's case, the *tabatière* design meant that the breech block slid sideways over the end of the cartridge, complicating the job of making the block fit tightly against the head of the cartridge. This, it was thought, increased the stress upon the head of the cartridge and the risk of catastrophic failure. In response, Colonel Boxer created a multipiece cartridge that the British used in one form or another for the next twenty years. It consisted of a double base-cup of brass secured to a varnished iron base by a percussion cap that was wedged through holes in each.

The body of the cartridge was a coil of thin brass foil, cemented inside of a paper case. After the cartridge was filled with powder, a wad of wool sealed it and then a lubricated bullet was seated in the cartridge's neck. Upon firing, the brass foil expanded to assist the base-cup in obturating the breech.[6]

The best thing that can be said about Boxer's ungainly cartridge was that it somehow worked. It was obviously inferior to the simple one-piece metallic cartridges produced in the United States, but was defended as being cheaper because it used less metal.[7] This is puzzling, since the labor of making the complicated Boxer cartridge at least partly offset any savings in materials. The more likely reason for the Boxer design was that the British, like the French and others, were having trouble drawing metallic cartridge cases and opted to continue using a variant of the traditional paper cartridge. Once committed to the peculiarities of the wrapped foil Boxer cartridge, the British stuck with it until 1885.

THE MARTINI-HENRY

Even while it was considering the merits of the Snider, Britain's War Office began looking for a new arm to replace it. In October 1865 it published an invitation to gun-makers to submit their breech loader designs in a "Prize Competition." There were specifications for the weight, recoil, accuracy, and rapidity of fire. The prizes that were promised (either £600 or £1,000, depending on the circumstances) were modest, even assuming that the War Office would live up to them anyway.[8]

Over one hundred designs were submitted in response to the War Office's invitation. After several rounds of testing, the only rifle that came out well was the Snider itself, which was there only as a control of sorts anyway. The committee decided that no one deserved the top prize of £1,000. Nevertheless, the Edinburgh gun-maker Alexander Henry was awarded £600 because the rifle he had submitted was the best of the disappointing lot.[9]

The committee needed to regroup. Somewhat by indirection, it ended up selecting the ammunition, breech system, and rifling scheme separately. Recent civilian target-shooting competitions had confirmed that smaller-caliber rifles were more accurate than large-caliber ones and, going back to the days of the P1853 Enfield, the War Office had a long-standing preference for heavy bullets. This led the committee to conclude that the ideal round would be a 480-grain bullet with an 85-grain powder charge fitted to a .45-caliber barrel. The next step was to determine what rifling scheme worked best within these constraints. The committee conducted accuracy tests at ranges of 300, 500, 800, and 1,000 yards and found, at the end, that the best rifling system was one Henry had submitted, which had wide lands and narrow grooves.[10]

Now, it remained only to find the best breech mechanism. This effort was complicated by the fact that the committee's deliberations had taken so long that now there were new breech-loading designs to try out. After starting all over again, the committee finally settled upon the breech-loading system proposed by Swiss gun-maker Friedrich von Martini. Martini's design, though, was not in fact entirely his own: it was a version of the American Peabody falling-block rifle, but with a better extractor and an internal firing pin that cocked automatically when the gun's lever dropped the breech block for loading.[11]

The exceptionally strong Peabody breech was well-suited for the heavy round the committee had chosen. However, the specifications for that round meant that the cartridge would end up being remarkably long and narrow. This became a problem for two reasons. The first was that the British were committed to the wrapped foil Boxer cartridge, whose fragility would only get worse the longer and narrower it was. The second was that in a falling-block design like the Peabody, the cartridge had to be inserted into the barrel at an angle. Loading ammunition of any length would be awkward and, if nothing else, reduce the rate of fire. The solution was to change to shape of the cartridge. The committee adopted a shorter "bottle necked" cartridge, so called because the cartridge was wide at the base and then narrowed at its midsection, a geometry that allowed ammunition-makers to put a larger powder charge in a shorter cartridge.[12] The cartridge's base was the same .577 iron disc and brass cup arrangement found in the Snider cartridge, but about two-thirds up the base the case gradually narrowed to .439 inch at the shoulder, thus keeping the case length to barely 2¼ inches and the loaded cartridge itself to less than 3¼ inches.[13]

There was outrage in some quarters at the committee's decision, in part because the Martini-Henry, as the arm was to be known, was disliked by the troops who experimented with it. Soldiers complained about its severe recoil, which left shoulders bruised and noses bloodied. There was enough truth to these criticisms that it was five more years before the Martini-Henry was Britain's officially adopted infantry arm. Nevertheless, the Martini-Henry became one of the most successful military arms of the nineteenth century, admired today almost to the point of idolatry. Its large powder charge, heavy bullet, sturdy breech, excellent rifling, and general ruggedness made the Martini-Henry an especially deadly weapon. Contemporary tests of the rifle showed that it had a muzzle velocity as high as 1,365 feet per second and devastating penetration. In the hands of an experienced soldier, the Martini-Henry could fire forty unaimed shots a minute, better than the Remington's thirty or the Chassepot's nineteen. The Martini-Henry was considered accurate to 800 yards and thought to have an outside range of 1,500. Its trajectory was flat enough that aiming the gun at a target 500 yards away required only a slight elevation and, at that distance, the mean deviation from the target was just 11 inches or so.[14] Whatever its shortcomings, the Martini-Henry's ballistics lent themselves to the longstanding British doctrine of indirect fire, where the rifle was aimed in the direction and at the distance of massed enemy forces, and rapid fire and heavy bullets did the rest.

MANUFACTURING

Notwithstanding its expansion during the American Civil War, Britain's small-arms industry remained heavily dependent upon artisanal methods. Besides the government armory at Enfield, only the London Armoury Company had been fully mechanized, and it closed not long after the Confederacy folded.[15] The Birmingham Small Arms Company, with official encouragement, began construction of a modern armory in 1863 and by 1865 or so had a contract to supply 20,000 Snider conversions to Turkey. After trying with little success to develop and market a breech loader of its own, BSA got a boost when the British Ordnance Board began placing orders for converted and new Sniders. By 1871, the firm had converted 156,000 muzzle loaders, and made another 52,000 new rifles.[16] Although BSA struggled in its manufacturing over the years, it became enough of a competitor to take at least one large contract away from its American rivals.

Another competitor formed with at least tacit government support was the National Arms & Ammunition Company, which was organized in 1872 specifically to manufacture Martini-Henry rifles for the British army. The company took over the Birmingham operations of British gun-maker Westley Richards, licensed patent rights to the Martini breech and Henry rifling systems, and made plans to manufacture as many as 2,000 Martini-Henry breech systems a week. National Arms' managing director was Major General W. M. H. Dixon, the officer who had been the superintendent of the small-arms works at Enfield for the past seventeen years. National Arms planned to become a fully mechanized operation, although when John Anthony visited its plant in December 1874, he found that its 1,000-man workforce could produce but 250 rifles a day and lagged behind the United States in manufacturing methods.[17]

Nevertheless, English arms-makers had a level of direct government support that their American competitors did not enjoy. Britain was a global power with overseas diplomatic and military interests to protect, while the United States was embarking on a decades-long process of consolidating and developing its internal empire in North America. Thus, in the coming years, Britain saw its domestic private arms business as an important element of its national security, while the United States government—which already owned the largest rifle factory on the planet—had other things on its mind.

CHAPTER 16

The Dreams of Ismail

IN THE LATE 1860S AND EARLY 1870S, THERE WERE FEW PLACES IN THE world more important than Egypt. Cotton exports during the Civil War made Egypt rich, and the newly opened Suez Canal put it in the middle of international trade and politics. Egypt "produced a harvest of gold richer and vaster than ever came from Ophir or California," the expatriate Samuel Lockett wrote.[1] "Everybody wanted to go to Egypt." And, remarkably, many Americans did. Robert E. Lee's eldest daughter Mary lived in Cairo for a while; a fugitive from Lincoln's assassination, John Surratt, was finally arrested in Alexandria in 1866; Mark Twain visited in 1867; William Tecumseh Sherman came in 1872; and Ulysses S. Grant twice stopped in Egypt during his world tour of 1877–1879. And the feelings were reciprocated. Egyptian authorities hired dozens of former Union and Confederate officers to reform Egypt's military, develop its infrastructure, and expand the boundaries of its empire. And Egypt bought immense numbers of rifles from the United States.

Egypt had been conquered by the Ottoman Turks in the early sixteenth century, but Ottoman authority was weak now. Napoleon invaded in 1798 in hopes of impeding Britain's expansion in India, only to be driven out by a combination of British and Ottoman forces. In the ensuing power vacuum, an ambitious Ottoman officer named Muhammad Ali became the *wāli* (governor) of Egypt. Muhammad Ali consolidated Egypt's economy, reformed its army, and took steps to develop an industrial economy. He built armories to copy European arms, foundries to cast cannon, mills to make gunpowder, and yards to build warships. With his military machine in place, Muhammad Ali made war on behalf of, and then against, the Turkish Sultan. The Ottoman government asked the European powers for support, and they ultimately curtailed Muhammad Ali's ambitions. But Egypt still had hopes. After Muhammad Ali's son Sa'id Pasha became *wāli* in 1853, he recruited the French ballistician Étienne-Claude Minié to build an armory in Cairo to manufacture rifled muskets. Minié ran the armory for years, even expanding it in 1865 with machinery from a defunct English firm that had been working for the South.[2]

After Sa'id died in 1863, his nephew Ismail became *wāli*, although Ismail soon claimed (and, later, was granted) the honorific title of *Khedive* (Viceroy). His succession came at a crucial time, when two unrelated events propelled Egypt—and Ismail himself—to center stage.

COTTON AND THE CANAL

The first was the American Civil War. Southern cotton was a mainstay of European textile mills until the Union blockade choked it off. But the climate and soil of the Nile delta were ideal for raising the crop, and the country's much-oppressed peasantry—the *fellahin*—were but a half-step above slave labor anyway. Ismail expanded his cotton plantings as fast as he could, and British and European mills bought as much cotton as Egypt could grow. Egyptian cotton was then, as now, prized for its long staple, and there was still demand for it even after the war ended.[3] By the late 1860s, Ismail had—or thought he had—more money than he could spend.

This avalanche of wealth coincided with the construction of the Suez Canal. A French-run company began digging the canal in 1859, and it opened ten years later. The canal's military and commercial importance was self-evident. By materially shortening sailing time between Europe and Asia, the canal drove commerce to, and through, Egypt. It also had profound geopolitical consequences. The historic trade routes between Europe and Asia were along the coast of Africa and around the Cape of Good Hope. Thus, the European powers, particularly Great Britain, had established strings of bases and colonies around Africa to support their interests. But the Suez Canal changed this calculus. Now, the eastern Mediterranean, the Red Sea, and the Horn of Africa were the choke points, and the elaborate systems that had previously guided trade with India, the East Indies, and China were less relevant. The fact that ocean commerce and warships were increasingly powered by steam instead of wind also meant that everything now happened faster and on a bigger scale.

Britain, in particular, had long opposed and feared the Suez Canal's construction. The United Kingdom did not yet have in the eastern Mediterranean Sea the strongholds it enjoyed at Gibraltar, Malta, and Minorca in the west, and the diversion of trade through the canal both detracted from British sea power and empowered almost every one of its rivals. Russia, in particular, was to be feared. If, for any reason, it could topple the Ottoman Empire, there was little to stop the tsar from extending his power to the eastern reaches of the Mediterranean and threatening Britain's communications with the Indian subcontinent, East Asia, and the Pacific. And, in the meantime, the canal might give Egypt ideas, and Egypt was the Ottomans' richest possession.

THE KHEDIVE ISMAIL

With his wealth and his country's strategic position, Ismail thought the time had come for Egypt to take its place among the family of nations. Indeed, he said, the Suez Canal all but detached Egypt from Africa; now it was part of Europe. Ismail constructed thousands of miles of irrigation canals, railroad tracks, and telegraph lines and even built a new district of Cairo mimicking Paris. (Ismail had been educated in Paris and was a devout Francophile.) He constructed a new opera house in Cairo, commissioned Giuseppe Verdi to write *Aida*, and attended its premier there in December 1871. Ismail was unfazed by the expense of all this. He was the largest individual landowner in the world, which made him in the eyes of many the wealthiest man on earth. With Egypt's prospects so bright, English and French banks happily loaned Ismail all the money he wanted. Obviously, no ruler with Ismail's wealth and position could bear continued subservience to the Ottoman Sultan and continue to fork over the large yearly tribute the Sultan commanded.[4] The time had come for Egypt to free itself from Turkey and conquer an empire of its own. With barely concealed ambition, Ismail began building an army.

The success of the Great Exhibition of 1851 prompted France to stage an Exposition Universelle in 1855, which Britain answered with an International Exhibition in 1862, causing France to organize yet another Exposition Universelle in Paris in 1867. Ismail mounted a lavish exhibition there—it had a Bedouin camp and a full-scale model of a pharaonic temple—and he enjoyed a reception worthy of his extravagance when he arrived in June. But he mixed business with pleasure. Every major arms-maker had come to Paris to show off its new weapons, and this was a perfect opportunity to start making plans. Ismail's entourage included a contingent of military officers, including army commander in chief Ratib Pasha and his ordnance experts Hassan Aflatoun and Étienne Minié.[5]

Ismail was interested in buying volumes of these new rifles, and he undoubtedly inspected them during his visits to the exposition. As a matter of national pride, it would be necessary to test them properly in Cairo, but in the meantime Ismail asked the French government to handle a set of trials for him. The competition began in Vincennes in late December 1868 and lasted until the end of January 1869.[6]

The Great Powers generally thought that whoever controlled the munitions of a developing country would control its military policy, too, so managing Egypt's choice of a new breech loader was a matter of importance to France and Britain alike. The French put forward the Chassepot, while the British offered their still-unperfected Martini-Henry. The board quickly rejected both, leaving only the Americans. The three finalists were Berdan, Peabody, and Remington, although the Berdan quickly fell out because its maker, Colt, was tied up with a big contract for Russia.[7]

The next round of trials was held a few months later at the Toura Artillery School near Cairo. Possibly at Ismail's invitation, Samuel Remington sailed to Cairo to attend the trials and there put his innate salesmanship to good use. Remington evidently represented to Ismail that the rolling block had been adopted as the standard rifle for the US Army, a statement which—although false—helped to win the business.*

---

* J. Dunn, "Egypt's Nineteenth Century Arms Industry," 9. A year later, when Ismail learned the truth, he angrily exclaimed "then they have lied to me again!" (US DOS Archives, G. H. Butler [Alexandria] despatch to H. Fish [Washington, DC], December 30, 1870, NAID211442158/ Images 104–5).

Ismail made a triumphal European tour in May and June 1869 to personally invite the continent's nobility to the festivities surrounding the opening of the Suez Canal. During the trip, the indefatigable Samuel Norris met the equally ubiquitous Ratib Pasha in the smoking room of Buckingham Palace to sign a contract for 60,000 Remingtons at 70 shillings apiece. The price Ratib agreed to pay was high for a gun as simple as the Remington rolling block. Only weeks before, Russia had signed a contract for 30,000 Berdan IIs—a more complex gun—at 65 shillings and later Remington sold rolling blocks to Egypt for 60 shillings.[8] There was an enduring suspicion that E. Remington & Sons freely paid bribes to get business, and Remington's price may well have included an allowance for a commission to the notoriously venal Ratib. There had been joking from the outset about such under-the-table payments; the editor of a French military journal commented at the time on "the rumors that have circulated about certain financial operations," but went on dryly to assure his readers that "everything will happen in the most honest, least oriental way in the world, that is to say without *bahschich*." In any event, the order was placed, and Colonel Minié was dispatched to Ilion to supervise the guns' inspection.[9]

Even if the price was inflated, the decision to order the Remington was a good one. The rolling block was a sturdy and reliable rifle and almost soldier-proof in its simplicity. It was accurate, had a good rate of fire, and was easy to maintain. It was not uncommon for foreign militaries to insist on some customization of the guns they ordered, and the Egyptians did so here, specifying changes to the gun's ammunition, which came to be known as the Egyptian .43 cartridge.[10]

"THERE IS NO NORTH OR SOUTH HERE"

This was the beginning of a long, if occasionally tortuous, relationship between Remington and Ismail. As a sign of favor, Ismail presented Samuel Remington with a plot of land in a fashionable quarter of Cairo. Remington was duty-bound to build a suitably lavish residence, which became a gathering place for Cairo's American society. It was a pleasant spot, a Confederate veteran wrote, "because there is no North or South here."[11]

Ismail needed a professional army as much as he needed modern weapons. Somehow, he was introduced to an adventurer named Thaddeus Mott, the son of a respected American doctor who once had been a court physician in Constantinople. Mott had a life worthy of a novel. He fought for Garibaldi in Italy as a teenager, then worked on a clipper ship, after that joined the Mexican army, and, finally, distinguished himself as a Union officer during the Civil War. He came to Egypt in April 1869, and Ismail quickly made him a *ferik* (akin to a major general). Before long, Mott was off to the United States to recruit veteran officers for the Egyptian army. For this, he enlisted the help of his friend William T. Sherman. Sherman did not discriminate between Union and Confederate, but the men he recommended tended to be officers who had been treated unjustly or otherwise fallen on hard times. The contingent was led by Sherman's West Point classmate Charles P. Stone, whose unfair scapegoating by Edwin Stanton—if not by Lincoln himself—in the recent war almost rose to the level of personal malice. There were two former Confederate generals, William W. Loring and Henry H. Sibley, who had been similarly ill-treated by the Rebel authorities, and underneath these three generals were about forty other veterans. Twenty of these men became colonels in Ismail's army, three lieutenant colonels, eleven majors, three captains, and three surgeons[12]

In Cairo and Alexandria, the American officers found an army and bureaucracy of studied disorganization. To the extent cultural and religious limitations permitted, they set to work modernizing what they could. Seeing that the country was defenseless against a naval attack, they built coastal defenses, brought a torpedo expert over to start a submarine school, and created a system of military railroads. They repaired lighthouses, established powder works and a cartridge plant, built an armory "with machinery for producing the latest Remington arms," and began acquiring ships to start a navy of sorts. General Stone took steps to create a general staff, including a staff college. To improve the quality of the infantry, he opened schools to educate the lower ranks and was surprised to find that within four years three-quarters of the infantry could read and write. Knowing Ismail's ambitions to expand his control to the south, Stone sent exploration details and surveying parties up the Nile and into Somalia.[13]

With Egypt apparently awash in wealth, it was inevitable that the Americans there would be drawn into arms-dealing. The American Consul General in Alexandria was George H. Butler, the nephew of the much-disliked Massachusetts politician Benjamin F. Butler. Mott enlisted George Butler in his effort to sell the Khedive 9,566 Colt revolvers, 10,278 Winchester carbines, and an equal number of Winchester rifles, plus a suite of cartridge-making machinery for a total of $717,386. In addition to whatever portion of the profits Mott agreed to share, Butler stood to benefit because his uncle's recently formed U.S. Cartridge Company would help provide the copious volume of ammunition these 30,000 guns would require. General Stone—by all accounts an honest and diligent man—opposed the purchase on the grounds that the Winchester's intricate mechanism and light ammunition were unsuitable for the Egyptian army. The Khedive was persuaded, and Egypt stayed with Remington. Perhaps in retaliation, Butler did his best to undermine Stone before fleeing Egypt in 1872 after joining a melee where one of the Confederate veterans was wounded.[14]

But other arms-makers did make sales in Egypt. Colt, using Remington as its sales agent, provided dozens—perhaps as many as 120— six-barreled large-caliber Gatling guns to the Khedivate. These were .58 caliber and presumably used the same ammunition as Egypt's Snider conversions. A few years later, Colt developed a light Gatling gun that could be mounted on a camel, much like the *zamburak* swivel-guns that had been used for centuries in the Middle East and South Asia. Colt offered these to Egypt and other customers, although it is unclear how many it sold.[15]

Dissimulation

Egypt's resort to American weaponry and advisers alarmed the British, who concluded that Ismail was preparing for a war of independence against Turkey. They probably were right. Ismail had indeed toyed with the idea of seceding from the Ottoman Empire, and there are suggestions that he timed his moves with whatever the Russians were doing to stir up trouble with Turkey. The Americans, for their part, thought this was exactly why Ismail had bothered to hire them in the first place. This was intolerable to the European powers, and in late 1869 British diplomats insisted that Ismail stop it. Perhaps at the urging of British or French diplomats, the Sultan ordered Ismail to surrender his breech loaders—the Sultan thought he had 200,000—and turn over two ironclads building in France. Ismail nimbly dodged the demand. He offered up the ironclads if the Ottomans would pay for them; as for the breech loaders, he said he had but 40,000 and these already had been distributed to his troops. With the surrender of the warships, the Sultan relented on the breech loaders, but to be safe Ismail canceled the unfulfilled portion of his order with Remington. Estimates of that number vary, but probably all but 15,000 to 20,000 guns already had been delivered. Fortuitously, war between France and Prussia soon broke out and Remington was able to offer Ismail's guns to the beleaguered French at $1.50 more than the Egyptians had agreed to pay.[16]

Ismail's obeisance to the Sultan was, obviously, just a gambit. Even while the Franco-Prussian War was raging, he inquired of George Butler whether he could get another 100,000 rolling blocks and, as soon as the war ended, Remington resumed shipping guns to him. Ismail decided that the best course of action was to dissimulate about his intentions, and he proceeded to flood diplomatic and military channels with disinformation. Some were led to believe that Russia was selling him arms, while others heard stories that Ismail had ordered 200,000 Chassepots from a merchant in Leghorn. Ismail assured the British Consul General that he had canceled his contract with Remington and had no plans for any new guns, while he was in fact having Remington transship arms to him through Liverpool with misleading markings suggesting that the crates contained only hardware or were destined for Yemen. Meanwhile, the British Minister to Constantinople wrote the Foreign Minister that Ismail already had 160,000 breech-loading rifles on hand, "amply sufficient for all his legitimate wants." Writing in 1877, one observer concluded that Ismail had 80,000 soldiers armed with rolling blocks and another 200,000 in store in his arsenals.[17]

Ismail's concealment efforts were successful enough that to this day no one really knows how many rifles Remington sold him. It is relatively safe to say that he ended up with the full complement of the 60,000 guns Ratib had contracted for in June 1869. Egypt put in an order for 55,000 rifles in 1874, which might have been for the renewal of the 1869 contract or a new contract altogether. At some point in these years, Egypt canceled a contract for an unknown number of rifles before Remington got to work on it, with Ismail paying Remington an indemnity of £30,000 to £35,000. There were others after that. After the terrible losses of its abortive invasion of Ethiopia in 1875 and 1876, Egypt had to restock its arsenals, and it may have signed yet another contract about that time; in 1877 the Khedive settled a dispute with Remington for overdue payments of £E71,000, an amount sufficient to pay for about 23,000 rifles. After that, Egypt contracted for 100,000 rolling blocks at £3 apiece, of which 54,100 were delivered. Samuel Remington later claimed that altogether he sold $3 million worth of guns and machinery to Egypt, and his firm was still owed $1 million for various reasons. Writing in 1893, Samuel Norris remembered that Remington sold Egypt "near 200,000 arms." Working through all of this—and the details are hard to track—suggests that Remington sold Egypt between 150,000 and 175,000 rolling blocks between 1870 and 1878.[18]

DISASTERS AND DEBT

Having avoided a direct confrontation with Turkey, Ismail shelved his ambitions of independence and turned his attention to creating a vast empire in northeast Africa. Sudan already was nominally an Egyptian possession, and in 1874 Ismail expanded his territory by annexing Darfur to the west. But his larger ambition was to swallow the entire Nile valley, which meant war with the Ethiopian emperor Yohannes IV. Ismail now had more Remingtons than ever and a well-trained army to boot, so the conquest of Ethiopia promised to be a straightforward affair.[19]

In November 1875, Ismail sent a force of a few thousand men by sea to Massawa in Egyptian-held Eritrea. Led by a mélange of Danish, American, Swiss, Austrian, and Egyptian officers, the force was massacred at a place called Gundat. To avenge the defeat, Ismail send a second, larger force of about 11,000. Ismail's third son, Prince Hassan, nominally led the force, but its commander in chief was the cunning Ratib Pasha, with former Confederate general William Wing Loring reluctantly agreeing to serve as Ratib's chief of staff. Of the three, only Loring had the capability to command, but Ratib's prevarication, inexperience, indecisiveness, and dissipation turned the expedition into—in Loring's words—a "military comedy." Predictably, the expedition ended in disaster at the Battle of Gura in March 1876, where Prince Hassan was captured by Yohannes and thousands of Egyptian soldiers were killed. Ratib's incompetence was the principal reason for the disaster, but in the subsequent finger-pointing the tenure of the American officers slowly came to an end.[20]

Financial dependence upon the European powers slowly strangled Ismail's Egypt and gave the Europeans the opportunity they needed. A *firman* from the Sultan in June 1873 had removed all limitations upon Ismail's ability to borrow and, before long, Egypt was hopelessly in debt.[21] To raise money, Ismail sold his controlling stake in the Suez Canal Company to the British government in November 1875 for about £4 million, but this was only a drop in the bucket. The following year, a commission of European diplomats and bankers took control of Egypt's treasury to manage the country's finances. Ismail remained Khedive, if something of a figurehead. When dissatisfaction with European interference erupted into a popular uprising, Ismail did little to stop it and, in the eyes of some, tacitly encouraged it. Egypt was too important strategically for Britain and France to tolerate such perfidy, and they prevailed upon the Sultan to remove Ismail in June 1879.

The British historian Keith Brown has pointed out a critical thing about weaponry: guns last a long time and they turn up in inconvenient places. The Egyptian Remingtons are a case in point. In 1881, the son of poor Nubian boat builders named Muhammad Ahmad proclaimed that he was the long-awaited Mahdiyya, or Mahdi, divinely ordained to prepare the world for the second coming of Jesus and to reunite all Moslems. Ahman instigated a jihadist revolt in Sudan that resulted in the destruction of several armies sent to subdue him, the capture of Khartoum, and the death of British General Charles ("Chinese") Gordon. One reason

Ahman did so well was that he was remarkably well-armed with weapons the Ethiopians had captured from the Egyptians years before and which Ahman's jihadists had then taken from the Ethiopians. Ahman died in 1885, but his successor, known as the Khalifa, continued the struggle, ultimately defeating the Ethiopian army and killing Yohannes himself in 1889. Having had enough of this, in 1898 British authorities dispatched a combined British-Egyptian force under General Herbert Kitchener to Sudan to suppress the Khalifa for good. Kitchener defeated the Khalifa's 60,000-man force that September at Omdurman, in a battle covered by the young journalist Winston Churchill. The exact number of dervishes killed can only be guessed, but after the shooting had stopped, Kitchener's forces collected 15,000 Remington rifles from the battlefield.[22]

CHAPTER 17

An Onion Dome

Motorists driving through Hartford, Connecticut, on the Interstate 91 overpass might for a second think they were in Moscow. To the west of the road there is a large, shapely onion dome, azure and embellished with gold stars. On top, there is a gilded weathervane in the shape of a rampant colt clenching a broken lance in its teeth. This, it is said, is a reference to Alexander the Great's horse, Bucephalus, who seized an enemy's lance to save his master. A reliable colt, it suggests, will always protect you.

Samuel Colt erected his dome in 1855 to announce his success in selling arms to Russia.* In 1853, Colt's friend Thomas Seymour was appointed to the post of United States Minister to Russia just as the Crimean War broke out. Seeing opportunity, Colt got to know Russia's Minister to the United States, Eduard de Stoeckl, a consummate diplomat who happened to take an acute personal interest in any business Americans were doing in Russia. With help from Stoeckl and Seymour, Colt took several trips to St. Petersburg between 1854 and 1858, usually returning with some business in hand. He sold thousands of revolvers to the Russian army and navy, got a contract to convert 50,000 old smoothbore flintlocks into percussion rifles, and sold the Tsar about three-dozen machines to equip his armory at Sestoretsk. Colt even developed something of a personal relationship with the Romanovs. When Tsar

---

* The original dome burned down in 1864 along with the rest of Colt's East Armory. Colt's widow, Elizabeth Hart Colt, insisted that the armory—dome, weathervane, and all—be rebuilt. The work was finished by 1867.

Alexander II was crowned in St. Petersburg in September 1856, Colt and his family attended ceremonies as official guests of Colt's friend Seymour. In 1858 Colt returned to Russia, using the occasion as an opportunity to lavish extravagant presentation revolvers on the Tsar and his brothers, the Grand Dukes Michael and Constantine, and receiving profuse gifts in return.[1]

STRANGE BEDFELLOWS

For much of the nineteenth century, the United States and Russia were on the best of terms. The United States remained neutral in the Crimean War and Russia in the Civil War. Tsar Nicholas I emancipated Russia's serfs in 1861, and he saw parallels in America's efforts to do the same for its enslaved peoples. Britain was a common nemesis. To Americans, Britain was a trade rival that actively worked to subvert the Union during the Civil War. Russia saw Britain as an impediment to the Tsar's ambitions in the Balkans, a not-so-secret supporter of the tottering Ottoman Empire, and a rival in what came to be known as the Great Game in Central Asia. Both Russia and the United States were in the process of creating continental empires, but there was no geopolitical space where the two countries competed. The world, in those days, was big enough for both.

The two countries' political, social, and economic systems could not have been more different. Russia would have been considered a third-world county, ruled by a hereditary autocrat surrounded by a reactionary nobility sitting atop a quasi-feudal economy. It was woefully behind Europe in terms of industrialization and, to some, it was an open question whether Russia considered itself part of Europe anyway. Its main assets were an immense amount of land, an enormous population, bottomless potential, and a certain strategic immunity against invasion. The United States, by contrast, was a rapidly industrializing republic that had a continent pretty much to itself. Protected by two oceans and preoccupied with internal political strife and the allure of untapped natural resources, America might have been considered the more inward-looking of the two places, except for the fact that its entrepreneurial culture propelled its merchants and traders to look for opportunities abroad.

Armaments were one area where the two nations' interests converged. Until the mid-nineteenth century, Russia had been self-sufficient when it came to arms, but its army was shocked into reform by the bitter experience of the Crimean War, and then further shaken when Prussia so quickly dispatched the Austro-Hungarian army in 1866.[2] Armies now had breech-loading rifles, metallic ammunition, repeating rifles, and even rudimentary machine guns. A military revolution was underway, and Russia lacked the industrial capacity to keep up.

In November 1866, the Tsar dispatched a contingent of officers under the command of Colonel Alexander Gorloff to the United States with instructions to study American guns and machinery and bring back what they could. It was not immediately clear how far Gorloff's charge extended, since there was a fuzzy line between his authority as an army officer and Eduard de Stoeckl's as the Tsar's representative in the United States. Although the amount of trade between the United States and Russia was minimal, Stoeckl kept a close watch on things since, like other diplomats of the time, he supplemented his government salary by taking commissions on business deals.

This led to a curious dynamic. Gorloff was an honest and meticulous officer, determined to get the best rifle he could, while Stoeckl was equally determined to get a cut of whatever arms deals Russia made. In choosing a rifle, Gorloff decided to deal with whoever held patent rights to the various systems, while Stoeckl set up meetings to lock up the contract to manufacture whatever guns Gorloff chose. Stoeckl particularly favored Colt, and upon learning the details of Gorloff's charge—it turned out that he was to order 30,000 rifles, buy gun-making machinery, and secure patent rights on whatever system Russia chose—he assured Colt vice president General William B. Franklin that Colt would get the contract. He also advised Franklin to have nothing to do with Gorloff until he came to Hartford.[3] Stoeckl added that he wanted no specific bid from Colt on the guns, only a general one for the entire transaction. The not-so-subtle message was that Stoeckl's influence would determine who got the contract.

But this was easier said than done because most of the patent rights Gorloff was dealing with already were licensed to someone other than

Colt. Thus, before Colt could manufacture guns for Russia, it needed a gun to manufacture. Franklin looked into trapdoor systems, in part to take advantage of the large market for converting muzzle loaders. Hiram Berdan was a good person to start with, since Berdan had patents on such a gun, not to mention a center-fire metallic cartridge that worked with it. Once he got deeper into the issue, though, Franklin began to fear that Berdan's gun would infringe patents held by Theodore Laidley, William Mont Storm, Benjamin Roberts, William Morgenstern, and William Miller, to name just a few. So, while Gorloff was inspecting all manner of breech-loading systems, Franklin and Berdan were negotiating with an array of inventors to clear a path to manufacture the Berdan design. Meanwhile, Berdan was cutting a separate deal with Marcellus Hartley to license his cartridge.*

Stoeckl and Franklin's careful plans were upset in May 1867, when Gorloff announced that he was leaning decidedly toward Providence Tool's Peabody rifle. Stoeckl swore that this would not happen; he vowed to Franklin that Colt would have "any order for guns given in this country by his government." Stoeckl may well have been playing both sides but, in any event, he informed Providence Tool that as the Russian representative in the United States, he would refuse to sign a contract for the Peabody unless he was paid a large commission. Perhaps mindful of Senator James Simmons's extortion efforts in 1861, John Anthony refused to pay the bribe and lost the contract to Berdan and Colt. In his somewhat stilted style, Anthony wrote, "This was a great disappointment to us, but gave us some insight into the methods by which gun orders are secured."[4]

The final contract was for 30,000 rifles, with accoutrements, at $22.85. It was a complicated multiparty affair with Russia paying Berdan ₽50,000 for his patent rights, Berdan and Colt buying licenses to quiet various patent claims, and Berdan redesigning his gun to circumvent yet another patent.[5] The rifle Russia ended up with—known as the Berdan I rifle to distinguish it from a bolt-action gun Berdan licensed to Russia a few years later—was a well-regarded gun despite its twisted genealogy.

---

* And Stoeckl was bargaining with American Secretary of State William H. Seward to sell Alaska to the United States. Treaty Concerning Cession of Russian Possessions in North America, 15 Stat. 539 (March 30, 1867).

Dispensing with an external hammer, it had instead a spring-loaded sliding one within a mechanism that also locked the breech block when the trigger was pulled. The Berdan I's barrel was .42 caliber, and it fired a bottlenecked metallic cartridge with a 370-grain bullet and about 77 grains of powder.[6]

Stoeckl, presumably, got his commission, although it is unclear who—Colt or Berdan himself—actually paid him. However, Franklin was a career army officer with a record unblemished by accusations of personal corruption, while Berdan's character had few defenders. Ordnance Chief Alexander Dyer, for example, thought Berdan "thoroughly unscrupulous and unreliable," and a diplomat whom Berdan tricked in Berlin in 1874 wrote Secretary of State Hamilton Fish that "the man is a charlatan."[7] Some of Berdan's later correspondence with Franklin, moreover, discusses with some candor his kickbacks to influential parties. It is worth remembering, though, that even if Franklin did not himself pay off Stoeckl, he undoubtedly knew about it. Ultimately, the arms business tainted everyone.

The Russian contract was not an especially large one, but Franklin thought that it was a promising first step. Even while Gorloff was testing various rifles, Franklin began negotiating a contract with Russia for twenty of the new multibarrel guns Colt was starting to make under its license from Dr. Richard Gatling. Moreover, any country that bought rifles would need revolvers, too, and no one—so Franklin thought—could match Colt in that department.

WILLIAM FRANKLIN AND THE BERDAN II

Colt was managed in these years by the retired general William Buel Franklin. Of Quaker extraction, Franklin nonetheless chose a military career and, through the offices of future president James Buchanan, received a place at West Point. He graduated first in his class in 1843, where he made a lifelong friend of classmate Ulysses Grant. Franklin became a military engineer, managing such projects as completion of the dome of the US Capitol and construction of the new Treasury Department building. In the chaotic early days of the Civil War, the task of making sense of the flood of volunteers was assigned to then-captain

Franklin, who came up with the plan for the organization of the new Union army. Franklin was pulled away from his engineering work to command combat troops in the Civil War. He suffered more than most in the army's administrative upheavals and took blame for blunders he did not commit. Nonetheless he was a brevetted major general in the regular army when he retired in March 1866 to take the job as Colt's vice president and general agent.[8]

Colt was in trouble when Franklin came aboard. Samuel Colt had died suddenly in 1862, the company's pistol works burned down two years later, the Civil War's end killed demand for guns of all types, and, at a time when metallic cartridges appeared, Smith & Wesson controlled the dispositive Rollin White patent. In all probability, the reason Colt survived at all was Franklin's attentive management. He drew up the plans for a new pistol works and superintended its construction; hired engineers to come up with new revolver designs; lobbied to prevent White from extending his patent; bought the rights to manufacture the Gatling gun; and took steps to have Colt develop its own breech-loading rifle. Franklin did all of this at a time when the entire industry was in distress and such household names as Burnside, Sharps, Spencer, and Whitney disappeared. Franklin managed Colt for twenty-three years and, largely due to his efforts, Colt was one of the few major American gun manufacturers that avoided liquidation.

After landing the contract for the Berdan I, Franklin turned his attention to getting further business from Russia. As a military man, he undoubtedly had expected some degree of professionalism from his Russian counterparts, but instead he found that dealing with Russia was a headache. At the top, the Russian military was a snake pit of intrigue, if not a sump of privilege, ineptitude, and corruption. It was difficult at any given time to know who was in power and who was scheming against whom for advantage. Although Alexander Gorloff was a dedicated officer, he also was a fussy perfectionist who constantly tinkered with gun designs and all too often took more credit than he was due for the incremental improvements he insisted upon. Gorloff become notorious for constantly demanding small changes to the weapons Russia ordered, for rejecting guns with insignificant flaws, and for refusing to accept once-rejected guns that had been fixed. (In fact, Colt had 5,000 surplus Berdan I's for sale in 1870, probably guns Gorloff had refused.) Nor could Franklin rely upon his own agents. Hiram Berdan ostensibly was Colt's partner in the company's dealings with the Russians, but in fact he was intent on establishing an independent relationship with the Tsar's military men, all the while keeping Gorloff in the dark.[9] The Russians, for their part, had no intention of becoming dependent upon Colt, viewed trapdoor designs like the Berdan I as primitive, and were more interested in buying gun machinery for their armories than anything else.

Franklin thought Colt could get a contract of some sort: after all, his factory was tooled to mass-produce the Berdan I, and any kinks in production had been worked out. However, Berdan had his own agenda. In 1868 he had patented the bolt-action Berdan II that he was promoting on his own account.[10] In February 1869, Berdan had a prototype of his gun made in England, which he submitted for trials in France. But Russia was the main prize, and evidently through Berdan's influence Russia made a tender to the Birmingham Small Arms Company in June 1869 for a large number—some say as many as 300,000—of Berdan IIs at 55 shillings each, with an additional 5-shilling royalty to Berdan. BSA countered with a proposal of 62 shillings (later raised when the bayonet was changed) plus, somewhat mysteriously, an even-higher 6-shilling royalty to Berdan. A contract for 30,000 Berdan IIs on these terms was signed on October 24, 1869. In keeping with Russia's long-term objectives, it also planned to buy BSA's tooling and production machinery at the end of the contract run.[11]

It is unclear how much of this Franklin knew, but in late 1869 he went to St. Petersburg with his top salesman Frederick von Oppen (Franklin thought von Oppen was the only man he could trust) to meet with Berdan and officials of the Russian military. Berdan told him about BSA's Berdan II contract, but then said that patent issues might prevent BSA from performing the contract, reopening the door for Colt. This, of course, was a strange thing for Berdan to say, but Franklin's more fundamental question was whether the Berdan II was even fit for service.[12] Old soldier and engineer that he was, Franklin knew that extensive testing and modification was required of any gun before it went into production, and that any armory that invested in tooling before a design was final was likely to go broke. Franklin made some proposals to manufacture the Berdan II, but nothing came of it.

Birmingham Small Arms did, in fact, receive the contract for the Berdan IIs and fought its way through patent litigation, including a lawsuit Samuel Norris brought for infringement of the patents on the Mauser rifle. But, as Franklin had thought, the contract was a poison pill. Long after milestones had come and gone, the Russians were tinkering with the Berdan II. Approval of a final design did not come until February 1, 1871, which happened to be the very deadline for finishing the contract. Meanwhile, BSA had invested so much in machinery and tooling that it was required to close its plant and lay off its workforce in mid-April of that year. After that, the Russians complained about the poor quality of BSA's work compared to Colt's. One Russian inspector wrote that half of BSA's barrels and gunstocks, almost one-third of the receiver frames, a quarter of the breech mechanisms, and 15 percent of the ramrods were defective. Unsurprisingly, with these rejection rates, BSA lost money on the contract, and there was no order for additional guns beyond the original 30,000.[13]

But there were some successes out of this messy story. The Birmingham machine tool firm of Greenwood & Batley did well by selling BSA the machinery it needed to manufacture the Berdan IIs, and then equipping Russian armories with even more machines. In April 1871, the company signed a ₽1.5 million contract for about 850 machine tools, including rifling machines, screw drop hammers, boring machines, and lathes. The Americans, though, were not completely excluded. Knitting these machines into an efficient production system was an enormous challenge that had bedeviled the Russians for a long time. Thus, even before it had executed its contract with the Tsar, Greenwood & Batley reached out to the American James Burton, who had been instrumental in modernizing Britain's Enfield armory years before. (Burton had spent the Civil War as a lieutenant colonel in the Confederate Ordnance Department.) Greenwood & Batley hired Burton to work on production of tools for Russia, oversee their installation at Sestroretsk, and then, circumstances permitting, expand the capacity of the Tula armory to 300 Berdan IIs a day. Within a few years, the new armories were in full production, although by then failing health had sent Burton back to Virginia.[14]

Despite the many hiccups, Russia's resolve to make its own guns paid off. The cost of rifles fell by half, and Russia recouped its investment within a decade. During the Russo-Turkish War, the Tsar's armories were able to produce over 150,000 Berdan IIs, and by the time Russia's rearmament was complete in 1884, about one million Berdan IIs had been made. Familiarly known as the "Berdanka," it became a treasured arm of the Russian soldier for decades thereafter.[15]

But for Colt, Russia offered one disappointment after another. As it turned out, the Berdan I's were the only rifles Colt ever sold to the Tsar, and Russia even went elsewhere for its revolvers. Once a trophy, Samuel Colt's azure blue onion dome became a haunting reminder of dashed hopes.

CHAPTER 18

Money to Be Had

"IT IS AS REGULAR A BUSINESS TO BUY ARMS IN THE CITY OF NEW YORK as it is to buy corn," Colonel Stephen Vincent Benét (the poet's grandfather) told Senator Hannibal Hamlin, chairman of the Senate committee investigating sales of government ordnance stores to France in late 1870 and 1871. Benét was not exaggerating by much: almost $14 million worth of American munitions, including 711,612 small arms, $1.5 million of heavy ordnance, and massive quantities of ammunition, were shipped directly to France from New York.[1] The war matériel packed twenty steamships to capacity and partially filled many more. Because of difficulties in collecting and loading so much matériel, barely a vessel sailed from New York on schedule during late 1870.

This was, of course, a repeat of sorts of the rash of arms-buying that the North and the South had indulged in a decade earlier, and it had the same measure of price inflation, double-dealing, and dissimulation. Now, though, the flow went the other way. Whenever someone wonders what became of the vast amount of war matériel that piled up during the Civil War, the answer is that a great deal of it ended up in France. It is questionable how much good all of this did France, but its boost to the American arms industry was undeniable. Arms-makers could sell as many guns as they could make and, not to be left out, even the federal government got into the business.

France and Prussia

The cause of all of this was the conflict now known as the Franco-Prussian War. Overlooked today, its historical importance was immense. Before the war, France had been the leading land power in Europe; afterwards, it was Germany. Foolishly, the Germans humiliated France by demanding large reparations and grabbing French territory, sparking a desire for revenge that contributed to the catastrophe of World War I.

The underlying reason for the war was the expansion of Prussian power during the 1860s and the ambitions of its chancellor, Count Otto von Bismarck, to unify the disparate German principalities into a single empire. For Bismarck's plan to succeed, France had to be humbled. Bismarck picked a fight in 1869 by arranging for an obscure Prussian nobleman to become king of Spain. Almost as eager for conflict as Bismarck, French Emperor Napoleon III declared war on July 19, 1870.

Germany had the larger army, but most observers thought France would win. France had studied the recent Austro-Prussian War and took to heart the advantages the needle-gun had given Prussia over Austria's muzzle loaders. On a crash basis, the French rearmed themselves with the modern Chassepot Model 1866. French military strategy hinged on entrenching their troops and decimating the attacking Prussians with withering small arms-fire.[2] Prussia, still using the antiquated *Zundnadelgewehr*, would be in trouble.

But Prussia, too, had studied the recent war. The Austrian forces had been incompetently led, but surprisingly stubborn thanks to their skillful use of artillery. The main lesson of this war, the Prussians concluded, was not that their needle-gun was better, but instead that their artillery was worse. Relying upon the ingenuity of the Krupp steelworks, Prussia began deploying rifled breech-loading field artillery obturated by a closure invented by (and stolen from) the American Lewis Broadwell, who by now was a European salesman for the Gatling Gun Company.[3]

The war was a one-sided affair. As predicted, the Chassepot easily outclassed the needle-gun, but the Prussians had correctly concluded that, at least in this particular war, breech-loading artillery bested breech-loading rifles. As French troops waited in their trenches, they were slowly pounded to bits by the Krupp fieldpieces.[4] In quick succession, the

The American exhibition at the Crystal Palace, 1851
DICKINSONS' COMPREHENSIVE PICTURES OF THE GREAT EXHIBITION (1852)

The Robbins & Lawrence armory on Mill Creek in Windsor, Vermont. Robbins & Lawrence was an incubator of machine tool technology and American armory practice. AMERICAN PRECISION MUSEUM, WINDSOR, VERMONT

Samuel Colt, the inveterate promoter who improved and popularized the revolver. Colt's broad patent and his influence in Washington, DC, forced competitors to explore new designs for repeating arms. NEW YORK PUBLIC LIBRARY DIGITAL COLLECTION

The azure Onion Dome Samuel Colt constructed in 1855 to commemorate his success in selling arms to the tsar of Russia WIKIMEDIA COMMONS

Illustration of the interior of the Colt armory, showing the shafting and belts that powered the machine tools and the extent and arrangement of the machinery. TENTH CENSUS OF THE UNITED STATES (1880): MANUFACTURES, VOL. 2, 1883

1854, 1855 & 1856.

ROPE MANTELET USED BY THE RUSSIANS TO PROTECT THE GUNNERS FROM RIFLE SHOTS.

A Russian gun emplacement during the Crimean War. Note the rope mantelets that were erected to protect the gun crews from the fire of rifled arms. MAJOR RICHARD DELAFIELD, REPORT ON THE ART OF WAR IN EUROPE IN 1854, 1855, & 1856. WASHINGTON GEORGE W. BOWMAN 1860.

General James Wolf Ripley. Ripley managed the Springfield Armory for fourteen years and headed the Union Ordnance Department for the first half of the Civil War. WIKIMEDIA COMMONS

Union dragoons fighting dismounted. Note that they are carrying Sharps carbines.
LIBRARY OF CONGRESS

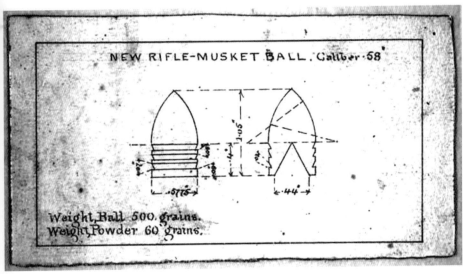

Diagram of the Burton bullet. WIKIMEDIA COMMONS

Marcellus Hartley, the New York merchant and arms dealer who was sent to England during the Civil War to buy arms for the Union. Hartley later founded the Union Metallic Cartridge and his firm, Schuyler, Hartley & Graham, became the United States's leading arms dealer. WIKIMEDIA COMMONS

Samuel Remington, the best known of the three Remington brothers. Remington moved to London in 1867, and for the next decade managed his firm's foreign sales. WIKIMEDIA COMMONS

Cutaway of the Remington rolling block breech mechanism. The breech block snaps down to expose the breech and is locked in place by the shoulders of the gun's hammer when the trigger is pulled. C. NORTON, AMERICAN INVENTIONS AND IMPROVEMENTS IN BREECH-LOADING SMALL ARMS (1880)

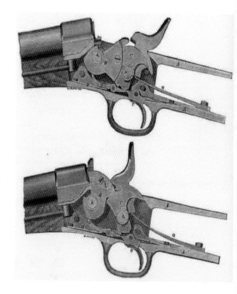

Ismail, the Khedive of Egypt from 1863 to 1879. Enriched by cotton exports during the American Civil War, Ismael hired dozens of Union and Confederate officers to modernize his army and ordered perhaps as many as 175,000 rifles from Remington.
WIKIMEDIA COMMONS

Mathew Brady portrait of Hiram Berdan, ca. 1860–1865. Berdan organized a regiment of sharpshooters in the Civil War and, in the postwar years, patented designs for cartridges and breech-loading rifles.
WIKIMEDIA COMMONS

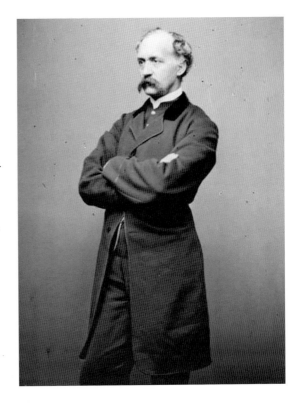

The Russian Grand Duke Alexis posing with George Armstrong Custer during Alexis' buffalo-hunting trip to Nebraska, 1872. They were joined on the trip by Buffalo Bill Cody and Chief Spotted Tail of the Brulé band of Sioux. WIKIMEDIA COMMONS

Leon Gambetta, Charles May, and William Reynolds departing from Paris by balloon on October 7, 1870. May and Reynolds's balloon, the *Georges Sand*, is on the right.
COLLECTION OF THE MUSÉES DE LA VILLE DE PARIS

A view of Ilion, New York, and the Remington armory, ca. 1874. FROM REMINGTON ARMS ARCHIVES

Barrel forging shop at the Remington armory, Ilion, New York, circa 1874. Remington was still using relatively crude trip hammers for forging work, long after other gun companies were using more modern methods. FROM REMINGTON ARMS ARCHIVES

Remington barrel machine room. In the foreground are unfinished barrels. At the back left is a set of vertical drill presses for boring or reaming barrels. On the right are what appear to be a series of rifling machines. FROM REMINGTON ARMS ARCHIVES

Remington Rifle Assembly Room No. 3. Sitting at the benches by the windows, the fitters put Remington's rolling blocks together. Note the racks of parts and the dollies holding assembled guns. FROM REMINGTON ARMS ARCHIVES

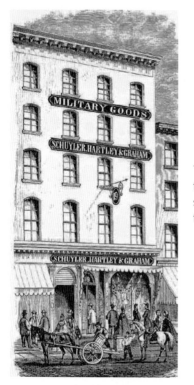

The premises of Schuyler, Hartley & Graham in downtown Manhattan. Although ostensibly a sporting goods store, the firm was one of the largest arms dealers in the world. WIKIMEDIA COMMONS

Lithograph of cartridge production at the Union Metallic Cartridge plant in Bridgeport, October 1877. HARPER'S MAGAZINE, OCT. 13, 1877

Providence Tool Company's president John Brayton Anthony (1829–1904). Beginning as a clerk in a hardware business, Anthony turned Providence Tool into one of the largest gun-makers in the world. UNIVERSITY OF RHODE ISLAND, MANUSCRIPT COLLECTION, GRACE CHURCH, PROVIDENCE, RI

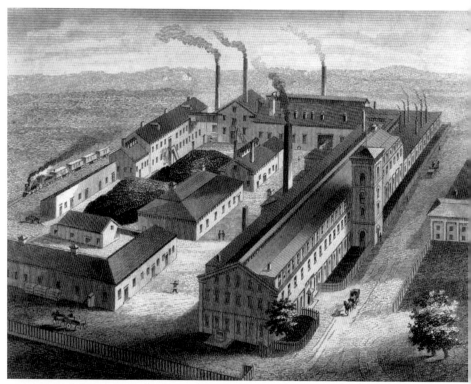

Engraving of the Providence Tool Company armory. Providence Tool manufactured over 600,000 Peabody-Martini rifles for the Ottoman Empire between 1874 and 1879. Note the enormous piles of coal in the left courtyard. AUTHOR'S COLLECTION

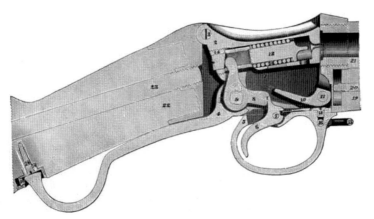

Cutaway view of the Peabody-Martini rifle. The lever dropped the breech block and automatically cocked the firing pin. C. NORTON, AMERICAN INVENTIONS AND IMPROVEMENTS IN BREECH-LOADING SMALL ARMS (1880)

Turkish General Osman Pasha, who commanded the Turkish forces at Plevna and brought the Russian invasion to a standstill for five months. WIKIMEDIA COMMONS

Lithograph of Russian attack at the Third Battle of Plevna, September 11, 1877. Note the casualties Russian troops are taking even at this distance rom the Turkish entrenchments and redoubts. *HARPER'S WEEKLY*, SEPT. 21, 1877

French lost three battles on their eastern border and were soon bottled up in their fortress at Metz. An army sent to relieve Metz was destroyed at Sedan on September 2, and Napoleon III and 80,000 of his soldiers were taken prisoner. When Metz itself surrendered in late October, the war clearly was over.

Or so it seemed. When news of the disaster reached Paris, there was a popular revolt. Napoleon III was overthrown, a new Third Republic was declared, a Government of National Defense was formed, and plans were made for a continued resistance. To avoid the advancing Prussians—they were soon at the gates of Paris—the French government relocated itself 140 miles away to Tours and made plans to continue the fight with newly raised armies. The question remained, though, where their weapons would come from.

Even before war was declared, American arms dealers had been at work. Marcellus Hartley's firm began upping its inventory of arms, buying up whatever stocks of weapons companies like Sharps and Spencer still had. In early July, Schuyler, Hartley & Graham wrote one of its Paris agents, Charles May, that it had over 25,000 rifles and pistols in stock—"all *entirely new*"—and "*want you* to press the sale of these goods." At first, French authorities had no interest, but their attitude soon changed; the only question was how many arms SH&G could get its hands on. Sensing a window of opportunity, the firm packaged up a collection of samples and dispatched a salesman, William W. Reynolds, to join May in Paris.[5]

The new French government formed a Commission of Armament, and on September 15 May and Reynolds signed a contract with the commission for thousands of Spencer, Sharps, and Remington breech loaders, as well as 1,500 converted Springfield and Enfield muskets and an immense amount of ammunition. This was, everyone guessed, just the beginning.[6]

ESCAPE FROM PARIS

The German army's encirclement of Paris already was underway, and within a few days the city was completely invested. Telegraph lines were cut, and Paris was isolated from the outside world. Although May had no reason to doubt that the text of his contract had reached Hartley before the telegraph lines went, there was no way to know for sure, so it made sense to get a hard copy of the document—and himself—to safety.[7]

Parisians soon realized that even if it was impossible to pass through Prussian lines, you could still float over them. Soon, a thriving balloon industry emerged. Working in vacant churches and train stations, seamstresses turned old curtains, bedsheets, and theater scrims into balloon envelopes, while workmen fashioned the balloon's skirts, uprights, and baskets and distillers produced volumes of buoyant coal gas. When conditions were favorable, winds carried the balloons to the outside world with bundles of letters and important documents and—for return mail—cages of homing pigeons. Understandably, there was a waiting list for balloons, but after some searching May found one in storage left over from the 1867 Exposition Universelle and bought it for F5,000. He planned to leave on October 5, but his plans were upended when the Interior Minister, Leon Gambetta, commandeered May's balloon to make his own escape from Paris. Fortunately, Gambetta happened to have a balloon of his own under construction, which he gallantly promised to May as a substitute.[8]

Weather grounded both aircraft until October 7, when "aeronauts" piloting Gambetta and his secretary Eugène Spuller in the *Armand-Barbès* and May, Reynolds, and a third passenger in the *Georges Sand* rose from the Place Saint-Pierre in Montmartre before an audience of well-wishers, including the American Minister to France, Elihu Washburne. Carried away by a northerly wind, the ships came under Prussian fire and were chased for a while by cavalry until their altitude (now 2,000 yards) and speed left the angry Germans behind. May and Reynolds landed at the town of Roye, caught the train to Amiens, and reached Tours that evening.[9]

THE "FRENCH LOAN"

But all of this begged the question of how France was to pay for this mountain of war matériel. With its capital besieged and its government in tatters, where would the money come from to pay for the small arms, artillery, ammunition, cavalry accoutrements, food, uniforms, and medical stores France needed? The government calculated that it required no less than £10 million, but worried that no bank would extend itself on behalf of a defeated country. In October, Gambetta and his ministers had their fears confirmed in London. Their usual bank, Rothschilds, flatly rejected the idea of a loan, and Baring Brothers could not help because Prussia was a client. With the top banks balking, the French turned to a smaller one run by an American, Junius Spencer Morgan. Morgan's bank, known as J. S. Morgan & Co., was mainly known for financing trade with the United States and underwriting the sale of bonds issued by American railroads. Nevertheless, Junius Morgan was respected for his honesty and common sense, and he had the additional advantage of a brilliant son, whom we know as J. P. Morgan, working at his correspondent bank in New York.

The French found the idea of an American bank appealing since so many of their new armaments probably would be coming from the United States anyway. And Junius Morgan, for his part, was not worried about France's creditworthiness. Before agreeing to make the loan, Morgan studied the history of French finances and determined that—despite its political turmoil and succession of governments reaching back to the Bourbon kings—not one of the dozen governments since the French Revolution had ever repudiated loans taken out by a predecessor. "There was no gamble," Morgan later said. "I thought it was a safe operation as it turned out."[10] Whatever else one might say about the French, they paid their debts.

Events proved Morgan right. Demand for the loan was surprisingly strong, and it quickly was syndicated to investors. Morgan earned a £275,000 commission, and he later made another £1.2 million when the French redeemed at par volumes of bonds Morgan had scooped from panicked investors after Paris fell in January 1871. Junius's grandson, J. P. Morgan Jr., later reflected that the "French loan" was the House of Morgan's first great windfall.[11]

SAMUEL REMINGTON

The volume of purchases expected from the French set off a land rush of gun-makers, salesmen, and adventurers to France. "Comparatively speaking," Reynolds wrote back to New York on September 8, 1870, "France is unarmed, there will be a big chance for somebody after this is over." No one saw this more clearly than Samuel Remington, who offered his services to France as its American purchasing agent. He was hired on September 24 or 25.[12]

Hard-nosed American arms dealers had few illusions about France's chances of success, but that was not their business anyway. They began scouring the country for anything they could box up and ship to Le Havre. At first, it was easy. Because of their foreign sales, many of the private armories were tooled up for gun production, and they threw themselves at this new opportunity. Providence Tool churned out 38,000 Peabodys within a few months.[13] Remington expanded its factory and ran multiple shifts twenty hours a day. In a period of just seven months, employing as many as 1,400 workers, it diverted production from Egypt, Spain, and other customers and shipped about 155,000 rifles to France. Even plants that rolled bayonets or stamped out sabers profited, and ammunition-makers, as always, thrived.[14]

But this was not enough: it was obvious that the only way to meet France's needs was to open the doors of the US government's arsenals. Seldom has there been a more willing seller. The War Department had finished the Civil War with over 1.2 million rifles and carbines in its depots, not to mention huge numbers of pistols and 282 million rounds of ammunition. With war debts to retire, Congress had urged the War Department to unload as much as it could. Although the Ordnance Department quickly went to work right after the Civil War—obligingly, it even refurbished its surplus weapons for foreign governments—its efforts had barely made a dent in the pile of munitions. Secretary of War William Belknap later reported to Congress that at the time the Franco-Prussian War broke out in July 1870, his department still had on hand over 890,000 muzzle loaders, 69,462 pistols, and tens of thousands of old breech loaders, not to mention huge amounts of every other imaginable type of war matériel.[15]

The Ordnance Department welcomed the newfound interest in its abundant surplus. In late September and early October, it sold

Remington 50,000 Springfield muskets at $5 apiece; Oliver Winchester 5,000 Spencer carbines at $23; W. S. Starr 35,000 Enfields at $3.50 to $4 and 5,000 Spencer carbines at $20; and SH&G thousands of Enfields and Spencer carbines at the same prices. This demand pushed up prices, and by mid-October Spencer carbines were up to $25.25 and the price of Springfield muskets had doubled.[16]

The Chief of Ordnance, Alexander B. Dyer, knew all too well that the arms he was selling were headed to France, but he saw no reason not to wring every cent he could for the US Treasury. Until then, the department had been somewhat casual about selling surplus weapons. Now, Dyer began timing arms sales to drive the market ever-higher and did what he could to encourage competitive bidding. On October 12, he advertised a massive sale of 310,000 Springfields and 100,000 Enfield muskets. Offers poured in at prices as high as $15.25 for new Springfields, and someone even bid $5.30 each for a lot of 30,000 used Enfields. Dyer was pleased at how well this worked: on October 6, Remington had offered him $7 apiece for 250,000 "good quality" Springfields but, using his leverage, Dyer ultimately got $12.30.[17]

France was indignant at these high prices and decided to do something about it. On October 12, the Government of National Defense issued a decree threatening to confiscate all arms entering the country and to pay only fair market value for them. This, they hoped, would drive out speculators and restore prices to reasonable levels. Remington's purchases were handled on this side of the Atlantic by Philo Remington's son-in-law, Watson Squire. Armed with this diktat (which, one guesses, he probably wrote himself), Samuel Remington sent a cable to Squire instructing him to suspend his purchases until the decree had settled the market. However, in an exceptionally obtuse move, Squire decided to convince Dyer of the futility of competitive sales by showing him Remington's cable. This backfired spectacularly. Dyer, knowing exactly what Remington was up to, showed the telegram to Secretary of War Belknap, who saw it as proof—as if there had been any doubt—that Remington was an agent of a belligerent power. As a neutral party, therefore, the United States could no longer could sell any arms at all to Remington.[18]

It is tempting, of course, to extol Dyer and Belknap as exemplary public servants who recoiled at the very thought that their government had been finagled into selling arms to a belligerent country through a secretive agent in violation of its solemn pledges of neutrality. In reality, they would have been fools if they had not seen what was going on, but they were not about to give up the high prices their useless surplus weapons now commanded. By pushing Remington out of the way, they again opened the bidding to speculators.

If Belknap and Dyer were astute enough to see that Remington was simply an agent of the French government, they knew equally well that Remington soon would resume its purchases through fronts and third parties. This it did. In bids accepted in late October, the Ordnance Department sold a total of 300,000 Springfields to SH&G, Boker & Co., and Austin Baldwin, as well as a quantity of old Gallagher and Warner breech-loading carbines. When a Senate committee examined witnesses from those firms, they freely admitted that they had been fronts for Remington, that their purpose had been to deceive the Ordnance Department, and that they were handsomely paid for their efforts. Perhaps the most egregious case was the department's sale in December of 24,000 Springfield breech-loading rifles, 1,600 Joslyn breech loaders, and 580 Spencers to one Thomas Richardson. No one had heard of Richardson, and it later turned out that he had never before bid on guns, nor knew much about them. And, improbably, he happened to be from tiny Ilion, New York (population 2,876), which by chance was Remington's headquarters. The Ordnance Department's man in New York, Colonel Silas Crispin, never actually met Richardson, but he later testified that someone—it turned out to be Watson Squire—told him that Richardson was a "gentleman of standing and not connected with the firm of E. Remington & Sons." This turned out, unsurprisingly, to be completely false: Richardson was a front, as Squire later candidly admitted, "to avoid raising any suspicion." Richardson made $15,000 for his work.[19]

The gun dealers themselves did not let questions of conflicts of interest interfere with their business opportunities. At the same time that Schuyler, Hartley & Graham was buying muzzle loaders from the Ordnance Department to feed to France, Marcellus Hartley—as he delicately put it—"offered these goods to Count Bismarck." A stickler for appearances, Hartley did not make the offer himself, but instead hired Herman Boker & Co. as his agent. A partner in the Boker firm, Herman Funke, traveled to Washington to call upon the Prussian minister, Baron von Gerolt, to see if Prussia might be interested in bidding for surplus arms. Gerolt asked Berlin for instructions, and on October 17 learned that Bismarck did not want the arms "because [he] could get them cheaper by taking them from the French on the banks of the Loire."[20]

Once the doors of the government's depots were opened, there was no stopping it. On December 13, Austin Baldwin & Co. received 2,600 Joslyn carbines, 10,000 Remington revolvers, 20,000 Starr's revolvers, 1.85 million Spencer cartridges, and 7.1 million pistol cartridges. And then things got serious. On February 1, 1871, Austin Baldwin took delivery of 180 ten-pounder Parrot guns and 120 twenty-pounders, plus the gun carriages, limbers, caissons, buckets, wrenches, pinchers, pole-pads, prolonges, vent punches, traveling forges, harnesses, and other equipment that went with them, not to mention over 200,000 shells and canister shot. On top of this, the Ordnance Department rid itself of unimaginable quantities of gunpowder and lead. The itemization of the surplus stores the department sold between July 1, 1870, and June 30, 1871, ran to twenty-one single-spaced printed pages.[21] As Watson Squire observed, "[O]ur Government could not have sold those arms within fifty years except under just the precise combination of circumstances that then existed."

THE NAVY REMINGTONS

But this was 1871, and France did not really want old Springfields or Enfields. Faced as they were with a well-equipped Prussian army, the French needed the Americans' fast-firing breech loaders. Inventories of these were gone, though, and private armories could not make new guns fast enough. The only place to get modern rifles was the US government itself.

In the aftermath of the Civil War, Congress was more tight-fisted than ever when it came to military spending and, for years, the Ordnance Department was prohibited from paying for new small arms for the army.

But the marines got better treatment. In March 1869, Navy Ordnance Chief John Dahlgren appointed a board of officers to determine which breech-loading arm the navy should use, with the admonition that the marines' gun should have the same weight, caliber, and ammunition as the regulation army rifle. After trials in 1869, the board recommended a rifle that used the Remington rolling-block breech and the standard .50-caliber barrel from the Springfield Armory. Since Springfield had time on its hands, the navy agreed to have 10,000 of the guns made there, with the navy paying the Ordnance Department $14.75 per rifle, plus a $1 royalty to Remington. Springfield got started on the project in mid-1870, and by the end of the year, a few thousand of the Navy Remingtons had been distributed to the marines.[22] As supplies of breech loaders dwindled in late 1870, though, Samuel Remington devised a plan to persuade the navy to hand their rifles over to him.

There was, of course, the threshold question of whether the navy was interested in selling its 10,000 rolling blocks at all. The Navy Secretary then was George M. Robeson, a New Jersey politician generally thought to be highly corrupt. On a salary of $8,000 a year, Robeson's net worth had soared from $20,000 when he was nominated in 1868 to $100,000 two years later, despite the money he spent generously entertaining guests in his Washington mansion. Of all the suspicious characters in the presidential administration of Ulysses S. Grant, there were few castigated more often or investigated more thoroughly than Robeson. During his tenure as Navy Secretary, he was subject to congressional investigations in 1872, 1876, 1878, and 1878–1879, the record of which ran to 5,675 pages.[23] All conceivable sins were ascribed to Robeson from suborning false claims and over-purchasing matériel to raking off commissions on contracts. Nevertheless, nothing ever stuck, and Robeson stayed in office for the entire eight years Grant ruled.

Barred from directly dealing with the federal government, Remington engaged the Baltimore firm of Poultney Trimble & Co. to handle the matter for him. In December 1870 or January 1871, Thomas Poultney decided to approach Robeson to see if the navy had anything for sale. In the first of several fishy moves, Poultney concluded that the best way of doing this was to hire, for a fee of $10,000, a friend of Robeson's named

MONEY TO BE HAD

Albert W. Markley. Markley was a New Jersey politician who knew nothing about guns, never had been in the arms business, and, when summoned before a Senate investigating committee, had no idea why Poultney had hired him. Markley did not do much to earn his fee. As he testified:

> Walking around to the Navy Department, I met the Secretary on the street, and asked him if he had any guns to sell, and told him that Mr. Poultney, of the firm of Poultney & Trimble, had told me the Department had some for sale. He said he did not know anything about it, and he had better communicate, and he would refer the matter to his Chief of Ordnance. I went back to the hotel and told Mr. Poultney, and he communicated, I suppose. That is about all I know about it. I got my money when the transaction was closed. That is all the trouble I had about it.

To many, it made no sense that a seasoned arms dealer like Poultney would pay such a large fee (about $250,000 today) for so little, and the whole arrangement sounded like a way to somehow put money in Robeson's pocket. It began to look even worse after it emerged that Markey had laundered Poultney's checks through a New York bank where his brother happened to work. But Markey stoutly denied that he had split his fee with anybody, and no amount of cross-examination could shake him.²⁴

The next step of the plan was to give the navy a pretext to get rid of the rifles. On January 18, 1871, the Navy Chief of Ordnance, Admiral Augustus Ludlow Case, wrote to the naval officer supervising the manufacture of the Remingtons at Springfield to inform him that "the Messrs. Remington" had told him that the position of the rear sight on the new navy rifle "weakens the arm, and does not permit an accurate sighting beyond point blank." There were several problems with this statement. The first was that it was Remington—in fact, it was Watson Squire himself—who had supplied the model of this gun to the navy when the ordnance board had conducted its gun trials. The second was that the Springfield Armory's rigorous inspection system would easily have picked up any defects in the arm or disparity between the pattern gun and the finished ones. And, most fundamentally, the officer supervising the production of the guns, Lieutenant Commander Frederick Pearson, rejected Remington's criticisms of the gun, pointing out that there was no weakening of the barrel, that the placement of the sight conformed with the barrel of the model gun, and that only marines "with weak eyes" would have a problem with the placement of the sight. Admiral Case responded that the sight must be moved, and ignored Pearson's other points.[25]

By then, Poultney & Trimble already had made an offer to Robeson for the 10,000 rifles, which Robeson accepted immediately. The entire transaction was strange. There was, of course, no public announcement of the sale or auction of the arms, and it was generally known in the trade that Poultney & Trimble were middlemen for the Remingtons. When questioned later, Admiral Case admitted that the original arm "was a good one" and had only a "slight defect." Poultney & Trimble's offer was odd: in return for the 10,000 original rifles, Poultney & Trimble agreed to provide the navy with about 12,500 new ones; however, the new rifles, like the original ones, were not to be made by Remington or Poultney & Trimble but instead by the government's Springfield Armory. But since the production run of the *original* rifles was far from completed, the armory would have to finish making the rest of the 10,000 allegedly defective guns before it could start on the new ones. This meant, at bottom, that the government employees at the armory were working for Poultney & Trimble, and any doubts on the matter were erased when it became clear that Poultney had agreed to pay any overtime wages incurred in the manufacture or reworking of the guns.[26]

And Remington made money coming and going. It charged the government a royalty of $1 a gun for the use of its patents and had collected this $10,000 for the 10,000 original rifles. Despite the fact that Remington was about to reap a windfall from reselling the 10,000 rifles, it also insisted on charging the navy the $1 royalty on each of the 12,000 new guns (inexplicably, the number had fallen from 12,500). When questioned about this, Robeson gave a confusing and evasive answer to the effect that the navy was not double-charged because Poultney & Trimble ended up covering the royalties when it paid for the arms, but there was a general sense that there had been some sharp dealings. Meanwhile, the marines were ordered to ship back to Springfield the 3,480 Remingtons they already were carrying and, presumably, return to using muzzle loaders. Between February 25 and April 15, 1871, the armory sent Poultney & Trimble the 10,000 rifles, which were duly loaded on ships and sent off to France.[27]

When the smoke cleared, the reality of the transaction was painfully obvious. Putting to one side the distinct possibility that Robeson had been bribed, the navy agreed to the transaction because it got 2,000 more breech loaders than it had before, and the Ordnance Department signed on because it kept the Springfield workforce busy at a time when the department was not permitted to buy new guns. But what all of this really meant was that the United States government had somewhat eagerly entered into the international arms business by selling weapons to agents of France during a time of war and, in effect, leasing its national armory to a firm whose letterhead identified it as "Arms-Dealers."[28]

SCANDALS AND INVESTIGATIONS

In the confusion of war, France's system for acquiring arms abroad was incomplete, inefficient, and inviting to corruption. Funds to buy arms were borrowed in London from J. S. Morgan & Co., deposited in New York with Morgan, Dabney & Co. and August Belmont & Co., and then disbursed on the authority of the French consul in New York, a man named Victor Place. Place's job was to inspect invoices and, if he approved them, instruct the banks to pay the amounts due. But Place aspired to more, and early on tried to deal in arms himself, taking commissions from Schuyler, Hartley & Graham in return for approving sales of obsolete weapons at excessive prices.[29]

Place came from a distinguished French family (he was fond of pointing out that his brother was the Archbishop of Marseilles), and he left behind in his diplomatic career one mishap after another. Among Place's shortcomings for the consulship in New York was the fact that he spoke no English, and so he hired as his assistant a man named Chauviteaux, who in turn hired a man named Church as his clerk. At each stage, someone demanded a commission. Remington was entitled to 5 percent (which he later voluntarily reduced to 2.5 percent), while Place took kickbacks from shipping lines he hired at inflated prices and helped himself to a 2 percent "consular commission" on all purchases in the United States. Chauviteaux, for his part, also insisted upon a commission of 1 percent, and most of a 25-cent-per-arm fee Place imposed on Remington.[30]

There was enormous social and political turmoil in France in the aftermath of the Franco-Prussian War. The French knew they had paid top dollar for tremendous quantities of mostly useless American weapons. Equally troubling was the fact that something like $1.5 million of the funds borrowed to pay for arms had gone missing. In June 1871, a French legislative committee submitted a report critical of Place, and he was criminally charged in October. At trial, Place accused Remington of diverting enormous sums through false bookkeeping and other devices, and he further implied that at least some of the money had gone to bribe federal officials. There was no truth in this and, in the end, Place's tactic did him no good. He went to prison for two years and, it seems, was fined F1,000,000. But Place's accusations set off a political storm in America.[31]

This was at the end of the first term of President Ulysses Grant, whose administration had a well-deserved reputation for graft. On Monday, February 12, one of Grant's political foes, Massachusetts Senator Charles Sumner, rose in the Senate to offer a resolution that the Ordnance Department's sales during 1870 and 1871 should be investigated, if only because there seemed to be a great deal of missing money and "the good name of the American Government seems to be seriously compromised." Sumner read several damning documents into the *Congressional Globe* including a telegram from Watson Squire bragging of "the strongest influences" working for Remington and a cable from Samuel Remington boasting how he had talked the Ordnance Department into manufacturing ammunition for France. The next week, Sumner's resolution was pressed by Missouri Senator Carl Schurz, a Prussian-born liberal Republican angered at the support the Ordnance Department had shown France. The Senate passed the resolution and a select committee was formed under the chairmanship of Maine Senator (and former vice president) Hannibal Hamlin to investigate the Ordnance Department's arms sales. Not to be outdone, the House of Representatives began an investigation of its own the following week.[32]

The Senate committee held thirty-one days of hearings and the House eleven. The clear objective of the Republican majority in each committee was to deflect blame from the War Department and Grant administration. The committees' few Democrats did what they could to pick apart witnesses' testimony. There were dozens of witnesses and much of the testimony was about the role Samuel Remington had played in the arms sales; inexplicably, Remington himself never showed up. The record of the committees' proceedings ran to over 1,000 pages, and the story it revealed was more one of evasiveness than anything else. Other than, perhaps, the $10,000 Albert Markley made for his one-minute conversation with Navy Secretary George Robeson, there was no evidence of official corruption. Splitting hairs, Hamlin's committee concluded that the Remingtons "were not the agents of France, but were contractors furnishing arms to France, and buying from our Government to fulfill their contracts with France." This, obviously, was ridiculous, but with France's money—about a quarter billion dollars today—now safely in the Treasury, it was best to close the book on the entire episode. It had been a windfall for all concerned, except, of course, for France itself. "[T]here was never a demand like that in this country except in our own war," Marcellus Hartley reflected, "and never will be, I guess, in the life of man again."[33]

CHAPTER 19

A Prince Visits

IN THESE YEARS, THE RUSSIANS WERE LOOKING FOR A NEW SIDEARM, and William Franklin had every right to think Colt would get the business. After all, the Tsar was a longtime customer, Colt was the leading maker of revolvers in the world, and its armory had been rebuilt with the newest machinery. What possibly could go wrong? The answer, unfortunately for Colt, was patents.

Samuel Colt had built his business on the breadth and strength of his original 1836 patent, but that had expired years ago. Metallic cartridges were now standard, and Smith & Wesson held the rights to the revolvers that used them. As long as Rollin White's patent was valid, Smith & Wesson had an unassailable position in the pistol market.

White's patent had a term of fourteen years, suggesting that the field would open up by April 1869. But things were not so simple. The Patent Act of 1836 provided that the Patent Office could extend a patent's term by seven years if a board concluded that the inventor, through no fault of their own, had failed to obtain "a reasonable remuneration" for the work they had put into the invention. Cleverly, Daniel Wesson wrote his license with White to impose upon White the trouble and expense of defending his patent. Ultimately, there was so much patent litigation that White was left with little for his efforts. Accordingly, he petitioned the Patent Office in 1867 for a seven-year extension of his patent term. This was denied, possibly due to the energetic opposition of other gun-makers and the Ordnance Department itself. Nevertheless, before long, Congress passed a bill ordering a retrial of White's claim. President Grant vetoed the bill on January 11, 1870, upon the advice of Chief of Ordnance A. B. Dyer, who complained that White, Smith, and Wesson already had profited handsomely, that the government had "suffered inconvenience and embarrassment" during the Civil War because other manufacturers were unable to use the patent, and that extension of the patent would impose unfair costs on the government. Although this seemed convincing enough, the Senate voted in late May to override the veto, thus resurrecting White's hopes. It was only when the House refused to override Grant's veto on June 22 that the matter finally was put to rest and competitors could sell revolvers with bored-through cylinders without fear of litigation.[1]

Because of the confusion surrounding White's patent extension, Colt put off development of a new metallic cartridge revolver until Grant's January 11, 1870, veto. This proved to be a bad decision. In August and October 1869, the army ordered that an ordnance board be convened under the authority of Major General John M. Schofield to report on the best small arms, including sidearms, for the service. The board, which came to be named after Schofield, required that sample arms be submitted to the St. Louis arsenal by March 1, 1870. This timing was ideal for Smith & Wesson, which had been working for some time on a new large-caliber (.44) single-action, top-break revolver that came to be known as the Smith & Wesson Model 3.[2] However, the schedule was an unfortunate one for Colt, which did not yet have a competing arm. Thus, the field came down to the new Smith & Wesson revolver and a few competing designs from Remington, Whitney, and the National Arms Company. Among these, the Model 3 was the clear winner. The Schofield Board wrote that the Model 3 was "decidedly superior to any other revolver submitted" and needed only to be converted from a rim-fire to a center-fire gun. Bolstered by this accolade, Smith & Wesson sent samples of the Model 3 to various dealers and, more importantly, to Alexander Gorloff in Hartford.[3]

Russia was at the time in the midst of choosing a new sidearm, a convoluted process characterized by the disorganization that so often bedeviled the tsarist regime. The decision to adopt a new pistol went back several years to an unsuccessful attempt to assassinate Tsar Alexander II.

Alarmed authorities rushed to rearm the country's gendarmerie, which led the Russian army to conclude that perhaps the time had come for the cavalry also to have a better pistol, or even a revolver. Since he was already in America, Alexander Gorloff was instructed to study the matter. Meanwhile, a commission was formed in Russia to test different weapons, but had trouble deciding how to go about it. After no small amount of indecision, it finally settled upon the Smith & Wesson Model 3, mostly because of the Schofield Board's favorable report. Colt, it seems, was never in the running.[4]

On the first of May, 1871, Gorloff signed a contract for 20,000 Model 3s at $13.02 each, paid in gold, with a $50,000 advance to help Smith & Wesson pay for tooling. As usual, Gorloff and his deputy—the aptly named Captain Konstantin Ordinetz—had a list of changes to the design, which Smith & Wesson wisely complied with. Some, such as Gorloff's demand that the barrel stamp and proof marks for the guns be in Cyrillic, not English, were fairly trivial. More significant was Gorloff's insistence that the Model 3's cylinder should be re-chambered for the cartridge that came to be known as the .44 S&W Russian. Even after production started, Gorloff and Ordinetz continued to demand changes, greatly complicating Smith & Wesson's manufacture of the gun. To the Russians' credit, many of these suggestions—such as a larger trigger pin, bigger cylinder retainer, stouter teeth in the extractor gear, and a more ergonomic pistol grip—were good ideas that became permanent features of the Model 3. However, this resulted in ongoing tooling changes and such a profusion of minor differences among successive production runs that even the great authority on Smith & Wesson firearms, Roy Jinks, confessed that he could not cover them all in his history of the company.[5]

Smith & Wesson completed the initial contract in the fall of 1872. Russia then gave a series of further orders, starting with two for 20,000 revolvers at $15.35 each in January and December 1873, and then one in October 1874 for 11,138 of an improved model. This led to even further orders in 1876 and 1877 for yet another 60,000 guns. All told, Smith & Wesson manufactured at least 131,138 Model 3 revolvers for Russia in these years, establishing the company as one of the preeminent gun-makers in the world. Soon, the company received orders for thousands of pistols from Japan, Turkey, and other countries.[6]

With its armory operating at full capacity filling foreign orders, Smith & Wesson somewhat neglected the American firearms market. This did not mean, however, that the Model 3 was unknown within the United States. Gorloff, Ordinetz, and the other Russian inspectors remained irritatingly demanding, rejecting guns for even trifling flaws. Rather than quarrel with its best customer, Smith & Wesson dutifully ground off the guns' Cyrillic markings and resold them domestically. Prominent and respected citizens such as Jesse James, Dallas Stoudenmire, and Texas Jack Omohundro all carried the Smith & Wesson Model 3.[7]

ALEXEI ALEXANDROVICH

In the midst of all this, one of the odder interludes in Russian-American relations occurred when the Tsar's son, Grand Duke Alexei Alexandrovich, came to tour the United States. The idea of an official visit seems to have had its genesis when a squadron commanded by Admiral David Farragut visited St. Petersburg in 1867. This called for a reciprocal courtesy and, since Alexei had naval training, it was resolved that he should lead it. Alexei's trip was notable less for the fact that he was the son of the Tsar of Russia than that this seems to have been the first visit made to America by the child of a sitting European emperor.

The Grand Duke arrived in New York on November 19, 1871, where he received salutes from the giant cannon on Governor's Island, a fleet review, official welcomes, and a parade with music provided by the bands of nineteen infantry regiments. In what became a wearisome routine, Alexei and his entourage suffered through multiple receptions, speeches, dinners, and galas. From New York, Alexei proceeded to Washington, where President Grant received him at the White House, and then to Annapolis, where he rejoined his squadron and sailed back to New York.[8]

Alexander Gorloff—now a general—was a member of Alexei's entourage, signaling the importance of American weapons to the Tsar's rearmament plans. On December 8, a train took Alexei's party to Bridgeport so he could inspect the Union Metallic Cartridge plant. Gorloff led Alexei through the factory, showing him step-by-step, in the words of one chronicler, how "gunpowder, manufactured for the Russian Government at one point near New York, is converted into cartridges at Bridgeport, for use in pistols made in Springfield." Alfred Hobbs presented Alexei with gifts, including a sporting rifle in a rosewood case and a shadow box showing Russian cartridges in every state of the production process. And, as if there were a need for anything more, Richard Gatling, too, was on hand to give Alexei a personal demonstration of his ferocious multibarrel gun.[9]

Alexei's visit was a long-remembered event at UMC. The company made room in the factory for a banqueting hall and treated the Russian delegation to lunch. Most of UMC's workforce were women, and for the occasion they adorned their machinery with flowers, bows, and ribbons and wore their finest dresses. With some hyperbole, a corporate historian later wrote that "[m]any a girl spent more time, thought, and money on her costume for the occasion than on her wedding gown." Alexei, who was something of—if, as history later sadly would show, nothing but—a ladies' man, was said to have been less impressed by the manufacturing miracle of a plant that spat out 400,000 brass cartridges daily than "the sight of the female machine operators in silk dresses and hair ribbons."[10]

Alexei's next stop was Springfield. In a harbinger of Colt's ongoing disappointment, the Grand Duke's train passed through Hartford but did not bother to stop. Instead, Alexei's object was Smith & Wesson. Horace Smith and Daniel Wesson delighted Alexei with the gift of a gold-inlaid revolver with a mother-of-pearl grip displaying the arms of Russia and the United States. Alexei was escorted through the Smith & Wesson facilities by Captain Ordinetz, who explained the process of pistol manufacture machine-by-machine. Smith and Wesson had hoped to give Alexei a demonstration of the accuracy of their revolvers, but this was dashed when the Grand Duke was forced to attend a banquet hosted by Springfield's city fathers. There, the Russian Minister to the United States, the boorish Konstantin Catacazy, managed to offend everyone by toasting the hospitality of "a city with remarkable facilities for preparing to kill people."[11]

From Springfield, Alexei's party proceeded to Boston, Ottawa, Chicago, Cleveland, and St. Louis. Finally, though, it reached its high point in Omaha, Nebraska, where the strangeness of Alexei's trip took on a whole new dimension.

GEORGE CUSTER, BUFFALO BILL, AND SPOTTED TAIL

Although the background is murky, it seems that the artist Albert Bierstadt somehow learned that Alexei might enjoy a trip to hunt buffalo—with Indians, too—on the Great Plains, and suggested as much to the Commanding General of the United States Army, William T. Sherman. Secretary of War Belknap agreed to use War Department funds to pay for the expedition and put General Philip Sheridan in charge of arranging it. Sheridan advised Belknap that winter was a bad time of year for a hunt, but obligingly went to work anyway. As to Indians, Sheridan hoped to enlist Spotted Tail, a chief of the Lakota Sioux, and a few hundred members of his Brulé band, and the general reached out to the Interior Department's Office of Indian Affairs for help. Spotted Tail leapt at the opportunity—it seems that he and his people already were hunting in the area illegally—but still demanded 10,000 rations of coffee, sugar, and flour and 1,000 rations of tobacco.[12]

A true buffalo hunt, of course, required an authentic buffalo hunter, so Sheridan hired William "Buffalo Bill" Cody. As if that was not enough, Sheridan then decided to have Lieutenant Colonel George Armstrong Custer join the expedition as well, presumably—and ominously—because of Custer's reputation as an Indian-fighter.[13]

By now, the project had ballooned to enormous size, involving 600 Brulé, dozens of cavalrymen, enormous volumes of food and equipment, and countless horses. Ensconced in Pullman cars, Alexei's party left Omaha for the hunt on the afternoon of January 12, 1872, accompanied by an unknown number of American military officers and the superintendents of the Union Pacific Railroad and Western Pacific Telegraph Company. They arrived in North Platte, Nebraska, the next day, where "[t]he three or four hundred rustic inhabitants who form the settlement were all out in the gray twilight of morning to see and welcome the Imperial visitor" and "simultaneously removed their hats" when the Grand Duke alighted from the train. There, Alexei met Buffalo Bill Cody who, in the florid prose of the time, was seated on a spanking charger, and with his long hair and spangled buckskin suit he appeared in his true character of one feared and beloved by all for miles around. White men and the barbarous Indians are alike moved by his presence, and none of them dare do aught in word or deed contrary to the rules of law and civilization.

"At exactly a quarter past eight General Sheridan gave the word to move, and Buffalo Bill advanced on a galloping steed, followed closely by the Duke's and the other conveyances." Altogether, there were 125 in the party.[14]

It was an eight-hour ride to the campsite on Red Willow Creek on January 13, with a stop along the way for sandwiches and champagne. Especially given its remoteness and winter conditions, Camp Alexis was surprisingly well appointed. There were large tents with carpeted floors for the guests and officers and smaller ones for the enlisted men, all arranged in military order. As Alexei's party approached, the band of the Second Cavalry struck up the Russian national anthem. After warming themselves around a bonfire, the party retired to the dining tents, where there were fine wines and a supper of game, including a prairie chicken bagged by Custer himself.[15]

By chance, the next day was Alexei's birthday, and it was understood that he should have the honor of shooting the first buffalo. Although accounts of the hunt are garbled, it seems that Custer charged into the buffalo herd to scatter the animals and chose a particular bull for Alexei to kill. Alexei shot the hapless bull with his revolver, presumably the one Horace Smith and Daniel Wesson gave him, but only wounded it; to end the creature's life, Buffalo Bill handed Alexei his trusty .50-caliber Springfield rifle, which he had named "Lucretia Borgia." The American press had some fun at Alexei's expense about the first day of the hunt, but Alexei seems to have been genuinely thrilled about the entire experience. There was a celebration that evening, with champagne and other indulgences, followed by a buffalo steak supper.[16]

The hunt continued over the next few days, but now in the company of Spotted Tail and eight of his chosen warriors. Alexei seems to have brought down several more buffalo, and he impressed everyone with his fearless horsemanship. Dinner on January 15 was followed by a demonstration of a ceremonial dance by the Brulé warriors, "ornamented with blankets, buffalo robes, and trinkets, their faces colored with red and yellow paint." Spotted Tail presided with his wife and his pretty sixteen-year-old daughter. Custer, in particular, was reported to have been enamored of "Miss Spotted Tail," as the newspapers called her, placing upon her a pair of earrings and giving her a kiss.[17]

The hunting party broke camp on the morning of January 16, 1872. Before leaving, Alexei presented handsome gifts to Spotted Tail and his family and gave each of the eight Brulé warriors in his hunting party an ivory-handled knife of the type made for the Tsar's imperial huntsmen. By all accounts, this was the highlight of Alexei's trip to America. He later wrote his brother Vladimir that he had "had such emotions that it is now even humorous to recall" and sent him a photograph taken with Custer. From Nebraska, the Grand Duke and his party proceeded to Denver, then to Topeka, Louisville, and New Orleans (where Alexei arrived in time to enjoy Mardi Gras), and then onward to Florida where they met the Russian squadron for the continuation of their trip to the Far East before alighting at Vladivostok on December 5.[18]

As disappointing as Alexei's visit was for Colt, it was a boon for Union Metallic Cartridge and Smith & Wesson. Revolvers and cartridges from Connecticut were a mainstay of Russian armament for years to come.

CHAPTER 20

Remington Triumphant

SAMUEL REMINGTON RULED THE SMALL-ARMS BUSINESS IN 1872. HE knew every military man worth knowing in Europe, rubbed elbows with royalty, and even had a marble palace in Cairo. From his perch in London, he supervised a network of sales agents across the globe. Any doubts about his influence were dispelled when, within the space of seven months, Remington had managed the transfer of astounding numbers of weapons to France, including 155,000 of Remington's own rolling blocks. His family's armory covered almost fifteen acres of floor space that, when working at full blast, could produce 1,500 rifles a day. Remington also had a profitable line of revolvers and now was expanding into such things as agricultural implements, cotton gins, sewing machines, and a contraption called the "typewriter."[1] And if there were a standard military rifle in the 1870s, it was the rolling block. Remington had sold over a million of them, and orders came in from everywhere.

The Franco-Prussian War affected Remington in more ways than the sheer amount of business it generated. So profitable was Remington's work in 1870 and 1871 that the Remington brothers paid themselves a stupefying $2 million dividend when it was over. Moreover, because the firm's work for the French had displaced other business, there was now a big backlog of orders. In 1870, Persia had contracted to buy 10,000 guns and Greece 15,000, both orders that now needed to be put into production. Although Egypt had terminated its 60,000-rifle order for the mutual convenience of the Khedive and Remington, deliveries probably resumed after the war. There were even significant domestic orders. Fighting off the influence of members of the Tweed Ring (who controlled the rights on domestic sales of the Allin rifle), Remington got an order from New York in 1872 for 21,000 guns for the state militia. In fact, it is hard to find places that did *not* order rifles from Ilion. Even the Papal Guard—charged with defending the tiny Vatican state—bought rolling blocks in 1874.[2]

This had the effect of driving competitors from the market. Some, like Winchester and Colt, did not seriously compete in the same space as Remington, and others like Spencer and Sharps already were gone, or soon would be. Remington's most serious competitor, Providence Tool, soured on gun-making after the end of the Franco-Prussian War saddled it with thousands of unsold Peabody rifles. Tired of a business that was so "spasmodic," the company's directors voted to dispose of its arms operation and sell its machinery and tools. Clothes wringers, sewing machines, and textile machinery, they thought, were safer lines of business.[3]

SPAIN

Although other countries were well on their way to self-sufficiency, declining powers like Spain remained dependent upon foreign arms, and it became Remington's most dependable customer. As early as 1866, Remington converted 10,000 Civil War muzzle loaders into rolling blocks for Spain. This, of course, was only a toe in the water. A slow-moving Spanish ordnance board began looking at breech loaders in 1868, putting Berdan, Gallagher, Palmer, Peabody, Remington, Sharps, Spencer, and other rifles through the customary tests of accuracy, range, rate of fire, recoil, penetration, cartridge extraction, fouling, durability, upkeep, economy, and imperviousness to water, dirt, dust, and sand. But for Remington, it was worth the wait. The board finally settled upon the rolling block in August 1870; although beset by various emergencies, the Spanish authorities placed interim orders for other guns in the meantime.[4]

The Spanish Remington was typical of the reduced-bore rifles developed in the mid-1860s. It was the same caliber (.433) as the Chassepot, with a bullet that was slightly heavier (396 grains) and a charge that was a little lighter (74 to 78 grains). Like other breech loaders of the time, the Spanish Remington had a muzzle velocity in the neighborhood of 1,350 feet per second.[5]

Samuel Norris was Remington's agent for the Spanish sales. In an article he wrote decades later, he remembered winning progressively larger contracts from Spain between 1868 and 1874 for 10,000, 50,0000, and 130,000 rifles, although an equally good source wrote that there was a Spanish order for 85,000 rolling blocks in 1867 and another 130,000 in 1874. Whatever the numbers, the guns saw much use. Spain still had restive overseas possessions in the Philippines, Puerto Rico, and Cuba, and it was beset by problems of royal succession at home. In Cuba, a rebellion of the island's upper classes against colonial rule in 1868 instigated the so-called Ten Years' War. The rebellion was especially challenging for the Spanish, partly because the insurgents were wealthy enough to buy weapons in New York and to hire a former Confederate general to lead them. Contemporaneous accounts say that Spanish forces in Cuba had 30,000 rolling blocks on hand by mid-1870.[6]

In 1872, a conflict known as the Third Carlist War erupted in Spain over a question of royal succession. Before it ended four years later, the Spanish government had placed an order for 130,000 guns, some of which probably went to Cuba or to Spanish forces in Puerto Rico. Spain tried to cut this back to 50,000 guns in 1874 because it now had more guns than it needed, prompting Norris to make an emergency trip from St. Petersburg through the Carlist lines to Madrid to talk them out of it. Norris's account of the incident suggests that he was exceptionally persuasive; even though Spain was all but bankrupt, the Council of State reversed its decision, accepted the arms, and paid for them "with a good degree of promptness." Norris noted that his "relations with all the Spanish officials were always pleasant," leading one to speculate on why they liked him so much.[7]

The Americas also became fertile ground. "Take the South American governments," as Marcellus Hartley put it in 1872, "the outs are in and the ins are out. They lose their arms, and they are buying all the time." Between 1871 and 1874, Chile ordered 12,000 guns, Columbia 6,800, Peru 5,000, and the newly independent Dominican Republic 5,000. The Spanish possessions of Cuba and Puerto Rico each ordered 10,000 rifles, and other countries like Argentina, Brazil, Honduras, and Venezuela bought unknown numbers. There were insurrections in some of these countries, too, and reports that Remingtons were being sold—probably by gun dealers—to rebels as well as the governments they were rebelling against. The biggest single buyer was Mexico, which placed orders in the mid-1870s amounting—depending on what source one uses—to somewhere between 14,000 and 50,000 rifles.[8]

All the while, Remington was producing guns for brokers like Schuyler, Hartley & Graham, who sold weapons in places and to people Remington itself could not or did not want to deal with directly. We can only guess at those numbers, but they were unquestionably substantial. China alone, some sources say, imported tens of thousands of rolling blocks.[9]

MANUFACTURING

One reason for Remington's profitability was its focus on controlling its costs. No perfectionist, Philo Remington cut capital spending by using less-specialized machine tools and by improvising fixtures and tools instead of buying sophisticated ones. Remington also pushed its machine tools to their limit, which increased productivity at the cost of wearing machines out prematurely. Felicia Deyrup observed that this seemingly wasteful approach probably reflected the fact that advances in machine tool technology quickly rendered older machines obsolescent anyway. As other armorers found when they left the business, gun-making machinery was highly specialized, wore out quickly, and was worth little on the open market. Tooling, usually useful only for specialized work anyway, barely had scrap value.[10]

Precision work on even minor gun parts had long been required by the US government and practiced by New England armorers. The Ordnance Department's 1878 memoranda governing fabrication of the 1873 Springfield rifle required even such small parts as the screws for the bayonet clasp, bolster, butt plate, and guard-bow swivel to be polished before they were done. The barrel went through two polishings, even though, at the end of the process, it was given a brown coat to prevent rust. These practices carried over to the private armories. In fulfilling its contract to manufacture Peabody-Martini rifles for Turkey in the mid-1870s, Providence Tool gave the weapons such a high finish that Ottoman troops called them the "Aynali Martini"—the "shiny Martini."[11]

Remington's standards of workmanship were different. In contrast to its competitors, Remington confined precision work to where it mattered. In 1871, a foreman sent from the Springfield Armory to visit the Remington works reported:

> The general workmanship is rough and will not compare favorably with ours. They do but little filing, polishing the parts as they come from the milling and profiling machines, without removing the burrs. In milling and profiling the parts, they in most cases force their machines beyond their capacity to do good work.

But this did not affect the guns' quality. The French commentator Achille Thomas-Anquetil, writing about the Vincennes trials in 1869, described the rolling block as "[v]ery easy to handle, elegant, well made in terms of gunsmithing," even though he personally favored the Peabody. Similarly, the Remington easily held its own in one trial after another, regardless of who was testing it. In 1869, a US Navy ordnance board chose the Remington over a host of other breech loaders, including the army's M1868 Springfield, and the next year reported that "Remington rifles are being distributed to the service to the exclusion of all other small arms."[12]

Remington also differed from the New England armories in how it ran its factory. Long after other gun-makers curtailed the practice, Remington continued to rely upon an "inside contracting" system where significant portions of its production were handled by third parties paid on a piecework basis. Remington provided the work space, power, raw materials, and machinery, while the contractors made their own tooling, jigs, and fixtures and were responsible for the oil, rags, abrasives, and other supplies they needed in their work. There were any number of advantages to the system. Remington put this work out to bid, assuring that it would get the best prices. It also let the company shift the burdens of hiring and paying its labor force onto outsiders, and it left up to the contractors whom they would hire. The Springfield inspector who came by the Remington plant in 1871 wrote that many of the workers were "lads, from twelve to twenty years old" and that "[t]hese boys with a little experience, can operate the machines and produce as much work as good mechanics."[13]

If harsh, the system reduced Remington's capital investment, streamlined its management, and simplified labor relations. Since the contractors were paid by the piece—and only for work that passed inspection—they had an incentive to find ways to improve their productivity. Similarly, some of the skilled machinists had developed shortcuts that they harbored as personal trade secrets. They were loath to share tricks of the trade with a faceless employer, preferring instead to keep them in the family.

Remington's efficiency was remarkable. In 1870, it estimated that it could manufacture between one and two hundred rifles a day with a capital investment of $30,000 to $35,000. The Springfield Armory, on the other hand, reported that it required over $175,000 in machinery to do the same.[14] Springfield, of course, was saddled with enormous legacy costs from its expansion during the Civil War, but it still compared badly.

Prosperity in Ilion

In any event, Remington seemed to be immensely profitable. Samuel Remington calculated that one-third of the contract price on his Egyptian deals was net profit. The firm's success transformed Ilion from a village into a prosperous small town. Its population grew from less than 2,900 in 1870 to 4,000 six years later. In 1870, a 1,000-seat opera house was put up, and a street railway appeared the next year. Eliphalet and Philo Remington gave generously to the town's churches, schools, libraries, and other institutions, and Philo built himself a somewhat monstrous stone mansion (on Remington Avenue) overlooking the town.[15]

Coming on top of large sales to France and China, the Spanish contracts pushed E. Remington & Sons and the town of Ilion to their zenith. In gratitude for its prosperity, Ilion celebrated the completion of their Spanish contracts with a ball, given December 18, 1874, that was totally disproportionate to the town's modest size. Remington spared no expense. It brought Pat Gilmore's 22nd Regiment Band in from New

York for the occasion and sent gowns for the Spanish officers' wives from Paris. The result, wrote the local *Herkimer Democrat*, was "a combination of beauty, pleasure, music, mirth, fashion, fancy, and rare social enjoyment." The *New York Graphic*, perhaps given to hyperbole, exclaimed, "It is a question whether the famed Brussels Ball, given on the eve of the Battle of Waterloo, excelled the Spanish Ball."[16] Surely, these were golden times for Ilion and the Remingtons.

CHAPTER 21

The Sublime Porte

No COUNTRY HAD GREATER STRATEGIC IMPORTANCE IN THE 1870s than Turkey, yet none seemed less organized to defend itself. From the time they appeared on the fringes of Europe in the thirteenth century, the Turks had expanded their grasp until, at its height, their Ottoman Empire embraced the southern and eastern perimeters of the Mediterranean, Egypt, the Levant, Greece, the Balkans, Cyprus, Crete, central Hungary, parts of Ukraine, and some of southern Russia and Crimea. As late as 1683, the Turks besieged Vienna itself. Ottoman power then steadily ebbed. Turkey lost war after war during the 1700s and early 1800s—four to Russia alone—and faced uprisings everywhere. By 1861 the empire was in the hands of a final set of faltering Sultans whose government—known as the "Sublime Porte" after the palace doorway from which proclamations had been announced centuries before—stumbled along as best it could. Still, Russia could not expand to the south as long as Turkey was in the way. Whatever the Ottomans' problems, Turkey remained the cork in the bottle of Russian ambitions.

The Ottoman government began preparing for a renewed war with Russia in 1869.[1] With memories of its loss in Crimea still fresh, Russia was looking to redress its grievances. But more was at stake, the Russians said, than mere geographic aggrandizement. The Tsar also was motivated by the belief that Russia was the cultural and religious guardian of the Slavic people themselves, millions of whom had long suffered under brutal Turkish rule in the Balkans. The time was coming, Russia thought, when the Ottoman Empire should be split up and Christian peoples freed from Moslem oppression. Thus, Russia spent the 1870s modernizing its army with new rifles, Krupp artillery, and Gatling guns and constructing military railroads to its southern frontiers. Few people gave Turkey much of a chance against Russia. The Ottomans were broke, moribund, corrupt, backward, and beset by ethnic strife. Yet serious geopolitical issues hinged upon Turkey's fate. Austria-Hungary—itself a polyglot empire with restive Slavic populations—depended upon Balkan stability for its own security, and Britain considered Turkey its protection against Russian expansion in the eastern Mediterranean. The confounding matter of what to do with the crumbling Turkish Empire was so complicated and prevalent in the minds of European diplomats that it was simply called the "Eastern Question."

The job of rearming Turkey would take years, and it was frustrated by the country's insolvency and endemic corruption. Yet Turkey ended up surprising everyone. Under pressure from Britain, Austria, and other powers, the Sublime Porte took the challenge seriously, and much of the money it raised in its periodic state financings went to buy weapons.[2] Between 1869 and 1878, no country bought more arms abroad than did Turkey and, as events would prove, probably no one did a better job.

SPRINGFIELDS

The advent of breech-loading rifles alarmed Turkey no less than anyone else and, either on its own or following British advice, the Ottomans decided to adopt the Snider. Before the Ottomans could convert muzzle loaders to breech loaders, though, they needed the muzzle loaders to begin with. Fortunately, the United States had plenty for sale. Working through their minister to the United States, the exotically named Blacque Bey, the Ottomans negotiated a deal with the Ordnance Department in mid-1869 to purchase 125,000 Springfields at $7 each.* The department was delighted to get this price, and it let the Turks have the pick of the litter. Before long, the Porte bought another 114,000 surplus Enfield muskets

---

* Blacque Bey was, in fact, a Frenchman of Scottish descent named Edouard Blacque. His first wife, Olivia (1830–1855), was the daughter of Dr. Valentine Mott, an American who served as an Ottoman court physician in the late 1830s and early 1840s. Blacque, thus, was the brother-in-law of Thaddeus Mott, whose work for Khedive Ismail was described earlier.

from the department, to which it added 100,000 more Springfields in January 1870. (Evidently having not much else to do, the Springfield Armory obligingly cleaned and repaired at least 60,000 of the Enfields.) Soon, the Sublime Porte added as many as 100,000 more Springfields to its inventory when Prussia sold off muzzle loaders it had captured from the French at a bargain price of $1 each.[3] Turkey evidently continued to buy Springfields and Enfields when it could and, according to one authority, had amassed over 500,000 by 1872.[4]

It is not entirely clear where the rifles were converted. A few years earlier, Birmingham gun-makers had sold Turkey 21,000 Snider conversions and breech mechanisms for 6,000 more, but by the late 1860s they were tied up with work for the British government. Many American gun-makers would have liked the work, but conversion in the United States was complicated by the fact that Jacob Snider's widow, Angelina, had taken out a US patent on the Snider system in October 1867 and certainly would demand a royalty. To the extent they could, the Turks converted some muzzle loaders to Sniders at their Tophane armory in Constantinople, although gun collectors also have found Turkish Sniders that were evidently altered in Liege.[5]

WINCHESTERS

In early 1870, the Turkish army dispatched Colonel Rustem Bey to the United States to look into buying breech-loading arms and ammunition. Rustem, unfortunately, did not speak English, and so was thrown upon the graces of Turkey's somewhat self-appointed consul in New York, Christopher Oscanyan. The position of consul was an honorary one, and Oscanyan supplemented his income by charging a commission for his services when an opportunity arose. Despite its obscurantist reputation, the Ottoman Empire could be surprisingly cosmopolitan, and it troubled no one that Oscanyan was an Armenian Christian with a degree from New York University. Because of Rustem's inability to communicate in English, Oscanyan soon took over the business end of his work.[6]

Rustem's assignment and Oscanyan's role were no secret, and in June 1869, Oliver Winchester contrived an impromptu meeting with Rustem and Oscanyan in Schuyler, Hartley & Graham's showroom in downtown

New York. Winchester quickly hired Oscanyan as his agent and agreed—in writing—to pay him a 10 percent commission on all arms and ammunition he sold Turkey.[7] This promised to be a lucrative deal, and Oscanyan made no secret of it.

An impediment to Winchester's hopes was that Rustem simply did not like the Winchester rifle. Although we do not know Rustem's particular objections, the Winchester had any number of well-known shortcomings and it was expensive. In January 1870, officials in Constantinople told Rustem that the heavier Spencer repeater looked like a better option, if only because the United States government was selling off its inventory of Spencers at distress prices. Believing this would sidetrack the Winchester, Oscanyan asked Rustem to send in a report condemning the Spencer. In fact, Rustem continued to dislike the Winchester, but as a favor to Oscanyan he nonetheless included it among the specimens he sent back to Constantinople and placed an order for 1,000.[8]

AZARIAN PÈRE ET FILS

Unbeknownst to Oscanyan, Oliver Winchester had concluded that he stood a better chance of getting a Turkish contract if he approached officials directly in Turkey. Thus, he sent one of his salesmen, Thomas Addis, to Constantinople and engaged the influential banking firm Azarian Père et Fils to assist him.

Azarian Père et Fils had been started decades before by an Armenian named Hovannes Azarian. He had five sons. One, Stepanos, rose to become the Patriarch of Catholic Armenians in Constantinople, and the others went into the family business. Seeing the potential of trade between Turkey and the United States, Hovannes sent at least two of his sons to Boston to open an office in 1851. In 1854, the eldest son, Aristakes, became an American citizen, although he probably did not advertise the fact back home, since he specifically agreed in his petition for citizenship "to renounce forever all allegiance and fidelity" to "Abdul Mejid, Sultan of Turkey." Aristakes returned to Constantinople, probably upon the death of his father in 1864, to take over the firm. His brother Vincent, though, remained in Boston and ran the firm's branch there.[9]

It was challenging to do business with the Ottomans without the Azarians' help. Oliver Winchester's son-in-law Thomas Bennett described the Azarian firm as a "very curious one."

> It is comprised of Aristakes A, his two sons Pier & Joseph & his brother Joseph. No clerks are kept in the office the business being entirely of a confidential nature. Every step is the resultant of the combined opinions of the firm. When a telegram is to be worded it is done by all hands at once. They shout, stamp, gesticulate, solo, uno, trio, quatro, and just as you expect to see them punch each others heads the noise ceases and the point is settled.

This apparent pandemonium concealed Aristakes Azarian's influence. The Azarian firm became the Rothschild bank's representative in Constantinople and, when the Constantinople Chamber of Commerce was organized in 1879, Aristakes became its first president. Aristakes's sway with the Sublime Porte was such that he almost figured as a government official himself. According to one story, Aristakes traveled to Bridgeport in 1872 for what seemed to be a courtesy tour of Union Metallic Cartridge's plant. At the end of the visit, he identified himself as a representative of the Ottoman government and summarily placed an order for ten million cartridges. His status in Constantinople was undeniable. According, again, to Thomas Bennett, "he walks into the War Dept in his muddy boots when all others must take off their shoes or go in slippers made expressly. All the Ministers and members of the council defer to him and gather round while he speaks."[10]

Arms sales could be a seedy business, and it was at its worst in Constantinople. The "Government was honeycombed with corruption," the English author Sir Edwin Pears later wrote. "Large rewards must be given to Ministers to make contracts," SH&G salesman William Saint Laurent wrote in 1871, "on that condition alone depends success." The head of the government was the Grand Vizier, without whose support progress was impossible. But even getting in the door required some out-of-pocket expense. "Money will be absolutely wanted at the Palace," Saint Laurent wrote. "We can not go there without giving the usual *backshiche* to the employees." An array of Ottoman officials had a say in the choice of weapons, partly because it expanded the opportunities to demand bribes. The Sultan himself made the final decision in a somewhat ritualistic process. In the presence of the Grand Vizier, the gun salesman presented a pair of the arm in question—gold-plated—as a gift to the Sultan. The guns ordinarily were set in a fancy case, engraved with the Sultan's arms and lined with crimson silk. There had to be one hundred cartridges for each gun, silver- or gold-plated and similarly engraved. If he liked the arm, the Sultan would issue a verbal *irade*, or secret edict, to the effect that it was his pleasure that the gun should be adopted. Only when court officials worked out all details of the contract would anything be put into writing and "then a written irade is presented to the sultan, and he takes a long reed, makes a flourish and the transaction is ended."[11]

Winchester sent six specially engraved guns—some gilded and some silver-plated—to Aristakes Azarian in the spring of 1870. They were presented to Sultan Abdulaziz on April 18, 1870, and he issued an *irade* the next day ordaining that the guns should be ordered, subject to field trials. These were held on July 3 in Constantinople. The Winchesters were put through the usual gauntlet of tests to determine their sturdiness, accuracy, and serviceability. One of these was the so-called sand test, where sand was poured into the gun's action to jam it. No gun could pass unless its promoter could demonstrate that a common soldier, using only the simplest tools at his disposal, could clear the action. According to one story—which may be apocryphal, since it is told about many guns and many tests in many countries—Thomas Addis first tried to clear the action by pouring water into it from a canteen, only to be told that Turkish soldiers did not carry canteens. Resourcefully, Addis then cleared out the sand by urinating into the gun, pointing out that Turkish soldiers surely had bladders.[12]

Whatever the truth of this, the government placed an order for 15,000 Winchester rifles and 5,000 carbines for $28 and $20, respectively, on November 9, 1870, as well as some ammunition, appurtenances, and, possibly, machinery.[13] The total contract amount was just short of $595,000 "payable ready money in gold."[14] An even larger $846,000 contract followed the next August for 30,000 rifles and more ammunition.[15] Winchester's success may have been due to the qualities of his repeating rifle, but there probably were other reasons. The British, upon whose advice Turkey relied, had a low opinion of repeating rifles in general and the Winchester in particular, and it is unlikely they would have counseled the Ottomans to make a large purchase of the guns. A more likely cause was the influence of Aristakes Azarian and, considering the venality of Ottoman officials, the purse of Thomas Addis.

The gun Winchester was offering was the Model 1866, an updated version of the original Henry rifle patented in 1860. The Model 1866 incorporated several improvements, including a magazine that was sealed to keep out dirt and a side gate in the receiver that let the user load the magazine from the breech. The gun's receiver was made from a bronze alloy called gunmetal, which gave it the nickname "yellow boy." (Bronze was a relatively expensive material, but easier to forge and machine than iron.) However, the Model 1866 still used the .44 Henry rim-fire cartridge, which was essentially a pistol cartridge; its bullet, in fact, was lighter than that of the Smith & Wesson Model 3 revolver.[16]

The Turkish orders came at a propitious time for Oliver Winchester. His armory was still small and, compared to the orders Remington and Providence Tool had pulled in, sales of his Model 1866 had been slow. Even during the Franco-Prussian War, when Samuel Remington was buying every gun he could find, Winchester shipped only 6,000 guns to France. The Turkish orders, though, changed all of that. During the winter of 1870, Winchester's factory ran two ten-hour shifts and spit out something like 1,000 guns per week, despite the fact that Winchester moved his machinery to a new armory in the middle of production. Winchester was able to keep his plant busy even after that as he began to fulfill the larger second contract. In a letter he sent John Anthony in October 1872, Winchester wrote that his sales were about $810,000 in 1871 and $1,015,000 in 1872, his profit margin over 25 percent, and his return on capital around 50 percent.[17]

Ordinarily, this spate of business should have delighted Christopher Oscanyan; after all, he had a written agreement promising him a 10 percent commission. Yet Oliver Winchester was in something of a bind. Not only was this a lot of money, but he owed a commission to Aristakes

Azarian and probably also owed something to Thomas Addis. Winchester decided to stiff Oscanyan, who sued in 1874 for the enormous sum of $144,095.50. The case wended its way through the court system, with Oscanyan maintaining that having done what he agreed to do, he should be paid the monies called for by his contract, and with Winchester reaching for whatever excuses he could find. Things finally found their way to the United States Supreme Court, which in 1880 decided in Winchester's favor. The Court gave short shrift to Oscanyan's arguments that he should be paid on his contract, condemning it as "corrupt" and "obnoxious." "It is the naked case of one officer of a government, to secure its purchase of arms, selling his influence with another officer in consideration of a commission on the amount of the purchase." Relying upon the logic of its decision in the case where Samuel Norris unsuccessfully sued Providence Tool years before, the Supreme Court simply refused to enforce the contract. It made no difference that such things might be perfectly legal in Turkey. "A contract to bribe or corruptly influence officers of a foreign government will not be enforced in the courts of this country."[18] Winchester did not owe Oscanyan a cent.

The Winchester guns began arriving in Constantinople in 1871, and Oliver Winchester's company in later years cultivated the story that these rifles were a devastating weapon that held a huge Russian army at bay. As we will see later, this is a fiction and myth. The Winchester rifle and carbine were too fragile to fire the heavy, high-velocity rounds required of a standard infantry arm and, whether justly or unjustly, soon were considered unfit for general service. Instead, in the following years, they were gradually taken out of infantry service and distributed to Turkey's gendarmerie, cavalry, and irregular troops.

A FRONT-LINE ARM

In 1872, Turkish authorities announced that they planned to conduct trials toward the adoption of a new breech-loading infantry weapon. The initial contract, it was assumed, would be for about 200,000 guns, with additional orders to follow.[19] Surely, this would be the largest arms deal of them all.

Overshadowing everything was the notorious inefficiency, indecisiveness, and dishonesty of the Ottoman regime. The American Minister to the Sublime Porte, George Boker, described Turkey in August 1872 as "a land where all things are corrupt." A British army officer wrote a few years later:

> The administration, or, more correctly, mal-administration, in the Turkish army is enveloped in such a mass of confusion and intrigue as to render elucidation impossible. So systematically and unblushingly are the principles of peculation, cunning, greed, and ambition carried out in every branch of military administration, that nothing but disorder and chaos can result.

As important as it was, Turkey's choice of a new arm probably would turn upon everything except the merits of the guns being tested.[20]

Given the stakes, every gun-maker descended upon Constantinople, rifle in hand. Remington came, promoting its rolling-block rifle. The opportunity was inviting enough that Providence Tool reconsidered its decision to exit from the armaments business and hired Schuyler, Hartley & Graham agent William Saint Laurent to promote the Peabody. Colt and the Birmingham Small Arms Company both offered to sell Turkey the Berdan, while Oliver Winchester urged the Porte to buy more of his repeating rifles.[21]

The trials seem to have followed the customary pattern. On June 18, William Saint Laurent wrote, "The trials of guns are going on, and will last all week. 2,000 rounds are fired from each gun." Yet there was a pervasive sense that bribery would win the day. Laurent's dispatch went on to say that Samuel Remington was in Constantinople and "is spending money right and left to secure a favorable report for his gun." A few years later, a British intelligence report complained that the Turks could have made their new guns themselves at two-thirds the cost, but then "no consideration would have passed into individual hands." Corruption was endemic. "Every officer except two," Saint Laurent reported, were against one particular gun "not because it is a bad gun, but on account of getting no bribery." Laurent himself, of course, was far from rectitudinous. His weekly letters to SH&G's home office mention employing the son of a minister "with the knowledge of the Minister," "having the very best influences" near the Grand Vizier, and bragging that another influential minister "is my friend & is willing to accept *backshish*." In August, American Minister George Boker wrote Secretary of State Hamilton Fish that three American contractors were vying for the huge Turkish order and "[i]t is said that one American contractor has expended 15,000 pounds in *backshiesh*, without obtaining the contract." Saint Laurent reported that Samuel Remington personally came to Constantinople to push for adoption of his arm and withdrew £14,000 from the bank "and it is supposed to have been spent here." Conflicts of interest bothered no one. The Azarians represented Winchester, Remington, and their English competitors. SH&G was hired to represent Providence Tool but also proposed to sell the Berdan, and, on the side, its agent Saint Laurent tried to broker a deal of his own for a vast number of Snider conversions.[22]

And there was skullduggery. BSA's efforts to sell the Berdan II were foiled when its agent—probably the Azarians—allegedly arranged to delay delivery of BSA's gun "long enough to ruin its chances, as better discounts were being offered by the American manufacturers." Oliver Winchester complained of Saint Laurent's "dishonorable course," "rascalities," and "mean acts," but nonetheless spread word that Providence Tool was too busy making sewing machines to fulfill any gun contract and Colt had floundered in making Berdan I's for Russia. Saint Laurent complained of "[t]his infernal Winchester," threatening that "he will find some difficulty in finishing his contract for the last 39,000 rifles of his." (In fact, Turkey did indeed stop paying Winchester for a while.) Saint Laurent also bragged in a report back to headquarters that he had just seen Samuel Remington and "killed his gun forever in Turkey" by planting a derogatory article about it in the newspapers. Meanwhile the Azarians were accused of stealing "tenders & prices of unaware strangers" by bribing interpreters. Everybody, it seems, thought that their gun had prevailed at the trials. Saint Laurent first believed that the Peabody had a slight edge on the Berdan, then that he was "positively certain securing contract . . . [for] either Peabody [or] Berdan," then that Turkey would choose the Berdan because Russia had, and finally that the Grand Military Council—which would decide the matter—favored the Peabody. Samuel Norris remembered that "three commissions in Constantinople decided on the Remington," while Saint Laurent wrote that the

"Remington gun is condemned." Meanwhile, British Ambassador Henry Elliot wrote in early July that the Berdan, Remington, and Peabody rifles had all been "definitively rejected."[23]

In fact, what happened surprised everyone. As John Anthony later wrote:

> To end the tedious investigation which was going on, and to stop also the numerous intrigues relating to the subject which seemed to prevent prompt official action, His Majesty the Sultan suddenly dismissed the Board and declared the "Martini-Henry" Rifle, of the British model, definitely adopted.

This, of course, infuriated the Americans. The company line in Ilion was that, just as Remington was about to sign a contract, someone close to the Sultan demanded "a bonus of fifty cents per gun, which the company refused to pay." Samuel Norris complained that the triumph of the British arm had been the result of "an intrigue at the palace of the Sultan" and Saint Laurent that "it was through a trick at the Palace that the gun was ordered." In fact, Saint Laurent maintained, the Martini-Henry had been rejected by all of the government commissions and had never even been tested at all.[24]

Some of this must be taken as sour grapes, but what seems to have happened was that a newly formed British firm, the National Arms & Ammunition Company, somehow slipped into the palace and carried away the prize, or at least so it seemed. National Arms had been spun off earlier that year from Westley-Richards "for the manufacture breech-loading rifles and other arms," particularly Britain's newly adopted Martini-Henry rifle. The head of National Arms was former major general W. M. H. Dixon, the respected officer who had run the Enfield armory since 1865.[25]

According to a dispatch Saint Laurent sent to New York, General Dixon "had a magnificent gun presented the Sultan & from that Sample he ordered." This is a little simplistic, but not inconsistent with the manner in which arms were presented to the Sultan, nor with the subterfuge of the Sublime Porte generally. Yet there are still problems with this version of things. The Porte was impatiently waiting to rearm, but there was little chance National Arms could fill the order. Estimates of Turkish needs were as high as a half-million guns, yet the British army and reserve forces alone might need as many as one million Martini-Henrys, and they were ahead of Turkey in line. National Arms, moreover, was not the state-of-the-art armory it professed to be, but was in fact still a quasi-artisanal operation that was years away from implementing true mass production. Dixon tacitly admitted as much. Almost as soon as the Sultan decided that Turkey would adopt the Martini-Henry, Dixon suggested to Saint Laurent that many of them would have to be made in America.[26] This leads, then, to the obvious question why Dixon and National Arms would try for a contract that they could not perform and so readily admit that its American competitors would end up with a large chunk of the work.

Although we can only speculate, one reason for the Porte's precipitous choice of the Martini-Henry may have been the military influence of the British. Russia's preparations for war were no secret, and given the imbalance of forces between the two countries, if Turkey were to hold its own it would need the best arms money could buy. The British had been improving and perfecting the Martini-Henry for years and, by 1872, they believed they had developed an almost-ideal infantry rifle. By contrast, with the exception of the Peabody (which was the basis of the Martini-Henry anyway), the British were unimpressed with the American offerings. The Winchester, they thought, was at best an arm for cavalry. The Berdan I was outdated and the Berdan II still untested. The British disliked the Remington's design because the breech block was locked only indirectly (by the gun's hammer) and the rearward thrust of the exploding cartridge was leveraged by the placement of the hammer's pivot.[27] Beyond that, the prevalent version of the rolling block, the .43 Egyptian or Spanish, had a lighter bullet, smaller powder charge, and less range than the Martini-Henry. But perhaps most important, the credibility of the June gun trials had been so ruined by bribery and scheming that no outcome could be considered legitimate. With so much at stake, it would have been surprising if the British government had not taken steps to intercede, and it would have been hard to find anyone to do so more credentialed than a decorated major general who had long managed the great Enfield armory.

CHAPTER 22

Arming an Empire

THE SULTAN'S CHOICE OF THE MARTINI-HENRY LEFT OPEN THE QUES-
tion who would make it. National Arms quickly fell out of the race. It
was far from ready to handle production at this level, and it would be
occupied making Martini-Henrys for the British army for years to come.
In the United States, it seemed that only Providence Tool could make the
gun. The Martini-Henry was based on the Peabody system, and Providence Tool undeniably controlled the two Peabody patents. The Turkish
Minister, Blacque Bey, met with John Anthony in New York to negotiate
a contract and, it seems, educate him on Ottoman practices. "Our interview today has been more free than before," Anthony wrote, "and I have
learned better the Turkish way of doing things."[1]

During July 1872, Anthony and Blacque worked out the details of
an agreement, with Providence Tool promising to make 100,000 guns for
$15 each, plus the cost of bayonets and minus a 50-cent discount. On July
25, this was slightly reduced to 63 shillings (about $15.75) for the rifle
and a quadrangular bayonet. Anthony thought the bargaining was over,
but he may not really have understood the Turkish way of doing things
after all. At the same time the Turks were negotiating with Providence
Tool, they also were talking to Birmingham Small Arms and its affiliated
firm, the London Small Arms Company, who had made a bid "at the
request of the British Government who wished to retain ties with Turkey." Similarly, they were negotiating with Oliver Winchester, who was in
Constantinople in connection with his earlier contracts. Probably leaked

the details of Anthony's offer, Winchester underbid it by one shilling, and grabbed the contract out from under Providence Tool.[2]

THE FIRST CONTRACT

The contract Winchester executed with the Sublime Porte was handwritten on a single large folio of parchment in parallel columns of Turkish and French, festooned with seals, stamps, and insignia. Azarian Père & Fils signed it on Winchester's behalf on August 1, 1872. This was the first of three contracts for guns, but it served as the model for the others.

The initial order was for 200,000 rifles, with quadrangular bayonets and accessories, at a price of 62 shillings. The contract provided that Turkey would provide Winchester with three sample guns from the English government's workshops at Enfield, and that the rifles Winchester produced must match the samples in all respects and have interchangeable parts. The contract left open the question of which cartridge the gun would use. Although much else about the contract had British fingerprints on it, the Turks did not commit themselves to the Boxer cartridge. Instead, the contract stated that the gun's chamber must fit whatever cartridge the Ottoman government decided to present.[3]

The Ottomans imposed a convoluted system for inspection: US Ordnance Department inspectors were to inspect and prove the rifles in accordance with British government regulations while a team of Turkish inspectors looked over their shoulders. Once accepted, the rifles were to be oiled to prevent rust then packed in zinc-lined, waterproof, double-reinforced crates and shipped to New York, all at Winchester's expense.[4]

The contract specified that Turkey would provide the sample Martini-Henrys and its new cartridge within two months, and that Winchester would begin shipping rifles six months later. Fifty thousand guns would be delivered during the following six months and 12,500 rifles shipped every month thereafter until all 200,000 were done. The contract had an elaborate system of escalating penalties if Winchester was late in its deliveries. Moreover, if for any reason Winchester failed to perform its obligations under the contract, there would be a penalty of 30 percent of the contract price. To secure this obligation, Winchester was required to post a bond in this amount with the Ottoman legation in Washington. The contract also specified that Winchester was obligated to perform the contract even if his workers went on strike or if he was sued for patent infringement.[5]

The Ottoman government agreed to pay for the rifles by establishing a series of credits with "a Notable bank in London" generally matching the delivery schedule of the rifles. Each week, as the Ottoman inspectors approved the rifles and supervised their packing into the zinc-lined crates, they were to give Winchester a receipt and send a duplicate receipt to the bank in London. Winchester, in turn, would submit a claim to the London bank for this amount and expect payment within seventy-five days. There was no provision in the contract to penalize Turkey for late payment or nonpayment, an odd omission since Turkey already was behind in paying Winchester for the guns he was making for them.[6]

THE PROBLEM OF PATENTS

It is puzzling why a savvy businessman like Oliver Winchester went to the trouble of bidding on the Turkish contract. He may not have had the capacity—industrial or financial—to meet the terms of the contract. But Winchester's main problem was that Providence Tool controlled the patents to the underlying Peabody system. Had he tried to make the guns in the United States, he would have faced an injunction and forfeiture of his large performance bond.

Winchester apparently believed that having left the arms business, Providence Tool would sell him its rights to the Peabody patent, or possibly be happy with a modest royalty. In fact, Providence Tool wanted the business for itself, and Anthony told anyone who would listen that he would do everything in his power to prevent Winchester from manufacturing Martini-Henrys in the United States. For a time, Winchester blustered and prevaricated. He wrote Anthony that Providence Tool would not get a dollar out of him in a patent suit and professed that his goal all along was just a patriotic desire to see the Turkish arms manufactured in the United States. This, of course, was incredible. Anthony also knew that he held the high cards in any negotiation, not the least because the company's lawyer, Benjamin Thurston, was known to be one of the best patent attorneys in the country.[7]

Winchester gave up quickly and soon, it seemed, he was trying to talk Anthony into taking the contract off his hands. Winchester suggested that Providence Tool might be able to get the Turks to pay another shilling for the rifles and, in any event, it would not have to pay SH&G a sales commission, since Saint Laurent had been unsuccessful. He told Anthony on September 28 that he was traveling to Washington to see Blacque Bey about the contract and suggested that Anthony might "get a friendly letter to him" right away. Winchester also recommended that Anthony write "General Dixon," presumably to address any reservations the British or Turks might have about the contract being transferred to Providence Tool.[8]

Despite Oliver Winchester's bluster, it seems that he liked Anthony and wanted to do business with him. More fundamentally, it might have been Winchester's plan all along to subcontract out much of the work, since his own armory was ill-equipped to make a gun like the Martini-Henry in the numbers Turkey wanted. Confidentially, Winchester even proposed a business deal. To avoid the expense of buying more machinery and to finesse the issue of patent rights, Winchester suggested that Providence Tool might take a sizable stake in his company's stock and hire Winchester to make the guns. It is unclear how serious Winchester was; previously, he had blown hot and cold on the arms business, and possibly this was really a feeler to see if Providence Tool might want to buy his gun-making operations altogether. Although Oliver Winchester bragged about how profitable his company was, his guns were not selling well, he was getting on in years, money was short, and—like Marcellus Hartley—Winchester was preparing to enter the ammunition business in a big way. In any event, nothing came of the idea, and soon Anthony and Winchester were hammering out the details of transferring Winchester's contract to Providence Tool.[9]

But this still left Winchester with the job of persuading the Ottomans to go along. He spun the novel argument that it really was Turkey's fault that his company could not make the 200,000 Martini-Henrys, and not because of any pesky issues having to do with patents. Instead,

Winchester wrote Blacque that he was "powerless to carry out the contract for the 200,000 Martini-Henry Guns" because the Turks had yet to pay him "the large amount of money due us" under the contracts for the guns he had sold them a year before. This, of course, was an obvious ploy to excuse Winchester's inability to perform the contract and, with any luck, get paid whatever the Turks owed him. Two weeks later, Winchester was more direct. "Prefer to have Anthony to take Martini contract," he cabled Azarian. "Am too feeble to take a contract for the Martini alone[.] I can get no help on it."[10]

The Porte, though, did not see things the same way. On October 25, the Azarians informed Winchester that the Turkish officer in charge of the Martini-Henry contract, Essad Pasha, looked to him as the contracting party (and, by the way, would take care of the money Winchester was owed) and, not knowing much about Anthony or Providence Tool, still wanted Winchester in the middle of things.[11] Essad's view was that Winchester should stick to his contract and make the necessary arrangements to perform it.[12]

All of this may well have simply reflected the Turkish way of doing things, but it also seems that Oliver Winchester had led the Porte to believe that he planned to construct a large armory in Constantinople to manufacture the Martini-Henry rifles there. Possibly, Winchester offered this to mollify the Porte's concerns about the patent problems he would face in the United States, or even to make his bid more appealing. However, the Ministry of War called his bluff, offering to grant Winchester "suitable land to build a factory and manufacture the guns here." This, of course, was the last thing Winchester wanted. He could not possibly construct an armory in time, the cost of equipping it would have ruined him, and Turkey had neither the skilled toolmakers nor the experienced plant superintendents necessary for mass production.[13]

There had been talk all along that the huge contract should be divided up among two or three arms-makers, and Winchester's tone suggests that this was his intention. The Ottomans knew little of Providence Tool and were skeptical of the firm's abilities to perform the contract; perhaps to bury the issue Azarian suggested that Winchester assign the contract to Providence Tool and then have Providence Tool subcontract production of the rifles to Remington. But in the end this all was too complicated. After mulling it over, the Ottomans agreed to Winchester's demand that they pay him the money they owed him and let him assign the contract to Providence Tool.[14]

Providence Tool's board of directors accepted the transfer on November 23.[15] And here was a significant difference between a family-owned company like Colt, Remington, or Winchester and a firm like Providence Tool Company. As surprising as it may now seem, Rhode Island was one of the wealthier and more influential places in the United States in the 1870s. It was the cradle of the American textile industry and, as competition arose from other places, Rhode Island capitalists had climbed the value chain from spinning yarn to weaving cloth to printing calicos, and now they were expanding into such high-tech fields as machine tools, textile equipment, precision instruments, and locomotives. Providence Tool was backed by these new capitalists, flush with money and looking for opportunity.

The Turkish contract was formally transferred on January 1, 1873, a simple affair that required only the separate endorsements of Blaque Bey, Oliver Winchester, and John Anthony. No money changed hands; Providence Tool got the business for free. The day before, Anthony and three of his fellow directors had posted a bond of £186,000 with the Ottoman legation in Washington, a number that was to triple within the year as additional contracts came in. Providence Tool's directors were under no illusions about the challenge they had taken on. As Anthony put it, they agreed to close ranks against misfortune and to hold each other's estates in case of death.[16]

As it had been in the Civil War, the matter of getting follow-on contracts was crucial if Providence Tool were to get the most out of its investment. Anthony needed someone with pull at the Porte, so in March 1873 he hired Azarian Père et Fils. As events later would prove, this was a wise choice; Providence Tool came to rely extensively upon Aristakes Azarian in the troubled years that lay ahead.[17]

Perhaps expedited by Aristakes Azarian's ability to cut through red tape, two other contracts followed in quick succession. On June 6, 1873, there was one for 300,000 rifles and on August 23 another for 100,000, both at 60 shillings. In most particulars, the orders were the same, except now the guns' sights were to be calibrated as high as 1,500 meters (from 1,300), probably as a result of ballistics testing the Turks had done earlier in the year.

THE PEABODY-MARTINI

An odd turn to the Sultan's decision was that, despite Turkey's urgent need for new rifles, he had chosen a weapon that was still being refined. The Martini-Henry that existed in 1872 was the second pattern of the Mark I model, and it still had problems with its trigger, block pin, sights, and firing pin.[18]

The schedule imposed on Providence Tool, however, did not admit of such delay; under the contract, deliveries were to start in early 1874, and there were long lead times in buying machinery, setting up a production line, and crafting the tooling. Thus, while the British were fixing the Mark I's shortcomings, the gun was being independently modified in the United States. The most important change was the cartridge. The Turks disliked the "ugly and clumsy" Boxer cartridge, and they began testing the Berdan cartridge at Union Metallic's plant in Bridgeport. They settled on a solid brass cartridge less awkward than the Boxer, but with the same weight of powder and ball. Besides being about 5 percent lighter than the Boxer's, the case of the UMC cartridge was of smaller caliber at the head (.587 versus .672) and at the junction of the shell and the bullet (.481 versus .507). The Berdan cartridge's thicker walls slowed down the heating of the firing chamber, which was a problem with the foil-wrapped Boxer. In keeping with the change in ammunition, Providence Tool also made a "radical" change to the rifle's extractor mechanism.[19]

Other preliminaries also had to be resolved. One was the problem of the United States patents Friedrich von Martini had been granted in 1869 and 1871 claiming improvements to the Peabody breech system. This required Providence Tool to hammer out a royalty arrangement with him. There was a similar dispute with the Scottish gunsmith Alexander Henry, who won a United States patent for his rifling system in October 1871. More stubborn than Martini, Henry took the matter to court where, after years of litigation, Benjamin Thurston had Henry's patent thrown out. With this cleared up, Providence Tool decided that the rifle it made should have an American name. It was the "Peabody-Martini."[20]

TOOLING UP

Anthony thought, correctly, that the first Turkish contract was just the beginning; he had been led to believe, in fact, that the Ottomans might buy as many as a million rifles.[21] Tooling for production at these levels required an immense amount of preparation and investment, but having constructed an armory from scratch during the Civil War, Anthony had a good idea how to do it. But the outlay was enormous: altogether the company added an additional $2 million of capital.[22]

In late 1873, inspectors from the United States and Turkish armies began to arrive in Providence; ultimately, there would be as many as forty American and two dozen Turks examining and testing the Peabody-Martinis. The job of supervising the inspection of the arms from the Turkish side was given to a Turkish intellectual, mathematician, and military engineer named Husseïn Tevfik. Born in Bulgaria in 1832, Tevfik was educated in Constantinople's military school and then sent to Paris as the Turkish legation's military attaché. Although his duties included inspecting guns and ammunition, he seems to have had sufficient spare time to study mathematics at the Sorbonne and join the French Mathematical Society. In 1872, Tevfik—by now a colonel—was assigned the task of supervising the inspection of the guns and ammunition being manufactured for Turkey in the United States. He moved to Providence, where he became something of a fixture for the next six years.

Tevfik by all accounts was an impressive and charming man. After he mastered English, he joined the Rhode Island Historical Society, where he gave talks about Turkish and Islamic culture and customs. At heart, though, he was an academic, and he spent much of his time in Providence writing a monograph on three-dimensional algebra.[23]

The experience of the Turkish inspectors, though, was more mixed. Alone in a strange land, they were left to their own devices in Providence and were remembered for many years. Townspeople recalled that the inspectors rode to and from work as a group, then gathered nightly at the bar of their hotel to drink, talk, and, on occasion, brawl. After one particularly memorable session, Joseph Azarian dispatched his son to Providence to keep watch over the Turkish inspectors. Despite the younger Azarian's best efforts, all difficulties could not be avoided. One of the Turkish officers hanged himself from a bridge in 1874, possibly out of shame, after being arrested for drunkenness. Four years later, another stabbed his mistress in a hotel room and, upon learning that he had been ordered back to Turkey, died by suicide. An inspector named Omer Mustapha fell in love with an innkeeper's daughter and, after being discharged from the army, returned to Providence to marry her. All of this was exaggerated in sensationalist newspaper accounts of the inspectors' time in Providence, which spoke of the Turks' fierce expressions, bushy beards, and red fezzes.[24]

ECONOMICS

Things started off late and then slowed down. The Turks did not provide the pattern guns on time; finally, in January 1874, they agreed to use a pattern gun Providence Tool itself supplied. The Ottomans were tardy as well in providing a £50,000 bond that the contract required before production would begin. The first shipment of 1,000 rifles was not made until March.[25]

There is a remarkable amount about John Anthony's life scattered across various archives and sources. Personally, he was a trim man of average size for the time: a passport application from November 1874 described him as five-foot-seven, with a high forehead, light hair, fair complexion, oval face, and blue eyes. There are few photographs of him, but he comes across as resolute, if not somewhat stubborn, in appearance. The documentary record of his business dealings shows him to be an intelligent, religious, civic-minded, and basically honest man whose formative experiences were learning how to grow a manufacturing operation and sell its products. (In the 1880 census, John Anthony gave his occupation as "Iron.") But now Anthony was in uncharted territory. However carefully he managed its business, Providence Tool was exposed to macroeconomic problems that few could foresee and none control. As he later said to J. P. Morgan, "[T]here was always a mountain just ahead of me."[26]

The blows came in quick succession. The first was the Panic of 1873, a global depression caused by economic overexpansion and triggered in America by the failure of the banking house of Jay Cooke & Company. Troubled conditions lasted most of the decade, and the United States was especially hard hit because it had no central bank. A coinage act passed in early 1873 committed the United States to the gold standard, so liquidity and credit depended upon how much gold was available. Gold, though, was scarce, partly because Germany was converting to the gold standard and France was buying gold to help pay off the $1 billion punitive indemnity that the victorious Prussians had imposed on it after the Franco-Prussian War. Anthony noted in his history of Providence Tool that this shortage of gold cut into the profits the company expected from its Turkish contracts, probably because his suppliers were reluctant to extend trade credit and his banks demanded 7 percent interest.[27]

More haunting was Turkey's chronic insolvency. For twenty years, Turkey had been borrowing in London and Paris to pay for arms, suppress revolts, and balance its budget. The amounts steadily rose to levels its economy could not sustain, and the Ottomans began borrowing money to pay interest on earlier loans. In 1873, Turkey borrowed 30.6 million gold lira (nearly £30 million) to cover its budget deficits, and it was evidence of Turkey's sorry state that the security for the loan included, among other things, a tithe on tuna and a cattle tax. Soon, the Ottomans' inability to pay Providence Tool fully and on time led to a succession of missed deadlines, work stoppages, interruptions of deliveries, partial payments, and renegotiations. It quickly became apparent that actually manufacturing huge volumes of rifles was the least of Providence Tool's problems.[28]

Anthony's optimism about the ultimate outcome of his contracts, though, remained essentially unshaken. In his history of Providence Tool, he wrote that the company had 1,700 machines installed in its plants by 1875 and sometimes employed more than 1,800 workers. This was, by any standard, an enormous operation, all the more impressive for the speed with which it was put together. "So far as we know," Anthony wrote, "no private establishment has ever undertaken contracts of such magnitude as ours." In view of later events, Anthony's upbeat tone seems unwarranted, but it was not unreasonable. The surviving Providence Tool records show that Anthony and his colleague William Dart carefully priced out their cost of production, subcontracted parts when it made sense, and bought finished barrels or barrel moulds from England. The size of the contract was enormous—at least $250 million in today's currency—and, at a time of financial panic in the United States, Providence Tool would be paid in gold-backed British pounds. Although the Ottomans were obviously strapped financially, it was no secret that war was coming, and the one thing a country facing invasion would pay for was guns. Having committed itself to the Peabody-Martini, Turkey could not back out now and, Anthony probably concluded, it would find the money that it needed.[29]

"This Noteworthy Visit"

Providence Tool manufactured 54,600 rifles in 1874, and when the Ottomans opened a £450,000 credit in December, it seemed that their financial problems might be behind them. With "[t]he Turkish gun work . . . now going on with great vigor," Anthony resolved to travel to Constantinople to see if Providence Tool might get a fourth contract. Accompanied by his wife, elder daughters, and Providence Tool's plant superintendent Benjamin R. Thurston (not to be confused with his lawyer, Benjamin F. Thurston), Anthony left Hoboken on December 10 on the Hamburg Line's *Holsatia*. He recorded the trip in a diary he kept, chronicling the adventures of a somewhat buttoned-up group of New Englanders on a visit to one of the more exotic places on the planet.[30]

His first stop was London, where Anthony had business to attend to. On December 22, he met with J. S. Morgan & Co., through whom Turkey's payments were to be handled, and added cryptically that he "saw Remington." He and Thurston went the next day to Birmingham where they visited the National Arms & Ammunition Company, which had been so instrumental in persuading the Sultan to choose the Martini-Henry. There he learned that National Arms' 1,000-man workforce could produce 250 rifles a day, but that it was still far behind the United States in manufacturing methods. Despite its size National Arms had only twenty-one machines and employed 250 workers whose job it was simply to file parts to gauge.[31]

Anthony was back in London for Christmas Eve, sourly noting "Weather dismal. The Holiday season interrupts everything." Later in the week, he had an "especially agreeable" interview with an officer of the Imperial Ottoman Bank, which was the conduit for payments from Constantinople. Interestingly, on December 31, Providence Tool placed an order for an immense amount—ten tons per week—of English steel for receivers, as well as one for thousands of barrels and the barrel moulds used in rolling barrels.[32]

The Anthonys spent the next month touring Europe. From Dover, they went to Paris, Modena, Turin, Bologna, and Ansona, visiting cathedrals, touring cities, and buying art, furniture, and luxury items. Proceeding south, they were stuck for a few days in Brindisi—Anthony noted in his diary that it was the birthplace of Virgil—and then boarded the SS *Ettore* for Constantinople. Passing through the Greek islands, Anthony noted that he saw a "sun worshipper," by which he probably meant a nude sunbather, perhaps a shock to a rectitudinous Rhode Islander. Something of a romantic, his diary recorded the moment the *Ettore* passed the plains of Troy, entered the straits of the Dardanelles, and approached the Golden Horn.[33]

The Anthonys arrived in Constantinople on Friday, January 22, 1875, and spent a few weeks there. Ellen Miller Anthony and her three eldest daughters—Mary, Annie, and Ellen—were admitted to the palace *seraglio* and encouraged to wear the robes, jackets, and sashes worn by Ottoman ladies. They attended social functions, a highlight of which were weddings where the girls threw gold confetti to the newlyweds. For a family raised in the insular world of mid-century Providence, it was an extraordinary experience. We need not guess what Constantinople looked like to them, though, because Mark Twain had passed through there just a few years before. In *The Innocents Abroad*, he wrote:

> People were thicker than bees, in those narrow streets, and the men were dressed in all the outrageous, outlandish, idolatrous, extravagant, thunder-and-lightning costumes that ever a tailor with the delirium tremens and seven devils could conceive of. There was no freak in dress

too crazy to be indulged in; no absurdity too absurd to be tolerated; no frenzy in ragged diabolism too fantastic to be attempted.

And for Ellen, Mary, Annie, and Ellen Anthony, the Turkish women "drifting noiselessly about . . . draped from chin to feet in flowing robes, and with snowy veils bound about their heads, that disclose only the eyes" must have been a mysterious sight. It was, Twain concluded, "an eternal circus."[34]

John Anthony spent January 23 at the Azarians' office, then called upon Turkey's interim War Minister and met the Grand Vizier. He reached an agreement for yet another 200,000 rifles, although the Porte's precarious financial conditions prevented the contract from being signed. Anthony busied himself with meetings for the balance of his stay, apologizing to his diary that he was too occupied sightseeing and conducting business to make daily entries. However, he did note on Saturday, January 30, that he visited the "church where Winchester guns are stored." The family left Constantinople on February 13 on the SS *Ceres*, which took them to Athens and Naples, from which they saw Rome, Florence, Milan, Turin, Geneva, Lausanne, and then Paris. They sailed for home on May 8.[35]

Anthony considered the trip a success. He wrote that he "received most unusual attentions from the heads of the different departments of the Government and further contracts were agreed upon." Anthony also was decorated with the Order of Osmanieh, the highest honor the Ottoman regime could confer upon a foreigner. He was thought to be the second infidel to receive the honor, the first having been Alfred Krupp, whose firm was supplying Turkey with hundreds of steel breech-loading field guns to go with the rifles Providence Tool was manufacturing.[36]

Disappointment
The credits Turkey established in December 1874 ran out midway the next year and, thereafter, funds came only sporadically. There were unending cycles of late payment, unfulfilled promises, threats, curtailment of production, and letters from lawyers. By 1875, Turkish public debt amounted to £200 million, and half of the country's revenue—£12 million—was

spent on debt service alone. In October, Turkey imposed a moratorium on paying its foreign debts, effectively declaring bankruptcy.[37]

Providence Tool was now out on a limb. The company finished the last of the 200,000 Peabody-Martinis of the first contract on November 9, 1875, but the Turks had still not paid for all of them and showed no sign of opening the credits for the second contract. To force the issue, Providence Tool kept 59,000 Peabody-Martinis in its warehouses as security. Whatever its effect as a pressure tactic, it did not help Providence Tool pay its bills. Hoping to avoid the expenses of stopping production and closing its armory, though, the company forged ahead with the second contract even though it was desperately short of cash.[38]

By mid-November, Providence Tool had 77,000 rifles on its hands. As usual, Turkey assured the company that new credits were imminent and pleaded for the rifles be shipped to Constantinople. When no money appeared, the company canceled orders for materials and reduced production to a trickle. Perhaps to make its point that it, at least, was complying with the terms of the contract, Providence Tool continued to submit drafts on the Imperial Ottoman Bank. On November 29, four drafts, totaling £40,000, were refused. "The effect on the Tool Company was immediate and disastrous," Anthony later wrote. The company's financial position deteriorated rapidly and, before long, Providence Tool's creditors began to attach its assets.[39]

To allay its creditors' worries, Providence Tool issued a public statement in mid-December 1875 about its financial affairs. Somewhat defensively, it noted that it had a contract to manufacture 600,000 rifles, "with the option of accepting an additional order for 200,000." Its capacity was 4,000 rifles per week, and it employed 1,800 men. The company had acted responsibly. It had reduced its debt to $600,000 and added $300,000 to "its general assets." "A combination of unfortunate circumstances . . . has placed the company under financial embarrassment, and compels it to ask its creditors to grant such extension as will enable it to carry to successful result the enterprise in which it is engaged." The company went on to point out that its principal stockholders were personally liable for the company's debts and they had property worth $5 million. Meanwhile, out of either loyalty or resignation, Providence Tool's workforce signed a petition "voluntarily & cheerfully relinquishing all claim to wages due them for work in the month of December 1875 until such time as the circumstances of the company improve."[40]

Instead, the company was able to arrange an extension of its bank loans, albeit at a high interest rate. Lenders, of course, demanded collateral, and the best Providence Tool could do was to pledge completed rifles. This alarmed the Ottomans, since it meant rifles they desperately needed might be auctioned off at a moment's notice. They came up with £154,000, an amount which helped pay off their arrears but was quickly eclipsed as more credits came due. By February 1876, Turkey was £446,000 behind. With the original system for financing arms production in shambles, the Azarians proposed a new plan. On March 25, 1876, the Turkish government agreed to pay the £1,035,400 remaining on the contracts week-by-week over the next few years. This freed the Turks from periodic dependence on large loans and enabled them to rely upon internal sources of revenue. For its part, Providence Tool would match its production schedule to these payments. In addition, as a guarantee of its obligations Turkey was to deposit a £50,000 bond and allow Providence Tool to retain 30,000 paid-for rifles.[41]

Both Turkey and Providence Tool had little choice but to accept the new system, since the company had invested millions in rifle production and the Turks were desperate for arms. However, it could not mask the fact that payments from Turkey would be few and far between. It is an interesting question why Providence Tool continued to manufacture rifles at all. The most likely reason was legal. Turkey had certainly breached its contracts with Providence Tool, and the company was entitled to rescind the contract if it wished. But that would leave it with a silent plant and large debts still to pay. Perhaps at this point, or soon thereafter, Anthony and Thurston settled upon a legal strategy that they kept to themselves. Providence Tool would continue to produce Peabody-Martinis and collect what money it could from Turkey as it went along. Still, it would hold the Ottomans liable for the damages their breach of the contract had caused and retain enormous numbers of guns the Porte already had paid for to make sure Turkey was good for the legal judgment when the day came. In the meantime, the looming Russian invasion would motivate the Turks to scrape together as much money as they could.

But there was a cost to making guns on this system, since Providence Tool was spending more making guns than it was receiving for them. As an expedient, the company borrowed money, pledging the guns it made as collateral for the loans. Essentially, guns were being manufactured to meet loans made to Providence Tool to produce guns—the company was arming banks, not soldiers. Indeed, when a Drexel, Morgan loan of £45,000 came due, Anthony's only option was to renew it with even more collateral—now 70,000 rifles—than before. Things on both sides became increasingly desperate. With the Russian threat looming, the panicked Ottomans pleaded for the Peabody-Martinis to be shipped, while Providence Tool demanded cash in advance. Finally, in November 1876, Providence Tool stopped work altogether.

This stalemate continued until it became apparent that war was imminent. Its back to the wall, the Ottoman government came up with £108,000 in February 1877, which enabled Providence Tool to release most of the unaccepted rifles from its inventory and restart production. But the company's health was irreparably damaged. It made just 73,000 guns in the first six months of 1877, and in July again stopped work and took steps to sell off 14,000 rifles the Turks had not yet accepted. Ottoman Minister of War Mahmoud Pasha somehow found some money and instructed Hussein Tevfik to load the steamer *Middleton*, already waiting in New Haven, with the guns and munitions he so urgently needed. No sooner had the Turks opened the new credits than they accidentally sunk two steamships on the Danube belonging to the *Middleton's* owners. The shipowners impounded the *Middleton's* cargo as indemnity and dispatched an agent to Constantinople to negotiate a settlement. The Ottomans outmaneuvered the steamship company's representative, however, declaring—with good reason—that since they were in default, the munitions did not belong to them but to the Azarians and Providence Tool, who had sunk no ships at all. This worked, and the *Middleton* sailed within a week.[42]

CHAPTER 23

Plevna

WHILE THE OTTOMANS WERE SCRAMBLING TO FIND MONEY TO PAY
for guns, the Russians were planning a war. Turkey's large navy—a
major cause of its insolvency—controlled the Black Sea, so the Russian
invasion would come by land. To the east, the Tsar's army would attack
from its bases in the Caucasus and march into Anatolia. In the west,
the Russians would make their way south through Roumania, cross the
Danube, invade the Turkish province of Bulgaria, and fight their way
to Constantinople itself.

As wars went, this was one of the worst-kept secrets ever. Through-
out the 1870s, Russia had been extending its rail lines to the Roumanian
border and modernizing its army. Russia finally declared war on April 24,
1877, and sent 100,000 men through Roumania toward the Danube. In
keeping with Russian tradition, the army was commanded by a Romanov,
in this case the Tsar's brother, Grand Duke Nicholas Nikolaevich.[1]

The Russian army forced a crossing of the Danube on June 27 and
28 and, now in Bulgaria, it headed to Nikopol to secure its right flank.
Almost simultaneously, in a daring attack, Russian divisions raced south
and captured the critical Balkan mountain passes. The two great bulwarks
of the Turkish defenses in the west were now irrelevant. With the Danube behind them and the passes secure, there was little to hold the Tsar's
army back from its next objective, the Turkish city of Adrianople.[2]

Upon learning of the Russian invasion, the Turkish military governor of Widdin on the Bulgarian-Serbian border marched his garrison

southeast to join Ottoman troops coming from the west. The Widdin force was large, well-equipped, and battle-hardened. More important was their general, a forty-year-old professional soldier named Osman Pasha. The Russians did not know much about Osman; if they had heard of him at all, they would have learned he was something of a religious fanatic and had "a violent dislike of foreigners." He was "[s]hort, but of commanding presence, dignified, taciturn, grave and abrupt of speech and manner, rather disdainful in looks and words, and had naught about him of the petty forms of politeness." And now, as the writer Rupert Furneaux succinctly put it, Osman was about "to wreck the whole Russian plan of campaign."[3]

Osman left Widdin on Friday, July 13, 1877, planning to reinforce the garrison at Lovatz, but the town fell before Osman could reach it. This meant that the Russians from Nikopol could now move south, unite with the force at Lovatz, and pour through the Balkan passes. But, as it happened, the way from Nikopol to Lovatz was through a town that soon would be world famous. This was Plevna, and success would depend upon who reached Plevna first. Wasting no time, Osman ordered a forced march, and occupied Plevna the morning of the 19th. He immediately deployed his men to the heights north and east of town.[4]

Russian pickets already had reported that a large Turkish force was heading to Plevna, but no one seemed worried by the news. Grand Duke Nicholas gave desultory instructions to Lieutenant General Schilder-Schuldner to occupy Plevna, and Schilder-Schuldner took his time in doing so. Scattered over a distance of seventeen miles, his 6,500 troops were disorganized and, inexplicably, he had no cavalry. The Russian expedition stumbled into Plevna on the afternoon of the 19th. There was a short, sharp fight in which one Russian regiment was nearly annihilated. Unaware that Osman's force was larger than his own, Schilder-Schuldner renewed his assault at dawn the next day. The Russian attack—which came to be known as the First Battle of Plevna—soon folded under ferocious counterattacks. Turkey lost 2,000 men, but the Russian force had 3,000 killed, including most of its officers.[5]

Grand Duke Nicholas was now in a bind. Osman's still-growing force could cut off Russian lines of communication to the Danube; unless

Osman was dislodged, the Russian invasion would come to a stop. But Plevna would be hard to take. Surrounded on the north and east by a ring of hills, and protected on the south by a deep ravine, it was a natural fortress. Plevna could not be bypassed, and taking it would require a bigger army than Nicholas had on hand.[6]

Both sides started preparing. General Nikolai Krudener's corps descended from Nikopol, joined by forces under Prince Carol of Roumania, some of whom were carrying the Peabody rifles Providence Tool had sold Roumania a few years earlier. By the end of August, Nicholas had 35,000 men and 176 cannon. But Osman now had at least as many soldiers and dozens of artillery pieces of his own. More importantly, his engineers had been furiously building earthen redoubts and digging miles of trenches. Nor was he short of ammunition. Commenting on the Turkish defense of Plevna after the fact, any number of observers noted that—whatever other privations the Turks endured—they never ran out of cartridges.[7]

The front line at Plevna was a horseshoe about fifteen miles long, but the key to its defense were two large redoubts on the commanding Grivitza ridge. Krudener questioned the wisdom of a frontal assault, only to be rebuked by Nicholas for his hesitancy. With some resignation, Krudener sent his troops forward on the afternoon of July 30. The Russians carried the outer trench lines, but faltered when they encountered the final entrenchments and formidable redoubts. It was here that the Russians first faced the full force of the American rifles. "[V]olley succeed volley with terrific rapidity and murderous effect," wrote the English soldier of fortune William Herbert, "and back went the Russian lines in a state of hopeless chaos, the ground strewn with dead and dying." On the right flank, one battalion reached the parapet of a redoubt, but within a few minutes lost 26 officers and 1,006 men. On the other flank, one regiment got no closer than 400 yards from the Grivitza redoubts and a second did not progress even that far. At sunset Krudener ordered a final assault in desperation, and then gave the order to retire.[8]

"Thus ended in complete failure the battle of July 30th," reported the American military attaché accompanying the Russian forces. Turkish casualties have been estimated at 2,000; of the 30,000 Russian soldiers thrown into battle, 169 officers and 7,136 men were killed or wounded. Accounts of the battle refer to the Turkish infantry's "murderous fire," men who "loaded and discharged astonishing celerity," "quickfire," "merciless fire," "rapidity of fire," and "volley upon volley." There were bitter recriminations among the Russian commanders, and anguish about what should be done next. Reluctantly, the Tsar decided to mobilize another 120,000 men, call out 26,000 militia, and bring up even more artillery. In addition, he appealed for help to Roumania, which dispatched 32,000 infantrymen, 5,000 cavalry troops, and 84 cannon.[9]

AMERICAN GUNS
It is odd that the array of weaponry Americans sold to Russia, Turkey, Roumania, Egypt, and other places should meet in Bulgaria. Nevertheless, Berdan, Winchester, Peabody, Remington, and Peabody-Martini rifles and carbines, Smith & Wesson revolvers, Snider-converted Springfield rifles, Ames bayonets, and ammunition from Winchester and Union Metallic Cartridge all came together on a single battlefield. The obvious, if insensitive, question is how well these arms worked.

Despite many disruptions, Providence Tool managed to ship an impressive number Peabody-Martinis to Turkey in time to see action. According to one dependable source, the Ottomans had 334,000 of them at the beginning of the war, and another 100,000 arrived during it.[10] This was sufficient, a British analyst later wrote, to arm three-quarters of the Turkish infantry. However, at Plevna, the mixture (between regulars and reservists) of Osman's forces may have been such that a smaller percentage carried Peabody-Martinis, although as casualties mounted, reservists probably picked up the Peabody-Martinis of fallen troops.[11]

In keeping with British doctrine, the Martini-Henry was designed to deliver a heavy bullet at long range; the Peabody-Martini, with the same weight of powder and ball and the added benefit of the Berdan cartridge, was probably better. The contracts between the Sublime Porte and Providence Tool provided that the gun would be sighted up to 1,500 meters (1,640 yards). Aiming over iron sights at such ranges was pointless, but moot anyway because Turkish infantry seldom bothered to aim at all. Instead, "orders were, briefly, as follows: 'As soon as you know or suppose the enemy to be within the range of your rifles, cover the space . . . with quickfire, independent of distance, duration, difficulty or aim, probability of hitting, and consumption of cartridges.'" Turkish soldiers "frequently opened fire at a range of 2,000 yards when occupying field works, and were accustomed to keep up an uninterrupted fusilade [*sic*], often without raising their heads over the parapet to aim."[12]

The rate of fire from the Turkish lines was beyond anyone's experience. Correspondents and survivors writing about Plevna commonly used descriptions such as "murderous," "overwhelming" and "withering" gunfire, "hailstorm of bullets," and "showers" and "avalanches" of lead. Individual Turkish soldiers sometimes shot as many as 500 rounds in a single engagement, and "[i]t was not rare to find 200 to 300 empty cartridge shells by the side of a dead Turk." William Herbert wrote that this was the decisive feature of the campaign: "the quick-fire of the Turkish infantry, of such power, duration, and effect as had never before been dreamt of."[13]

Matched with the Peabody-Martini's rate of fire was its long range. A reporter from the *Times* of London wrote that "[t]he American rifles used by the Turks have a tremendous range; I have seen dug out of a hard clay bank bullets which had penetrated sixteen inches after traversing a distance of over 2,000 yards." "This power of penetration," London's *Daily News* reported, "is owing to the shape of the ball":

It is not, properly speaking, a conical ball, but a solid cylinder of lead, an inch long, and about the diameter of the chassepot bullet, simply rounded at the forward end. Although not larger in diameter than the Russian Berdan, it is nearly twice the weight, and this, combined with the necessary increase in the charge of powder, gives it a fearful power of penetration. One of these bullets will travel a mile, and then go through a horse and any number of men who should happen to be in its line of march.

At this range, almost every bullet was in some sense a stray, but it made little difference. Foreign military observers learned that the "Turks could inflict equal or perhaps greater losses on the enemy by not aiming when they shot." Prussian observer Major Viktor von Lignitz estimated that random rifle fire cost the Russians 200 men a day. Almost unanimously, reporters and military observers alike concluded that "[t]he rifles carried by the Turkish infantry were the best in existence."[14]

Winchesters

A pervasive myth about Plevna is that, somehow, the Turks' Winchester rifles and carbines were decisive.[15] In fact, they may not have been used much at all. It is difficult to pin down the source of this legend, but it was likely the result of Winchester's marketing efforts after Plevna had become a household word in the United States and Europe. In any event, it is certainly untrue.[16] Even the unpublished history of Winchester prepared by its de facto official historian George Watrous years ago acknowledged that the Winchester "would have been no match in the hands of the regular troops against the Russian infantry armed with the single shot Krenk and Berdan rifles."[17]

It is worth remembering that the Winchesters in question were the Model 1866, and not the later versions of the arm. It had few admirers. The American observer at Plevna, Lieutenant Francis Greene, wrote that the Winchester carried by the Turkish cavalry, "although a repeating arm, has such a small charge and short range as to make it a very inferior weapon." British military observers said the same thing, adding that the gun had to be carried with the muzzle up to avoid damaging the magazine spring and that the Winchester usually was used as a single-shot weapon because the weight of the cartridges in the magazine unbalanced the gun. In the field, the Winchester suffered by comparison to the Berdan and the Peabody-Martini. The Englishman William Herbert, serving on the Turkish side, wrote of the "frequent complaints" against the Winchester, and British army Captain George Clarke wrote in 1880 that the Winchester was "inferior to the Berdan carbine of the Russian Cavalry." Francis Greene, attached to the Russian forces, spoke of two fights a week apart. During the first one, between Turkish Circassian cavalry and Russian Cossacks, the Cossacks felled one Turk after another with their Berdans, while staying wholly out of range of the Turks' Winchesters. Yet a week later at the same place, Greene saw an exchange where the

Russians lost fifty or sixty men because "now it was the Turkish infantry opposed to us, armed with the Peabody-Martini rifle, a splendid weapon which carries with deadly effect to 2,000 yards."[18]

It was perhaps for these reasons that, according to the semi-official Turkish account of Plevna, the Winchester was "found to be so defective that, before the end of the war, they were removed from the cavalry, and replaced with the Martini." And, of the many contemporaneous accounts of Plevna, not one recites that the Turkish regulars carried the Winchester rifle or carbine. As if there were any remaining doubt, the Turkish history—which had been written with Osman's help and sources—put it starkly: "It is untrue that the infantry [at Plevna] used the Winchester rifle."[19]

Turkey had 39,000 Winchesters at the beginning of the Russo-Turkish War. By then, Winchesters were carried by the Turkish and Circassian cavalry, the dragoons, the militia, field artillery, the gendarmerie, and the Ottoman's infamous *başıbozuks*.[20] Various sources confirm that Osman's cavalry and dragoons at Plevna used the Winchester, suggesting that anywhere from 1,000 to 2,350 of his men had it. This would have been a small percentage—probably not much more than 5 percent—of the Turkish force and, it is worth noting, there is no evidence that Osman deployed his scarce mounted troops in the trenches and redoubts surrounding the town. Although the Winchester could rapidly fire the contents of its magazine, once those cartridges were gone, the rifle was not much quicker than any other single-shot gun.[21]

There is an interesting contract that sheds some light upon the issue. Signed on March 29, 1876, between Hussein Tevfik on one side and Oliver Winchester and Marcellus Hartley on the other, the agreement provided that Winchester and UMC would join forces to build within ten months a "complete plant of machinery" to manufacture small arms ammunition.[22] This was to be a major project for the cash-strapped Ottomans—the price was £52,250 and the document listed the dozens of machines the Americans were to ship over—and it almost certainly reflected the Turkish army's needs and expectations. The contract specified that the plant was to have a daily capacity of 300,000 Martini-Henry or Snider cartridges, but only 20,000 Winchester rounds. Certainly, by 1876, the Snider and Peabody-Martini were the Turks' principal rifles.

This is not to say that there were no Winchesters at Plevna. The English surgeon Charles Ryan, asked to join a cavalry squadron in late September to reconnoiter the Russian lines south of Plevna, wrote of firing away with his Winchester when they happened upon a superior Russian force. As late as December 9, Osman had about 1,200 surviving cavalrymen, which would have left as many as 1,000 of the guns available for issue to others. On the eve of Osman's attempted breakout on December 9, he had Winchester carbines handed out to his officers. But these are the exceptions that prove the rule. In none of the published accounts of the earlier battles at Plevna does any writer—on either side—say anything about the use of Winchesters other than as a cavalry weapon, and none includes the Winchester among the rifles that were so lethal to the attacking Russian troops on July 20, July 30, or September 11.[23]

Sniders and Krnkas

The workhorse of the Turkish army was the Snider conversion, which was carried by the reserves known as the Rediff. The Snider mechanism was simple, easy to operate, and could fire a dozen rounds a minute. The Turkish Snider was sighted for 1,300 yards, which probably was ambitious. Calculations of the numbers of Sniders at Plevna vary between 7,500 and 30,000. Not much was written about the Snider at Plevna, although this may be more a function of which soldiers used which rifles than anything else. The Russian counterpart to the Snider was the Model 1867 Krnka rifle, a conversion of the muzzle-loading .60 Model 1857 rifle-musket. Few observers had much to say about the Krnka, and fewer yet said anything good. It was slow-loading and fired a ponderous 550-grain bullet. However, it could still kill you. Charles Ryan, an English surgeon working in the ranks of Osman's army, spoke of Turks who attacked Russian positions being driven back by the "murderous fire of the Krenke and Berdan rifles."[24]

Berdan Rifles

Russian troops who could get one carried the Berdan rifle. There were, of course, two Berdan rifles, although they "had the same caliber and nearly the same cartridge, and consequently about the same qualities of range, trajectory, etc." Thirty thousand Berdan I rifles, made by Colt, had been issued to troops earlier in the decade, and almost certainly some were used by Russian soldiers at Plevna. The Berdan II was the bolt-action rifle Russia adopted in 1869. After the Birmingham Small Arms Company finished making the first 30,000 Berdan IIs, its machinery was sent to Russia and the War Ministry took over production. The ministry's goal was to manufacture 300 Berdan IIs a day, but production lagged. As Russia began preparing for war, the War Ministry belatedly ordered its armories to manufacture rifles "night and day at fever heat." At the war's outset, the Berdan had been issued to a quarter of the Tsar's front-line troops. Only mounted troops and special rifle brigades carried the weapon on the Bulgarian front until Berdan-equipped reinforcements began to arrive in August 1877. In the course of the war, the Tsar's factories made about 150,000 Berdan IIs.[25]

The Berdan II was a first-rate weapon in its own right, if designed for a different type of battle. The rifle was likened to the Chassepot because of its small caliber and bolt action, and Hiram Berdan probably copied elements of it. The Berdan II had the smallest caliber (.42) of the common infantry rifles of the 1870s, its bullet (370 grains) was the lightest, and its charge of powder (78 grains) among the lowest. The idea behind the rifle was to solve for accuracy by maximizing muzzle velocity and flattening the bullet's trajectory, producing a gun that was lethal at short range and accurate at longer distances. At short and intermediate range, the Berdan II stood up well to the Martini-Henry. Its muzzle velocity was around 1,450 feet per second, better than the Martini-Henry's, although at 500 yards the bullets' velocities were about equal and after that the Martini-Henry outperformed it. The penetrating power of the Berdan II was certainly less than the Martini-Henry, although it is difficult to find a direct comparison. At forty yards, the Martini-Henry round could pass through twenty-two and a half one-inch pine boards, while at 200 paces, the Berdan II could go through eight.[26]

The Berdan II suffered by comparison to the Peabody-Martini. Although there are countless stories of the deadliness of the Peabody-Martini at 2,000 yards, there are almost none for the Berdan II. Watching a strong Russian force attack outnumbered Turkish troops in the Balkans, the Scottish war correspondent Archibald Forbes saw the Peabody-Martini stagger the Russian columns and even prevent skirmishers from advancing. "[T]he Peabody-Martinis," he wrote, "had the advantage of the Russian Berdans." After the fall of Plevna, some Russian regiments voted with their feet and began using captured Peabody-Martinis.[27]

Gatling Gun

A puzzling thing about Plevna was the ineffectiveness of the Gatling gun. Especially in view of the frontal charges both sides mounted, one would assume that it would have made an appearance.

There were plenty of them. Covering the war for the *North American Review*, retired general George B. McClellan recorded that the Tsar's invasion force had fifty-seven batteries of "Gatlin guns," although not all of these would have been with the Grand Duke's forces in Bulgaria. Despite these numbers, there is virtually no mention of the Gatling gun at Plevna. Osman had his troops maintain a "ceaseless fire" over the Russians day and night, but this evidently was done with the Peabody-Martini. The Russians did move their Gatling guns to their forward lines after they invested Plevna, but they mainly used them at night "probably with the intention of keeping the Turks occupied, so as to relax the tensions on the infantry in the trenches." Again, what is significant is the absence of reporting. Not one of the participants or observers present at Plevna wrote of any instance of a Gatling gun being used in battle; as the historian Maureen O'Connor observed, after conducting a sweeping review of the dispatches written by foreign military observers at Plevna, "mitrailleuses were rarely employed in the war."[28]

Revolvers and Rolling Blocks

There was no shortage of short-range engagements at Plevna, and there are occasional references to officers carrying and using revolvers. Russian officers, of course, had the heavy Smith & Wesson Model 3 revolver that was made in such enormous numbers, but the arm is not mentioned by name in the principal accounts of Plevna, nor of the Russo-Turkish War itself. The Turks were said to have carried the pin-fire Lefaucheux revolver and also purchased quantities of Smith & Wesson revolvers, which they issued to artillery drovers and horsemen. But, again, not much more is said about them.[29]

The record is equally silent about Remington rifles. After the Russian invasion, the Sultan summoned troops from around his empire, including thousands from Egypt. Accounts differ as to when and how many Egyptians soldiers came, although 12,000 seems to be a reliable number. Fairly or not, the fighting qualities of the Egyptian troops were denigrated, and it seems that many were given rear duty. However, Egyptian soldiers fought at the critical battles around Shipka Pass, and one of the rare references to the rolling blocks was from an engagement there where two battalions of Russian reinforcements "suffered severely from the hostile Remington rifles." There may also have been thousands of Remington rifles at Plevna itself, but they are not mentioned.[30]

Ammunition

The amazing rate at which Turkish troops fired their rifles was precisely the nightmarish waste of ammunition that had so bedeviled military thinkers for at least a century. Yet the Turkish response was simple: buy or make enormous quantities of cartridges and be sure that the front line always had more than enough. Turkey bought immense quantities of ammunition from the United States before the war. In 1873, Winchester had contracts with Turkey for 2 million blank training cartridges and 50 million Snider cartridges. Between 1874 and 1877, the Ottomans purchased 80 million Snider cartridges from Winchester and another 200 million primed Peabody-Martini cases and bullets for cartridges to be finished in Constantinople.[31] In 1877 and 1878, Turkey bought 210 million cartridges from UMC, and this was on top of what they had ordered before.[32]

Whatever the exact numbers, the one thing everyone agreed upon was that the Turks had acquired mountains of small-arms ammunition and found a way to deliver it where it was needed. In preparation for the Russian attack on September 11, each man was issued 600 cartridges, and boxes holding 1,000 cartridges each "stood in convenient positions in the trenches and the redoubt." In preparation for his breakout on December

9, Osman issued 130 cartridges to every soldier. Astonishingly, every battalion also had a reserve of 180,000 cartridges, which worked out to 450 rounds per man or a total of possibly 18 million cartridges.[33]

The Third Battle of Plevna

As the Tsar's officers licked their wounds in August, it is unclear whether they reflected upon the lessons of their first two defeats. Each time, they had mounted a frontal assault upon an entrenched enemy of equal strength, and each time their attacking troops had suffered appalling losses. From this, the Russians seem to have concluded that the answer was not to avoid frontal assaults on an entrenched enemy, but instead to attack with more troops.

Russian numbers grew day by day. By early September, there were 90,000 soldiers and over 440 artillery pieces. Osman had about two-thirds as many men and one-fifth the artillery. But during this interlude, Osman's chief of staff Tewfik Bey had "constructed the most elaborate and perfect system of field fortification that the world had ever seen." The walls of the redoubts were up to twenty feet high and twenty feet thick. The subsoil at Plevna was a heavy clay, ideal for the construction of such massive earthworks. Artillery shells buried themselves in the earth; what little damage they did was easily repaired at night by pushing the clay back into place. The redoubts were protected by deep and wide ditches, and beyond those were concentric rings of connecting trenches for shelter, communication, and riflemen.[34]

Tsar Alexander II had come to Plevna to watch the attack, which he observed from a special pavilion with a sweeping view of the battlefield. The attack was set for September 11, the feast day of his patron saint. That morning, the Tsar worried; his officers sipped champagne, enjoyed good food, and chatted in comfort; and his soldiers endured a cold, steady rain. Russian batteries had begun their bombardment of the Turkish lines on September 7, but the 30,000 shells they launched into the Turkish positions did little damage. After a final cannonade that "shook the ground, as if this globe were quivering," the assault began.[35]

The Russian plan was to attack at three places: the Grivitza redoubts in the northeast, the Omer Tabiya ("Omer Battery") in the southeast corner, and the redoubts around Krishin to the south. It began on a bad note; two Russian regiments attacked the Omer Tabiya prematurely and were wiped out, losing 2,300 of their 5,000 men. The *Manchester Guardian's* correspondent Francis Stanley watched the assault on one of the southern Krishin redoubts. Thirty-five thousand Russian troops poured fire into the Turkish trenches in preparation for their onslaught. But then,

[a]lurid flame burst from these like the sulphuric blaze of a great volcano, the whole ten battalions disappeared enveloped in its smoke, then flame after flame followed, lighting up with a fierce glow (so rapid and continuous was the rifle-firing) the dense dark smoke in which these ten devoted battalions were struggling; the loss of life was appalling, not one half the number got back, as with wild gestures of affright they rushed downwards and backwards followed by the merciless bullets.

There is, to be sure, some purple prose in this—after all, the *Guardian* had newspapers to sell—but it agrees with other accounts.[36]

One of the successes that day was the capture of the lower Grivitza redoubt, the Kanli Tabiya. Early on, Archibald Forbes "saw a spurt of Roumanian infantry in the direction of the Grivitza redoubt, which was promptly crushed by a most murderous rifle-fire by its defenders." Another assault was repulsed until, on a final try with Russian help, the Roumanians finally took the redoubt. Yet the Roumanians then learned that the Kanli Tabiya was servient to the Bash Tabiya 180 yards behind it. This they attempted to capture, but "its defenders poured an incessant hail of bullets from a triple line of rifle-barrels upon the attacking troops. . . . After a few minutes of this awful fire the Russian remnant broke and fled back." Later, the American observer Lieutenant Francis Greene saw that "[t]he terreplein of the redoubt as well as its ditch had a complete pavement of dead bodies." Altogether the Roumanians and Russians suffered almost 4,000 dead and wounded assaulting Kanli Tabiya.[37]

The boldest of the Russian generals, Mikhail Skobeleff, attacked the Kavanlik and Issa redoubts to the southeast of Plevna with 17,000 soldiers. After terrible losses, his men had carried both forts by midafternoon. They hung on overnight, exhausted, low on ammunition, and unreinforced. Meanwhile, the Turks counterattacked. After repeated Turkish assaults, Skobeleff began withdrawing his surviving troops under fire late on the 12th. When Skobeleff gathered his command the next day, he found that his losses were 160 officers and 8,000 men were missing.[38]

The Third Battle of Plevna was a worse defeat for the Tsar than the first two. Losses can only be guessed at, but the estimates made by William Herbert are as good as any. He calculated that in the two days of fighting, the Turks suffered 5,000 casualties and the Russians 20,000. All the Tsar had to show for this was the "barren triumph" of the single redoubt that the Roumanians had taken and held. Archibald Forbes, observing the battle near the eminence where the Tsar stood, saw Alexander "in solitary anguish . . . a spectacle of majestic misery."[39]

SIEGE AND SURRENDER

The Russians were now in disarray. Ignoring his panicked brother, who urged a retreat to the Danube, Tsar Alexander summoned to Plevna Russia's famed military engineer, Eduard Totleben. After examining Osman's fortifications, Totleben concluded that future assaults were pointless and Plevna could be taken only by siege.

As reinforcements arrived, the Russian army slowly enveloped the town. By October 24, it was wholly invested, with 180,000 Russians surrounding 34,000 Turks. From there, it was just a matter of time. On December 9, the Turks mounted an abortive breakout that was quickly crushed. The garrison surrendered the next day. The exact losses at Plevna cannot be known with any certainty, but probably about 100,000 died, of which one-third were Turks, over a half Russians, and the rest Roumanians.[40] As events would show, Plevna had not necessarily been a defeat for Turkey, nor was it really over. Osman's 143-day defense of the town would have lasting repercussions.

CHAPTER 24

Losing the Peace

WITH PLEVNA FINALLY OUT OF THE WAY, THE RUSSIAN ARMY SOON
reached Turkey itself. On January 20, 1878, they were at Adrianople, and
ten days later the Ottoman government signed an armistice. Alarmed by
the imminent collapse of the Ottoman Empire, Britain sent its Mediterranean fleet to the Dardanelles. The Russian army stopped short of
occupying Constantinople, instead setting up its camps at the suburb
of San Stefano. There, the Tsar negotiated a one-sided treaty that suggested that his war aims all along had been much more ambitious than
the humanitarian objectives he had previously championed. The Treaty
of San Stefano, signed March 3, 1878, carved up the Sultan's European empire, established a large quasi-independent Christian Bulgaria,
and, most worrisome to the British, provided that the Bosphorus and
the Dardanelles should be open at all times to merchant vessels of neutral
states heading to and from Russia's Black Sea ports. This last provision, of
course, seemed innocent enough, except that everyone well knew that it
was just a foot in the door. Russia's larger ambitions, bluntly expressed by
its long-serving minister to the Sublime Porte, Count Nikolay Pavlovich
Ignatyev, were "the command of Constantinople and the Straits" either
by diplomacy or conquest.[1]

Osman Pasha had been wounded in the abortive escape effort of
December 9 and became a Russian prisoner the next day. He was released
in late March and returned to a hero's welcome in Constantinople. Mobs
thronged the streets in hopes of glimpsing him. "It is difficult for a foreigner to realize the enthusiasm of the common people for this man,"

the American chronicler Henry Dwight wrote at the time. "Besides their admiration for the general whose fame rang through Europe for weeks, they have a holy veneration for the soldier who caused the deaths of many thousands of infidels." Osman was received and—in Ottoman custom—kissed on the eyes by the Sultan, upon which Osman was said to have fallen on his knees, weeping. The Sultan conferred the title of Gazi ("Victorious") upon Osman, promoted him to the rank of field marshal, admitted him to the Order of the Medjidiye, and presented him with a gold medal and a gilded sword. At that, Osman and his chief of staff, the often-overlooked Tewfik Bey, dined with the Sultan.*

THE DIPLOMATIC SOLUTION

The hand of Britain had been evident for a while. The Sultan's abrupt decision in 1872 to adopt the Martini-Henry suggests that some political or diplomatic pressure came into play. And, as mentioned before, it is hard to understand why Major General Dixon of the National Arms Company would have gone to great lengths to urge the Sultan to buy an arm his company was not in a position to sell.

Wherever the truth lies, few gambits have worked out better than whatever British diplomats and military advisors did in mid-1872 to persuade the Sultan to adopt the Martini-Henry. It is possible, of course, that other rifles would have performed just as well at Plevna, but the fact of the matter is that the Peabody-Martini—and a remarkable quantity of ammunition—was the deciding weapon there. Without it, even Osman probably could not have held off the Russian army for almost five months.

And these months made the difference. While the Tsar was detained in Bulgaria, other countries went to work forging a diplomatic solution to the now-unbalanced power structure in Europe. The details of this work—which involved endless negotiations, secret side-deals, and tacit understandings—are blindingly intricate.[2] However, Britain cobbled

---

* Osman barely missed crossing paths with Ulysses S. Grant, whose world tour took him to Constantinople on March 5, where he stayed about a week. It is tempting to think about what such a meeting between the great generals would have been like, although it must also be remembered that Osman disdained infidels and foreigners. H. Dwight, *Turkish Life*, 271–75; John Russell Young, *Around the World with General Grant* (New York: American News Company, 1879), 346.

together enough support to convene a conference of nations to adjust the provisions of San Stefano. For this it enlisted the help of newly unified Germany, whose chancellor, Otto von Bismarck, saw an opportunity in the shifting configuration of European boundaries and alliances.

The diplomatic assembly, which came to be known as the Congress of Berlin, met for a month in the summer of 1878. It was unusual, as one historian put it, because its purpose "was to dictate terms to the victors rather than to the vanquished." The result of the Congress was the Treaty of Berlin, which reset some of the national boundaries drawn in San Stefano and, critically for Britain, removed San Stefano's provision about freedom of navigation in the straits.[3] When everything was over, Roumania, Serbia, and Montenegro became independent; Bosnia, Hercegovina, and parts of Montenegro were handed over to Austria-Hungary; Macedonia was returned to Turkey; the newly created Principality of Bulgaria was reduced by half; Cyprus was awarded to Britain; and Russia got to keep some of the lands it gained in San Stefano. But the net result was the preservation of the Ottoman Empire itself.

The Congress of Berlin undid many of the Tsar's gains, rewarded Austria-Hungary and Britain for no apparent reason, led to rancor and recriminations in Russia, and denied the Tsar an outlet to the Mediterranean. One school of historians believes that it was the five-month interruption of the Russian invasion that bought Britain the time it needed to mount this successful diplomatic counterattack. Oxford scholar A. J. P. Taylor wrote:

Most battles confirm the way that things are going already; Plevna is one of the few engagements which changed the course of history. It is difficult to see how the Ottoman Empire could have survived in Europe if the Russians had reached Constantinople in July; probably it would have collapsed in Asia as well. Plevna gave the Ottoman Empire another forty years of life.[4]

CHAPTER 25

Philadelphia, 1876

Almost twenty-five years to the day after London's Great Exhibition opened, Americans inaugurated the first world's fair held in the United States. The Centennial International Exhibition of 1876, marking a century of independence, occupied a large and elaborate complex by the Schuylkill River in Philadelphia. Like the great European expositions, the Centennial Exposition was a celebration of accomplishment, and it was an opportunity for the country to show off its industrial strength. The symbol of it all was the Corliss Centennial Steam Engine, a 1,400-horsepower, 45-foot-tall colossus with two 44-inch-diameter pistons, each with a 10-foot stroke. The immense machine had been built, coincidentally, across an alley from the armory where Providence Tool was making the Sultan's Peabody-Martinis.[1]

All of the nation's industries had exhibits at the Centennial, not the least being the country's arms-makers. Union Metallic Cartridge, Remington, Providence Tool, Winchester, Sharps, Whitney, Gatling, Ames, Colt, U.S. Cartridge Company, and the Ordnance Department itself showed off their work. The Springfield Armory mounted an exhibition where visitors could watch rifles being made, and the Frankford Arsenal had a production line of nineteen cartridge-making machines, which "constituted the first public display of automation as we now know it."[2] Private armorers offered everything from revolvers, shotguns, and military rifles to machine guns and multibarrel cannon. From obscurity in 1851, the American small-arms industry was now second to none.

But this was its peak. It stood to reason that, sooner or later, nations that could produce their own arms would do so and countries required to buy arms abroad would have what they needed. An acute observer could tell that the arms market was slowly winding down. Samuel Remington moved back to the United States in 1877, and Samuel Norris returned for good the next year. Winchester completed the last of its foreign military contracts in 1878 and thereafter concentrated on ammunition sales and the domestic gun market. That same year, a group of gun-makers—Winchester, Providence Tool, Whitney, Sharps, and Ames among them—formed a group called the Association of Manufacturers of Arms, Ammunition, and Equipments of the United States and launched a lobbying campaign to shut down the Springfield Armory on the premise that they could do the job better.[3] This, of course, failed; Springfield kept going until 1968.

Before long, the two biggest private arms-makers—Providence Tool and Remington—were both in trouble. Within ten years, one was gone and the other sold for a knock-down price at auction.

PROVIDENCE TOOL COMPANY

The Peabody-Martini's success at Plevna did not rescue Providence Tool. Turkey's payments remained unpredictable, and the company's production of guns sporadic. There was yet another stab at a final resolution in April 1878—by then the Turks owed £307,346—with money coming from sources as diverse and random as fees from men paying to avoid military conscription, money raised by selling off the personal effects of soldiers killed in battle, and a contribution from the Company for Opening Railroads in Roumelia. This was deemed the last and final settlement, but no one really believed it and, in fact, it never happened.[4] Instead, payments dribbled in and arms trickled out as they were paid for.

As if its other problems were not enough, Providence Tool suffered yet another blow on October 18, 1878, when the steamer *John Bramhall* was wrecked in a gale on Long Island Sound. The *Bramhall* was packed with arms and munitions for Turkey, including 25,100 Peabody-Martinis, a huge store of ammunition, and 200 boxes of Hussein Tevfik's papers and personal effects. (Tevfik himself had returned to Turkey two months earlier.) The cargo was insured, but John Anthony maintained that the wreck still cost his firm $100,000.[5] This, of course, only further complicated the convoluted finances—and by now the term "Byzantine" was uniquely appropriate—afflicting Providence Tool and Turkey alike.

There is an unusual document stemming from the *Bramhall* wreck. Providence Tool had $400,000 of notes due at the end of 1878, yet the *Bramhall's* insurers were dragging their feet in paying up. This required a visit to Providence Tool's banker, and the banker was J. P. Morgan. Anthony wrote Providence Tool's treasurer, William Dart, about his meeting at the bank, which offers a rare description of Morgan's personality:

> I found Mr. Morgan engaged in an excited discussion about an insurance matter this morning in which I often heard the name of Oliphant & Co. When he turned and recognized me, I said I would wait a little while, until he got cooled off, perhaps he would then come over and sit down on the sofa by me, which was evidently a more comfortable place.
>
> Presently he came and sat down. . . . I told him we were annoyed about the delay in adjusting our loss, and it was now only three weeks to the first of January when we had $400,000 of notes to pay. "My dear fellow," said he, "Don't you worry about that. I expect the loss will be settled before that time and the money paid, but if it is not, I will advance you upon your policy all the money you need for the 1st of January to the extent of $350,000 for a consideration." I asked him what he meant by "a consideration"? and he replied there might be a little matter of interest, if the money was not due, but he thought not.
>
> I told him I was happy—and both he and Mr. Fabri repeated "you always get what you ask for here."
>
> Mr. Morgan said "where is that gun you was going to send me for my boy?" I asked him if he wanted one for sporting purposes or target shooting? And he replied for sporting. I described our "Kill Deer" rifle and told him I would have his sons' [*sic*] monogram engraved upon one (J.P.M. Jr.). He said now put one up in a nice box and do it up right. This I promised to do. I asked him if the 'Kill Deer' would be the right thing? He said "not kill the dear boy," but kill some of those animals in the Adirondacks.—Ask James to fit up a rifle.[6]

The almost endless round of promises, defaults, renegotiations, short-term solutions, and further defaults continued into 1879. Finally, they were resolved when Osman Pasha himself became Ottoman Minister of War. Osman, of course, knew better than anyone his army's staggering losses of guns and matériel during the Russo-Turkish War and the need to replenish weapon stocks. He chartered the steamship *Norman Monarch* and instructed Tevfik to immediately load 59,100 rifles, all the bayonets, several million cartridges, three boilers, and anything else going to Constantinople. At the same time, Osman negotiated a settlement with the Azarians, to whom he agreed to pay £18,000 immediately and £39,000 after the *Norman Monarch* put to sea.[7]

Providence Tool, though, was in a bind. Although its assets nominally exceeded liabilities by $1.8 million, most of these assets were machinery, tooling, and inventory of questionable value.[8] Specialized for rifle production, the machinery and tooling were not worth much, and its merchandise probably should have been written down, too. But the most troubling problem was the company's illiquidity. Out of $3 million of assets, less than $20,000 was cash or "bills receivable." It also recorded $162,533.06 of accounts receivable, but it is unclear how collectible these were. By any standard, Providence Tool was insolvent. The huge risk it had taken on the Turkish contract depended upon favorable interest rates, economies of scale, and—most of all—prompt payment. The Panic of 1873 and Turkey's defaults doomed the company from the beginning, and all that kept it going was John Anthony's determination to see the matter through.

On May 7, 1879, Providence Tool notified Tevfik it had resumed manufacture of the rifles. It finished the last of them on Christmas Eve. Anthony informed the new head of the Turkish inspectors, Major Hassan Basseri, that Providence Tool had manufactured 625,817 rifles: the 600,000 called for by the three contracts, 5,000 for the Sultan's mother, 680 ordered by patriotic Turkish citizens, 37 purchased by General Tevfik himself, and 20,100 to replace those lost on the *Bramhall*. A year later, the balance of the money owed Providence Tool was paid by the Ottoman government.[9]

It would seem that, at long last, this saga was at an end. But John Anthony had been playing a long game. The Turks owed him money for their chronic defaults, but the only way of collecting against the Ottomans was to put a lien on whatever assets they had in the United States, and those assets happened to be 48,617 Peabody-Martinis sitting in a Brooklyn warehouse. Even after receiving Turkey's final payment in December 1880, Anthony refused to turn over the guns. The essence of Providence Tool's claim was that Turkey's breaches of contract had driven the company to the brink of bankruptcy, it had borrowed heavily to stay afloat, and the undelivered rifles were now pledged as security to its banks. Damages, Providence Tool said, were as high as $1 million. To avoid going to court, the Ottomans offered a contract for a further 50,000 rifles, but the idea went nowhere.[10]

In late 1882, Providence Tool repaid its loan from Drexel, Morgan & Co. with $165,000 borrowed from the American National Bank of Providence, which then took control of the pledged rifles and a large number of bayonets. In November, the Sultan sued Providence Tool and the bank, but lost on a legal technicality in August 1883.[11] Ultimately, the Turks paid a final settlement, the rifles were released, and the long story of Providence Tool and the Turkish contracts was finally over.

By then, Providence Tool was in the hands of its lenders. On April 22, 1882, Anthony convened a meeting of the company's creditors to tell them the company no longer could meet its obligations. This precipitated a cascade of claims and attachments, and soon a creditors committee began methodically dismembering the company. The armory and equipment were sold to a machine tool firm, the hardware business reconstituted as the Rhode Island Tool Company, and its sewing machine operations went to a group of investors. What was left was sold off for 50 cents on the dollar, and Providence Tool was dissolved in 1885.[12]

Probably around 1878, Anthony wrote a short history of Providence Tool, perhaps reflecting on what an odyssey it all had been. Starting as a clerk in a small ironworks, he had been pulled into great events of his day. He was in the War Department the morning after Bull Run; did business with Marcellus Hartley, Oliver Winchester, and Samuel Remington and was on familiar terms with J. P. Morgan; his firm armed Canada,

Switzerland, Roumania, Spain, and any number of other countries; and it had completed what one contemporary authority called "the most important order for arms known in the history of the industry." Anthony's account reflected the disappointments that had come, one after the other, since he was awarded the Order of Osmanieh in 1875: "The Grand Vizier with whom I was brought personally in contact, and who personally presented the decree and decoration, was afterward assassinated, and the Sultan who conferred it was deposed." "The benefits which we expected would come from this noteworthy visit," Anthony added, had vanished with "[t]he many misfortunes which have since fallen upon the Empire."[13] These many years later, there is something still poignant in this. The Turkish contract ruined John Anthony, but without Providence Tool, there might have been no Plevna.

REMINGTON

Enthusiastic town boosters rightly declared that the Spanish Ball of 1874 was the most extravagant event Ilion had ever seen, but they did not know there would never be another one. With its Spanish business done, Remington's enormous factory again needed large contracts; so great was its capacity that even orders for a few thousand weapons could be filled within weeks. The only country of any size in the market now was Egypt, with whom Remington had a long, if mixed, history. Probably in 1876, Samuel Remington signed a contract with the Khedive for 100,000 rifles at £3 each.[14]

It was evidence of Remington's apprehensiveness that he reached for this business. By now, the Khedive's reckless borrowing had caught up with him: Egypt's economy was now run by a committee of European diplomats and bankers. In any event, Remington took on the work, which Egypt quickly found it could not pay for. As early as June 1876, Samuel Remington wrote a personal note to Ismail, complaining that Egypt's failure to pay for the rifles "was creating a very present and dangerous situation for my company." By August, he was making trips to Cairo to see the Khedive and demanding that the American State Department use its official resources to help him collect his money. Patiently, the US Consul General in Cairo, Elbert E. Farman—remembered today as the man who persuaded Ismail to gift Cleopatra's Needle to the United States—used what little leverage he had to persuade the Egyptians to free up money to pay Remington. For a while, payments slowly came in, and by May 1877 the Khedive at least had paid Remington for the guns delivered to date.[15] In retrospect, Remington should have stopped there, but instead it kept producing guns, and as these piled up in the United States and foreign ports, Samuel Remington's desperation grew.

One reason Remington had kept production going may have been the Russo-Turkish War. By now, it was raging in the Balkans, and possibly Remington thought it would be a repeat of the windfall his firm had enjoyed a few years earlier when he brokered the flood of American weapons to France during the Franco-Prussian War. If so, he was not alone. Indifferent to whose side they were on, gun salesmen from Hiram Berdan to Samuel Norris traveled to Constantinople and combed the Balkans in search of sales.[16] But the war ended too suddenly, no orders came in, and Samuel Remington was soon back in Cairo.

Farman was an easy scapegoat for Remington to blame, and Remington harshly complained about him to Secretary of State William Evarts. Perhaps to appease a fellow New Yorker, Evarts sent more than one imperious missive to Farman, oblivious to how hard Farman had worked for Remington and how helpful he had been. Farman responded with detailed dispatches describing all he had done. In one, he pointed out that members of the consulate had accompanied Samuel Remington to no less than one hundred meetings with the Egyptian authorities and had managed to cajole £71,000 out of the Khedive between June 1876 and June 1877.[17]

But this still left Remington short, and he seems to have had something of a breakdown. According to a dispatch Farman sent Evarts in May 1878, the Khedive's chief of staff, General Charles Stone, begged to have Remington leave Egypt. In a meeting with the head of Egypt's ordnance department, Aflatoun Pasha, Remington became agitated when he learned that Egypt could not accept rifles as quickly as their contract stipulated and needed the delivery schedule relaxed. According to Stone, "a sword was standing in one corner of the room, which Mr. Remington sprang and seized and unsheathing it, apparently tried in the wildest manner to kill himself." After Aflatoun and a nearby soldier wrestled the sword away from him, Remington collapsed on a nearby couch in exhaustion, leaving in confusion after the Egyptians revived him. Samuel Remington, Farman implied, had his back against a wall. He was "constantly in the receipt of telegrams and letters to the effect that his firm would fail, if money was not sent immediately" and "often in such a state of mind, probably in consequence of his financial embarrassment, that he annoyed us extremely."[18]

With so many creditors demanding payment, Remington was lucky to get anything out of Egypt, and Farman spent two years negotiating a deal on the firm's behalf. In the end, he arranged for Egypt to pay Remington £65,000 and for the company to keep its undelivered guns and a quantity of machinery. This was substantially less than the £159,874 Samuel Remington thought he was owed, but in the circumstances still a miraculous recovery. Problematically, though, it left Remington with 19,340 undelivered guns, plus another 26,000 or so unfinished ones.[19]

For all intents and purposes, the rolling block's great run was over. Remington's salesmen still journeyed far and wide chasing orders, but there were few to be had now. The last large rolling block purchase came in 1879 from Argentina, which bought perhaps as many as 20,000. Yet the Remingtons were not ready to give up yet on the gun business. Technology had moved on, and the world's militaries were starting to replace their single-shot rifles with bolt-action guns using magazines. Perhaps, Remington thought, this would be yet another revolution in arms like the Minié rifles of the 1850s or the breech loaders of the 1860s. In 1878, the firm began promoting a bolt-action rifle designed by New Jersey inventor John W. Keene, which used a tubular magazine resembling the Winchester's.[20]

Meanwhile, Remington designer James Paris Lee was working on a bolt-action system of his own that used a detachable metal-box magazine that fed cartridges to the breech through a channel cut through the bottom of the receiver. In Lee's design, each time a spent shell was ejected, a new cartridge was pushed up into the breech from below, and when the whole magazine was emptied, a new one could be snapped into place. In November 1879, Lee was awarded a patent with broad claims, including rights to a magazine that was spring-loaded, detachable, and configured to feed cartridges through the bottom of the receiver. Although Lee was working with Remington at the time, he somehow kept the rights to his invention and, to Remington's annoyance, he licensed them to P. T. Barnum's Sharps Rifle Company. The US Navy agreed to purchase 300 Lee rifles from Sharps, but Sharps failed before it could complete the order. Remington then bought the incomplete contract and rights to the rifle, which they renamed the Remington-Lee.[21]

Evidently thinking they had another success on their hands, Philo and Eliphalet Remington (Samuel had died in December 1882) began retooling their plant to make the gun. Ultimately their capacity grew to 200 guns a day. But the Remington-Lee got off to a slow start, and as late as 1887 no more than 50,000 had been sold.[22]

Disaster

But there were glimmers of hope. The Ottoman Empire, of all places, was slowly rebuilding from the ruins of war, and its Minister of War now was Osman's former chief of staff, Tewfik Pasha. By the mid-1880s, Turkey's finances had improved enough that it began considering a major weapons purchase. There were rumors that Turkey would order at least 400,000 rifles, and possibly as many as 600,000.[23]

Remington quickly went after the business, promoting the Remington-Lee and doing whatever it could to remove any impediment to getting the order. One roadblock was Providence Tool's still-pending claim against the Ottomans for their breaches of contract; as long as this was around (and now it was in the hands of Providence Tool's creditors), any guns made in the United States for the Turks might be attached. Adroitly, the Remingtons (or, perhaps, their ally Marcellus Hartley) used their influence to help the two sides settle their differences, opening the way to having the new guns made in America.[24]

A second problem was the shaky state of Remington's finances. With revenues from their weapons business dwindling, Remington's debts had mounted steadily, first consuming the firm's reserves, then the brothers' personal fortunes. By 1885, the company was borrowing to meet overhead expenses and operating costs. Remington's financial weakness undermined its credibility and threatened to derail the one opportunity that would get the firm back on its feet. To help put its house back in order, Remington sold its promising typewriter business to a partnership of former employees for $186,000. But this backfired. Remington's creditors, worried about its dissipation of assets, demanded immediate payment of their notes. Remington went into receivership in April 1886.[25]

The Remingtons deserve credit for having seen that the gun business alone would not support an industrial dynasty. Early on, they had broadened their business and expanded into new areas. The arms operation had a sister operation that produced agricultural equipment, and the Remington works made and sold everything from prefabricated bridges to fire engines and trolley cars. Remington had a line of sewing machines and, to its credit, in 1873 entered the typewriter business. But each of these required capital investment, and they all encountered headwinds. There was plenty of competition in agricultural machinery, and Remington was too far from the burgeoning Midwest to be competitive. An unsuccessful effort to market a reversible mower cost Remington $350,000 and a failed cotton gin project made things worse. Virtually every gun firm had a sewing machine, too, and "ruinous competition" made it impossible to make money selling them. After looking at Remington's books years later, a retired Remington employee, Albert Russell, guessed that the company had lost $1 million on sewing machines alone. And, as promising as the typewriter was, it took years to perfect.[26]

Before long, troubling details emerged about Remington's finances. On paper, it had substantial assets in land, tooling, machinery, and even patents. But there was not much cash and, as it turned out, Remington's liquidity problems were beyond what anyone could have imagined. For the past decade or so, Remington had in essence been printing its own money, a scrip it called "orders." Remington's workers and contractors were paid in scrip, and so respected was the company that local merchants accepted Remington "orders" as it they were cash. With time, the scrip displaced government currency in Ilion. In the words of one newspaper:

> The method has been for an employee to give an order on the Remington firm for his boots, his coat, his bed, his board, his cigar and his

minister. These orders after three months, during which they drew no interest, were changed for a short time note of the company's, which at the end of three or four months, was paid or renewed. Very many of the short notes have been changed into long-time notes, . . . so that the creditors of the corporation are very many of them the residents of Ilion, most of them, as it is believed.[27]

Some—probably the Remingtons themselves—defended the practice as a means of insulating their workforce and community from the ups and downs of the US dollar during the Panic of 1873 and the roiled years that followed it. But it also meant that the Remingtons were, in essence, borrowing from their own workers and neighbors and, probably, understating their liabilities. When the edifice came crashing down, the townspeople, as well as the Remingtons themselves, were broke.

There was no federal bankruptcy code in those years, so the matter of restructuring an insolvent firm was more complicated than it is now. An item in the August 6, 1886, *New York Times* reported that a committee of creditors was completing its work and planning to create a new organization to take over and operate the works in Ilion. Ordinarily, this was done by holding a public auction of the assets, at which the senior creditors would submit a "credit bid"—that is, having the debts they held treated as cash—and agree to contribute enough additional cash (in this case, it was 10 percent of the total debt) to provide working capital for the new enterprise. Behind the senior creditors, successive layers of creditors were to get tiers of preferred stock, "the members of the old Remington Company" being on the bottom. With this plan in place, E. Remington & Sons was declared legally bankrupt on April 26, 1887. Ostensibly, it had assets of $1,711,784, but these were illiquid and almost certainly overstated. Its liabilities—which by contrast were demands for cash—were $1,255,703. A new company, Remington Arms Company, was formed the next year, owned jointly by Winchester and Schuyler, Hartley & Graham. Marcellus Hartley was its president and Winchester's Thomas Bennett its vice-president. Eight years later, Winchester sold out to Hartley & Graham (Jacob Schuyler had died in 1887), and so now Marcellus Hartley controlled it all.[28]

MAUSER

Remington's efforts to bolster its finances probably were irrelevant anyway. Constantinople newspapers reported in late December 1886 that Ottoman War Minister Tewfik was in Berlin, and within a month, Turkey had signed a contract for 600,000 Mausers.[29] The Ottomans' decision to order Mausers probably had less to do with Remington's finances than with the growing ties between Turkey and Germany, which had started with Bismarck's intermediation at the Congress of Berlin. So close did the two countries become that Turkey allied itself with Germany in World War I.

In a business rife with ironies, there was a particular one when it came to the Mauser rifle. The Mauser firm was founded by two brothers, Wilhelm and Paul, who followed their father into the gunsmithing trade. (There were other brothers as well, including one who worked for a time in Ilion for Remington.) In 1867, an Austrian official showed Samuel Norris an interesting bolt-action rifle, "the invention of two brothers, Mauser by name." Thinking that the design might work as a system for converting the Chassepot into a metallic cartridge gun, Norris immediately went to Paris to see what the French thought. They showed enough interest that Norris traveled to the remote village of Oberndorf, in Württemberg, where the Mausers worked in a small government armory. "They looked like crushed men—poor and working hard for their living," Norris wrote decades later. "I found that the officials pooh-poohed their arm, and they had lost all hope."[30] Norris's account of things makes him out to be a thoughtful advisor to the Mauser brothers, and perhaps even a generous patron. In fact, it was somewhat the opposite: Norris proceeded to take advantage of the two in manner that was both underhanded and overbearing.

Norris seems to have led Wilhelm and Paul Mauser to think that he would market their gun all over Europe. He moved them from Oberndorf to Liege, where Remington had a small workshop. There, on September 28, 1867, a *notaire* drew up a one-sided contract among them. The document is a reflection both of the Mausers' naiveté and Norris's avarice; as Norris boasted to his wife, "I have what I came for and more if I desire." The contract gave Norris near total ownership and control of the Mausers' work. Ostensibly, the arrangement called for Norris to hire the brothers for a period of ten years at an annual salary beginning at F3,000 and climbing to F12,000. In return, Norris would have complete rights to their gun and all improvements. Yet Norris was under no obligation to keep the Mausers in his employ; he could let them go whenever he wanted. In that case, the Mausers would get their intellectual property rights back, except for the French patent, which Norris got to keep "as indemnity for his trouble." On June 2, 1868, Norris and the Mauser brothers secured a US patent on the Mauser system, although it is far from clear what part of the invention could be credited to Norris.[31]

Norris, of course, had no ability to manufacture the Mauser or any other gun. Various accounts suggest that Samuel Remington was furious with Norris for diverting the Mauser opportunity to himself, and that Norris either sold or gave Remington a share of his interest in the contract. Whatever it was, it seems that Norris depended upon Remington to promote the gun and, probably, make it. In this, he was frustrated by Samuel Remington's preference for the rolling block. In a piece Norris published in the *New York Times* in 1898, he wrote that Remington discouraged the Mauser's "presentation to military authorities, being anxious that the Remington should be the only arm to be energetically pushed." Privately, he was less diplomatic. The year before, Norris prepared a private account of the matter and called Remington "a man totally unfit for the important relation he had to his firm & whose selfishness & narrow views" caused him to miss out on the best opportunity of his life.[32]

One area where Norris could sell the Mauser system without the need to involve Remington was to license it for conversions, especially to the French. By 1869, though, it was clear that the French had no interest in the Mauser. Cutting his losses, Norris terminated his arrangements with the Mauser brothers, leaving Wilhelm and Paul to their own devices. The Mausers seem to have thought themselves rather cruelly used, but in Norris's telling they "became tired & disappointed" with the lack of progress and wanted to return home anyway.[33]

For Wilhelm and Paul Mauser, at least, it was a blessing in disguise. Wiser for the experience, they kept working on their rifle, which soon attracted the attention of the Prussian government. The rest, as they say, is history. Tens of millions of Mauser rifles were produced in the following years, and the design became a global standard. The only two countries where Norris held patent rights were France and the United States, but France rejected the Mauser and America only adopted features of it long after Norris's patent had expired.

This was the end of the reign of American arms-makers. By 1886 Providence Tool, Sharps, and Spencer were gone, and soon Winchester—now run by Thomas Bennett—would buy what was left of Whitney. Remington was much reduced and would become a part of Marcellus Hartley's empire. Colt, Winchester, and Smith & Wesson were still in business, but now focused on the domestic market.

Everyone involved sensed that they had been part of something important, but each struggled to capture what it was. Almost unexpectedly, commercial necessity pushed them abroad, where their technological advantage mixed with the geopolitics of the age to take them places they could never have imagined. Americans who in any other time would have contented themselves with more mundane matters traveled the world and met emperors and tsars, kings and khedives, sultans and grand viziers. Their weapons had started wars, decided battles, and changed the face of the nineteenth century. The fever, though, ended almost as quickly as it had begun, and in the ensuing silence, the arms sellers themselves were in some wonderment about it all.

EPILOGUE

Alexei Alexandrovich's later life did him no credit. The Grand Duke played a minor role in the Russo-Turkish War and was ineffective when he later was made the figurehead of the Russian navy. There were persistent allegations of misappropriation of official funds and wasteful spending on palaces, mistresses, and palaces for mistresses. After the Japanese made quick work of Russian fleets in the Russo-Japanese War of 1904, Alexei retired in disgrace and moved to Paris, where he died in 1908.

John Anthony was in his mid-fifties when Providence Tool was liquidated in 1885. He stayed with the fragments of Providence Tool for a time, and then took a job as treasurer for a calico printing firm. Widowed in 1891, he continued to live with three of his unmarried daughters, a grand-niece, and a few servants in a stately home at 72 Manning Street in Providence that housed the art and furniture he and his wife had amassed during their trip to Constantinople in 1875. Anthony may have choked on his breakfast the morning of August 12, 1892, when the papers reported the shocking news that his third cousin, Lizzie Borden, had been arrested for the grisly axe murders of her father and step-mother (herself a distant cousin). Anthony died at age seventy-five in 1904, apparently still working until the end. There were enough gunstocks left over from Providence Tool's gun business that the Anthony daughters used them as firewood for years.

Hiram Berdan remained a complicated figure. He patented more inventions, including torpedoes, torpedo boats, artillery fuses, and a semi-submersible gunboat. He prosecuted a long-running lawsuit against the United States government for infringing one of his patents, finally receiving a $95,000 award in 1890. Berdan continued to be something of a manipulative and self-delusionary character. After leaving the army under pressure in January 1864—and despite having been court-martialed and repeatedly accused of cowardice—he somehow was brevetted ex post facto as both a brigadier general and major general by President Andrew Johnson in 1869, although the Senate confirmed only the lower rank. Inexplicably, Berdan then campaigned to have Congress award him the Medal of Honor for valor at Gettysburg, despite the fact there was no evidence that he had done anything remotely valiant there or anywhere else. One of Berdan's daughters married the then-popular novelist Francis Marion Crawford and the other, living in Paris, became the Baroness Lepeltier-D'Aunay. Berdan died of a cerebral hemorrhage in 1893 at the Metropolitan Club in Washington, DC.

Notoriously unsuccessful as a general, **Ambrose Burnside** had a remarkable postwar career. He served three one-year terms as the governor of Rhode Island and was in his second term as a senator when he passed away in 1881. Burnside was active in veterans' organizations, and he was the first president of the National Rifle Association when it was organized in 1871.

George Armstrong Custer famously died at Little Big Horn on June 25, 1876. Spotted Tail was not present that day, but among the Sioux warriors who wiped out Custer's command were members of the Brulé band, including braves who had hunted with Custer and Alexei barely four years earlier.

Marcellus Hartley became one of the wealthiest men of his time. Beside his interests in Union Metallic Cartridge and Remington Arms, Hartley sat on the boards of various banks, trust companies, and insurers. Seeing the promise of electric lighting and power, he was a major investor in the firm that became Westinghouse. There he worked closely with Hiram Maxim, whose labors in the field of electric power generation preceded his fame as the designer of the Maxim machine gun. In the 1890s, Hartley loaned Adolph Ochs money to keep the *New York Times* afloat and, according to Hartley family tradition, suggested to Ochs the paper's enduring slogan, "All the News That's Fit to Print." Hartley died of a heart attack in 1902, hours before he was scheduled to meet with John Browning about his new autoloading shotgun.

Alfred C. Hobbs worked at Union Metallic Cartridge until his death in 1891. He remained a gifted inventor and, over the years, improved the company's cartridge designs and took out patents on a percussion cap, cartridge primers, and machines for loading cartridges and punching cartridge heads.

Ismail Pasha was deposed at the insistence of Great Britain and France in 1879. He went into exile near Naples, Italy, until he was allowed to move to Constantinople in 1885. Essentially confined to his palace, Ismail died in 1895.

Samuel Norris left the gun business after returning to Rhode Island in 1878. He then turned his attention to other opportunities, including a company that made wooden paving blocks. Norris remained bitter about Samuel Remington's refusal to promote the Mauser rifle and, before his death in 1902, wrote a series of essays and newspaper articles about his experiences as a gun salesman in Europe.

Osman Nuri Pasha died in 1900. He was buried in an elaborate tomb next to the Conqueror's Mosque in Constantinople, and is still considered one of Turkey's greatest generals.

Henry O. Peabody lived until 1903, wealthy from the royalties he received from his gun patents. Childless, he left his assets to a philanthropic trust with directions to fund a school for young women. The Henry O. Peabody School for Girls opened in Norwood, Massachusetts, in 1940 and remained in operation until changed circumstances forced it to close in 1989. (The school continues to exist as a charitable foundation that awards scholarships to young women pursuing a college or technical education.) Peabody invented other things besides guns, ranging from centrifuges for extracting honey to a machine for spreading fertilizer.

Large numbers of Turkey's **Peabody-Martini** rifles were seized by the Tsar's armies in 1878. They were used by Russian troops as late as

World War I when they, in turn, were surrendered to German troops. While going through captured German war records in the 1950s, Norman Rich learned that some of the Peabody-Martinis had been used by German reserve units in World War II.

After the Civil War, the **Springfield Armory** went into a period of decline. The army was satisfied with its Allin trapdoor breech loader and saw little need to adopt the more advanced rifles that other countries were using. The United States finally adopted the bolt-action Krag-Jørgensen in 1893 and set Springfield to work to manufacture it. After so many years of stasis, the job of retooling was a challenging one, but successfully implemented by the armory's new commandant, Colonel Alfred Mordecai, who had followed in his father's footsteps.

Watson Squire amassed large tracts of land in the Washington Territory in the mid-1870s and moved to Seattle in 1879. He served as territorial governor from 1884 to 1887, a period characterized by anti-Chinese rioting and martial law. After Washington became a state, Squire was elected senator, a position he held until 1897. He died in 1926 at eighty-eight.

Hussëin Tevfik remained in Ottoman service. After returning to Constantinople in 1878, he taught mathematics and published his monograph on multidimensional algebra. Tevfik became Turkey's Minister of Finance in 1880, its Minister to the United States in 1883, and, later, Minister for Public Works. After Turkey adopted the Mauser rifle in 1887, he headed the commission responsible for the guns' inspection. Tevfik was appointed to the rank of marshal in 1893, became Minister of Finance for a second time in 1897, and was an advisor to the Sultan at his death in 1901.

Oliver Winchester died in 1880, and management of his company devolved upon his son-in-law Thomas Gray Bennett. Winchester's only son passed away in 1881, and it was his daughter-in-law, Sarah Lockwood Winchester, who built the famous, if bizarre, Winchester Mystery House in San Jose, California.

NOTES

CHAPTER 1

1. Royal Commission for the Great Exhibition of the Works of Industry of All Nations, *Official Catalogue* (London: W. Clowes & Sons, 1851), vol. 1, "Plan of the Building."

2. Royal Commission, *Official Catalogue*, vol. 3, ex. nos. 7, 10, 84, 172, 239, 253, 274, and 359, pp. 1433–69; Yvonne Ffrench, *The Great Exhibition: 1851* (London: Harvill Press, 1950), 243–44; Clement Shorter, *The Brontës' Life and Letters*, vol. 2 (London: Hodder and Stoughton 1908), 215–16.

3. Franklin Parker, *George Peabody* (Nashville, TN: Vanderbilt University Press, 1971), 49; Benjamin Pierce Johnson, *Report of Benj. P. Johnson: Agent of the State of New York, Appointed to Attend the Exhibition of the Industry of All Nations, Held In London, 1851* (Albany, NY: C. Van Benthuysen, Public Printer, 1852), 13, 94.

4. B. Johnson, *Report*, 15.

5. Royal Commission, *Official Catalogue*, vol. 3, ex. no. 298, p. 1453; B. Johnson, *Report*, 139–40.

6. B. Johnson, *Report*, 140–43.

7. Nathan Rosenberg, *The American System of Manufactures* (Edinburgh: Edinburgh University Press, 1969), 10; B. Johnson, *Report*, 143.

8. N. Rosenberg, *American System*, 7; B. Johnson, *Report*, 93–94.

9. Royal Commission, *Official Catalogue*, vol. 3, ex. no. 321, p. 1454; Michael B. Schiffer, Power Struggles: Scientific Authority and the Creation of Practical Electricity Before Edison (Cambridge, MA: MIT Press, 2008), 124.

10. Jeffrey A. Auerbach, *The Great Exhibition of 1851: A Nation on Display* (New Haven, CT: Yale University Press, 1999); N. Rosenberg, *American System*, 15; James Rasenberger, *Revolver: Sam Colt and the Six Shooter That Changed America* (New York: Scribner, 2020), 284.

11. N. Rosenberg, *American System*, 18; B. Johnson, *Report*, 160.

12. Royal Commission, *Official Catalogue*, vol. 3, ex. no. 328, p. 1455 (emphasis added).

CHAPTER 2

1. Col. Berkeley Lewis, *Small Arms and Ammunition in the United States Service* (Washington, DC: Smithsonian Institution, 1956), 5–6. Felicia Deyrup, *Arms Makers of the*

Connecticut Valley: A Regional Study of the Economic Development of the Small Arms Industry, 1798–1870, Smith College Studies in History, vol. 23 (Northhampton, MA: Smith College, 1948), 229–30.

2. Alfred Mordecai, *Ordnance Manual for the Use of Officers of the United States Army* (Washington, DC: Gideon & Co., 1850), 196; Theodore T. S. Laidley, *The Ordnance Manual for the Use of the Officers of the United States Army* (Philadelphia: J. B. Lippincott & Company, 1862), 208; B. Lewis, *Small Arms*, 47; James G. Benton, *Course of Instruction in Ordnance & Gunnery* (New York: D. Van Nostrand, 1862), 294, 314–15; N. Rosenberg, *American System*, 120.

3. Gordon L. Jones, *Confederate Odyssey* (Athens: University of Georgia Press, 2014), 214–15; N. Rosenberg, *American System*, 39; Thomas F. F. Cottesloe, "Notes on the History of the Royal Small Arms Factory, Enfield Lock," *Journal of the Society for Army Historical Research* 12, no. 48 (Winter 1933–1934): 200–201; David Williams, *The Birmingham Gun Trade* (Stroud, UK: History Press 2009), 46; James Lewis, "The Development of the Royal Small Arms Factory (Enfield Lock) and Its Influence upon Mass Production Technology and Product Design C1820–C188" (thesis, Middlesex University, 1996), 58.

4. Kenneth Alder, "Innovation and Amnesia: Engineering Rationality and the Fate of Interchangeable Parts Manufacturing in France," *Technology and Culture* 38, no. 2 (April 1997): 273–311.

5. David A. Hounshell, *From the American System to Mass Production* (Baltimore: Johns Hopkins University Press, 1984), 5, 43, 261.

CHAPTER 3

1. F. Deyrup, *Arms Makers*; John P. Johnson, "Robbins & Lawrence Armory (American Precision Museum)," US Department of the Interior, National Park Service, HAER VT-39, 2009; Andrew J. B. Lee, "The U.S. Armory at Harpers Ferry Historic Resource Study," Harpers Ferry National Historical Park Archeology Program, 2006; Diana Muir, *Reflections in Bullough's Pond: Economy and Ecosystem in New England* (Hanover and London: University Press of New England, 2000); Merritt Roe Smith, *Harpers Ferry Armory and the New Technology: The Challenge of Change* (Ithaca, NY: Cornell University Press, 1980).

2. "From George Washington to the United States Senate and House of Representatives, 8 January 1790," Founders Online, National Archives, https://founders.archives.gov/documents/Washington/05-04-02-0361.

3. *Journal of the House*, vol. 1 (January 15, 1790), 141–42; Alexander Hamilton, *Report on the Subject of Manufactures* (New York: Cosimo Classics, 2007), 63–64; "Act to Provide for the Erecting & Repairing of Arsenals & Magazines," 3rd Cong., 2d Sess., Ch. 14, 1 Stat. 352, §§ 1 and 4.

4. Eli Whitney got into musket-making out of desperation; he was on the brink of personal bankruptcy and, to pay off his creditors, he needed the large advances the federal government was offering to anyone who would take an arms contract. Whitney never built the mechanized or modern armory he promised, nor ever in his life did he make a musket (or anything else) with interchangeable parts. Instead, when called upon to demonstrate

the quality of his arms, Whitney had his workers hand-finish a dozen or so until each of their parts matched. This dissimulation impressed government officials and gave credence to the iffy proposition that the technology of the day was adequate for the high level of precision that interchangeability required. It also bolstered Whitney's reputation as a technological oracle of sorts, and his advocacy legitimatized the Ordnance Department's costly and somewhat premature program to develop the machine-driven manufacture of arms. See Edwin A. Battison, "Eli Whitney and the Milling Machine," *Smithsonian Journal of History* 1, no. 2 (Summer 1966): 23; D. Muir, *Reflections in Bullough's Pond*, 124–25; Merritt Roe Smith, "Eli Whitney and the American System of Manufacturing," in *Technology in America: A History of Individuals and Ideas*, 6th ed., ed. Carrol W. Pursell Jr. (Cambridge, MA: MIT Press, 1986), 46–48; William P. Blake, *History of the Town of Hamden, Connecticut* (New Haven, CT: Price, Lee & Co., 1888), 131–34.

5. Constitution, Art. 1, § 8, Cl. 15; "Act Making Provision for the Arming of the Whole Body of the Militia of the United States," Ch. 60, 10th Cong., 1st Sess., 2 Stat. 490 (April 22, 1808); M. R. Smith, *Harpers Ferry*, 209; D. Hounshell, *American System*, 42; Robert S. Woodbury, "The Legend of Eli Whitney and Interchangeable Parts," *Technology and Culture* 1, no. 3 (Summer 1960): 236–37; Jeanette Mirsky and Allan Nevins, *The World of Eli Whitney* (New York: Macmillan, 1952), 108, 137–38; W. Blake, *History of Hamden*, 120–21; S. N. D. North and Ralph North, *Simeon North, First Official Pistol Maker of the United States* (Concord, NH: Rumford Press, 1913), 66; "Act to Establish a Quartermaster's Department," 12th Cong., 1st Sess., Ch. 66, 2 Stat. 696, §§ 3 and 5 (March 28, 1812); "Act for the Better Regulation of the Ordnance," 12th Cong., 1st Sess., Ch. 83, 2 Stat. 732, § 5 (May 14, 1812).

6. "Act for the Better Regulation of the Ordnance Department," 13th Cong., 3rd Sess., Ch. 38, 3 Stat. 203, §§ 9 and 10 (February 8, 1815) (emphasis added).

7. M. R. Smith, *Harpers Ferry*, 212; Michael S. Raber, Patrick M. Malone, Robert B. Gordon, and Carolyn C. Cooper, *Conservative Innovators and Military Small Arms: An Industrial History of Springfield Armory, 1794–1968* (South Glastonbury, CT: Raber Associates, 1989), 67.

8. See F. Deyrup, *Arms Makers*; Charles H. Fitch, *Report on the Manufacture of Fire-arms and Ammunition* (Washington, DC: Government Printing Office [hereinafter "GPO"], 1882); Robert B. Gordon, "Simeon North, John Hall, and Mechanized Manufacturing," *Technology and Culture* 30, no. 1 (January 1989): 179–88; D. Hounshell, *American System*; Robert A. Howard, "Interchangeable Parts Reexamined: The Private Sector of the American Arms Industry on the Eve of the Civil War," *Technology and Culture* 19, no. 4 (October 1978): 633–49; David R. Meyer, *Networked Machinists: High Technology Industries in Antebellum America* (Baltimore: Johns Hopkins University Press, 2006); Charles R. Morris, *The Dawn of Innovation* (New York: Public Affairs, 2012); M. Raber, et al., *Conservative Innovators*; N. Rosenberg, *American System*; Joseph W. Roe, *English and American Tool Builders* (New York: McGraw Hill Book Co., 1916); M. R. Smith, *Harpers Ferry*; Merritt Roe Smith, "Army Ordnance and the 'American System' of Manufacturing, 1815–1861," in *Military Enterprise and Technological Change* (Cambridge, MA: MIT Press, 1985); Paul Uselding, "Elisha K. Root, Forging, and the 'American System,'" *Technology and Culture* 15, no. 4 (October 1974): 543–68.

9. R. Woodbury, "Legend of Eli Whitney," 247–48; Robert B. Gordon, "Material Evidence of the Manufacturing Methods Used in Armory Practice," *IA: The Journal of the Society for Industrial Archeology* 14, no. 1 (1988): 32; Robert B. Gordon, "Who Turned the Mechanical Ideal into Mechanical Reality?" *Technology and Culture* 29, no. 4 (October 1988): 773, 774 fig. 10; C. Fitch, *Report*, 3, 15; M. Raber, et al., *Conservative Innovators*, 141–42.

10. J. Roe, *Tool Builders*, 168–69, 189–91, 220–21; Asa Waters, "Thomas Blanchard, The Inventor," *Harper's New Monthly Magazine* 43, no. 374 (July 1881), 255; Henry Howe, *Memoirs of the Most Eminent American Mechanics* (New York: Harper & Brothers, 1852), 201–5; Carolyn Cooper, *Shaping Invention: Thomas Blanchard's Machinery and Patent Management in Nineteenth-Century America* (New York: Columbia University Press, 1991), 17–19, 79–81; M. R. Smith, *Harpers Ferry*, 205–7, 209, 225–41; D. Williams, *Birmingham Gun Trade*, 65; R. Gordon, "Simeon North," 179–88; M. Raber, et al., *Conservative Innovators*, 333–34; C. Fitch, *Report*, 22, 26–27.

11. C. Fitch, *Report*, 28–29; F. Deyrup, *Arms Makers*, 154; N. Rosenberg, *American System*, 136, 178.

CHAPTER 4

1. J. Lewis, "Development of the Royal Small Arms Factory," 127–28; N. Rosenberg, *American System*, 40–41 and nn. 1 and 2.

2. J. Rasenberger, *Revolver*, 294–95; Russell I. Fries, "British Response to the American System," *Technology and Culture* 16, no. 3 (1975): 377n2; N. Rosenberg, *American System*, 45–46.

3. J. Lewis, "Development of the Royal Small Arms Factory," 13; James A. Nasmyth, *James Nasmyth, Engineer: An Autobiography* (New York: Harper & Brothers, 1883), 365–66; N. Rosenberg, *American System*, 31n4, 43–53, 91–98.

4. N. Rosenberg, *American System*, 99, 101, 113, 197.

5. N. Rosenberg, *American System*, 91–97, 100–4, 122–23, 180–81, 196; Peter G. Smithurst, *The Guns and Gun-Making Machinery of Robbins & Lawrence* (Windsor, VT: American Precision Museum, 2007), 5; J. Nasmyth, *Autobiography*, 365–66; George W. Cullum, "James W. Ripley," in *Biographical Register of the Officers and Graduates of the U.S. Military Academy at West Point, N.Y.*, vol. 1, 3rd ed. (Boston and New York: Houghton, Mifflin, 1891), 121.

6. N. Rosenberg, *American System*, 196; "Military Commission to Europe in 1855 and 1856, Report of Major Alfred Mordecai," Sen. Ex. Doc. No. 60 (Washington, DC: George W. Bowman, 1860) [hereinafter A. Mordecai, "1856 Military Commission Report"], 164 (Ser. Set 1037).

7. A case in point was Samuel Colt's frustration with his London revolver factory. Despite its use of American methods, the London armory never matched the success of Colt's Hartford plant, largely because Colt's dependence upon machinery was alien to England's cultural traditions. The London armory became a drain on the company's work, and Colt closed it in 1857. J. Rasenberger, *Revolver*, 101–4, 261, 266–68, 282–84, 294–95, 301, 309–10, 319–20, 323–44; R. Fries, "British Response to the American System," 377n2.

8. M. R. Smith, *Harpers Ferry*, 110.
9. C. Fitch, *Report*, v, 2–3, 16–17; N. Rosenberg, *American System*, 365.
10. C. Fitch, *Report*, 6; N. Rosenberg, *American System*, 136, 180–87.
11. US Patent No. 5,763 (September 12, 1848); Benjamin Huger, et al., *Reports of Experiments with Small Arms for the Military Services* (Washington, DC: A. O. P. Nicholson,1856), 24–25 and errata; "Weapons of War," in Office of the Royal Artillery, *The Technical Educator, an Encyclopædia* (London: Cassell, Petter & Galpin, 1880), 194.
12. J. Roe, *Tool Builders*, 192 and app. A, 287–88; *Rowan v. Sharps Rifle Manufacturing Co.*, 35 Conn. 127 (1868), Record on Appeal (Brighton, MI: Cornell Publications, 2005), 2, 17–20, 38–46.
13. N. Rosenberg, *American System*, 103, 115.
14. J. Roe, *Tool Builders*, 189–91; "Superintendents of National Armories," H. R. Misc. Doc. No. 76, 33rd Cong., 1st Sess. (Washington, DC: A. O. Nicholson, 1854), 259 (Ser. Set 741).
15. N. Rosenberg, *American System*, 117, 136, 180–91.
16. Thomas K. Tate, *From Under Iron Eyelids* (Central Milton Keynes, UK: Author-House, 2005), 82–84, 97; A. Mordecai, "1856 Military Commission Report," 107 (Ser. Set 1037).
17. P. Smithurst, *Robbins & Lawrence*, 6.
18. J. Roe, *Tool Builders*, 192–93, 288; P. Smithurst, *Robbins & Lawrence*, 6–7.
19. *Rowan v. Sharps*, Record on Appeal, 22–23, 28–29, 52–61; J. Roe, *Tool Builders*, 192, 194, app. A, 288; Guy Hubbard, "The Influence of Early Windsor Industries Upon the Mechanic Arts," *Proceedings of the Vermont Historical Society for the Years 1921, 1922 & 1923* (Montpelier, VT: Capital City Press, 1924), 175–76.

CHAPTER 5

1. B. Lewis, *Small Arms*, 89, 91; N. Rosenberg, *American System*, 40–41 and n. 2; Sir James Emerson Tennant, *The Story of the Guns* (London: Longman, Green, Longman, Roberts & Green 1864), 6–7; Major Richard Delafield, *Report on the Art of War in Europe in 1854, 1855, and 1856* (Washington, DC: George W. Bowman, 1860), 8.
2. "Weapons of War," *Technical Educator*, 65; Great Britain, War Office, *Text Book on the Theory of the Motion of Projectiles* (London: HM Stationery Office, 1863), 10–12; S. V. Benét, "Rifle Target Practice in the Army," *Army and Navy Journal* 20, no. 8 (September 23, 1882): 176; Robert L. O'Connell, *Of Arms and Men: A History of War, Weapons, and Aggression* (Oxford: Oxford University Press, 1989), 158; Joseph Bradley, *Guns for the Tsar* (DeKalb: Northern Illinois University Press, 1990), 47.
3. J. Benton, *Course of Instruction*, 275; John Gibbon, *The Artillerist's Manual* (New York: D. Van Nostrand, 1860), 125, 128–29; Great Britain, War Office, *Text Book*, 14–15.
4. Benjamin Robins, *New Principles of Gunnery* (London: W. Wingrave, 1805), 179–83, 182n*, 254; Brett D. Steele, "Muskets and Pendulums: Benjamin Robins, Leonhard Euler, and the Ballistics Revolution," *Technology and Culture* 35, no. 2 (April 1994), 361; H. W. S. Cleveland, *Hints to Riflemen* (New York: D. Appleton, 1864), 73–79; B. Robins, *New Principles of Gunnery*, 191–92, 258–59.

5. O. H. Creighton, L. Evis, M. Kingdom, C. J. McKenzie, I. Watt, and A. K. Outram, "The Face of Battle? Debating Arrow Trauma on Medieval Human Remains from Princesshay, Exeter," *Antiquaries Journal* 100 (2020): 183; J. Gibbon, *Artillerist's Manual*, 126, B. Lewis, *Small Arms*, 7–9, 45, 92; C. H. B. Pridham, *Superiority of Fire*, 9; R. O'Connell, *Arms and Men*, 171–72.

6. B. Robins, *New Principles of Gunnery*, 336–37; J. Benton, *Course of Instruction*, 308; B. Lewis, *Small Arms*, 7–8, 12; R. O'Connell, *Arms and Men*, 171–72; Great Britain, War Office, *Text Book*, 112–13.

7. Mark Urban, *Fusiliers: The Saga of a British Redcoat Regiment in the American Revolution* (New York: Walker & Co., 2007), 318; "Act to Establish a Uniform Militia," 2d Cong., 1st Sess., Ch. 33, 1 Stat. 271, § 4; "Act to Raise for a Limited Time an Additional Military Force," 10th Cong., 1st. Sess., Ch. 63, 2 Stat. 481, §§ 1 and 2 (April 12, 1808); Peter G. Smithurst, *The Pattern 1853 Enfield Rifle* (Oxford: Osprey Publishing, 2011), 6; B. Lewis, *Small Arms*, 49; Great Britain, War Office, *Text Book*, 112; J. Benton, *Course of Instruction*, 308, 317; Maj. James Irvine Hicks, *Notes on U.S. Ordnance*, vol. 2 (1776–1941) (Greens Farm, CT: Modern Books, 1941), 63; B. Huger, et al., *Reports of Experiments*, app. I, 1 (Panôt); A. Mordecai, "1856 Military Commission Report," 172 (Ser. Set 1037); Kenneth Alder, *Engineering the Revolution: Arms & Enlightenment in France, 1763–1815* (Chicago: University of Chicago Press, 1997), 111.

8. R. O'Connell, *Arms and Men*, 191; "Weapons of War," *Technical Educator*, 65; B. Lewis, *Small Arms*, 13–14; J. Benton, *Course of Instruction*, 311; A. Mordecai, "1856 Military Commission Report," 173 (Ser. Set 1037); William W. Greener, *Gunnery in 1858: Being a Treatise on Rifles, Cannon, and Sporting Arms* (London: Smith Elder & Co., 1858), 348–49; Great Britain, War Office, *Text Book*, 114–15.

9. Great Britain, War Office, *Text Book*, 114–15; J. Benton, *Course of Instruction*, 311–12; B. Lewis, *Small Arms*, 14; A. Mordecai, "1856 Military Commission Report," 157–58, 162–63 (Ser. Set 1037).

10. Hew F. A. Strachan, *From Waterloo to Balaclava: Tactics, Technology, and the British Army, 1815–1854* (Cambridge: Cambridge University Press, 1985), 31, 40.

11. H. Strachan, *From Waterloo to Balaclava*, 23.

12. H. Strachan, *From Waterloo to Balaclava*, 44; Sir Alexander Hamilton Gordon, *Remarks on National Defence, Volunteers and Rifles: With a Report on Experiments with Small Arms, Carried on at the Royal Manufactory at Enfield in 1852* (London: Parker, Furnivall & Parker, 1853), 3.

13. A. H. Gordon, *Remarks on National Defence*, 43; A. Mordecai, "1856 Military Commission Report," 170 (Ser. Set 1037); Captain Jervis-White Jervis, *The Rifle-Musket* (London: Chapman & Hall, 1854), vii n. *, 9–10; Vivian Dering Majende, *The Arms and Ammunition of the British Service* (London: Cassell, Petter & Galpin, 1874), 9; "Weapons of War," *Technical Educator*, 66; H. Strachan, *Waterloo to Balaclava*, 46; N. Rosenberg, *American System*, 41n.

14. B. Huger, et al., *Reports of Experiments*, 11, 12, 14–15, 30–32, 39, 41–75.

15. The official tolerance for the M1855's bore was .0025 inch and that of the P1853 .001 inch, meaning that the M1855's actual caliber could range from 0.5775 to 0.5825 and the P1853's between .576 and .578 (T. Laidley, *Ordnance Manual*, 183; A. Mordecai,

NOTES

"1856 Military Commission Report," 173–74 (Ser. Set 1037); D. Williams, *Birmingham Gun Trade*, 47). The Springfield's bullet had a specified diameter of 0.5775 inch, while that of the P1853 was .568 inch (later reduced to .55), although all of these measurements became somewhat meaningless once the gun barrel began to foul (T. Laidley, *Ordnance Manual*, 270; P. Smithurst, *Pattern 1853 Enfield Rifle*, 68). For reference, the diameter of a human hair averages about .001 inch.

16. 1855 Rept. Sec. War, 34th Cong., 1st Sess., Sen. Ex. Doc. No. 1 (Washington, DC: Beverley Ticker, 1855), 551–53 (Ser. Set 811); B. Huger, et al., *Reports of Experiments*, 74, 77, 85–86; J.-W. Jervis, *Rifle-Musket*, 45; J. Gibbon, *Artillerist's Manual*, 130; A. Gordon, *Remarks on National Defence*, app. 43; Norm Flayderman, *Flayderman's Guide to Antique American Firearms*, 9th ed. (Iola, WI: Gun Digest Books, 2007), 567–58; P. Smithurst, *Pattern 1853 Enfield Rifle*, 12.

The weight of the Springfield was a little more than the Enfield. Some of this may have been because the American weapon adopted a device called the Maynard tape primer. Invented by Washington, DC, dentist and inventor Edward Maynard, the tape primer was intended to speed up reloading by automating the process of mounting the percussion cap on the gun's cone. It did so with a series of fifty pellets of primer pasted between two paper strips, forming a roll of tape that the soldier inserted into a cavity in the gun's lock plate. There, a feed mechanism linked to the gun's hammer advanced the tape each time the hammer was cocked, placing a new pellet atop the cone. In theory, this dispensed with the need for the soldier to manually put a new percussion cap on the cone with each reloading. Despite the Ordnance Department's reservations about the device's shortcomings, it acquiesced to Jefferson Davis's views and included it among the specifications for the M1855. Experience proved the department right. The primer tape was not completely waterproof, and the Maynard mechanism itself easily fouled. William R. Edwards, *Civil War Guns* (Secaucus, NJ: Castle, 1982), 16–17; 1855 Rept. Sec. War, 551–53 (Ser. Set 811); G. Jones, *Confederate Odyssey*, 26.

17. P. Smithurst, *Pattern 1853 Enfield Rifle*, 15–16; A. Gordon, *Remarks on National Defence*, app. 45; 1855 Rept. Sec. War, 551–53 (Ser. Set 811).

18. "Weapons of War," *Technical Educator*, 66; A. Mordecai, "1856 Military Commission Report," 175 (Ser. Set 1037); J. Hicks, *Notes on U.S. Ordnance*, 36.

19. J. Benton, *Course of Instruction*, 314–15; J. Gibbon, *Artillerist's Manual*, 222–24; Brett Gibbons, *The Destroying Angel* (privately published, 2019), 41–43, 72–73; Cadmus M. Wilcox, *Rifles and Rifle Practice: An Elementary Treatise Upon the Theory of Rifle Firing, Explaining the Causes of Inaccuracy of Fire, and the Manner of Correcting It* (New York: D. Van Nostrand, 1859), 181, 202; Lt. Col. Earnest C. Wilford, *Three Lectures Upon the Rifle* (London: John W. Parker & Son, 1859), 43–44.

20. B. Gibbons, *Destroying Angel*, 41–42, 71; Lt. Henry Charles Watson, *Eight Lectures Delivered at the School of Musketry, Hythe* (Hythe, UK: W. S. Payne, 1862), 48–49; E. Wilford, *Three Lectures*, 43–44.

21. S. Benét, *Rifle Target Practice*, 176; B. Gibbons, *Destroying Angel*, 65–78.

22. B. Gibbons, *Destroying Angel*, 36; A. Mordecai, "1856 Military Commission Report," 176 (Ser. Set 1037).

CHAPTER 6

1. Great Britain, War Office, *Text Book*, 129–32.

2. B. Lewis, *Small Arms*, 11; A. Mordecai, "1856 Military Commission Report," 172–73 (Ser. Set 1037); J. Gibbon, *Artillerist's Manual*, 123; Great Britain, War Office, *Text Book*, 129–30.

3. B. Lewis, *Small Arms*, 58; J. Gibbon, *Artillerist's Manual*, 124; J. Bradley, *Guns for the Tsar*, 47.

4. J. Gibbon, *Artillerist's Manual*, 132.

5. A. Mordecai, "1856 Military Commission Report," 159 (Ser. Set 1037); H. Strachan, *Waterloo to Balaclava*, 38; "Feats of Fire-arms," *Scientific American* 13, no. 1 (September 12, 1857): 6.

6. J. Rasenberger, *Revolver*, 46–49.

7. B. Lewis, *Small Arms*, 9; Mark Twain, *The Innocents Abroad* (Hartford, CT: American Publishing, 1869), 125.

8. B. Lewis, *Small Arms*, 53–54; F. Deyrup, *Arms Makers*, 123–24; J. Rasenberger, *Revolver*, 192–23, 237–39; Samuel Colt, "On the Application of Machinery to the Manufacture of Rotating Chambered-Breech Fire-Arms, and their Peculiarities," *Proceedings of the Institution of Civil Engineers*, vol. 11 (London: William Clowes & Sons, 1855), 11.

9. *Providence Tool Co. v. Norris*, U.S. Sup. Ct., Dec. Term, 1863, No. 208, Record on Appeal [hereinafter "*Norris* Rec."], 94–95. Warner was one of the leading armorers of the time. He had begun his career at Springfield as a boy in 1811, and he rose to become its master armorer (*Norris* Rec., 93–106; Arcadi Gluckman and L. D. Saterlee, *American Gun Makers* [Harrisburg, PA: Stackpole Co., 1953], 227). He was instrumental in Springfield's success in finally attaining practical interchangeability with the Model 1842 musket, developing the gauges and overseeing the tooling. Warner resigned in 1843 to enter the gun business himself, and by the time of the Mexican War he had a contract to manufacture rifles for the Ordnance Department. Warner later indicated he had redesigned the Colt Walker to make it easier to manufacture (*Norris* Rec., 94–97).

10. J. Rasenberger, *Revolver*, 244–45, 258, 330.

11. D. Muir, *Reflections in Bullough's Pond*, 130–31; J. Rasenberger, *Revolver*, 250, 257–58; J. Roe, *Tool Builders*, 168–69.

12. F. Deyrup, *Arms Makers*, 150–57; J. Roe, *Tool Builders*, 169; J. Rasenberger, *Revolver*, 330–31.

13. J. Rasenberger, *Revolver*, 145, 237–39; F. Deyrup, *Arms Makers*, 123–24.

14. US Patent No. 9430X (February 25, 1836); *Colt v. Massachusetts Arms Co.*, 6 F. Cas. 161, 163 (1851); Roy Jinks, *History of Smith & Wesson* (North Hollywood, CA: Beinfeld Publishing, 1977), 11.

15. James M. McPherson, *Battle Cry of Freedom* (Oxford: Oxford University Press, 1988), 226; J. Rasenberger, *Revolver*, 354; "The Colt Patent Extension," *Scientific American* 13, no. 33 (April 24, 1858): 261; "Colt's Extension—Curious Rumors," *Scientific American* 13, no. 36 (May 15, 1858): 284; 1859 Rpt. Sec. War, 36th Cong., 1st Sess., Sen. Exec. Doc. No. 2 (Washington, DC: George W. Bowman, 1860), 11 (Ser. Set 1024); 1860 Rpt. Sec. War, 36th Cong., 2d Sess., Sen. Exec. Doc. No. 1 (Washington, DC: George W. Bowman, 1860), 9 (Ser. Set 1079); Appropriations Act of June 23, 1860, 36th Cong.,

1st Sess., Ch. 205, 12 Stat. 103–4, § 3; Appropriations Act of March 2, 1861, 36th Cong., 2d Sess., Ch. 84, 12 Stat., 214, 220, § 10; B. Lewis, *Small Arms*, 63.

16. J. Rasenberger, *Revolver*, 313–14, 335.

17. R. Jinks, *Smith & Wesson*, 1–6, 13, 23–24, 18–20, 34; J. Roe, *Tool Builders*, app. A, 287; George R. Watrous, "History of Winchester Repeating Arms Company," vol. 1, pt. A (typescript, Winchester Arms Company records, n.d.), 3; Edwin A. Battison, "Robbins & Lawrence Armory and Machine Shop: An International Historic Mechanical Engineering Heritage Site" (address delivered May 28, 1987, to the American Society of Mechanical Engineers), 8.

18. US Patent No. 12,529 (March 13, 1855); US Patent No. 5,763, 1 (September 12, 1848); *White v. Allen*, 29 Fed. Cases 969, 974–75 (D. Mass. 1863).

19. *White v. Allen*, 29 Fed. Cases at 973; US Patent No. 12,648 (April 3, 1855).

20. US Patent No. 11,496 (August 8, 1854); R. Jinks, *Smith & Wesson*, 34, 36–37; "Message of the President," 41st Cong., 2d Sess., Vol. 1, Sen. Exec. Doc. 23 (Washington, DC: GPO, 1870), 2–3 (Ser. Set 1405).

21. R. Jinks, *Smith & Wesson*, 37; Colt Patent Fire Arms Manufacturing Company [CPFAMC] Papers, W. B. Franklin Diary, April 18 and 19, 1866.

22. US Patent No. 14,491 (March 25, 1856), fig. 3 and cl. 2; W. Edwards, *Civil War Guns*, 114.

23. "Appropriations for the Support of the Army," 33rd Cong., 1st Sess., Ch. 267, 10 Stat. 576, 579 (August 5, 1854); Brig. Gen. Stephen V. Benét, *A Collection of Annual Reports and Other Important Papers Relating to the Ordnance Department*, vol. 2 (Washington, DC: GPO, 1878), 643; Carl L. Davis, *Arming the Union: Small Arms in the Civil War* (Port Washington, NY: Kennikat Press, 1973), 115–16; C. Wilcox, *Rifles and Rifle Practice*, 217; Benjamin P. Poore, *Life & Public Service of Ambrose E. Burnside* (Providence, RI: J. A. & R. A. Reid, 1882), 83–87.

24. B. Poore, *Ambrose Burnside*, 87–88; G. Cullum, "Ambrose Burnside," *Biographical Register*, vol. 2, 318; George B. McClellan, *McClellan's Own Story* (New York: Charles L Webster, 1887), 162; Charles Leroy Brown, "Abraham Lincoln and the Illinois Central Railroad, 1857–1860," *Journal of the Illinois State Historical Society* 36, no. 2 (June 1943): 146–48.

25. United States War Department, *The War of the Rebellion: A Compilation of the Official Records of the Union and Confederate Armies* (Washington, DC: Government Printing Office 1899), Series III, Volume I, 264 [hereinafter "WR: (*series*)/(*volume*)/(*page*)"].

CHAPTER 7

1. F. Deyrup, *Arms Makers*, 128.

2. Emory M. Thomas, "The Greatest Service I Rendered the State," *Virginia Magazine of History and Biography* 94, no. 3 (July 1986): 348. Stuart was in town hoping to sell the War Department his recently patented "Improved Method of Attaching Sabers to Belts" (US Patent No. 25,684).

3. M. R. Smith, *Harpers Ferry*, 35, 105.

4. M. R. Smith, *Harpers Ferry*, 75, 85, 101, 253–56, 279; A. Lee, "U.S. Armory at Harpers Ferry," 43, 47–55; Act of August 5, 1854, 33rd Cong., 1st Sess., Ch. 257, 10 Stat. 576, 578; T. Tate, *From Under Iron Eyelids*, 73.

5. M. R. Smith, *Harpers Ferry*, 318–19; "Act Providing for Sale of the Lands, etc., Near Harper's Ferry," 40th Cong., 3rd Sess., Ch. 2, 15 Stat. 265, § 1 (December 15, 1868).

6. Jonathan Elliot, ed., *The Debates in the Several State Conventions on the Adoption of the Federal Constitution*, vol. 3, 2d ed. (printed for the editor, 1836), 422–24; Alan Taylor, *The Internal Enemy: Slavery and War in Virginia* (New York: W. W. Norton, 2013), 113–14, 414–15.

7. Commonwealth of Virginia, *Journal of the Virginia House of Delegates, of the State of Virginia for the Session of 1859–1960* (Richmond, VA: William F. Ritchie, 1859), 24, 181, 187, 190; M. R. Smith, *Harpers Ferry*, 310.

8. WR: III/I/1; William Maynadier, *Reply to the Charges in the Potter Committee* (Washington, DC: H. S. Bowen, 1862), 5–6.

9. W. Maynadier, *Reply*, 4; WR: III/I/2–4, 13, 39, 45.

10. WR: III/I/6–13, 51–52; W. Maynadier, *Reply*, 6–8.

11. W. Maynadier, *Reply*, 3–4; WR: I/LIII/504–5; WR: III/I/15.

12. WR: III/I/15, 21, 33, 51–52; "The Robbery of Indian Bonds," *New York Times*, February 13, 1861, 1; *The Floyd Acceptances*, 774 U.S. (7 Wall.) 666 (1869); Robert M. Hughes, "John B. Floyd and His Traducers," *Virginia Magazine of History and Biography* 43, no. 4 (October 1935): 328; "The National Crisis," *New York Times*, December 31, 1860, 1.

13. C. Davis, *Arming the Union*, 40–41; W. Maynadier, *Reply*, 5–8; H. T. Miller, "Small Arms Procurement in the Civil War," *Military Engineer* 25, no. 139 (January-February 1933): 71; Ulysses S. Grant, *Personal Memoirs of U.S. Grant* (New York: Library of America, 1990), 150–51.

14. WR: I/VII/301–4; Lewis Wallace, "The Capture of Fort Donelson," in *Battles and Leaders of the Civil War* (New York: Century Co., 1887–1888), 415–18.

15. WR: III/I/1.

CHAPTER 8

1. John George Nicolay, *An Oral History of Abraham Lincoln: John G. Nicolay's Interviews and Essays* (Carbondale: Southern Illinois University Press, 2006), 41; Anonymous, *Diary of a Public Man* (Chicago: private printing for Abraham Lincoln Book Shop, 1945), 73–77, 105; Robert Bruce, *Lincoln and the Tools of War* (Indianapolis, IN: Bobbs-Merrill, 1956), 28; WR: III/I/102; "Purchase of Arms," 37th Cong., 2d Sess., H.R. Exec. Doc. No. 67 (Washington, DC: GPO, 1862), 31 (Ser. Set 1131).

2. G. Cullum, "James W. Ripley," *Biographical Register*, vol. 1, 119; M. Raber, et al., *Conservative Innovators*, 61n104, 64, 67.

3. G. Cullum, "James W. Ripley," *Biographical Register*, vol. 1, 121; Jacob Abbott, "The Armory at Springfield," *Harper's New Monthly Magazine* 5, no. 26 (July 1852): 161; R. Bruce, *Lincoln*, 25; M. Raber, et al., *Conservative Innovators*, 29, 192; F. Deyrup, *Arms Makers*, 240 (tables 1 and 2), 245 (table 4), 246 (figure 2), 247 (table 5); "Appropriations for the Support of the Army," 33rd Cong., 1st Sess., Ch. 267, 10 Stat. 576, 578 (August 5, 1854).

4. C. Davis, *Arming the Union*, 14–20; Major Clarence E. Dutton, "The Ordnance Department," in *The Army of the United States*, ed. Theodore F. Rodenbough and William L. Haskin (New York: Argonaut Press, 1966), 132; see, for example, WR: III/II/849–59.
5. WR: III/I/42–43; C. Davis, *Arming the Union*, 41.
6. 1859 Rep. of the Sec. War, 3 (Ser. Set 1024); 1860 Rep. of the Sec. War, 5 (Ser. Set 1079); WR: III/I/22, 67–68, 145–46, 301, 304; "Act to Provide for Calling Forth the Militia," 3rd Cong., 2d Sess., Ch. 36, 1 Stat. 424, § 4 (February 28, 1795); Emery Upton, *The Military Policy of the United States* (Washington, DC: GPO, 1912), 229.
7. WR: III/I/55, 260, 322.
8. E. Upton, *Military Policy*, 243–46; "Act to Authorize the Employment of Volunteers," 37th Cong., 1st Sess., Ch. 9, 12 Stat. 268, § 1 (July 22, 1861); "Act in Addition to Act to Authorize the Employment of Volunteers," 37th Cong., 1st Sess., Ch. 17, 12 Stat. 274 (July 25, 1861); "Act to Increase the Present Military Establishment," 37th Cong., 1st Sess., Ch. 34, 12 Stat. 279, § 1 (July 29, 1861); "Appropriation for the Purchase of Arms," 37th Cong., 1st Sess., Ch. 29, 12 Stat. 283 (July 31, 1861).
9. C. Davis, *Arming the Union*, 50–53.

CHAPTER 9

1. Henry Brooks Adams, *The Education of Henry Adams* (Boston: Houghton Mifflin, 1918), 114–15, 123, 166.
2. US House of Representatives, 76th Cong., 2d Sess., Appendix to the Congressional Record, November 3, 1930, 352. See Earl Russell to Lord Lyons, December 19, 1861, Treaty of Washington, Tribunal of Arbitration, "Counter Case of Great Britain," reprinted in 42nd Cong., 2d Sess., H.R. Ex. Doc. No. 282 (Washington, DC: GPO, 1872) [hereinafter "Counter Case of Great Britain"], 904–5 (Ser. Set 1521); The Queen's Neutrality Proclamation, Downing Street, London, February 1, 1862, https://www.loc.gov/item/scsm000229.
Within months, British shipyards had begun fitting out commerce raiders for the South and, in 1863, launched two formidable ironclad rams the Confederacy had ordered. This time, Charles Adams's diplomacy prevented the yard from delivering the ships to the South, probably because the North by then had prevailed at Gettysburg and Vicksburg, and the British government decided that the time had come to switch sides.
3. "The Rebel Loan," *New York Times*, December 9, 1865, 1; Marc D. Weidenmier, "The Politics of Selective Default: The Foreign Debts of the Confederate States of America," Claremont Colleges Working Papers in Economics, No. 2000–13 (Claremont, CA: Claremont McKenna College, Department of Economics, 2000), 21–22, table 1.
4. CPFAMC Papers, Letters, F. von Oppen to Colt, April 4, 1861; Caleb Huse, *The Supplies for the Confederate Army* (Boston: T. R. Marvin & Son, 1904), 9–10; WR: IV/I/§ 1/220, 332–33.
5. WR: III/I/621–22; *Norris Rec.*, 55, 197; C. Davis, *Arming the Union*, 58–59; WR: IV/I/§ 1/538–39; G. Jones, *Confederate Odyssey*, 214–15; W. Edwards, *Civil War Guns*, 69; A. Mordecai, "1856 Military Commission Report," 170 (Ser. Set 1037). Ironically, the one European power that did not have an "Enfield" of its own was France.

Although French had developed the Minié ball in the 1840s, they did not generally adopt it until 1857, and even then in an unusually large caliber (.702).

6. C. Huse, *Supplies*, 22–23; WR: III/I/621–22.

7. WR: IV/II/382; David Burt, *Major Caleb Huse C.S.A. and S. Isaac Campbell & Co.* (Central Milton Keynes, UK: AuthorHouse, 2009) 25–26. It was risky for the Armoury Company to confine itself to a single customer, but its options were few by then. It collapsed a year after the Confederacy itself, going out of business in 1866. G. Jones, *Confederate Odyssey*, 237.

8. C. Davis, *Arming the Union*, 50; "Purchase of Arms," H.R. Exec. Doc. No. 67, 4–13, 29–30 (Ser. Set 1131); see WR: III/II/855–56; G. Cullum, "Daniel Tyler," *Biographical Register*, vol. 1, 222, 228; WR: III/I/245, 262–63, 273, 277–78, 418–19, 445–46.

9. To his credit, Schuyler talked his co-owners out of their plan to melt down the heavy silver cup to strike commemorative medals for themselves; instead, they gifted the cup to the Yacht Club and established the famous America Cup challenge. "George L. Schuyler Dead," *New York Times*, August 1, 1890, 1.

10. WR: III/I/355, 418–19, 621–22; "Purchase of Arms," H.R. Exec. Doc. No. 67, 227–29 (Ser. Set 1131); "Counter Case of Great Britain," H.R. Ex. Doc. No. 282, 908–9 (Ser. Set 1521); C. Davis, *Arming the Union*, 53.

11. C. Huse, *Supplies*, 34; WR: III/I/273, 418–19, 675–76; C. Davis, *Arming the Union*, 53; "Purchase of Arms," H.R. Exec. Doc. No. 67, 76 (Ser. Set 1131).

12. About 18,000 were obsolete Austrian arms and another 17,000 were French and Prussian guns of too great a caliber to be useful. Of the lot, the only serviceable weapons were about 25,000 .55 and .58 Austrian rifles or rifled muskets. "Purchase of Arms," H.R. Exec. Doc. No. 67, 83 (Ser. Set 1131).

13. "Purchase of Arms," H.R. Exec. Doc. No. 67, 7, 81–83, 235 (Ser. Set 1131); C. Davis, *Arming the Union*, 55; "Counter Case of Great Britain," H.R. Ex. Doc. No. 282, 909 (Ser. Set 1521).

14. Commission on Ordnance and Ordnance Stores, "Government Contracts," US House of Representatives, 37th Cong., 2d Sess., H.R. Rep. No. 2, at LXXVIII, LXXIX (July 1, 1862) (Ser. Set 1143).

15. "Purchase of Arms," H.R. Exec. Doc. No. 67, 229–35 (Ser. Set 1131); C. Davis, *Arming the Union*, 53–55; "Counter Case of Great Britain," H.R. Ex. Doc. No. 282, 908–9 (Ser. Set 1521).

16. "Purchase of Arms," H.R. Exec. Doc. No. 67, 235 (Ser. Set 1131); W. Edwards, *Civil War Guns*, 70.

17. WR: III/II/112–13; Joseph W. Hartley, *Marcellus Hartley, A Brief Memoir* (New York: privately published, 1903), 28–29.

18. J. Hartley, *Marcellus Hartley*, 9–10, 18. The "Schuyler" in Schuyler, Hartley & Graham was Jacob Rutsen Schuyler, who was no relation to George L. Schuyler.

19. J. Hartley, *Marcellus Hartley*, 33–34, 46–47.

20. J. Hartley, *Marcellus Hartley*, 33–35.

21. J. Hartley, *Marcellus Hartley*, 30–34, 39–40, 46–48; "Counter Case of Great Britain," H.R. Ex. Doc. No. 282, 940–43 (Ser. Set 1521).

22. "Purchases by Ordnance Department," 40th Congress, 2d Sess., H.R. Exec. Doc. No. 99, (Washington, DC: GPO, 1869), 764 (Ser. Set 1338); J. Hartley, *Marcellus Hartley*, 46–47.

23. "Counter Case of Great Britain," H.R. Ex. Doc. No. 282, 949, 955–58 (Ser. Set 1521); G. Jones, *Confederate Odyssey*, 212–13.

24. 1866 Rept. Sec. War, 39th Cong., 2d Sess., H.R. Ex. Doc. No. 1 (Washington, DC: GPO, 1866), 663–64 (Ser. Set 1285); C. Davis, *Arming the Union*, 64; M. Raber, et al., *Conservative Innovators*, 69; G. Jones, *Confederate Odyssey*, 214–15, 411; Patrick George Griffith, *Battle Tactics of the Civil War* (Marlborough, UK: Crowood Press, 2014), 79.

CHAPTER 10

1. "Purchase of Arms," H.R. Exec. Doc. No. 67, 32 (Ser. Set 1131).

2. WR: III/I/264–65, 278–79; "Purchase of Arms," H.R. Exec. Doc. No. 67, 30 (Ser. Set 1131).

3. A "stand" generally meant the firearm and certain accoutrements. In this case, the contract called for Colt to deliver "one wiper, one screwdriver, one spare cone, and one tompion to each musket, and one ball-screw, one spring-vice, and one tumbler and wire-punch to every ten muskets." "Purchase of Arms," H.R. Exec. Doc. No. 67, 36, ¶ 3 (Ser. Set 1131).

4. WR: III/I/264; "Purchase of Arms," H.R. Exec. Doc. No. 67, 36–39 (Ser. Set 1131); F. Deyrup, *Arms Makers*, 196.

5. "Purchase of Arms," H.R. Exec. Doc. No. 67, 15, 47–52, 74–5 (Ser. Set 1131).

6. "Purchase of Arms," H.R. Exec. Doc. No. 67, 33–34, 93–99, 133–34, 135–37, 137–39, 144–46, 154–68, 171–75 (Ser. Set 1131).

7. J. B. Anthony Papers, "Quarter Century Report, President of Providence Tool Company" (1878) [hereinafter "Anthony Papers, Q.C.R."] 1, 1865; *Norris Rec*, 121; Thomas W. Bicknell, *History of the State of Rhode Island and Providence Plantations* (New York: American Historical Society, 1920), 237.

8. *Norris* Rec., 8, 10, 121–23, 158, 288; Anthony Papers, Q.C.R., 2.

9. *Norris* Rec., 2, 230, 238–39; J. Johnson, "Robbins & Lawrence Armory," 30; Gerald M. Carbone, *Brown & Sharpe and the Measure of American Industry* (Jefferson, NC: McFarland & Co., 2017), 29; J. Roe, *Tool Builders*, 195.

10. *Norris* Rec., 17–18, 135–37; "Report of the Commission on Ordnance Contracts & Claims," 37th Cong., 2d Sess., Sen. Exec. Doc. No. 72 (Washington, DC: GPO, 1862) [hereinafter "Senate Holt Rep."], 167–68 (Ser. Set 1123).

11. *Norris* Rec., 39, 137, 205–7, 212, 231; "Purchase of Arms," H.R. Exec. Doc. No. 67, 39 (Ser. Set 1131).

12. *Norris* Rec., 139–40; J. Roe, *Tool Builders*, 195–96; Guy Hubbard, "Development of Machine Tools in New England," *American Machinist* 60, no. 12 (March 20, 1924): 439–40; G. Carbone, *Brown & Sharpe*, 29.

13. *Norris* Rec., 240–41, 138–39.

14. Forging barrels traditionally had been the hardest part of gun-making because it involved smithing flat iron blanks ("skelps") into seamless tubes. By the 1840s, English

gun-makers had developed a means of turning skelps into gun barrels by squeezing them between heavy iron rollers. Each roller had a series of progressively narrower, deeper, and more rounded channels, matching a complementary channel on the opposite roller. After being heated to working temperature, the skelp was drawn repeatedly through the rollers, each time being shifted to a tighter channel until it finally was a long, tapered tube. To keep the walls of the skelp from collapsing, workmen inserted steel rods known as mandrels inside the skelp as it took its tubular form. The ends of the mandrels had large, egg-shaped finials that were too big to pass through the rollers and, thus, stayed behind as the skelp was drawn. When the red-hot skelp came out of the rollers, workmen grabbed it with tongs, reheated it, and then reran it through the rollers as needed. After the rolling was completed, the barrel was straightened, turned on a lathe, put against a grinding wheel, bored, reamed, and, finally, rifled. C. Fitch, *Report*, 9–10; "How a Rifled Musket Is Made at the Providence Tool Company's Armory," pt. 1, *Scientific American 9*, no. 19 (November 7, 1863): 293–94.

15. *Norris* Rec., 67, 140, 240.

16. *Norris* Rec., 138, 239–41.

17. *Norris* Rec., 142–43, 242–45; F. Deyrup, *Arms Makers*, 56, 93, 194; R. Gordon, "Mechanical Ideal," 773–74.

18. *Norris* Rec., 143–44, 148; Senate Holt Rep., Sen. Exec. Doc. No. 72, 166–72 (Ser. Set 1123).

19. *Norris* Rec., 145–48, 247, 267, 275, 277, 289.

20. *Norris* Rec., 106–21, 165–74; A. and L. Saterlee, *American Gun Makers*, 105, 227.

21. 69 U.S. (2 Wall.), 45.

22. *Norris* Rec., 291; Senate Holt Rep., Sen. Exec. Doc. No. 72, 17 (Ser. Set 1123); *Tool Co. v. Norris*, 69 U.S. at 55–56.

23. *Norris* Rec., 245; "How a Rifled Musket Is Made at the Providence Tool Company's Armory," pt. 2, *Scientific American 9*, no. 20 (November 14, 1863), 308; T. Laidley, *Ordnance Manual*, 184–85; F. Deyrup, *Arms Makers*, 59; M. Raber, et al., *Conservative Innovators*, 218–19, 221.

24. "Arms & Munitions for Army & Militia," 45th Cong., 3rd Sess., Sen. Ex. Doc. No. 17 (Washington, DC: GPO, 1879), 15 (Ser. Set 1828); "How a Rifled Musket Is Made," pt. 2, 308–10; "How a Rifled Musket Is Made," pt. 1, 293; "How a Rifled Musket Is Made," pt. 2, 308; Luther D. Burlingame, "The Universal Milling Machine," *American Machinist* 34, no. 1 (January 5, 1911): 9.

25. Anthony Papers, Q.C.R., 1865; "Arms & Munitions for Army & Militia," Sen. Ex. Doc. No. 17, 15 (Ser. Set 1828); WR: III/IV/§ 2/1280.

26. Anthony Papers, Q.C.R., 1864, 1865; U.S., Tax Assessment Lists, R.I., Dist. 1, "Annual, Monthly and Special Lists," May 1864, 109.

27. Senate Holt Rep., Sen. Exec. Doc. No. 72, 312–14, 315, 317–18 (Ser. Set 1123).

28. Senate Holt Rep., Sen. Exec. Doc. No. 72, 315 (Ser. Set 1123).

29. WR: III/I/264–65.

30. "Arms & Munitions for Army & Militia," Sen. Ex. Doc. No. 17, 15 (Ser. Set 1828).

31. WR: III/I/260, 402 § 5; C. Davis, *Arming the Union*, 69; G. Cullum, "Alexander B. Dyer," *Biographical Register*, vol. 1, 666–67.

32. Earl J. Hess, *The Rifle Musket in Civil War Combat: Reality and Myth* (Lawrence: University Press of Kansas, 2008), 45; F. Deyrup, *Arms Makers*, 240 table 1, 245 table 4; C. Davis, *Arming the Union*, 69–71; M. Raber, et al., *Conservative Innovators*, 33, 285; *Norris* Rec., 60–70.

33. The first of these was the Model 1861, which dispensed with the cumbersome Maynard primer system. After that Springfield incrementally improved the gun, producing the Model 1863 and Model 1864. Altogether, Springfield made 265,129 Model 1861s, 273,265 Model 1863s, and 255,040 Model 1864s. Claude Fuller, *The Rifled Musket* (New York: Bonanza Books, 1958), 6–7, 11, 23–25.

34. C. Davis, *Arming the Union*, 70, 173; 1863 Rept. Sec. War, 38th Cong., 1st Sess., H.R. Ex. Doc. No. 1 (Washington, D.C.: GPO 1864), 104 (Ser. Set 1184); 1864 Rept. Sec. War, 38th Cong., 2d Sess., H.R. Ex. Doc. No. 83 (Washington, DC: GPO, 1865), 114 (Ser. Set 1230); WR: III/IV/§ 2/801; P. Griffith, *Battle Tactics*, 79; F. Deyrup, *Arms Makers*, 178.

CHAPTER 11

1. 1863 Rept. Sec. War, H.R. Exec. Doc. No. 1, 107 (Ser. Set 1184); WR: III/III/1134; P. Griffith, *Battle Tactics*, 77; U. S. Grant, *Memoirs*, 384–85.

2. B. Gibbons, *Destroying Angel*, 18, 21, 29, 33, 85–87, 108–12; H. Strachan, *Waterloo to Balaclava*, 41.

3. Henry Heth, preface to *A System of Target Practice* (New York: D. Van Nostrand, 1862); S. Benét, "Rifle Target Practice," 176; C. Wilcox, *Rifles and Rifle Practice*, 237, 242–43; J. Gibbon, *Artillerist's Manual*, 220 (emphasis in original).

4. P. Griffith, *Battle Tactics*, 149–50, 189, 191; E. Hess, *Rifle Musket*, table 4.3, 108–13.

5. These accounts are anecdotal, but they are consistent with overall numbers. Estimates of the number of Confederate soldiers killed or wounded in battle are no higher than 350,000 (P. Griffith, *Battle Tactics*, 95). During the war years, the federal Ordnance Department issued to troops 679,456,187 cartridges for small arms (1863 Sec. War Rept., H.R. Exec. Doc. No. 1, 108 [Ser. Set 1184]; 1864 Sec. War Rept., H.R. Exec. Doc. No. 83, 118 [Ser. Set 1230]; 1865 Sec. War Rept., 39th Congress, 1st Session., H.R. Exec. Doc. No. 1, Vol. 2 [Washington, DC: GPO, 1866], 998 [Ser. Set 1250]). Eighty-five percent of small arms were muskets, rifles, and carbines, so it is a fair assumption that 85 percent of these cartridges—about 580 million—also were for shoulder arms. Even if one assumed that not one Confederate casualty resulted from artillery, sidearms, or edged weapons and further assumed that only 10 percent of the cartridges issued to Union troops ever were fired in battle, this still means that only about 0.6 percent of shots fired from shoulder weapons by federal troops hit a Confederate soldier. With more realistic assumptions, this success rate would be even lower. (See E. Hess, *Rifle Musket*, 116 [20 percent of casualties caused by artillery].)

6. Jeffrey C. Hall, *The Stand of the U.S. Army at Gettysburg* (Bloomington: Indiana University Press, 2009), 330; E. Hess, *Rifle Musket*, 116; P. Griffith, *Battle Tactics*, 83–85, see also 213n60, 214n14.

7. S. Benét, "Rifle Target Practice," 176.

8. Allen C. Guelzo, *Gettysburg: The Last Invasion* (New York: Vintage Books, 2014), 36–39; P. Griffith, *Battle Tactics*, 74–75, 88, 147–50, 208n48; B. Gibbons, *Destroying Angel*, 42–43, 80–81; C. Wilcox, *Rifles and Rifle Practice*, 202; J. Gibbon, *Artillerist's Manual*, 232; E. Hess, *Rifle Musket*, 59, 107–8, 108–13; WR: I/VII/341; C. Davis, *Arming the Union*, 148; J. Hall, *U.S. Army at Gettysburg*, 328, 331, 368–69n30.

9. "Feats of Fire-arms," *Scientific American*, 6; WR: III/I/264–65.

10. S. Benét, *Collection of Annual Reports*, vol. 2, 618–19; "Feats of Fire-Arms," *Scientific American*, 6; "Official Report on Firearms," *Scientific American* 13, no. 1 (October 24, 1857): 1; "Trial of Breech-loading Arms," *Scientific American* 13, no. 49 (August 14, 1858): 390; "Appropriations for Support of the Army," 35th Cong., 1st Sess., Ch. 156, 11 Stat. 332, 335 (June 12, 1858); 1859 Sec. War Rept., Sen. Exec. Doc. No. 2, 3, 11 (Ser. Set 1024); 1860 Sec. War. Rept., Sen. Exec. Doc. No. 1, Vol. 2, 9 (Ser. Set 1079).

11. B. Huger, et al., *Reports of Experiments*, 94, 102, 105–6, 108; compare A. Mordecai, *Ordnance Manual* 163 (1840 musket .6 pound heavier); P. Griffith, *Battle Tactics*, 81; C. Davis, *Arming the Union*, 118; J. Gibbon, *Artillerist's Manual*, 224–25; M. Raber, et al., *Conservative Innovators*, 102; J. Benton, *Course of Instruction*, 449.

12. G. Delafield, *Report on the Art of War in Europe*, 8–9; WR: III/I/423; "Purchase of Arms," H.R. Exec. Doc. No. 67, 177–78 (Ser. Set 1131); "Purchases by Ordnance Department," H.R. Exec. Doc. No. 99, 946–49 (Ser. Set 1338); 1866 Rept. Sec. War, H.R. Ex. Doc. No. 1, 663–64 (Ser. Set 1285). The Ordnance Department also purchased about 1,450 "Sharps" carbines from the Philadelphia firm of Sharps & Hankins (Ord. Dept. Purch., 41). Christopher Sharps formed this company after leaving the Sharps Rifle Company in 1853. However, other than sharing his name, the Sharps carbines made in Hartford had little in common with those made in Philadelphia. C. Davis, *Arming the Union*, 79; W. Edwards, *Civil War Guns*, 301–2.

13. "Purchase of Arms," H.R. Exec. Doc. No. 67, 178 (Ser. Set 1131); "Purchases by Ordnance Department," H.R. Exec. Doc. No. 99, 722–23 (Ser. Set 1338).

14. G. Cullum, "James W. Ripley," *Biographical Register*, vol. 1, 123.

15. "Purchase of Arms," H.R. Exec. Doc. No. 67, 69–71, 178–82 (Ser. Set 1131); US Patent No. 17,644 (June 23, 1857) and No. 17,702 (June 30, 1857).

16. "Purchase of Arms," H.R. Exec. Doc. No. 67, 69, 182, 179–82 (Ser. Set 1131); "Purchases by Ordnance Department," H.R. Exec. Doc. No. 99, 722–24, 852 (Ser. Set 1338).

17. "Purchase of Arms," H.R. Exec. Doc. No. 67, 155, 183–92 (Ser. Set 1131).

18. "Purchase of Arms," H.R. Exec. Doc. No. 67, 176 (Ser. Set 1131); 1862 Ord. Dept. Rept., WR: III/II/849, 855–56; 1866 Report of the Secretary of War, H.R. Exec. Doc. No. 1, 663 (Ser. Set 1285).

19. Hiram Berdan letter to Lt. Gen'l Winfield Scott, June 13, 1861, reprinted in Roy Marcot, *U.S. Sharpshooters: Berdan's Civil War Elite* (Mechanicsburg, PA: Stackpole Books, 2007), 9; WR: III/II/643–44.

20. John H. Brown and Rossiter Johnson, eds., "Hiram Berdan," in *Twentieth Century Biographical Dictionary of Notable Americans*, vol. 1 (Boston: Biographical Society, 1904), 278; *Graves v. Berdan*, NY Court of Appeals, No. 78, Case on Appeal (1859), 3–4, 7, 24 (New York: Wm. C. Bryant & Co., 1859); "Mechanical Bakery at Baltimore," *Scientific*

American 13, no. 38 (May 29, 1858): 301; "Feeding the People by Machinery," *Chicago Tribune*, July 2, 1858, 1.

21. E. Upton, *Military Policy*, 248–51; Act of July 22, 1861, 37th Cong., 1st Sess., Ch. 9, 12 Stat. 268, § 2; WR: III/I/270.

22. R. Marcot, *U.S. Sharpshooters*, 11, 46–57; G. Jones, *Confederate Odyssey*, 326; R. Bruce, *Lincoln*, 154–55

23. G. Jones, *Confederate Odyssey*, 326; R. Marcot, *U.S. Sharpshooters*, 52–55, 58–59.

24. The English word *sharpshooter* seems to have come from the German term Scharfschütze, which described Napoleonic-era Austrian marksmen who fought on the side of the French. The term had been in common use in Britain and America for some time. See Charles Rogers, L.L.D., *The Modern Scottish Minstrel*, vol. 1 (Edinburgh: Adam & Charles Black, North Bridge, 1855), 126; A. Mordecai, "1856 Military Commission Report," 15–16, 180 (Ser. Set 1037); Anonymous, *Diary of a Public Man*, 83; "The Great Wolf Hunt," *New Hampshire Statesman* (Concord), April 21, 1860, reprinted in Sandwich Historical Society, "One Hundred Second Annual Excursion" (August 15, 2021), 29–33; S. Benét, *Collection of Annual Reports*, vol. 2, 382; WR: III/I/270.

25. WR: III/I/604; WR: III/II/574–75; William Freeman Fox, *Regimental Losses in the American Civil War, 1861–1865* (Albany, NY: Albany Publishing Co., 1898), 418–19; G. Jones, *Confederate Odyssey*, 327; R. Marcot, *U.S. Sharpshooters*, 59–60, 78, 80–82, 109–11, 114.

Berdan and his family moved in with his wife's parents in West Lebanon, New Hampshire. He soon began working in nearby Windsor, Vermont, for E. G., Lamson & Co., a successor firm to Robbins & Lawrence. Lamson hired Berdan to work with gun designer William Palmer on the Ball and Palmer breech-loading carbines (Carrie Brown, "Guns for Billy Yank: The Armory in Windsor Meets the Challenge of Civil War," *Vermont History* 79, no. 2 [Summer/Fall 2011]: 154–55). Probably in November 1866, Berdan moved to Ilion and became involved with the Remington plant there (CPFAMC Papers, W. B. Franklin Diary, November 3, 1866). On January 9, 1866, he received a US patent (No. 51,991) on an improvement to the rolling-block rifle, and he later sued Remington for infringement. His case was thrown out when the court concluded that it was Remington's workmen, and not Berdan, who had made the improvement in question. "He was not present when its necessity in that gun was discovered," the court ruled, "nor was he present when it was done" (*Berdan Fire-Arms Manufacturing Co. v. Remington*, 3 Fed. Cases 259, 260 [N.D.N.Y. 1873]). "Berdan did not invent it."

26. P. Griffith, *Battle Tactics*, 26; R. Marcot, *U.S. Sharpshooters*, 47.

27. Albert Ball of Worcester, Massachusetts, also patented a repeating arm in June 1863, which was manufactured in small numbers by the E. G., Lamson Company (US Patent No. 38,935). The Ordnance Department placed an order in June 1864 for 1,000 Ball's repeating carbines, but they were not delivered until after the war. "Purchases by Ordnance Department," H.R. Exec. Doc. No. 99, 244–45, 823 (Ser. Set 1338).

28. R. Marcot, *U.S. Sharpshooters*, 55–57; S. Benét, *Collection of Annual Reports*, vol. 2, 220, 256–57; J. Rasenberger, *Revolver*, 130; C. Davis, *Arming the Union*, 125; 1866 Sec. War. Rept., H.R. Ex. Doc. No. 1, 664 (Ser. Set 1285); "Purchases by Ordnance Department," H.R. Exec. Doc. No. 99, 730–33 (Ser. Set 1338).

29. One of the better known was the account of one Captain Wilson of the 12th Kentucky Cavalry, who kept a loaded Henry rifle across the road from his house in a corn crib. While dining with his family one day, Wilson was surprised by seven guerillas intent on killing him. He prevailed upon them to not shoot him in the presence of his family, and escorted them outside. At that, he ran to his corn crib, retrieved his Henry, and felled his assailants one by one. (It was not explained why Captain Wilson kept his Henry rifle outdoors in the corn crib.) Winchester also circulated reports from Colonel John Wilder of the effectiveness of the Henry rifle, which was odd since Wilder and his men actually used Spencers. Charles Winthrop Sawyer, *Our Rifles* (Boston: Williams Book Store, 1944), 278–80.

30. 1866 Sec. War. Rept., H.R. Ex. Doc. No. 1, 664 (Ser. Set 1285); Frank C. Barnes, *Cartridges of the World*, 12th ed., ed. Layne Simpson (Iola, WI: Gun Digest Books, 2009), 451; Martin Pegler, *Winchester Lever-Action Rifles* (Oxford: Osprey Publishing, 2015), 14–16; C. Davis, *Arming the Union*, 89–90; "Purchases by Ordnance Department," H.R. Exec. Doc. No. 99, 843 (Ser. Set 1338).

31. Lafayette Wallace Case, MD, *The Hollister Family of America* (Chicago: Fergus Printing Co., 1886), 316; US Patent No. 27,393 (March 6, 1860).

32. L. W. Case, *Hollister Family*, 317; C. Davis, *Arming the Union*, 91–92.

33. L. W. Case, *Hollister Family*, 316–17; WR: III/I/733–74.

34. Senate Holt Rep., Sen. Exec. Doc. No. 72, 425–26 (Ser. Set 1123); WR: III/I/733–74.

35. Senate Holt Rep., Sen. Exec. Doc. No. 72, 422–23, 425–30 (Ser. Set 1123); "Purchase of Arms," H.R. Exec. Doc. No. 67, 155 (Ser. Set 1131); "Purchases by Ordnance Department," H.R. Exec. Doc. No. 99, 963 (Ser. Set 1338).

36. L. W. Case, *Hollister Family*, 318; Eric Maurice, "Send Forward Some Who Would Fight" (master's thesis, Butler University, 2016), 41, 43; "Purchases by Ordnance Department," H.R. Exec. Doc. No. 99, 963 (Ser. Set 1338).

37. W. A. Bartlett, "Lincoln's Seven Hits with a Rifle," *Magazine of History* 19, no. 1 (1922): 71–73; L. W. Case, *Hollister Family*, 317–18; John Hay, *Letters of John Hay and Extracts from Diary*, ed. Andrew Dickson White, Clara Louise Hay, and Henry Adams (Washington, DC: privately printed, 1908), 93.

38. "Purchases by Ordnance Department," H.R. Exec. Doc. No. 99, 85–86, 573–76, 578 (Ser. Set 1338); 1866 Rept. Sec. War, H.R. Ex. Doc. No. 1, 663–64, 667 (Ser. Set 1285).

39. J. Roe, *Tool Builders*, 231, 237–38; William G. Lathrop, *The Brass Industry of Connecticut: A Study of the Origin and the Development of the Brass Industry of the Naugatuck Valley* (New Haven, CT: Price, Lee & Adkins, 1909), 102–4; N. Rosenberg, *American System*, 338–40.

40. C. Dutton, "Ordnance Department," 134; "Weapons of War," *Technical Educator*, 271.

41. *Norris Rec.*, 69–70, 76, 79–80, 141.

42. Theodore T. S. Laidley, "The Breech-Loading Musket," *United States Service Magazine* 3 (New York: Charles R. Richardson, 1865), 69 (emphasis in original); Major Thomas J. Treadwell, *Metallic Cartridges, as Manufactured and Tested at the Frankford Arsenal, Philadelphia, PA* (Washington, DC: GPO, 1873), 2; 1864 Rept. Sec. of Navy, 38th

Cong., 2d Sess., H.R. Ex. Doc. No. 1 (Washington, DC: GPO, 1864), 986–87, 992 (Ser. Set 1221); B. Lewis, *Small Arms*, 85–86; P. Griffith, *Battle Tactics*, 86.

43. Charles A. Stevens, *Berdan's United States Sharpshooters in the Army of the Potomac, 1861–1865* (St. Paul, MN: Price-McGill Company 1892), 461–62; R. Bruce, *Lincoln*, 284–87; G. Jones, *Confederate Odyssey*, 326–27; W. Fox, *Regimental Losses*, 419; Claude Fuller, *The Breech Loader in the Service 1816–1917* (New Milford, CT: N. Flayderman & Co., 1965), 206–11; Grady McWhiney and Perry D. Jamieson, *Attack and Die: Civil War Military Tactics and the Southern Heritage* (Tuscaloosa: University of Alabama Press, 1982), 5; C. Sawyer, *Our Rifles*, 278–79; E. Hess, *Rifle Musket*, 54–55; "Breech-Loading Rifles for the Army," *Scientific American* 10, no. 11 (March 12, 1864): 170. See Col. Berkeley Lewis, *Notes on Ammunition of the American Civil War 1861–1865* (Washington, DC: American Ordnance Association, 1959), 10–11 (accuracy of Maynard, Greene, Henry, and Spencer carbines).

44. C. Davis, *Arming the Union*, 137–38.

45. T. Laidley, "Breech-Loading Musket," 68.

46. G. Cullum, "James W. Ripley," *Biographical Register*, vol. 1, 259; Act of July 17, 1862, Ch. 200, 12 Stat. 594, 596 § 12; Ord. Dept. Purch., 798–99, 840–41, 841–42, 851–52, 919–20, 941, 945–49, 963–65, 995; 1866 Rept. Sec. War, H.R. Ex. Doc. No. 1, 663–64 (Ser. Set 1285).

47. WR: III/IV/§ 2/971–72.

48. WR: III/IV/§ 2/1280; Anthony Papers, Q.C.R., 1865; 1865 Rept. Sec. War, H.R. Exec. Doc. No. 1, Vol. 2, 996 (Ser. Set 1250).

49. 1866 Rept. Sec. War, H.R. Ex. Doc. No. 1, 657, 663–64 (Ser. Set 1285); Harold L. Peterson, *Notes on Ordnance of the American Civil War* (Washington, DC: American Ordnance Association, 1959), 2.

CHAPTER 12

1. Samuel Orcutt, *A History of the Old Town of Stratford and the City of Bridgeport, Connecticut*, vol. 2 (Bridgeport, CT: Fairfield County Historical Society, 1886), 887–88.

2. J. Hartley, *Marcellus Hartley*, 50–51.

3. WR: III/IV/§ 1/588; Col. Berkeley Lewis, "Small Arms Ammunition at the International Exposition Philadelphia, 1876," *Smithsonian Studies in History and Technology*, January 1972: 2.

4. WR: III/IV/§ 1/594, 618–19; B. Lewis, *Notes on Ammunition*, 10; Bill Jobbagy, "Ammunition Manufacturing in South Coventry, Connecticut," February 2017, 3–4, https://www.coventryct.org/DocumentCenter/View/2077/Ammunition-Manufacturing -in-Coventry?bidId=; Roy Marcot, "Marcellus Hartley: Merchant, Financier, Millionaire and Philanthropist," *American Society of Arms Collectors Bulletin* 83 (Fall 2000): 28; 1866 Report of the Secretary of War, H.R. Exec. Doc. No. 1, 666–67 (Ser. Set 1285); W. Lathrop, *Brass Industry*, 80, 87–88, 102–3; J. Hartley, *Marcellus Hartley*, 52; S. Orcutt, *History of Stratford*, 888.

5. See, for example, US Patent No. 56,332 (July 10, 1866).

6. R. Marcot, "Marcellus Hartley," 28; J. Hartley, *Marcellus Hartley*, 53; S. Orcutt, *History of Stratford*, 888–89; Charles R. Norton, *American Breech-Loading Small Arms* (New York: F. W. Christern, 1872), 281.

7. US Patent No. 27,933 (April 17, 1860); US Patent No. 29,108 (July 10, 1860); US Patent No. 30,446, 1 (October 16, 1860).

8. Robert Mermelstein, *Mermelstein's Guide to Metallic Cartridge Evolution* (Fort Wayne, IN: Sinclair International, 2004), 25; C. Norton, *American Breech-Loading Small Arms*, 280–81; F. Barnes, *Cartridges*, 451, 452–53.

9. B. Lewis, "Small Arms Ammunition," 7; US Patent No. 20,214 (May 11, 1858); US Patent No. 20,727 (June 29, 1858); Mermelstein, *Guide*, 25.

10. US Patent No. 53,388 (March 20, 1866) and No. 82,587 (September 29, 1868).

11. See *Berdan Fire-Arms Manufacturing Co. v. Remington*, 3 Fed. Case 259, 260 (N.D.N.Y. 1873); *U.S. v. Berdan Fire-Arms Manufacturing Company*, 156 U.S. 552 (1895), 557–58.

12. T. Treadwell, *Metallic Cartridges*, 3, 6, plate XVI; US Patent No. 82,587 (September 29, 1868).

Chapter 13

1. Edward H. Knight, *Knight's American Mechanical Dictionary*, vol. 1 (Boston: Houghton Osgood & Co., 1880), 855–60; J. Bradley, *Guns for the Tsar*, 14–15; US Patent Nos. 45,043, 45,105, and 45,123 (November 24, 1864); US Patent Nos. 65,607, 65,704, and 65,585 (June 11, 1867); 1867 Rept. Sec. War, 40th Congress, 2d Sess., H.R. Exec. Doc. No. 1 (Washington, DC: GPO, 1867), 18, 610 (Ser. Set 1324).

2. New York Board for Examination of Breech-Loading Small Arms, *Report of the Board for Examination of Breech-loading Small Arms* (Albany, NY: Weed, Parsons & Co., 1867), 57.

3. 40th Cong., 2d Sess., *Congressional Globe*, pt. 2 (February 19, 1868), 1284–85; "Appropriations for the Support of the Army," 40th Cong., 2d Sess., Ch. 52, 15 Stat. 64, 66.

4. C. Norton, *American Breech-Loading Small Arms*, 167 and fig. 1 and 2; US Patent No. 49,959 (Erskine Allin, September 19, 1865), 2; "Sale of Arms by Ordnance Department," 42d Cong., 2d Sess., Sen. Rep. No. 183 (Washington, DC: GPO, 1872), 531, 536 (Ser. Set 1497).

5. John C. Davis, "U.S. Army Rifle & Carbine Adoption between 1865 and 1900" (master's thesis, U.S. Army Command & General Staff College, Fort Leavenworth, 2007), 10–11.

The Springfield Armory developed a method of narrowing its .58-caliber muskets by boring out the rifling and brazing a thin-walled steel tube to reduce the barrel's diameter (J. Davis, "U.S. Army Rifle & Carbine Adoption," 11; New York Board for Examination of Breech-Loading Small Arms, *Report*, 47–48).

6. US Patent No. 49,959 (Erskine Allin, September 19, 1865), 2.

7. "Weapons of War," *Technical Educator*, 195. This was copied, apparently, from an idea patented by the American William Hubbell in 1844 (US Patent No. 3,649, July 1, 1844).

8. C. Dutton, "Ordnance Department," 134–35; "Weapons of War," *Technical Educator*, 272.

9. CPFAMC Papers, contract between F. Von Oppen and Efflatoun Bey (May 17, 1866), as amended October 17, 1866; "Sale of Arms & Ordnance Stores," 42d Cong., 2d Sess., H.R. Ex. Doc. No. 89 (Washington, DC: GPO, 1872), 11, 13 (Ser. Set 1511); F. Deyrup, *Arms Makers*, 212.

10. US Patent No. 20,073 (April 27, 1858), No. 37,501 (January 27, 1863), No. 45,797 (January 3, 1865), and No. 74,428 (February 11, 1868), 2.

11. US Patent No. 35,947 (July 22, 1862); Anthony Papers, Q.C.R., 1864.

12. F. Deyrup, *Arms Makers*, 209

13. "Weapons of War," *Technical Educator*, 66; 1866 Rept. Sec. War, H.R. Ex. Doc. No. 1, 698–701 (Ser. Set 1285); William W. Greener, *Modern Breech-loaders: Sporting and Military* (London: Cassell, Petter & Galpin, 1871), 199–202, 223; F. Barnes, *Cartridges*, 357–58, 360.

14. Barnes, *Cartridges*, 356–62; A. Mordecai, "1856 Military Commission Report," 170–71 (Ser. Set 1037); J. Gibbon, *Artillerist's Manual*, 224; "Weapons of War," *Technical Educator*, 333–34; "The New Martini-Enfield Rifle," *The Engineer* (July 2, 1886), tables at 16.

15. In a rifled gun, the caliber of the barrel "is the approximate diameter of the circle formed by the tops of the lands." Association of Firearm and Tool Mark Examiners, *Glossary*, 6th ed. (2013), 28.

16. These are the values given by Frank Barnes in his compendious *Cartridges of the World*, using modern black powder and instruments; see pp. 357–58 and 360–63. Contemporaneous measurements of muzzle velocities varied materially because of differences in the quality of gunpowder and the imprecision of the instruments used to calculate projectile speeds. In the case of the Chassepot, Martini-Henry, and Snider, for example, one authority calculated their respective muzzle velocities as 1,391, 1,365, and 1,262 feet per second, while another, writing five years later, had them as 1,369, 1,315, and 1,240. Compare "Weapons of War," *Technical Educator*, 336, and W. Greener, *Modern Breech-loaders*, 745. The muzzle velocity of the Berdan II was given as anywhere from 1,302 to 1,450 feet per second. William W. Greener, *The Gun and Its Development: With Notes on Shooting*, 3rd ed. (London: Cassell & Co., 1885), 745; "New Martini-Enfield Rifle," *The Engineer*, tables at 16; Francis Vinton Greene, *The Russian Army and Its Campaigns in Turkey in 1877–1878* (New York: D. Appleton & Co., 1879), 58.

CHAPTER 14

1. "Sales of Arms & Ordnance Stores," H.R. Ex. Doc. No. 89, 3–4, 6 (Ser. Set 1511); "Purchases by Ordnance Department," H.R. Exec. Doc. No. 99, 948–49 (Ser. Set 1338).

2. CPFAMC Papers, W. B. Franklin Diary, May 12, 1865.

3. 1867 Rept. Sec. Navy, 40th Cong., 2d Sess., H.R. Ex. Doc. No. 1 (Washington, DC: GPO, 1868), 144 (Ser. Set 1327).

4. William O. Achtermeier, *Rhode Island Arms Makers & Gunsmiths, 1643–1883* (Providence, RI: Man at Arms, 1980), 30–31, 33; 1866 Rept. Sec. War, H.R. Ex. Doc. No. 1, 700–701 (Ser. Set 1285); "Roberts Breech-Loading Musket & Carbine," 43rd Cong., 2d

Sess., H.R. Ex. Doc. No. 152 (Washington, DC: GPO, 1875), 4, 15, 18 (Ser. Set 1648); Thomas Heptinstall, "From Snider-Enfield, to Martini-Henry, to the Magazine Lee Metford: An Historical and Technical Overview of the Development of British Military Rifles from 1866 to 1895" (master's thesis, University of Huddersfield, 2016), 58–71; Achille Thomas-Anquetil, "Canons, Poudres, Engins, Armes Portative," in *Le Spectateur Militaire: Recueil de Science, d'art et d'Histoire Militaires* (Paris: Direction du Spectateur Militaire, 1869), 441–49; University of Rhode Island, Manuscript Collection, Records of St. Michael's Church, Bristol, Family Papers, Norris, Samuel, Msg. 185, Series X [hereinafter "Norris Family Papers"], Box 2/3, Fold. 37, October 22, 1893.

5. William P. Blake, ed., *Reports of the United States Commissioners to the Paris Universal Exhibition, 1867*, vol. 1 (Washington, DC: GPO, 1870), 270–72; Anthony Papers, Q.C.R., 11.

6. Samuel Norris, "Facts About Small Arms," *New York Times*, July 31, 1898, 22; "Purchases by Ordnance Department," H.R. Exec. Doc. No. 99, 849 (Ser. Set. 1338); Anonymous, *Representative Men and Old Families of Rhode Island* (Chicago: J. H. Beers & Company, 1908), 1030; *Norris Rec.*, 25–26; Norris Family Papers, Box 2/3, Fold. 37, 1–2; Albert N. Russell, "Ilion and the Remingtons," in *Papers Read Before the Herkimer County Historical Society 1896, 1897 & 1898* (Herkimer and Ilion, NY: Citizen Publishing Co., 1899), 83.

7. Pamela Haag, *The Gunning of America: Business and the Making of American Gun Culture* (New York: Basic Books, 2016), 124–25. No one knew Addis's real name, but his assumed one was a play on the name of a well-known New York politician of the day, Thomas Addis Emmett.

8. "T. G. Bennett Dead," *New York Times*, August 20, 1930, 19; Laura Trevelyan, *The Winchester: The Gun That Built an American Dynasty* (New Haven, CT: Yale University Press, 2016), 46–47, 57–59; W. Achtermeier, *Rhode Island Arms Makers*, 33; J. Rasenberger, *Revolver*, 303, 355–56; "Gen. Berdan Dead," *New York Times*, April 1, 1893, 1.

9. P. Haag, *Gunning*, 135; *Oscanyan v. Winchester Repeating Arms Co.*, 103 U.S. 261, 271 (1880); CPFAMC Papers, Foreign Correspondence (Unclassified), Box 1, Colt correspondence and Berdan correspondence, H. Berdan to W. Franklin, December 24, 1869, and H. Berdan to W. Franklin, October 5, 1870, and September 21, 1870; Rhode Island Historical Society, Providence Tool Records [hereinafter "RIHS, PTC Rec."], Box 3, Fold. 1, J. B. Anthony to William Saint-Laurent, February 5, 1872.

10. *Providence Tool Company v. Norris*, 69 U.S. 45 (1864); *Oscanyan v. Winchester Repeating Arms Co.*, 103 U.S. 261 (1880).

11. Connecticut Museum of Culture and History, Bennett-Winchester Family Papers, Ms. 87108, *Letters 1878–1879*, T. G. Bennett to H. J. W. Bennett, March 10, 1879, 2; March 22, 1879, 2; March 30, 1879, 3–4; and April 24, 1879.

12. W. Achtermeier, *Rhode Island Arms Makers*, 32–33; Herbert G. Houze, *Winchester Repeating Arms Company: Its History and Development from 1865 to 1981* (Iola, WI: Krause Publications, 1994), 57–59; Herbert G. Houze, "Brief Notes on Three Subjects," *American Society of Arms Collectors Bulletin* 108 (September 2013): 13–14. Winchester also seemed to have sold about 2,000 guns in South American about then; its corporate records

disclosed that it had $57,000 in Chilean-Peruvian assets in 1867 (G. Watrous, "History of Winchester," 89).

13. Anthony Papers, Q.C.R., 1867; S. Norris, "Facts About Small Arms."

14. Remington's corporate archives were destroyed in a fire in 1939, so we will never know with any certainty how many guns it sold (John Patrick Dunn, "Egypt's Nineteenth Century Arms Industry," in *Girding for Battle*, ed. Donald J. Stoker Jr. and Jonathan A. Grant [Westport and London: Praeger, 2003], 19n45; George Layman, *The Military Remington Rolling Block Rifle*, 4th ed. [Union City, TN: Pioneer Press, 1999], 35). Contemporary sources, moreover, do not always agree, and people writing today are often forced to piece together what evidence they can. As a result, numbers for Remington's foreign sales often are inexact and, at times, self-contradictory. In the case of Denmark, the size of its order varies from "42,000 stands of arms," to "between 35,000 and 40,000 arms," to "30,000 . . . which was followed by more contracts," to "42,000 rolling block rifles and carbines with the latter numbering only 1,800," to 30,000 rifles, 1,800 carbines, and 10,000 "systems," to 40,557 rifles and 1,800 carbines, to "forty-two thousand rifles" (A. Russell, "Ilion and the Remingtons," 82–83; C. Fitch, *Report*, 6; S. Norris, "Facts About Small Arms"; G. Layman, *Military Remington Rolling Block Rifle*, 4, 66; S. M. Alvis, "Remington Foreign Military Arms," typescript (1969), Remington Arms Company Corporate Records; Remington Arms–Union Metallic Cartridge Co., *A New Chapter in an Old Story* [New York: Remington Arms–Union Metallic Cartridge Co., 1912], 22). There is evidence that Remington sold small numbers of rolling blocks between 1867 and 1870 to Austria, Italy, the Netherlands, and Switzerland. These were likely to have been bought for field testing; there is no contemporaneous evidence of any of these countries purchasing significant numbers of the guns. In 1868, Japan ordered 820 rifles from Remington, possibly for the same purpose (G. Layman, *Military Remington Rolling Block Rifle*, 9, 98).

15. C. Fitch, *Report*, 6; G. Layman, *Military Remington Rolling Block Rifle*, 9, 66; S. Norris, "Facts About Small Arms"; A. Russell, "Ilion and the Remingtons," 83.

16. S. Norris, "Facts About Small Arms"; Norris Family Papers, Box 2/3, Fold. 37, 3–10 (October 22, 1893).

17. H. Houze, "Brief Notes," 108/18n12; G. Watrous, "History of Winchester," 83–84; C. Norton, *American Breech-Loading Small Arms*, 36, 399; Charles R. Norton, *American Inventions and Improvements in Breech-Loading Small Arms* (Springfield, MA: Chapin & Gould, 1880), 101–2; CPFAMC Papers, W. B. Franklin Diary, June 18 and 28, 1867; W. Achtermeier, *Rhode Island Arms Makers*, 33–34.

18. W. Achtermeier, *Rhode Island Arms Makers*, 30–31, 34–35; Anthony Papers, Q.C.R., 1868.

19. W. Achtermeier, *Rhode Island Arms Makers*, 36; Anthony Papers, Q.C.R., 1871.

20. W. Greener, *Gun and Its Development*, 137–38, 144, 745; "Weapons of War," *Technical Educator*, 336.

21. P. Ganidel, *Notice sur les Cartouches Pour Armes de Guerre et Notamment sur la Cartouche Pour Fusil Chassepot Dit Modèle 1866* (Paris: Dupont, 1873), 3–6, 10–11.

22. CPFAMC Papers, W. B. Franklin Diary, April 26, 1867; US Patent No. 65,607 (June 11, 1867); W. Achtermeier, *Rhode Island Arms Makers*, 34; Edward Hull, *Roberts Breechloading Firearms* (privately published, 2015), 44–45.

23. "Sales of Arms by Ordnance Department," Sen. Rep. No. 183, 531 (Ser. Set 1497).

24. C. Fitch, *Report*, 10–11; F. Deyrup, *Arms Makers*, 211; CPFAMC, folder labeled "Historical"; CPFAMC Papers, W. B. Franklin Diary, October 4, 1867.

25. James Carlile McCoan, *Egypt as It Is* (New York: Henry Holt & Co., 1877), 98; C. Fitch, *Report*, 10–11; J. Dunn, "Egypt's Nineteenth Century Arms Industry," 11; T. Tate, *From Under Iron Eyelids*, 325.

26. A. Thomas-Anquetil, "Armes Portative," 439; CPFAMC Papers, Gatling gun materials, R. Gatling to W. Franklin, March 24, 1868; CPFAMC Papers, Box 9, Von Oppen correspondence, F. Von Oppen to W. Franklin, April 14, 1869.

CHAPTER 15

1. Pennsylvania Academy of the Fine Arts, *Catalogue of the Memorial Exhibition of Portraits by Thomas Sully*, 2nd ed. (Philadelphia: Pennsylvania Academy of Fine Arts, 1922), 177; J. Scoffern, "Jacob Snider," *Belgravia* 1 (February 1867): 181; Charles M. Clode, *The Military Forces of the Crown*, vol. 2 (London: J. Murray, 1869), 532n2.

2. J. Scoffern, "Jacob Snider," 179–80; T. Heptinstall, "Snider-Enfield," 19–20; M. Drake, "Military Breechloaders," 440–41; "Weapons of War," *Technical Educator*, 194; C. Clode, *Military Forces*, 533.

3. T. Heptinstall, "Snider-Enfield," 31; J. Scoffern, "Jacob Snider," 175–78, 180, 182–83; Bennett Woodcroft, *Chronological Index of Patents Applied for and Granted for the Year 1862* (London: George Eyre & William Spottiswoode, 1863), 125; *Feather v. The Queen*, 6 B&S 257 (1865); C. Clode, *Military Forces*, 534–35.

4. T. Heptinstall, "Snider-Enfield," 42–43, 46–52; D. Williams, *Birmingham Gun Trade*, 103; "Weapons of War," *Technical Educator*, 195; Stephen Manning, *The Martini-Henry Rifle* (Oxford: Osprey, 2013) 6–7; J. Scoffern, "Jacob Snider," 175.

5. "Weapons of War," *Technical Educator*, 66, 271–72 and fig. 3; Brig. Gen. J. H. LeFroy, *Official Catalogue of the Museum of Artillery in the Rotunda* (London: George Eyre and William Spottiswoode, 1864), 77, ¶ 13; F. Barnes, *Cartridges*, 365.

6. "Weapons of War," *Technical Educator*, 195, 271; US Patent No. 91,818 (June 29, 1869); C. Norton, *American Breech-Loading Small Arms*, 289–92.

7. "Weapons of War," *Technical Educator*, 271.

8. T. Heptinstall, "Snider-Enfield," 58; S. Manning, *Martini-Henry Rifle*, 8.

9. T. Heptinstall, "Snider-Enfield," 58–65. Alexander Henry's rifle sometimes is confused with the rifle developed by Benjamin Tyler Henry. Alexander Henry's rifle used a breech system resembling that of the Sharps rifle (W. Greener, *Modern Breech-loaders*, 211).

10. T. Heptinstall, "Snider-Enfield," 68–71.

11. T. Heptinstall, "Snider-Enfield," 68–71; *Henry v. Providence Tool Company*, 11 Fed. Case 1182, 1183–84 (D. R.I. 1878); US Patent No. 90,614 (May 25, 1869).

12. It is unclear who can claim credit for coming up with the necked metallic cartridge. The inventor Brigham Payne of Crittendon & Tibbals patented a machine for necking

cartridge shells in October 1865 (US Patent No. 50,489) and the Spencer Repeating Rifle Co. began selling a necked rim-fire 56–46 sporting cartridge the next year (F. Barnes, *Cartridges*, 452). However, the idea behind a necked cartridge—to increase the load of powder while retaining a smaller-caliber bullet—only exacerbated the inherent weaknesses of rim-fire cartridges, and it was not until center-fire cartridges came along that necked cartridge became common. In September 1868, Hiram Berdan received a US patent (No. 82,587) for a cartridge that was illustrated as both center-fire and necked, although the patent made no claims about either. That same year, Russia adopted a necked cartridge for the Berdan I rifle, and soon Remington, Sharps, and others chambered rifles for necked ammunition as well (F. Barnes, *Cartridges*, 121, 137, 138, 357).

13. "The Cartridges for the New Rifle," *The Engineer* 28 (August 20, 1869): 125; "Weapons of War," *Technical Educator*, 335; W. Greener, *Gun and Its Development*, 133; United Kingdom, *Treatise on Ammunition* (London: HM Stationery Office, 1878), 253–54, plate at 362.

14. T. Heptinstall, "Snider-Enfield," 72–75; W. Greener, *Gun and Its Development*, 132–33, 137–38, 211; "Weapons of War," *Technical Educator*, 336.

15. Some of the gunsmiths from the Armoury Company formed their own firm, known as the London Small Arms Co., which continued to manufacture rifles for the British government, albeit on a limited scale.

16. John Walter, "The Rise of the Piled Arms: A Short History of the Birmingham Small Arms Company," pt. 2, *Guns Review* 24 (June 1984): 398.

17. "National Arms," *The Economist* 30, no. 1,484 (February 3, 1872): 159; T. Tate, *From Under Iron Eyelids*, 82–83, 94; Anthony Papers, Diary, December 23, 1874.

CHAPTER 16

1. J. Dunn, "Egypt's Nineteenth Century Arms Industry," 6.

2. J. Dunn, "Egypt's Nineteenth Century Arms Industry," 3–6, 11.

3. Sven Beckert, *Empire of Cotton: A Global History* (New York: Vintage Books, 2014), 293–94; "Egyptian Cotton," *New York Times*, June 26, 1864, 5.

4. Hans Busch, ed., *Verdi's Aida: The History of an Opera in Letters and Documents* (Minneapolis: University of Minnesota Press, 1978), 6; James Carlile McCoan, *Egypt Under Ismail: A Romance of History* (London: Chapman and Hall, 1889), 103–7; "Modern Progressive Egypt," *Scientific American* 28, no. 24 (June 14, 1872): 372; J. Dunn, "Egypt's Nineteenth Century Arms Industry," 7; J. McCoan, *Egypt as It Is*, 80–81.

5. Janet Abu-Lughod, "Tale of Two Cities: The Origins of Modern Cairo," *Comparative Studies in Society and History* 7, no. 4 (July 1965): 439; J. Dunn, "Egypt's Nineteenth Century Arms Industry," 9.

6. A. Thomas-Anquetil, "Armes Portative," 283–84.

7. A. Thomas-Anquetil, "Armes Portative," 283, 444–48.

8. Russia also paid Berdan a royalty of 6 shillings per gun (J. Walter, "Rise of the Piled Arms," 399).

9. S. Norris, "Facts About Small Arms"; C. Fitch, *Report*, 6; C. Norton, *American Breech-Loading Small Arms*, 42–43; J. Walter, "Rise of the Piled Arms," 399; US DOS Archives, E. E., Farman (Cairo) first despatch to W. M. Evarts (Washington, DC), June

22, 1880, NAID211429385/Images 132–34; A. Thomas-Anquetil, "Armes Portative," 284; J. Dunn, "Egypt's Nineteenth Century Arms Industry," 9.

10. F. Barnes, *Cartridges*, 360–61.

11. G. Layman, *Military Remington Rolling Block Rifle*, 11; J. Dunn, "Egypt's Nineteenth Century Arms Industry," 9.

12. Robin J. L. Buxton, "The American Efforts to Modernize the Egyptian Army under Khedive Ismail" (master's thesis, Portland State University, 1978), 28; "General Thaddeus Phelps Mott," *New York Times*, November 27, 1894, 6; William B. Hesseltine and Catherine H. Wolf, *The Blue and Gray on the Nile* (Chicago: University of Chicago Press, 1961), 9–18; WR: I/V/341–46; Charles Chaillé-Long, *My Life in Four Continents* (London: Hutchinson and Company, 1912), 38n1; Tarik Tansu Yiğit, "Reconstructing the Self and the American: Civil War Veterans in Khedival Egypt" (PhD diss., İhsan Doğramaci Bilkent University, 2020), 36–50.

13. W. Hesseltine and C. Wolf, *Blue and Gray*, 69–71, 84–88, 120–74; Frederick J. Cox, "The American Naval Mission in Egypt," *Journal of Modern History* 26, no. 2 (June 1954): 173, 175–77; J. McCoan, *Egypt as It Is*, 98, 292.

14. John Patrick Dunn, "'An American Fracas in Egypt': The Butler Affair of 1872," *Journal of the American Research Center in Egypt* 42 (2005/2006): 158–60; J. Dunn, "Egypt's Nineteenth Century Arms Industry," 12 and n. 68; T. Yiğit, "Civil War Veterans in Khedival Egypt," 113–15.

15. John P. Dunn, *Khedive Ismail's Army* (London: Routledge, 2005), 69; J. Dunn, "Egypt's Nineteenth Century Arms Industry," 12 and n. 68; C. Norton, *American Breech-Loading Small Arms*, 236, 268.

16. Frederick J. Cox, "Khedive Ismail and Panslavism," *Slavonic and East European Review* 32, no. 78 (December 1953): 153–54 and n. 19; W. Hesseltine and C. Wolf, *Blue and Gray*, 65–68; C. Chaillé-Long, *Life in Four Continents*, 38, 58; John Patrick Dunn, "Remington 'Rolling Blocks' in the Horn of Africa," *American Society of Arms Collectors Bulletin* 71 (Fall 1994): 20n52, 21; J. McCoan, *Egypt Under Ismail*, 101–2, 109–10; *May v. Schuyler*, N.Y. Super. Ct., No. 103, Case and Exceptions (New York: Foster & Epley, 1877) [hereinafter "*May* Rec."], 30–32, 392–93.

17. US DOS Archives, G. H. Butler (Alexandria) dispatch to H. Fish (Washington, DC), December 30, 1870, NAID211442158/Images 103–8; J. Dunn, "Egypt's Nineteenth Century Arms Industry," 10; TNA:PRO FO:78, H. Elliott to Lord Granville, April 20, 1871; J. McCoan, *Egypt as It Is*, 97.

18. A. Russell, "Ilion and the Remingtons," 84; US DOS Archives, E. E., Farman (Cairo) despatch to W. M. Evarts (Washington, DC), June 22, 1880, RG59/NAID211429385/ Images 132–34; US DOS Archives, E. E., Farman (Cairo) despatch to W. M. Evarts (Washington, DC), May 4, 1878, RG59/NAID211427877/Images 488–50; US DOS Archives, E. E., Farman (Cairo) despatch to W. M. Evarts (Washington, DC), June 22, 1880, RG59/NAID211429385/Images 132–34; US DOS Archives, W. M. Evarts instructions to E. E., Farman, March 28, 1878, RG59/NAID149304315/Images 54–56; Norris Family Papers, Box 2/3, Fold. 37, 3 (October 22, 1893); C. Fitch, *Report*, 6.

19. F. Cox, "Panslavism," 159; Czeslaw Jesman, "Egyptian Invasion of Ethiopia," *African Affairs* 58, no. 230 (January 1959): 76.

20. William W. Loring, *A Confederate Soldier in Egypt* (New York: Dodd, Mead, 1884), 301–5, 329–34, 344; J. McCoan, *Egypt Under Ismail*, 169–17; C. Jesman, "Egyptian Invasion," 75, 79; W. Hesseltine and C. Wolf, *Blue and Gray*, 228–34.

21. Thomas Erskine Holland, *The European Concert in the Eastern Question: A Collection of Treaties and Other Public Acts* (Oxford: Clarendon Press, 1885), 121–25; Evelyn Baring, *Modern Egypt* (London: Macmillan, 1908), 12.

22. Keith Brown, "What a 150-Year-Old Gun Tells Us about the End of Colt's AR-15," *Slate*, October 24, 2019; Winston Churchill, *The River War* (New York: Skyhorse Publishing, 2013), 269–300; S. Norris, "Facts About Small Arms."

CHAPTER 17

1. J. Bradley, *Guns for the Tsar*, 56–58 and n. 51; J. Rasenberger, *Revolver*, 336–37; Norman Saul, *Distant Friends: The United States and Russia* (Lawrence: University Press of Kansas, 1991), 213–14, 241–42; "Famous George Law Muskets," *Scientific American* 40, no. 5 (October 13, 1855): 37; A. Mordecai, "1856 Military Commission Report," 159 (Ser. Set 1037).

2. J. Bradley, *Guns for the Tsar*, 6, 20.

3. CPFAMC Papers, W. B. Franklin Diary, February 18, 1867.

4. CPFAMC Papers, W. B. Franklin Diary, May 10, 1867; Anthony Papers, Q.C.R., 1866.

5. CPFAMC Papers, Box 8, Contract of November 25, 1867; CPFAMC Papers, W. B. Franklin Diary, December 20, 21, and 24, 1867.

6. N. Flayderman, *Guide*, 119; F. Barnes, *Cartridges*, 357; C. Norton, *American Breech-Loading Small Arms*, 171.

7. United States Army, *Proceedings of a Court of Inquiry Convened at Washington D.C., Nov. 9, 1868. by Special Orders No. 217 War Department to Examine into the Accusations Against Brig. and Bvt. Major General A. B. Dyer, Chief of Ordnance* (Washington, DC: GPO, 1869), 431; R. Bruce, *Lincoln*, 297.

8. E. Upton, *Military Policy*, 234–35 and n. a; G. Cullum, "William B. Franklin," *Biographical Register*, vol. 2, 152.

9. Alden Hatch, *Remington Arms: An American History* (Ilion, NY: Remington Arms, 1956), 114; CPFAMC Papers, Box 9, Von Oppen correspondence, Norfolk Works to CPFAC, October 14, 1869; CPFAMC Papers, Foreign Correspondence (Unclassified), Box 1, Colt correspondence and Berdan correspondence, A. Gorloff to W. Franklin, February 29, 1869, and H. Berdan to W. Franklin, September 21, 1870; R. Jinks, *Smith & Wesson*, 67; *May Rec.*, 31–32.

10. Even here, Berdan could not escape accusations of stealing the ideas of others. Samuel Norris maintained that Berdan had simply copied the rifle he and the Mauser brothers had patented in June 1868 (US Patent No. 78,603), and a British engineering journal in 1871 dismissed the Berdan II as "merely a clumsy attempt to evade the patents of Bethel Burton." Norris Family Papers, Box 2/3, Fold. 39, 2 of 3 (n.d.); Edward Spon, et al., *Spons' Dictionary of Engineering, Civil, Mechanical, Military, and Naval*, vol. 4 (London: E. & F. N. Spon, 1871), 1485; E. Hull, *Roberts Breechloading Firearms*, 26.

11. US Patent No. 85,162 (December, 22, 1868); J. Bradley, *Guns for the Tsar*, 109; J. Walter, "Rise of the Piled Arms," 399; CPFAMC Papers, Box 9, Von Oppen correspondence, W. Franklin to CPFAC, December 3, 1869.

12. J. Bradley, *Guns for the Tsar*, 109–10; CPFAMC Papers, Box 9, Von Oppen correspondence, W. Franklin to Colt, September 18, 1869, November, 30, 1869, and December 3, 1869.

13. CPFAMC Papers, Box 9, Von Oppen correspondence, F. Von Oppen to W. Franklin, January 8, 1870; J. Walter, "Rise of the Piled Arms, 399; J. Bradley, *Guns for the Tsar*, 155. To make matters worse, Berdan led BSA into another disastrous contract that drove it into bankruptcy. He secured an order from Prussia for 40 million cartridge cases, which BSA duly prepared for by investing in suites of cartridge-making machinery. BSA soon ran into production problems which, again, led to losses. BSA was liquidated at the end of 1872, albeit a successor firm with a similar name rose from its ashes the next year (J. Walter, "Rise of the Piled Arms," 399; D. Williams, *Birmingham Gun Trade*, 97).

14. T. Tate, *From Under Iron Eyelids*, 323, 326, 328; J. Bradley, *Guns for the Tsar*, 157–58, 161.

15. Bradley, *Guns for the Tsar*, 159; Alexander Tarsaidze, "Berdanka," *Russian Review* 9, no. 1 (January 1950): 30–36.

CHAPTER 18

1. "Sales of Arms by Ordnance Department," Sen. Rep. No. 183, 129 (Ser. Set 1497); Pierre Lorain and Jean Boudriot, *Les Armes Américaines de la Défense Nationale 1870–1871* (Paris: Les Presses de l'Emancipatrice, 1970), 4, 90.

2. Geoffrey Wawro, *The Franco-Prussian War: The German Conquest of France in 1870–1871* (Cambridge: Cambridge University Press 2005), 53–55, 56–57.

3. G. Wawro, *Franco-Prussian War*, 57–58; Royal Commission for the Vienna Universal Exhibition of 1873, *Report, Part III* (London: HM Stationery Office, 1874), 881–94.

4. P. Griffith, *Battle Tactics*, 148.

5. "Sales of Arms by Ordnance Department," Sen. Rep. No. 183, 525 (Ser. Set 1497); *May* Rec., 22–25 (emphasis in original).

6. *May* Rec., 30–32, 44–46, 392–93.

7. "Sales of Arms by Ordnance Department," Sen. Rep. No. 183, 525 (Ser. Set 1497).

8. "Balloons and Carrier Pigeons," *New York Herald*, January 29, 1871, 5; *May* Rec., 71–72, 432, 437.

9. *May* Rec., 72–73; "Balloons," *New York Herald*, 5

10. Vincent P. and Rose C. Carosso, *The Morgans: Private International Bankers, 1854–1913* (Cambridge, MA: Harvard University Press, 1987), 131; George W. Smalley, *Anglo-American Memories*, 2nd Series (New York and London: G. P. Putnam's Sons, 1912), 216–17.

11. V. and R. Carosso, *Morgans*, 132.

12. *May* Rec., 10, 366; "Sales of Ordnance Stores," 42nd Cong., 2d Sess., H.R. Rep. No. 46, 207 (Ser. Set 1528).

13. Thirty-three thousand of these went to France, and Providence Tool was left with the other 5,000. Ultimately, the company was able to sell them to Connecticut and Massachusetts. Anthony Papers, Q.C.R., 1870, 1871.

14. Anthony Papers, Q.C.R., 1870; F. Deyrup, *Arms Makers*, 211; "Sales of Arms by Ordnance Department," Sen. Rep. No. 183, XXVII, 150 (Ser. Set 1497); "Sales of Ordnance Stores," H.R. Report No. 46, 86 (Ser. Set 1528).

15. WR: III/V/145; "Sales of Arms by Ordnance Department," Sen. Rep. No. 183, XXVII, 2, 30 (Ser. Set 1497); "Joint Resolution Directing Secretary of War to Sell Damaged or Unserviceable Arms," 40th Cong., 2d Sess., Jt. Res. 61, 15 Stat. 259 (July 20, 1868).

16. "Sales of Arms by Ordnance Department," Sen. Rep. No. 183, XXXIII–XXXVIII, 179–80 (Ser. Set 1497).

17. "Sales of Arms by Ordnance Department," Sen. Rep. No. 183, XXXIII–XXXVIII, 83–84, 89, 132–33 (Ser. Set 1497).

18. "Sales of Arms by Ordnance Department," Sen. Rep. No. 183, XVII–XVIII, 18, 140, 221–22, 231–22 (Ser. Set 1497).

19. "Sales of Arms by Ordnance Department," Sen. Rep. No. 183, XXXV, XXXIX, 183, 195, 222, 224, 308, 310 (Ser. Set 1497); "Sales of Ordnance Stores," H.R. Rep. No. 46, 78 (Ser. Set 1528).

20. "Sales of Arms by Ordnance Department," Sen. Rep. No. 183, 318–19, 527 (Ser. Set 1497); 42d Cong., 2d Sess., *Congressional Globe*, pt. 2 (February 16, 1872) (Washington, DC: Rives & Bailey, 1872), 1069.

21. "Sales of Arms by Ordnance Department," Sen. Rep. No. 183, XXXVII–VIII, XXXIX–XLII (Ser. Set 1497).

22. 1870 Rept. Sec. of the Navy, 41st Cong., 3rd Sess., H.R. Ex. Doc. No. 1, Pt. 3 (Washington, DC: GPO, 1870), 59, 60–62 (Ser. Set 1448); "Sales of Arms by Ordnance Department," Sen. Rep. No. 183, LXVI, 422, 432 (Ser. Set 1497).

23. "Sales of Arms by Ordnance Department," Sen. Rep. No. 183, LXVI, 238–39 (Ser. Set 1497); 1870 Rept. Sec. of the Navy, H.R. Ex. Doc. No. 1, Pt. 3, 65 (Ser. Set 1448); Charles. O. Paullin, "A Half Century of Naval Administration in America, 1861–1911," *U.S. Naval Institute Proceedings* 39, no. 3 (September 1913): 1228–29.

24. "Sales of Arms by Ordnance Department," Sen. Rep. No. 183, 504–5 (Ser. Set 1497); "Sales of Ordnance Stores," H.R. Rep. No. 46, 211–12 (Ser. Set 1528).

25. "Sales of Arms by Ordnance Department," Sen. Rep. No. 183, 502–3 (Ser. Set 1497); 1870 Rept. Sec. of Navy, H.R. Ex. Doc. No. 1, Pt. 3, 60 (Ser. Set 1448).

26. "Sales of Arms by Ordnance Department," Sen. Rep. No. 183, LXVI, 420, 422–24, 426, 428, 432–35 (Ser. Set 1497).

27. "Sales of Arms by Ordnance Department," Sen. Rep. No. 183, LXVI, 422–24, 426–28, 430–31, 533–35 (Ser. Set 1497).

28. "Sales of Arms by Ordnance Department," Sen. Rep. No. 183, LXVI, 421, 426 (Ser. Set 1497).

29. "Trial of Victor Place," *Bench and Bar* (New Series), October 1871–January 1872 (Chicago: Callaghan & Cockcroft, 1871): 31, 45–46.

30. "Trial of Victor Place," 31–33.

31. "Sales of Arms by Ordnance Department," Sen. Rep. No. 183, 273–74, 341 (Ser. Set 1497); 42d Cong., 2d Sess., *Congressional Globe*, pt. 2 (February 12, 1872) (Washington, DC: Rives & Bailey, 1872), 953; "Trial of Victor Place," 33–34, 49.

32. *Congressional Globe*, pt. 2 (February 12, 1872), 953; "Sales of Arms by Ordnance Department," Sen. Rep. No. 183, I–II (Ser. Set 1497); "Sales of Ordnance Stores," H.R. Rep. No. 46, 1 (Ser. Set 1528).

33. "Sales of Arms by Ordnance Department," Sen. Rep. No. 183, I, XII, XVIII, 22, 531 (Ser. Set 1497); "Sales of Ordnance Stores," H.R. Rep. No. 46, 1 (Ser. Set 1528).

CHAPTER 19

1. "An Act to Promote the Progress of Useful Arts," 24th Cong., 1st Sess., Ch. 357, 5 Stat. 117, § 18; "Message of the President," Sen. Exec. Doc. 23, 1–3 (Ser. Set 1405); 41st Cong., 2d Sess., *Congressional Globe* (May 31, 1870), 3949–50, and *Congressional Globe* (June 22, 1870), 4693–99.

2. The Model 3 was a top-break gun, meaning that it hinged below and behind the cylinder, thus exposing the rear of the cylinder for ejection of spent shells and reloading of new cartridges.

3. R. Jinks, *Smith & Wesson*, 62–65; "Roberts Breech-Loading Musket & Carbine," H.R. Ex. Doc. No. 152, 15 (Ser. Set 1648).

4. J. Bradley, *Guns for the Tsar*, 113–14.

5. R. Jinks, *Smith & Wesson*, 65–66, 68, 73–74; C. Norton, *American Breech-Loading Small Arms*, 182; F. Barnes, *Cartridges*, 297.

6. R. Jinks, *Smith & Wesson*, 67, 74–78, 80, 103; J. Bradley, *Guns for the Tsar*, 115–16. Gorloff wrote that Smith & Wesson made 142,333 Model 3s for Russia and that another 75,000 were made in Germany by the firm of Loewe and Loewe. During the 1880s and 1890s, Russia also may have manufactured as many as 400,000 Model 3s in its armory at Tula. The Smith & Wesson Model 3 remained the standard Russian sidearm until its army adopted the Belgian-made Nagant in 1895 (J. Bradley, *Guns for the Tsar*, 116, 159).

7. R. Jinks, *Smith & Wesson*, 67, 70, 75.

8. Anonymous, *His Imperial Highness the Grand Duke Alexis in the United States of America during the Winter of 1871–72* (Cambridge, MA: Riverside Press, 1872), 14–15, 19–20, 25–26, 31–33.

9. Anonymous, *His Imperial Highness*, 61–62; Lee A. Farrow, *Alexis in America: A Russian Grand Duke's Tour, 1871–1872* (Baton Rouge: Louisiana State University Press, 2014), 93–94.

10. Anonymous, *His Imperial Highness*, 62; L. Farrow, *Alexis in America*, 93–94; A. Hatch, *Remington Arms*, 116–17.

11. Anonymous, *His Imperial Highness*, 62–64; L. Farrow, *Alexis in America*, 95.

12. L. Farrow, *Alexis in America*, 145–46; George E. Hyde, *Spotted Tail's Folk* (Norman: University of Oklahoma Press, 1961), 194–95.

13. L. Farrow, *Alexis in America*, 146–47; Anonymous, *His Imperial Highness*, 155.

14. G. Hyde, *Spotted Tail's Folk*, 195–96; Anonymous, *His Imperial Highness*, 150, 154–56; L. Farrow, *Alexis in America*, 148.

15. L. Farrow, *Alexis in America*, 150–51; Anonymous, *His Imperial Highness*, 157.
16. L. Farrow, *Alexis in America*, 152–53; Anonymous, *His Imperial Highness*, 162–63.
17. L. Farrow, *Alexis in America*, 154–56; Anonymous, *His Imperial Highness*, 172–74.
18. G. Hyde, *Spotted Tail's Folk*, 196; L. Farrow, *Alexis in America*, 156; Anonymous, *His Imperial Highness*, 146–56 passim.

CHAPTER 20

1. C. Norton, *American Breech-Loading Small Arms*, 45; A. Hatch, *Remington Arms*, 147–48, 168; "Sales of Arms by Ordnance Department," Sen. Rep. No. 183, XXVII (Ser. Set 1497).

2. A. Russell, "Ilion and the Remingtons," 83; G. Layman, *Military Remington Rolling Block Rifle*, 12, 98; "Trial of Fire Arms," *Scientific American* 25, no. 21 (November 18, 1871): 320.

3. W. Achtermeier, *Rhode Island Arms Makers*, 36; Anthony Papers, Q.C.R., 1869, 1870, 1872.

4. G. Layman, *Military Remington Rolling Block Rifle*, 9; C. Norton, *American Breech-Loading Small Arms*, 37–38; Anthony Papers, Q.C.R., 1868; A. Thomas-Anquetil, "Armes Portative," 289; Vanessa M. Ziegler, "The Revolt of 'the Ever-faithful Isle': The Ten Years' War in Cuba, 1868–1878" (PhD diss., University of California Santa Barbara, 2007), 97; S. Norris, "Facts About Small Arms."

5. Spain tinkered enough with the ammunition that the Spanish .43 and the Egyptian .43 rounds, while closely related, were not interchangeable. C. Norton, *American Breech-Loading Small Arms*, 37–38; F. Barnes, *Cartridges*, 358, 360.

6. S. Norris, "Facts About Small Arms"; A. Russell, "Ilion and the Remingtons," 83–84; V. Ziegler, "Revolt," app. C; C. Norton, *American Breech-Loading Small Arms*, 38–39, 41.

7. S. Norris, "Facts About Small Arms."

8. "Sales of Arms by Ordnance Department," Sen. Rep. No. 183, 531 (Ser. Set 1497); G. Layman, *Military Remington Rolling Block Rifle*, 10, 12, 98; C. Fitch, *Report*, 6; S. Alvis, "Remington Foreign Military Arms," 1–2; A. Russell, "Ilion and the Remingtons," 84; Helmuth C. Engelbrechtl and Frank C. Hanighen, *Merchants of Death* (Garden City, NY: Garden City Publishing Company, 1937), 45, 48; Remington-UMC, *New Chapter*, 24, 35.

9. A. Russell, "Ilion and the Remingtons," 84; S. Alvis, "Remington Foreign Military Arms," 1; Remington-UMC, *New Chapter*, 24.

10. F. Deyrup, *Arms Makers*, 207; Norris Rec., 79–80, 148–49.

11. S. V. Benét, ed., *The Fabrication of Small Arms for the United States Service*, Ordnance Memoranda No. 22 (Washington, DC: GPO, 1878), 27, 80–82, 83, 86, 88, 94; Julian Bennett, "The 'Aynali Martini': The Ottoman Army's First Modern Rifle," *Anatolica* 44 (2018): 229–55.

12. F. Deyrup, *Arms Makers*, 207–8; A. Thomas-Anquetil, "Armes Portative," 447; 1870 Rept. Sec. Navy, H.R. Ex. Doc. No. 1, Pt. 3, 60–62 (Ser. Set 1448); 1871 Rept. Sec. Navy, 42d Cong., 2d Sess., H.R. Ex. Doc. No. 1, Pt. 3 (Washington, DC: GPO, 1871), 85 (Ser. Set 1507).

13. Warren E. Schulz, *Ilion—The Town Remington Made* (Hicksville, NY: Exposition Press, 1977), 17–18; F. Deyrup, *Arms Makers*, 207–8; D. Hounshell, *American System*, 49–50.

14. F. Deyrup, *Arms Makers*, 204.

15. US DOS Archives, E. E., Farman (Cairo) first despatch to W. M. Evarts (Washington, DC), June 22, 1880, NAID211429385/Images 132–34; A. Hatch, *Remington Arms*, 148–50.

16. A. Hatch, *Remington Arms*, 151.

CHAPTER 21

1. *Oscanyan v. Winchester Repeating Arms Co.*, US Supreme Court, Oct. Term, 1880, No. 262 [hereinafter "*Oscanyan* Rec."], Record on Appeal, ¶ 38.

2. Frederick Maurice, *The Russo-Turkish War, 1877* (London: S. Sonnenschein & Co., 1905), 16.

3. The Prussians also were busy trying to sell off the Chassepots they had seized from surrendering French troops. In August 1873, the British ambassador to Turkey, Sir Henry Elliott, reported that Germany had arranged to sell the Shah of Persia 100,000 captured Chassepots, with the proviso that Persia not sell them back to the French. TNA:PRO FO:78, H. Elliott to Lord Granville, August 27, 1873.

4. "1870 Rept. Sec. War, Part II," 41st Cong., 3rd Sess., H.R. Ex. Doc. No. 1, Part 2 (Washington, DC: GPO, 1871), 292 (Ser. Set 1446); "Sales of Arms by Ordnance Department," Sen. Rep. No. 183, 9, 23, 125, 133–34, 174–75, 532 (Ser. Set 1497); "Sales of Ordnance Stores," H.R. Rept. No. 46, 74 (Ser. Set 1528); "Sales of Arms & Ordnance Stores," H.R. Ex. Doc. No. 89, 11, 13 (Ser. Set 1511); F. Deyrup, *Arms Makers*, 212; J. Bennett, "Aynali Martini," 238–39.

5. J. Bennett, "Aynali Martini," 238; Joseph McKenna, *The Gun Makers of Birmingham, 1660–1960* (Jefferson, NC: McFarland & Co., 2021), 65; US Patent No. 69,941 (October 17, 1867).

6. *Oscanyan* Rec., Bill of Exceptions, ¶¶ 7, 9, 18, 39–40.

7. *Oscanyan* Rec., Bill of Exceptions, ¶¶ 9–10, 18, 40, 50.

8. *Oscanyan* Rec., Bill of Exceptions, ¶¶ 19, 44–45.

9. U.S. Circ. Court., D. Mass., Oct. Term, 1853, Naturalization Records, No. 7–445, A. Azarian Primary Declaration of Intent (May 1, 1854); Margaret Stevens Hoel, "The *Ticaret Odasi*: Origins, Functions, and Activities of the Chamber of Commerce of Istanbul, 1885–1899" (PhD diss., Ohio State University, 1973), 50; Haag, *Gunning*, 133–34. Joseph scandalized Boston by marrying the Brahmin Martha Baxter Bingham and, with his bride in tow, quickly returned to Constantinople. The Bostonians' main objection to Joseph was less that he was Armenian than that he was Catholic.

10. Connecticut Museum of Culture and History, Bennett-Winchester Family Papers, Ms. 87108, *Letters 1878–1879*, T. G. Bennett to H. J. W. Bennett, December 8, 1877, 3; M. Hoel, "*Ticaret Odasi*," 50; P. Haag, *Gunning*, 133–34.

11. Sir Edwin Pears, *Forty Years in Constantinople* (London: Herbert Jenkins, 1916), 5; William Saint Laurent Papers, CRKN, MG 29, Reel C-10338, Images 145 (May

29, 1871), 307 (February 21, 1872), and 392–93 (May 21, 1872); *Oscanyan* Rec., Bill of Exceptions, ¶ 44.

12. L. Trevelyan, *Winchester*, 60; *Oscanyan* Rec., Bill of Exceptions, ¶¶ 22, 55; S. Norris, "Facts About Small Arms"; P. Haag, *Gunning*, 134.

13. A letter Oliver Winchester wrote Blacque in October 1872 recited that the first contract was for 22,000 guns. RIHS, PTC Rec., Box 3, Fold. 1, O. F. Winchester to Blacque, October 12, 1872.

14. One reason Winchester got the contract was that his offer was, by accident, artificially low. An error in cabling the terms of the contract to Constantinople misrepresented the price of the carbines as $20 instead of $27. Winchester sued Western Union for the consequent $35,000 in damages, but lost his case. G. Watrous, "History of Winchester," 95n1; L. Trevelyan, *Winchester*, 58–59.

15. *Oscanyan* Rec., Bill of Exceptions, ¶¶ 11, 70; P. Haag, *Gunning*, 136.

16. F. Barnes, *Cartridges*, 297, 451.

17. F. Deyrup, *Arms Makers*, 213; P. Haag, *Gunning*, 137–38; RIHS, PTC Rec., Box 3, Fold. 1, O. F. Winchester to J. B. Anthony, October 4, 1872.

18. P. Haag, *Gunning*, 133–34, 137–38; *Oscanyan* Rec., Bill of Exceptions, ¶ 5; *Oscanyan v. Arms Company*, 103 U.S. 261, 271, 276–77.

19. *His Imperial Majesty, the Sultan of the Ottoman Empire, v. Providence Tool Co.*, E.D.N.Y., [hereinafter *"Sultan v. PTC"*], Answer to Amended Complaint, ¶ 17.

20. US DOS Archives, G. H. Boker (Constantinople) dispatch to H. Fish (Washington, DC), August 15, 1872, NAID188888272/Image 108; William Smith Cooke, *The Ottoman Empire and Its Tributary States, Excepting Egypt, with a Sketch of Greece* (London: W. Clowes & Son, 1876), 46.

21. J. Walter, "Rise of the Piled Arms," 399.

22. William Saint Laurent Papers, CRKN, MG 29, Reel C-10338, Images 424–25 (June 18, 1872), 432–35 (July 10, 1872), 306 (February 21, 1872), 325–29 (March 2, 1872), 321 (March 6, 1872), 342–43 (April 23, 1872), 356 (May 8, 1872), 380–81 (May, 18, 1872), 430–31 (June 28, 1872), 390–93 (May 21, 1872), and 383 (n.d.); CEH Vincent to Director Intelligence Department War Office, "The Offensive & Defensive Condition of the Ottoman Empire," October 1875, TNA:PRO WO:106; US DOS Archives, G. H. Boker (Constantinople) dispatch to H. Fish (Washington, DC), August 15, 1872, NAID188888272/Image 109.

23. J. Walter, "Rise of the Piled Arms," 399; RIHS, PTC Rec., Box 3, Fold. 1, O. F. Winchester to J. B. Anthony, September 17, 1872, and O. F. Winchester to J. B. Anthony, September 24, 1872; William Saint Laurent Papers, CRKN, MG 29, Reel C-10338, Images 380–881 (May, 18, 1872), 389R (May 19, 1872), 394 (May 26, 1872), 433–34 (July 10, 1872), 409 (June 7, 1872), 397–401 (May 27, 1872), 408 (June 3, 1872), 424–25 (June 18, 1872), and 430–31 (June 28, 1872); S. Norris, "Facts About Small Arms"; TNA:PRO FO:78, Henry Elliot to Lord Granville, July 8, 1872.

24. Anthony Papers, Q.C.R., 1874; S. Norris, "Facts About Small Arms"; A. Russell, "Ilion and the Remingtons," 85; Remington-UMC, *New Chapter*, 22; Saint Laurent Papers, CRKN, MG 29, Reel C-10338, Image 430 (June 28, 1872).

25. "National Arms & Ammunition Company, Abridged Prospectus," *The Economist* 20, No. 1,484 (February 3, 1872): 159; D. Williams, *Birmingham Gun Trade*, 103.

26. Saint Laurent Papers, CRKN, MG 29, Reel C-10338, Images 430 (June 28, 1872) and 391 (May 21, 1872); "National Arms," *The Economist*, 159.

27. W. Greener, *Modern Breech-loaders*, 190–91; T. Tate, *From Under Iron Eyelids*, 309; "The Paris Exhibition," *Scientific American* 17, no. 3 (July 20, 1867): 42.

CHAPTER 22

1. RIHS, PTC Rec., Box 3, Fold. 1, J. B. Anthony to Wm. Dart, July 25, 1872.

2. RIHS, PTC Rec., Box 3, Fold. 1, J. B. Anthony to Blacque, July 10, 1872, and Blacque to Server Pasha J. B. Anthony, July 11, 1872; RIHS, PTC Rec., Box 3, Fold. 1, Blacque to Minister of War, July 25, 1872; J. Walter, "Rise of the Piled Arms," 399; C. Norton, *American Inventions*, 62; W. Achtermeier, *Rhode Island Arms Makers*, 38; Contract between Winchester Repeating Arms Company and Dari Choura, dated July 20, 1872 [hereinafter "Winchester–Dari Choura Contract"], Art. 1, RIHS, PTC Rec., Box 7, Fold. 2.

3. Winchester–Dari Choura Contract, Arts. 1, 2, 6, 12.

4. Winchester–Dari Choura Contract, Arts. 3–5.

5. Winchester–Dari Choura Contract, Arts. 6–9.

6. Winchester–Dari Choura Contract, Arts. 10–12.

7. Anthony Papers, Q.C.R., 1872; RIHS, PTC Rec., Box 3, Fold. 1, O. F. Winchester to J. B. Anthony, September 24, 1872, and O. F. Winchester to J. B. Anthony, September, 1872; Edward Hull, *Peabody Firearms* (privately published, 2019), 126; W. Achtermeier, *Rhode Island Arms Makers*, 38–39; Saint Laurent Papers, CRKN, MG 29, Reel C-10338, Image 58 (July 29, 1872); RIHS, PTC Rec., Box 3, Fold. 1, J. B. Anthony correspondence with Blacque, July 11, 1872; US DOS Archives, C. Hale (Washington, DC) instructions to G. H. Boker (Constantinople), September 19, 1872, RG 59, NAID 149336895/ Images 233–34, and G. H. Boker (Constantinople) despatch to Hamilton Fish (Washington, DC), October 12, 1872, RG 59, NAID 188888272/Images 192–93; RIHS, PTC Rec., Box 3, Fold. 1, O. F. Winchester to J. B. Anthony, October 4, 1872; Rhode Island Historical Society, "Benjamin F. Thurston," in *Proceedings of the Rhode Island Historical Society (1890–1891)* (Providence: Rhode Island Historical Society, 1891), 98–101.

8. RIHS, PTC Rec., Box 3, Fold. 1, O. F. Winchester to J. B. Anthony, October 4, 1872, and O. F. Winchester to J. B. Anthony, September 28, 1872.

9. E. Hull, *Peabody Firearms*, 126; G. Watrous, "History of Winchester," 115; RIHS, PTC Rec., Box 3, Fold. 1, O. F. Winchester to J. B. Anthony, October 4, 1872.

10. RIHS, PTC Rec., Box 3, Fold. 1, O. F. Winchester to Blacque Bey, October 12, 1872; E. Hull, *Peabody Firearms*, 126–27; RIHS, PTC Rec., Box 3, Fold. 1, Azarian Père et Fils to O. F. Winchester, October 25, 1872.

11. According to the Azarians, Essad was skeptical of Providence Tool because he had "utter distrust" of its agent Saint Laurent (RIHS, PTC Rec., Box 3, Fold. 1, Azarian Père et Fils to O. F. Winchester, October 25, 1872). This may have been true, or it might have been the latest salvo in the bitter rivalry between the Azarians and Saint Laurent. On

May 27, 1872, Saint Laurent wrote a letter to the Azarians—almost certainly intended to be leaked to newspapers or shared with Porte officials—accusing them of every possible sin, ranging from inappropriate gifts to government officials to paying off interpreters to stealing competitors' commercial secrets to outright bribery (Saint Laurent Papers, CRKN, MG 29, Reel C-10338, Images 397–401 (May 27, 1872). Saint Laurent, of course, had often bragged about doing these things himself.

12. RIHS, PTC Rec., Box 3, Fold. 1, Azarian Père et Fils to O. F. Winchester, October 25, 1872.

13. RIHS, PTC Rec., Box 3, Fold. 1, Azarian Père et Fils to O. F. Winchester, October 25, 1872.

14. RIHS, PTC Rec., Box 3, Fold. 1, Azarian Père et Fils to O. F. Winchester, October 25, 1872; E. Hull, *Peabody Firearms*, 127.

15. Anthony Papers, Q.C.R., 1872.

16. Anthony Papers, Q.C.R., 1872, 1873. With his gun contract assigned to Providence Tool, Oliver Winchester turned his attention to the profitable pursuit of manufacturing ammunition. By 1873, he had expanded his operation to the point where it could make 250,000 metallic cartridges daily, and he had quadrupled even that by 1875 (G. Watrous, "History of Winchester," 112).

17. Anthony Papers, Q.C.R., 1873.

18. S. Manning, *Martini-Henry Rifle*, 11–12.

19. C. Norton, *American Inventions*, 66–67; S. Manning, *Martini-Henry Rifle*, 10.

20. US Patent No. 90,614 (May 29, 1869) and No. 115,546 (May 30, 1870); Anthony Papers, Q.C.R., 1873; US Patent No. 119,846 (October 10, 1871); *Henry v. Providence Tool*, 11 Fed. Case 1182 (D. R.I. 1878).

21. *Sultan v. PTC*, Answer to Amended Complaint, ¶ 17 (March 31, 1883), and J. B. Anthony Aff., ¶ 1.

22. Robert Wheeler, "When Providence Armed the Turks," *Providence Sunday Journal*, February 16, 1941, sec. 4, 1, 4. Capital demands of this magnitude all but doomed Providence Tool's earlier plans to diversify into other areas. In particular, Anthony had to find a way to back out of his commitment to manufacture sewing machines for the Singer-owned Domestic Sewing Machine Company. Providence Tool had begun making sewing machines in 1870 and had committed itself to delivering 300 daily (D. Hounshell, *American System*, 97; Anthony Papers, Q.C.R., 1872). However, by 1873, Anthony seemed worried about the risks Providence Tool was taking between the new gun contract and the work for Singer, and at the end of 1873, the demands of the Turkish contract preempted the Singer business (Anthony Papers, Q.C.R., 1873; D. Hounshell, *American System*, 97).

23. Hussein Tevfik, *Linear Algebra* (Constantinople: A. H. Boyajian, 1882).

24. "When Providence Armed the Turks," *Providence Sunday Journal*; C. Norton, *American Inventions*, 9.

25. Anthony Papers, Q.C.R., 1874.

26. RIHS, PTC Rec., Box 3, Fold. 4, J. B. Anthony to Wm. Dart, December 11, 1878.

27. Anthony Papers, Q.C.R., 1875.

28. Ercan Karakoç and Ali Serdar Mete, "The Effects of the Firearm Purchasing on the Ottoman Financial Structure During the Military Modernization (1853–1908)," *SUTAD* 49 (Ağustos 2020): 305.

29. Anthony Papers, Q.C.R., 1875.

30. *Sultan v. PTC*, Anthony Aff., ¶ 8; Anthony Papers, Q.C.R., 1874; Anthony Papers, Diary, December 9, 1874.

31. Anthony Papers, Diary, December 22 and 23, 1874.

32. Anthony Papers, Diary, December 24, 28, and 31, 1874.

33. Anthony Papers, Diary, January 2 and 19–21, 1875.

34. Anthony Papers, Diary, January 22 and February 13, 1875; M. Twain, *Innocents Abroad*, 164, 359.

35. Anthony Papers, Diary, January 23 and 30, 1875, and February 13–May 7, 1875; Anthony Papers, Q.C.R., 1875. However, Anthony did make a contract for 200,000 *yataghan*-style saber bayonets and scabbards, work which Providence Tool subcontracted to the Ames Sword Company of Chicopee and Springfield, Massachusetts (Anthony Papers, Q.C.R., 1875).

36. Anthony Papers, Q.C.R., 1874; E. Karakoçv and A. Mete, "Firearm Purchasing," 303.

37. Hasan Abdioğlu, "The Ottoman Public Debt Administration (OPDA) in Debt Process of Ottoman Empire," conference paper, December 2018, 2, 7; E. Karakoçv and A. Mete, "Firearm Purchasing," 306.

38. Anthony Papers, Q.C.R., 1875; *Sultan v. PTC*, J. B. Anthony Aff., ¶¶ 15–16 and Exs. 6–15 (April 1883).

39. *Sultan v. PTC*, J. B. Anthony Aff., ¶¶ 14 and 15, Ex. 18.

40. "The Providence Tool Company," *New York Times*, December 19, 1875, 1; RIHS, PTC Rec., Box 3, Fold. 22.

41. Anthony Papers, Q.C.R., 1875; *Sultan v. PTC*, Anthony Aff., Exs. 20–22 (April 1883), and Amended Bill of Complaint, dated March 23, 1883, Ex. 5.

42. *Sultan v. PTC*, Anthony Aff., ¶ 22 and Exs. 56–58 (April 1883).

CHAPTER 23

1. George B. McClellan, "The War in the East," *North American Review* 125, no. 256 (July-August 1877): 40–41; F. V. Greene, *Russian Army* 147; William V. Herbert, *The Defence of Plevna* (London: Longmans, Green, and Co. 1895), 114.

2. George B. McClellan, "The War in the East, Part II," *North American Review* 125, no. 258 (September–October 1877): 246–70; W. Herbert, *Defence of Plevna*, 115; F. V. Greene, *Russian Army*, 172–74.

3. W. Herbert, *Defence of Plevna*, 80–81, 118; Rupert Furneaux, *The Breakfast War* (New York: Thomas Y. Crowell, 1958), 39.

4. W. Herbert, *Defence of Plevna*, 121–24, 130–32, 135; R. Furneaux, *Breakfast War*, 43; F. V. Greene, *Russian Army*, 313.

5. R. Furneaux, *Breakfast War*, 44, 52; F. V. Greene, *Russian Army*, 189–92; G. McClellan, "War in the East, Part II," 262–63; W. Herbert, *Defence of Plevna*, 157–58.

6. W. Herbert, *Defence of Plevna*, 134

7. F. V. Greene, *Russian Army*, 192–93; R. Furneaux, *Breakfast War*, 63; G. McClellan, "War in the East, Part II," 263; Maureen P. O'Connor, "Vision of Soldiers: Britain, France, Germany and the United States Observe the Russo-Turkish War," *War in History*, July 1997: 283; W. Herbert, *Defence of Plevna*, 181.

8. F. V. Greene, *Russian Army*, 193–96; R. Furneaux, *Breakfast War*, 61; W. Herbert, *Defence of Plevna*, 187–90.

9. F. V. Greene, *Russian Army*, 200, 204–5; W. Herbert, *Defence of Plevna*, 151, 189–90, 198, 207.

10. Another source estimated that 200,000 Peabody-Martinis were received in the course of the conflict, but it is hard to know if this is true (F. V. Greene, *Russian Army*, 141). John Anthony's history of Providence Tool recites that the company had manufactured about 369,600 Peabody-Martinis by the end of 1876 and 506,600 by the end of 1877 (Anthony Papers, Q.C.R., "Guns," 1874).

11. Henry O. Dwight, *Turkish Life in War Time* (London: Wm. H. Allen & Co., 1881), 84–85; F. V. Greene, *Russian Army*, 141; C. Norton, *American Inventions*, 71–72; J. Bradley, *Guns for the Tsar*, 226n96; F. Maurice, *Russo-Turkish War*, 16–17, 269; Julian Bennett, "Debunking a Myth: The Winchester Repeating Rifle and the 'Plevna Delay,'" 10–11 (unpublished paper); W. Herbert, *Defence of Plevna*, 352.

12. W. Herbert, *Defence of Plevna*, 20–21, 281; F. Maurice, *Russo-Turkish War*, 17; M. O'Connor, "Vision of Soldiers," 282.

13. Archibald Forbes, *Czar and Sultan: The Adventures of a British Lad in the Russo-Turkish War of 1877–78* (Bristol, UK: J. W. Arrowsmith, 1894), 77–78, 174, 183; Francis Stanley, *St. Petersburg to Plevna: Containing Interviews with Leading Russian Statesmen and Generals* (London: R. Bentley, 1878), 189; London Daily News, *The War Correspondence of the "Daily News," 1877*, 2nd ed. (London: Macmillan and Co., 1878), 634; Thilo von Trotha, *Tactical Studies on the Battles Around Plevna*, trans. Carl Reichmann (Kansas City, MO: Hudson-Kimberly Co., 1896), 207; W. Herbert, *Defence of Plevna*, 281.

14. London Daily News, *War Correspondence, 1877*, 440, 477, 479, 634; London Daily News, *The War Correspondence of the "Daily News," 1877–78* (London: Macmillan and Co., 1878), 22; M. O'Connor, *Vision of Soldiers*, 282; C. Norton, *American Inventions*, 71–72; F. V. Greene, *Russian Army*, 141. That the Peabody-Martinis worked so well also is surprising given how poorly they were maintained by Turkish troops. On the war's eastern front, British observer Captain C. B. Norman wrote that they were "rarely cleaned, thrown down on rocks, piled carelessly, and unpiled violently; it, to me, is a simple marvel how the weapons stand it at all. I have constantly taken the rifles out of men's hands and examined them, finding them in a condition that would drive the captain of a line regiment into an early grave" (C. B. Norman, *Armenia and the Campaign of 1877* (London: Cassell, Petter & Galpin, 1878), 185). "I think the Providence Company may be congratulated on the success of their contract," he concluded."

15. Richard L. Trenk, "The Plevna Delay," *Men at Arms Magazine* 19, no. 4 (1997): 29–36; P. Haag, *Gunning*, 140–41; L. Trevelyn, *Winchester*, 64–67.

16. Much of the following discussion relies upon Julian Bennett's research and analysis in his thorough study of the subject. See J. Bennett, "Debunking a Myth."

17. G. Watrous, "History of Winchester," 115–16.

18. F. V. Greene, *Russian Army*, 141; TNA:PRO FO:78, A. H. Layard to Lord Stanley, "Memorandum on Technical Subjects," October 27, 1877; TNA:PRO WO:106, Captain Thomas Fraser, "Memorandum on Small Arms Used in the War of 1877," January 7, 1878; George S. Clarke, "Plevna," in *Professional Papers of the Corps of Royal Engineers*, vol. 5, ed. R. H. Vetch (London: Royal Engineer Institute, 1881), 7; W. Herbert, *Defence of Plevna*, 25; F. V. Greene, *Sketches of Army Life in Russia* (New York: C. Scribner's Sons,1885), 100–101.

19. J. Bennett, "Debunking a Myth," 16. This agrees with information from Turkey's eastern front. There, British observer Captain C. B. Norman wrote that irregular infantry carried the Peabody-Martini and cavalry, irregular cavalry and artillerymen Winchesters (C. Norman, *Armenia and the Campaign of 1877*, 72, 109, 112, 141).

20. Henry Dwight wrote as well that as the Russians approached Constantinople in July 1877, the city's policemen were issued Winchesters to use in the case of a civil insurrection. H. Dwight, *Turkish Life*, 136; London Daily News, *War Correspondence, 1887*, 189.

21. H. Dwight, *Turkish Life*, 84; F. Maurice, *Russo-Turkish War*, 18; J. Bennett, "Debunking a Myth," 11–12 and nn. 54–56, 16; Greene, *Sketches*, 100–101; London Daily News, *War Correspondence, 1887*, 106, 119, 510; W. Herbert, *Defence of Plevna*, 23, 161, 162, 168–69; A. Forbes, *Czar and Sultan*, 305; G. Clarke, "Plevna," 7, 123n*; W. Greener, *Modern Breech-loaders*, 188; W. Greener, *Gun and Its Development*, 137–38; New York Board for Examination of Breech-Loading Small Arms, *Report*, 61.

22. RIHS, PTC Rec., Box 3, Fold. 12. There is no evidence that the factory was ever built.

23. Charles S. Ryan, *Under the Red Crescent: Adventures of an English Surgeon with the Turkish Army at Plevna and Erzeroum* (New York: Charles Scribner's Sons, 1897), 260; A. Forbes, *Czar and Sultan*, 305; W. Herbert, *Defence of Plevna*, 352.

24. J. Bennett, "Debunking a Myth," 10–11; H. Dwight, *Turkish Life*, 84; T. Heptinstall, "Snider-Enfield," 23, 33–36; F. Maurice, *Russo-Turkish War*, 12, 17; W. Greener, *Modern Breech-loaders*, 223; G. Clarke, "Plevna," 123; F. V. Greene, *Russian Army*, 58; C. Ryan, *Under the Red Crescent*, 232.

25. F. V. Greene, *Russian Army*, 58; T. Tate, *From Under Iron Eyelids*, 323; D. Williams, *Birmingham Gun Trade*, 106; J. Bradley, *Guns for the Tsar*, 158–59; Sir Frederick Arthur Wellesley, *With the Russians in Peace and War* (London: E. Nash, 1905), 165; F. Maurice, *Russo-Turkish War*, 11–13.

26. W. Greener, *Gun and Its Development*, 149, 211, 745; "New Martini-Enfield Rifle," *The Engineer*, tables at 16; F. V. Greene, *Russian Army*, 58. As to muzzle velocities, see n. 16, p. 275.

27. A. Forbes, *Czar and Sultan*, 379, 406–7.

28. G. McClellan, "War in the East," 40–41; TNA:PRO WO:106, CEH Vincent to Director Intelligence Department War Office, "The Offensive & Defensive Condition of the Ottoman Empire," October 1875; F. Stanley, *St. Petersburg to Plevna*, 152–53; London Daily News, *War Correspondence, 1887*, 602, 606; C. Norton, *American Inventions*, 292; M. O'Connor, "Vision of Soldiers," 279.

29. C. Ryan, *Under the Red Crescent*, 167; Herbert, *Defence of Plevna*, 36, 150, 198; Clarke, "Plevna," 7; TNA:PRO WO:106, R. R. Lennox to H.R.M. Charge d'affairs, April 4, 1877; C. B. Norman, *Armenia and the Campaign of 1877*, 71–72, 191.

30. F. V. Greene, *Russian Army*, 140; London Daily News, *War Correspondence, 1887*, 24, 190, 427; A. Forbes, *Czar and Sultan*, 121; J. Bennett, "Debunking a Myth," 11; F. Maurice, *Russo-Turkish War*, 17; US DOS Archives, E. E., Farman (Cairo) despatch to W. M. Evarts (Washington, DC), May 30, 1877, RG59/NAID211427370/Images 479–84.

31. G. Watrous, "History of Winchester," 116–17. The empty cartridge cases were filled and the bullets seated at the Zeitinbornou Powder Works in Constantinople. The diarist Henry Dwight wrote in September 1877 that the Turks "fill the cartridge shells sent from New Haven. They cannot get enough lead here, and have not money to buy it abroad" (H. Dwight, *Turkish Life*, 161, 163).

32. M. O'Connor, "Vision of Soldiers," 283; F. Deyrup, *Arms Makers*, 210–11; G. Watrous, "History of Winchester," 116; J. Bennett, "Aynali Martini," 245n87; RIHS, PTC Rec., Box 3, Fold. 12; Remington-UMC, *New Chapter*, 33.

33. W. Herbert, *Defence of Plevna*, 232–33, 362; A. Forbes, *Czar and Sultan*, 285. See F. V. Greene, *Russian Army*, 301 (40,000 men at breakout).

34. F. V. Greene, *Russian Army*, 234–39, 423–26, 440; C. Ryan, *Under the Red Crescent*, 220–24; W. Herbert, *Defence of Plevna*, 177–78, 233–34; J. Bennett, "Debunking a Myth," 4n13.

35. A. Wellesley, *Russians in Peace and War*, 242–43; R. Furneaux, *Breakfast War*, 109–10; A. Forbes, *Czar and Sultan*, 175–76; C. Ryan, *Under the Red Crescent*, 221–22; Archibald Forbes, George Alfred Henty, and Arthur Griffiths, *Battles of the Nineteenth Century* (London: Cassell & Co., 1896), 684.

36. W. Herbert, *Defence of Plevna*, 243, 457n90; F. Stanley, *St. Petersburg to Plevna*, 192.

37. A. Forbes, *Czar and Sultan*, 174, 176–77; C. Ryan, *Under the Red Crescent*, 238; F. V. Greene, *Russian Army*, 245.

38. A. Forbes, *Czar and Sultan*, 183–92; W. Herbert, *Defence of Plevna*, 258–68.

39. W. Herbert, *Defence of Plevna*, 270–71; A. Forbes, *Czar and Sultan*, 176–77.

40. W. Herbert, *Defence of Plevna*, 209, 312, 362, 372–73, 406–7.

CHAPTER 24

1. Treaty of San Stefano, Articles VI, XIX, XXIV, reprinted in T. Holland, *European Concert*, 335–48; Benedict Humphrey Sumner, "Ignatyev at Constantinople, 1864–1874," *Slavonic and East European Review* 11, no. 32 (January 1933): 342–43.

2. See, for example, Alan John Percivale Taylor, *The Struggle for Mastery in Europe* (Oxford: Oxford University Press, 1971), 246–51.

3. Robert Howard Lord, "The Congress of Berlin," in *Three Peace Congresses of the Nineteenth Century* (Cambridge, MA: Harvard University Press, 1917), 48; T. Holland, *European Concert*, 226.

4. A. J. P. Taylor, *Struggle for Mastery*, 245.

CHAPTER 25

1. *Providence Tool v. Corliss*, 9 R.I. 564 (1870)

2. United States Centennial Commission, International Exhibition 1876, *Official Catalogue* (Philadelphia: Nagle & Co., 1876), 134–35; B. Lewis, "Small Arms Ammunition," 1.

3. A. Russell, "Ilion and the Remingtons," 84; Anonymous, *Old Families of Rhode Island*, 1031; G. Watrous, "History of Winchester," 117–18; "Arms & Munitions for Army & Militia," Sen. Ex. Doc. No. 17, 2 (Ser. Set 1828).

4. *Sultan v. PTC*, Anthony Aff., ¶ 24 (April 1883).

5. 1879 Rept. Sec. War, Report of the Chief Signal Officer, 46th Cong., 2d Sess., H.R. Exec. Doc. 1, Pt. 2 (Washington, DC: GPO, 1879), 71 (Ser. Set 1908); *Sultan v. PTC*, Affidavit of Husseïn Tevfik, ¶ 1 (July 2, 1883), and Answer of Providence Tool, ¶ 10.

6. RIHS, PTC Rec., Box 3 F. 4, J. B. Anthony to Wm. Dart, December 12, 1878.

7. *Sultan v. PTC*, Tevfik Aff., ¶¶ 19, 20.

8. Anthony Papers, Q.C.R., 1874.

9. *Sultan v. PTC*, Tevfik Aff., ¶¶ 21–22; Anthony letter to Hassan Basseri, December 24, 1879; and Anthony Aff., ¶ 67.

10. *Sultan v. PTC*, Hassan Basseri Aff., ¶¶ 7, 17–18 (July 2, 1883) and Tevfik Aff., ¶¶ 22–25.

11. *Sultan v. PTC*, Answer, ¶ 11 (December 23, 1882); *Sultan of the Ottoman Empire v. Providence Tool Co.*, 23 Fed. 572 (E.D. N.Y. 1883).

12. W. Achtermeier, *Rhode Island. Arms Makers*, 43.

13. Charles R. Norton, *American Inventions*, 62; Anthony Papers, Q.C.R., 1874.

14. US DOS Archives, E. E., Farman (Cairo) despatch to W. M. Evarts (Washington, DC), June 22, 1880, RG59/NAID211429385/Images 132–34.

15. E. Baring, *Modern Egypt*, 12; Dunn, "Egypt's Nineteenth Century Arms Industry," 13; US DOS Archives, E. E., Farman (Cairo) despatch to W. M. Evarts (Washington, DC), July 26, 1877, RG59/NAID211427877/Images 206–9, and E. E., Farman (Cairo) despatch to H. Fish, April 3, 1877, RG59/NAID211427370/Images 270–75.

16. Anonymous, *Old Families of Rhode Island*, 1031; C. Ryan, *Under the Red Crescent*, 308; US DOS Archives, E. E., Farman (Cairo) despatch to W. M. Evarts (Washington, DC), May 4, 1878, RG59/NAID 211427877/Image 506.

17. US DOS Archives, W. M. Evarts instructions to E. E., Farman, March 3, 1878, RG59/NAID149304315/Images 54–56, and E. E., Farman (Cairo) despatch to W. M. Evarts (Washington, DC), May 4, 1878, RG59/NAID211427877/Images 488–50.

18. US DOS Archives, E. E., Farman (Cairo) despatch to W. M. Evarts (Washington, DC), May 10, 1878, RG59/NAID211427877/Image 505, and E. E., Farman (Cairo) despatch to W. M. Evarts (Washington, DC), May 10, 1878, RG59/NAID211427877/ Images 505–6.

19. US DOS Archives, E. E., Farman (Cairo) second despatch to W. M. Evarts (Washington, DC), June 22, 1880, RG59/NAID211429385/Images 135–44.

20. G. Layman, *Remington Rolling Block Rifle*, 10; US Patent No. 147,945 (February 24, 1874); A. Russell, "Ilion and the Remingtons," 86.

21. US Patent No. 221,328 (November 4, 1879); John Walter, "James Paris Lee," *Classic Arms & Militaria*, August/September 2016: 21; G. Hubbard, "Influence of Early Windsor Industries," 175–76.

22. A. Russell, "Ilion and the Remingtons," 86; J. Walter, "James Paris Lee," 22.

23. CPFAMC Papers, "Correspondence with Gen'l McCook on Turkish guns," John McCook letter to William Franklin, November 9, 1886.

24. A. Russell, "Ilion and the Remingtons," 91.

25. A. Russell, "Ilion and the Remingtons," 91; Dmitra Doukas, *Worked Over: The Corporate Sabotage of an American Community* (Ithaca, NY: Cornell University Press, 2003), 84–85.

26. A. Russell, "Ilion and the Remingtons," 87–90.

27. *Utica (NY) Daily Press*, April 20, 1886, quoted in D. Doukas, *Worked Over*, 87–88.

28. A. Russell, "Ilion and the Remingtons," 92.

29. CPFAMC Papers, "Correspondence with Gen'l McCook on Turkish guns," John McCook letter to William Franklin, January 14, 1887.

30. Norris Family Papers, Box 2/3, Fold. 39, 4–6; S. Norris, "Facts About Small Arms."

31. S. Norris, "Facts About Small Arms"; Norris Family Papers, Box 2/3, Fold. 39, Contract, ¶¶ 1, 3, 6, 9, 10; US Patent No. 78,603 (June 2, 1868).

32. S. Norris, "Facts About Small Arms"; Norris Family Papers, Box 2/3, Fold. 39, 7, 10 (n.d.).

33. Norris Family Papers, Box 2/3, Fold. 39, 8 (October 22, 1893).

SELECTED BIBLIOGRAPHY

PRIVATE PAPERS AND CORPORATE RECORDS

John Anthony Papers. These papers consist of corporate records, papers from litigation between Providence Tool Company and Turkey, a diary Anthony kept of his travels to Europe and Turkey in 1874 and 1874, and a "Quarter Century Report" he wrote about Providence Tool around 1878. The papers originally were in the possession of Margaret Sims, who passed away years ago. They are believed to still be in private hands.

Bennett-Winchester Family Papers. Papers from the Bennett and Winchester family are in the collection of the Connecticut Museum of Culture and History, Hartford, Connecticut, categorized as the Bennett-Winchester Family Papers, MS. 87108.

Colt Papers. The archives of the Colt Patent Fire Arms Manufacturing Company (CPFAMC) are held in the Connecticut State Library, Hartford, Connecticut, generally under the classification RG103.

Norris Family Papers. Correspondence and other materials relating to the work of Samuel Norris are among the records of St. Michael's Church, Bristol, Rhode Island, which are held in the Manuscript Collection of the University of Rhode Island, catalogued under Msg. 185, Series X.

Providence Tool Company Records. The surviving records of the Providence Tool Company are in the collection of the Rhode Island Historical Society, classified as MSS 89.

Remington Arms Company Corporate Records. These materials were compiled by Samuel Alvis of Remington Arms decades ago and consisted mostly of unattributed secondary sources.

William Saint-Laurent Papers. Correspondence from William Saint Laurent is maintained by the Canadian Research Knowledge Network, under the heading "Fonds William Saint-Laurent, MG 29."

Winchester Repeating Arms Company Records. These were in the hands of the Olin Corporation in New Haven, Connecticut, years ago. The most important document there was George R. Watrous's typescript "History of Winchester Repeating Arms Company," which was given the call number 623.4409 (W677).

GOVERNMENT ARCHIVES
United Kingdom, The National Archives. The records formerly held in the Public Records Office were transferred to the UK's National Archives twenty years ago, where they are kept under the general category of TNA:PRO. For the most part, the records I have relied upon were correspondence between the Foreign Office and its representatives in Constantinople (FO:78) and correspondence between the War Office and its attachés in the Balkans (WO:106).

United States National Archives. The archival materials I have relied upon from the United States National Archives are diplomatic correspondence within the General Records of the US Department of State, Record Group 59. These are generally available online at https://catalog.archives.gov/id/[*NAID number/image number*]. Where I have cited these materials, I have provided the NAID numbers for them.

LEGAL RECORDS
I have followed standard forms of legal citation for reported cases, and if a reported judicial decision is properly cited in a footnote or endnote, I have not listed it here. However, I have referred to the appellate record from the following cases:

Graves v. Berdan, 26 N.Y. 498 (1863), No. 78, Case on Appeal (1859). New York: Wm. C. Bryant & Co., 1859.

May v. Schuyler, N.Y. Super. Ct., No. 103, Case and Exceptions. New York: Foster & Epley, 1877.

Oscanyan v. Winchester Repeating Arms Co., 103 U.S. 261 (1880), Record on Appeal.

Providence Tool Co. v. Norris, U.S. Sup. Ct., Dec. Term, 1863, No. 208, Record on Appeal.

Rowan v. Sharps Rifle Manufacturing Co., et al., 33 Conn. 1 (1865), 35 Conn. 127 (1868), Record on Appeal. Brighton, MI: Cornell Publications, 2005.

White v. Allen, 29 Fed. Cases 62 (D. Mass., 1863), Record on Appeal. Boston: Alfred Mudge & Son, 1863.

OFFICIAL UNITED STATES GOVERNMENT PUBLICATIONS
There is a wealth of information in reports the War Department and Navy Department submitted to Congress, as well as reports, transcripts, and other materials relating to congressional debates and the work of congressional committees.

Annual Reports of the Secretary of War were submitted to Congress at the end of each federal fiscal year and printed in the records of the Senate or House of Representatives. For convenience and reference, I have included the Serial Set (abbreviated "Ser. Set") volume numbers; however, if the report spans more than one volume, I have cited only the volume where the relevant material (usually the report of the Chief of Ordnance) is found. The volumes of the Serial Set can be accessed online at https://catalog.hathitrust.org/Record/006228203.

By year, they are cited and found as follows:

1855: Sen. Exec. Doc. No. 1, 34th Cong., 1st Sess. Washington, DC: Beverley Ticker, 1855 (Ser. Set 811).
1856: H. Rep. Exec. Doc. No. 1, Vol. II, 34th Cong., 3rd Sess. Washington, DC: Cornelius Wendell, 1856 (Ser. Set 894).
1857: Sen. Exec. Doc. No. 11, Vol. II, 35th Cong., 1st Sess. Washington, DC: W. A. Harris, 1858 (Ser. Set 920).
1858: Sen. Exec. Doc. No. 1, Vols. I and II, 35th Cong., 2nd Sess. Washington, DC: W. A. Harris, 1858 (Ser. Sets 975 and 976).
1859: Sen. Exec. Doc. No. 2, 36th Cong., 1st Sess. Washington, DC: George W. Bowman, 1860 (Ser. Sets 1024 and 1025).
1860: Sen. Exec. Doc. No. 1, Vol. II, 36th Cong., 2nd Sess. Washington, DC: George W. Bowman, 1860 (Ser. Set 1079).
1861: Sen. Exec. Doc. No. 1, 37th Cong., 2nd Sess. Washington, DC: Government Printing Office [hereinafter "GPO"], 1861 (Ser. Set 1118).
1862: H.R. Exec. Doc. No. 1, 37th Cong., 3rd Sess. Washington, DC: GPO, 1862 (Ser. Set 1159).
1862: Report of the Chief of Ordnance, WR: III/II/849–59.
1863: H.R. Exec. Doc. No. 1, 38th Congress, 1st Sess. Washington, DC: GPO, 1864 (Ser. Set 1184).
1864: H.R. Exec. Doc. No. 83, 38th Congress, 2nd Sess. Washington, DC: GPO, 1865 (Ser. Set 1230).
1865: H.R. Exec. Doc. No. 1, 39th Congress, 1st Sess., Vol. 2. Washington, DC: GPO, 1866 (Ser. Set 1250).
1866: H.R. Exec. Doc. No. 1, 39th Congress, 2nd Sess. Washington, DC: GPO, 1866 (Ser. Set 1285).
1867: H.R. Exec. Doc. No. 1, 40th Congress, 2nd Sess. Washington, DC: GPO, 1867 (Ser. Set 1324).
1868: H.R. Exec. Doc. No. 1, 40th Cong., 3rd Sess. Washington, DC: GPO, 1869 (Ser. Set 1367).
1870: H.R. Ex. Doc. No. 1, Pt. 2, 41st Cong., 3rd Sess. Washington, DC: GPO, 1871 (Ser. Set 1446).
1871: H.R. Exec. Doc. No. 1, Pt. 2, 42nd Cong., 2nd Sess. Washington, DC: GPO, 1871 (Ser. Set 1503).
1879: H.R. Exec. Doc. No. 1, Pt. 2, Report of the Chief Signal Officer, 46th Cong., 2nd Sess. Washington, DC: GPO, 1880 (Ser. Set 1908).

Annual Reports of the Secretary of the Navy are treated the same way as the Annual Reports of the Secretary of War:

1864: H.R. Ex. Doc. No. 1, 38th Cong., 2nd Sess. Washington, DC: GPO, 1864 (Ser. Set 1221).
1865: H.R. Ex. Doc. No. 1, 39th Cong., 1st Sess. Washington, DC: GPO, 1865 (Ser. Set 1253).

1867: H.R. Ex. Doc. No. 1, 40th Cong., 2nd Sess. Washington, DC: GPO, 1868 (Ser. Set 1327).
1868: H.R. Ex. Doc. No. 1, 40th Cong., 3rd Sess. Washington, DC: GPO, 1869 (Ser. Set 1369).
1869: H.R. Ex. Doc. No. 1, Pt. 1, 41st Cong., 2nd Sess. Washington, DC: GPO, 1869 (Ser. Set 1411).
1870: H.R. Ex. Doc. No. 1, Pt. 3, 41st Cong., 3rd Sess. Washington, DC: GPO, 1870 (Ser. Set 1448).
1871: H.R. Ex. Doc. No. 1, Pt. 3, 42nd Cong., 2nd Sess. Washington, DC: GPO, 1871 (Ser. Set 1507).
1873: H.R. Ex. Doc. No. 1, Pt. 3, 43rd Cong., 1st Sess. Washington, DC: GPO, 1873 (Ser. Set 1600).

REPORTS, HEARINGS, AND MATERIALS ON ORDNANCE DEPARTMENT PURCHASES OR SALES OF ARMS

The congressional Serial Set also contains a number of other reports and materials as follows:

"Arms & Munitions for Army & Militia," 45th Cong., 3rd Sess., Sen. Ex. Doc. No. 17. Washington, DC: GPO, 1879 (Ser. Set 1828).
"Government Contracts," Commission on Ordnance and Ordnance Stores, U.S. House of Representatives, 37th Cong., 2nd Sess., H.R. Rep. No. 2. Washington, DC: GPO, 1862 (Ser. Set 1143).
"Message of the President," 41st Cong., 2nd Sess., Vol. 1, Sen. Exec. Doc. 23. Washington, DC: GPO, 1870 (Ser. Set 1405).
"Military Commission to Europe in 1855 and 1856, Report of Major Alfred Mordecai," 36th Cong., 1st Sess., Sen. Ex. Doc. No. 60. Washington, DC: George W. Bowman, 1860 (Ser. Set 1037).
"Papers Relating to the Treaty of Washington," 42nd Cong., 2nd Sess., H.R. Exec. Doc. No. 89. Washington, DC: GPO, 1872 (Ser. Set 1554).
"Purchase of Arms," 37th Cong., 2nd Sess., H.R. Exec. Doc. No. 67. Washington, DC: GPO, 1862 (Ser. Set 1131).
"Purchases by Ordnance Department," 40th Congress, 2nd Sess., H.R. Exec. Doc. No 99. Washington, DC: GPO, 1869 (Ser. Set 1338).
"Report of the Commission on Ordnance Contracts & Claims," 37th Cong., 2nd Sess., Sen. Exec. Doc. No. 72. Washington, DC: GPO, 1862 (Ser. Set 1123).
"Roberts Breech-Loading Musket & Carbine," 43rd Cong., 2nd Sess., H.R. Ex. Doc. No. 152. Washington, DC: GPO, 1875 (Ser. Set 1648).
"Sales of Arms & Ordnance Stores," 42nd Cong., 2nd Sess., H.R. Exec. Doc. 89. Washington, DC: GPO, 1872 (Ser. Set 1511).
"Sales of Arms by Ordnance Department," 42nd Cong., 2nd Sess., Sen. Rep. No. 183. Washington, DC: GPO, 1872 (Ser. Set 1497).
"Sales of Ordnance Stores," 42nd Cong., 2nd Sess., H.R. Report No. 46. Washington, DC: GPO, 1872 (Ser. Set 1528).

Treaty of Washington, Tribunal of Arbitration, "Counter Case of Great Britain," reprinted in 42nd Cong., 2nd Sess., H.R. Ex. Doc. No. 282. Washington, DC: GPO, 1872 (Ser. Set 1521).
Because the titles of these reports are confusingly similar in some instances, they are cited in the footnotes by title, document number, and Serial Set number.

The War of the Rebellion

Between 1880 and 1901, the staff of the United States War Department published a 128-volume compilation of government documents from the Civil War. The full citation to the work is *The War of the Rebellion: A Compilation of the Official Records of the Union and Confederate Armies* (Washington, DC: Government Printing Office), and it can be accessed online at https://babel.hathitrust.org/cgi/mb?a=listis;c=106642625 and other places. The compilation is divided into six series (I through VI), and there are multiple volumes within each series. It is cited here as follows: WR: [*series*]/[*volume*]/[*page*].

PATENTS, STATUTES, CONGRESSIONAL DEBATES, AND OTHER UNITED STATES GOVERNMENT MATTERS

Various statutes, congressional debates and resolutions, and other actions are cited in the footnotes or endnotes and are not set forth here. Patents are cited by number and date of issue, but not by title or description.

PRIMARY AND SECONDARY SOURCES

The following is a selected bibliography and, for reasons of space, covers only materials referred to in the book's text, footnotes, or endnotes. Some materials (e.g., newspaper articles) are cited only in notes and are not listed here.

Abbott, Jacob. "The Armory at Springfield." *Harper's New Monthly Magazine* 5, no. 26 (July 1852): 145–61.
Abdioğlu, Hasan. "The Ottoman Public Debt Administration (OPDA) in Debt Process of Ottoman Empire." Conference paper, December 2018.
Abu-Lughod, Janet. "Tale of Two Cities: The Origins of Modern Cairo." *Comparative Studies in Society and History* 7, no. 4 (July 1965): 429–45.
Achtermeier, William O. *Rhode Island Arms Makers & Gunsmiths, 1643–1883*. Providence, RI: Man at Arms, 1980.
Adams, Henry Brooks. *The Education of Henry Adams*. Boston: Houghton Mifflin, 1918.
Alder, Kenneth. *Engineering the Revolution: Arms & Enlightenment in France, 1763–1815*. Chicago: University of Chicago Press, 1997.
———. "Innovation and Amnesia: Engineering Rationality and the Fate of Interchangeable Parts Manufacturing in France." *Technology and Culture* 38, no. 2 (April 1997): 273–311.
Anonymous. *Diary of a Public Man*. Chicago: private printing for Abraham Lincoln Book Shop, 1945.

Anonymous. *His Imperial Highness the Grand Duke Alexis in the United States of America during the Winter of 1871–72*. Cambridge, MA: Riverside Press, 1872.

Anonymous. *Ilion: 1852–1952*. Ilion, NY: Centennial Committee (privately published), 1952.

Anonymous. *Representative Men and Old Families of Rhode Island*. Chicago: J. H. Beers & Company, 1908.

Association of Firearm and Tool Mark Examiners. *Glossary*. 6th ed., 2013.

Auerbach, Jeffrey A. *The Great Exhibition of 1851: A Nation on Display*. New Haven, CT: Yale University Press, 1999.

Baring, Evelyn, Earl of Cromer. *Modern Egypt*. London: Macmillan, 1908.

Barnes, Frank C. *Cartridges of the World*. 12th ed. Edited by Layne Simpson. Iola, WI: Gun Digest Books, 2009.

Bartlett, Rev. William Alfred. "Lincoln's Seven Hits with a Rifle." *Magazine of History* 19, no. 1 (1922): 68–72.

Bartlett, W. A., and D. B. Gallatin. *Cartridge Manual: An Illustrated Digest*. Union City, TN: Pioneer Press, 1956.

Battison, Edwin A. "Eli Whitney and the Milling Machine." *Smithsonian Journal of History* 1, no. 2 (Summer 1966): 9–34.

———. "Robbins & Lawrence Armory and Machine Shop: An International Historic Mechanical Engineering Heritage Site." Address delivered on May 28, 1987, to the American Society of Mechanical Engineers.

Beckert, Sven. *Empire of Cotton: A Global History*. New York: Vintage Books, 2014.

Benét, Brig. Gen. Stephen V. *A Collection of Annual Reports and Other Important Papers Relating to the Ordnance Department*. Vol. 2. Washington, DC: Government Printing Office, 1878.

———. *Metallic Ammunition for the Springfield Breech-loading Rifle-musket*. Philadelphia: Frankford Arsenal and J. J. O'Reilly, 1868.

———. "Rifle Target Practice in the Army." *Army and Navy Journal* 20, no. 8 (September 23, 1882): 176.

Bennett, Julian. "The 'Aynali Martini': The Ottoman Army's First Modern Rifle." *Anatolica* 44 (January 1, 2018): 229–55.

———. "Debunking a Myth: The Winchester Repeating Rifle and the 'Plevna Delay.'" Unpublished paper.

Benton, James G. *Course of Instruction in Ordnance & Gunnery*. New York: D. Van Nostrand, 1862.

Bicknell, Thomas William. *The History of the State of Rhode Island and Providence Plantations*. New York: American Historical Society, 1920.

Blake, William P. *History of the Town of Hamden, Connecticut*. New Haven, CT: Price, Lee & Co., 1888.

———, ed. *Reports of the United States Commissioners to the Paris Universal Exhibition, 1867*. Vol. 1. Washington, DC: Government Printing Office, 1870.

Bradley, Joseph. *Guns for the Tsar*. DeKalb: Northern Illinois University Press, 1990.

Brown, Carrie. "Guns for Billy Yank: The Armory in Windsor Meets the Challenge of Civil War." *Vermont History* 79, no. 2 (Summer/Fall 2011): 141–61.

Brown, Charles Leroy. "Abraham Lincoln and the Illinois Central Railroad, 1857–1860." *Journal of the Illinois State Historical Society* 36, no. 2 (June 1943): 121–63.

Brown, John Howard, and Rossiter Johnson, eds. "Hiram Berdan." In *Twentieth Century Biographical Dictionary of Notable Americans*. Vol. 1. Boston: Biographical Society, 1904.

Brown, Keith. *Loyal Unto Death: Trust and Terror in Revolutionary Macedonia*. Bloomington: Indiana University Press, 2013.

———. "What a 150-Year-Old Gun Tells Us about the End of Colt's AR-15." *Slate*, October 24, 2019.

———. "Whose Gun Is This? Notes from the North American-Ottoman Arms Trade." Visiting seminar, University of Helsinki Anthropology, September 2022. https://blogs.helsinki.fi/anthropology/2021/10/07/keith-brown-whose-gun-is-this-notes-from-the-north-american-ottoman-arms-trade.

Bruce, Robert. *Lincoln and the Tools of War*. Indianapolis, IN: Bobbs-Merrill, 1956.

Burlingame, Luther D. "The Universal Milling Machine." *American Machinist* 34, no. 1 (January 5, 1911): 9–13.

Burt, David. *Major Caleb Huse C.S.A. and S. Isaac Campbell & Co*. Central Milton Keynes, UK: AuthorHouse, 2009.

Busch, Hans, ed. *Verdi's Aida: The History of an Opera in Letters and Documents*. Minneapolis: University of Minnesota Press, 1978.

Busk, Hans. *Hand-book for Hythe: Comprising a Familiar Explanation of the Law of Projectiles, and an Introd. to the System of Musketry, Now Adopted by All Military Powers: with Numerous Illustrations*. London: Routledge, Warne, and Routledge, 1860.

Carbone, Gerald M. *Brown & Sharpe and the Measure of American Industry: Making the Precision Machine Tools that Enabled Manufacturing, 1833–2001*. Jefferson, NC: McFarland & Co., 2017.

Carosso, Vincent P., and Rose C. Carosso. *The Morgans: Private International Bankers, 1854–1913*. Cambridge, MA: Harvard University Press, 1987.

"The Cartridges for the New Rifle." *The Engineer* 28 (August 20, 1869): 125.

Case, Lafayette Wallace, MD. *The Hollister Family of America*. Chicago: Fergus Printing Co., 1886.

Chaillé-Long, Charles. *My Life in Four Continents*. London: Hutchinson and Company, 1912.

Churchill, Winston. *The River War*. New York: Skyhorse Publishing, 2013.

Clarke, George S. "Plevna." In *Professional Papers of the Corps of Royal Engineers*. Vol. 5. Edited by R. H. Vetch. London: Royal Engineer Institute, 1881.

Cleveland, H. W. S. *Hints to Riflemen*. New York: D. Appleton and Company, 1864.

Clode, Charles M. *The Military Forces of the Crown*. Vol. 2. London: J. Murray, 1869.

Colt, Samuel. "On the Application of Machinery to the Manufacture of Rotating Chambered-Breech Fire-Arms, and Their Peculiarities." In *Institution of Civil Engineers, Proceedings*. Vol. 11. London: William Clowes & Sons, 1855.

Cooke, William Smith. *The Ottoman Empire and Its Tributary States, Excepting Egypt, with a Sketch of Greece*. London: W. Clowes & Son, 1876.

Cooper, Carolyn. "The Evolution of American Patent Management: The Blanchard Lathe as a Case Study." Prologue, *Journal of the National Archive* 19, no. 4 (Winter 1987): 345–59.

———. *Shaping Invention: Thomas Blanchard's Machinery and Patent Management in Nineteenth-Century America*. New York: Columbia University Press, 1991.

Cottesloe, Thomas Francis Freemantle. "Notes on the History of the Royal Small Arms Factory, Enfield Lock." *Journal of the Society for Army Historical Research* 12, no. 48 (Winter 1933–34): 197–212.

Cox, Frederick J. "The American Naval Mission in Egypt." *Journal of Modern History* 26, no. 2 (June 1954): 173–78.

———. "Khedive Ismail and Panslavism." *Slavonic and East European Review* 32, no. 78 (December 1953): 151–56.

Creighton, O. H., L. Evis, M. Kingdom, C. J. McKenzie, I. Watt, and A.K. Outram. (2020). "The Face of Battle? Debating Arrow Trauma on Medieval Human Remains from Princesshay, Exeter." *Antiquaries Journal* 100 (2020): 165–189.

Cullum, George Washington. *Biographical Register of the Officers and Graduates of the U.S. Military Academy at West Point, N.Y.* 3rd ed. Boston and New York: Houghton, Mifflin, 1891.

Daliba, James. "Armory at Springfield, Communicated to the House of Representatives March 3, 1823." *American State Papers*, series V, *Military Affairs*, vol. 2: 538–53.

Davis, Carl L. *Arming the Union: Small Arms in the Civil War*. Port Washington, NY: Kennikat Press, 1973.

Davis, John C. "U.S. Army Rifle & Carbine Adoption between 1865 and 1900." Master's thesis, U.S. Army Command & General Staff College, Fort Leavenworth, 2007, 10–11.

Delafield, Major Richard. *Report on the Art of War in Europe in 1854, 1855, and 1856*. Washington, DC: George W. Bowman, 1860.

Deyrup, Felicia. *Arms Makers of the Connecticut Valley: A Regional Study of the Economic Development of the Small Arms Industry, 1798–1870*. Smith College Studies in History, vol. 33. Northhampton, MA: Smith College, 1948.

Dodge, William Castle. *Breech Loaders versus Muzzle Loaders, or How to Strengthen Our Army and Crush the Rebellion*. Washington, DC: Ed. A. Stevens, 1864.

"Domestic Intelligence: The Report on Fire-Arms." *Harper's Weekly* 1, no. 43 (October 24, 1857): 678.

Doukas, Dmitra. *Worked Over: The Corporate Sabotage of an American Community*. Ithaca, NY: Cornell University Press, 2003.

Drake, Captain Mervin. "On the Military Breechloaders of Prussia, France, and England." *Royal United Services Institution Journal* 15, no. 64 (1871): 438–58.

Dunn, John Patrick. "'An American Fracas in Egypt': The Butler Affair of 1872." *Journal of the American Research Center in Egypt* 42 (2005/2006): 153–61.

———. "Egypt's Nineteenth Century Arms Industry." In *Girding for Battle*, edited by Donald J. Stoker Jr. and Jonathan A. Grant. Westport and London: Praeger, 2003.

———. *Khedive Ismail's Army*. London: Routledge, 2005.

———. "Remington 'Rolling Blocks' in the Horn of Africa." *American Society of Arms Collectors Bulletin* 71 (Fall 1994): 19–31.

Dutton, Clarence E. "Ordnance Department." In *The Army of the United States*, edited by T. Rodenbough and W. Haskin. New York: Argonaut Press, 1966.

Dwight, Henry O. *Turkish Life in War Time*. London: Wm. H. Allen & Co., 1881.

Edwards, William R. *Civil War Guns*. Secaucus, NJ: Castle, 1982.

Engelbrechtl, Helmuth C., and Frank C. Hanighen. *Merchants of Death*. Garden City, NJ: Garden City Publishing Company, 1937.

Farrow, Lee A. *Alexis in America: A Russian Grand Duke's Tour, 1871–1872*. Baton Rouge: Louisiana State University Press, 2014.

Ffrench, Yvonne. *The Great Exhibition: 1851*. London: Harvill Press, 1950.

Fitch, Charles H. *Report on the Manufacture of Fire-arms and Ammunition*. Washington, DC: Government Printing Office, 1882.

Flayderman, Norm. *Flayderman's Guide to Antique American Firearms*. 9th ed. Iola, WI: Gun Digest Books, 2007.

Forbes, Archibald. *Czar and Sultan: The Adventures of a British Lad in the Russo-Turkish War of 1877–78*. Bristol, UK: J. W. Arrowsmith, 1894.

Forbes, Archibald, George Alfred Henty, and Arthur Griffiths. *Battles of the Nineteenth Century*. London: Cassell, 1896.

Fox, William Freeman. *Regimental Losses in the American Civil War, 1861–1865*. Albany, NY: Albany Publishing Company, 1898.

Fries, Russell I. "British Response to the American System: The Case of the Small-Arms Industry after 1850." *Technology and Culture* 16, no. 3 (1975): 377–403.

Fuller, Claude. *The Breech Loader in the Service 1816–1917*. New Milford, CT: N. Flayderman & Co., 1965

———. *The Rifled Musket*. New York: Bonanza Books, 1958.

Furneaux, Rupert. *The Breakfast War*. New York: Thomas Y. Crowell, 1958.

Ganidel, P. *Notice sur les Cartouches Pour Armes de Guerre et Notamment sur la Cartouche Pour Fusil Chassepot Dit Modèle 1866*. Paris: Dupont, 1873.

Gibbon, John. *The Artillerist's Manual*. New York: D. Van Nostrand, 1860.

Gibbons, Brett. *The Destroying Angel*. Privately published, 2019.

Gluckman, Col. Arcadi, and L. D. Saterlee. *American Gun Makers*. Harrisburg, PA: Stackpole Co., 1953.

Gordon, Sir Alexander Hamilton. *Remarks on National Defence, Volunteers and Rifles: With a Report on Experiments with Small Arms, Carried on at the Royal Manufactory at Enfield in 1852*. London: Parker, Furnivall & Parker, 1853.

Gordon, Robert B. "Material Evidence of the Manufacturing Methods Used in 'Armory Practice.'" *IA: The Journal of the Society for Industrial Archeology* 14, no. 1 (1988): 23–35.

———. "Simeon North, John Hall, and Mechanized Manufacturing." *Technology and Culture* 30, no. 1 (January 1989): 179–88.

———. "Who Turned the Mechanical Ideal into Mechanical Reality?" *Technology and Culture* 29, no. 4 (October 1988), special issue, *Labor History and the History of Technology*: 744–78.

SELECTED BIBLIOGRAPHY

Grant, Jonathan. *Rulers, Guns and Money: The Global Arms Trade in the Age of Imperialism.* Harvard University Press, 2007.

Grant, Ulysses S. *Personal Memoirs of U. S. Grant.* New York: Library of America, 1990.

Great Britain, War Office. *Text Book on the Theory of the Motion of Projectiles, the History, Manufacture, and Explosive Force of Gunpowder, the History of Small Arms, the Method of Conducting Experiments.* London: HM Stationery Office, 1863.

Greene, Francis Vinton. *The Russian Army and Its Campaigns in Turkey in 1877–1878.* New York: D. Appleton & Co., 1879.

———. *Sketches of Army Life in Russia.* New York: C. Scribner's Sons, 1885.

Greener, William W. *The Gun and Its Development: With Notes on Shooting.* 3rd ed. London: Cassell, 1885.

———. *Gunnery in 1858: Being a Treatise on Rifles, Cannon, and Sporting Arms.* London: Smith Elder & Co., 1858.

———. *Modern Breech-loaders: Sporting and Military.* London: Cassell, Petter & Galpin, 1871.

Griffith, Patrick George. *Battle Tactics of the Civil War.* Marlborough, UK: Crowood Press, 2014.

Guelzo, Allen C. *Gettysburg: The Last Invasion.* New York: Vintage Books, 2014.

Guyer, Isaac D. *History of Chicago: Its Commercial and Manufacturing Interests and Industry.* Chicago: Church, Goodman & Cushing, 1862.

Haag, Pamela. *The Gunning of America: Business and the Making of American Gun Culture.* New York: Basic Books, 2016.

Hall, Jeffrey C. *The Stand of the U.S. Army at Gettysburg.* Bloomington: Indiana University Press, 2009.

Hamilton, Alexander. *Report on the Subject of Manufactures.* New York: Cosimo Classics, 2007.

Hartley, Joseph Wilfred. *Marcellus Hartley, A Brief Memoir.* New York: privately published, 1903.

Hatch, Alden. *Remington Arms: An American History.* Ilion, NY: Remington Arms, 1956.

Hay, John. *Letters of John Hay and Extracts from Diary.* Edited by Andrew Dickson White, Clara Louise Hay, and Henry Adams. Washington, DC: Printed but not published, 1908.

Herbert, William V. *The Defense of Plevna.* London: Longmans, Green, and Co., 1895.

———. "The Third Battle of Plevna." In Charles Ryan and William V. Herbert, *Conflict at Plevna.* UK: Leonaur, 2013.

Hess, Earl J. *The Rifle Musket in Civil War Combat: Reality and Myth.* Lawrence: University Press of Kansas, 2008.

Hesseltine, William Best, and Hazel Catherine Wolf. *The Blue and Gray on the Nile.* Chicago: University of Chicago Press, 1961.

Heth, Henry. *A System of Target Practice: For the Use of Troops When Armed with the Musket, Rifle-musket, Rifle, or Carbine.* New York: D. Van Nostrand, 1862.

Hicks, James Irvine. *Notes on U.S. Ordnance.* Vol. 2 (1776–1941). Greens Farm, CT: Modern Books, 1941.

Holland, Thomas Erskine. *The European Concert in the Eastern Question: A Collection of Treaties and Other Public Acts.* Oxford: Clarendon Press, 1885.

Houze, Herbert G. "Brief Notes on Three Subjects." *American Society of Arms Collectors Bulletin* 108 (September 2013): 13–19.

———. *Winchester Repeating Arms Company: Its History and Development from 1865 to 1981.* Iola, WI: Krause Publications, 1994.

Hounshell, David A. *From the American System to Mass Production.* Baltimore and London: Johns Hopkins University Press, 1984.

"How a Rifled Musket Is Made at the Providence Tool Company's Armory," pt. 1. *Scientific American* 9, no. 19 (November 7, 1863): 293–94.

"How a Rifled Musket Is Made at the Providence Tool Company's Armory," pt. 2. *Scientific American* 9, no. 20 (November 14, 1863): 308–10.

Howard, Robert A. "Interchangeable Parts Reexamined: The Private Sector of the American Arms Industry on the Eve of the Civil War." *Technology and Culture* 19, no. 4 (October 1978): 633–49.

Howe, Henry. *Memoirs of the Most Eminent American Mechanics.* New York: Harper & Brothers, 1852.

Hubbard, Guy. "The Influence of Early Windsor Industries Upon the Mechanic Arts." In *Proceedings of the Vermont Historical Society for the Years 1921, 1922 & 1923.* Montpelier, VT: Capital City Press, 1924.

Huger, Benjamin, et al. *Reports of Experiments with Small Arms for the Military Services: By Officers of the Ordnance Department, U.S. Army.* Washington, DC: A. O. P. Nicholson, 1856.

Hughes, Robert M., "John B. Floyd and His Traducers." *Virginia Magazine of History and Biography* 43, no. 4 (October 1935): 316–29.

Hull, Edward. *Peabody Firearms.* Privately published, 2019.

———. *Roberts Breechloading Firearms.* Privately published, 2015.

Huse, Caleb. *The Supplies for the Confederate Army, How They Were Obtained in Europe and How Paid For: Personal Reminscences and Unpublished History.* Boston: T. R. Marvin & Son, 1904.

Hyde, George E. *Spotted Tail's Folk.* Norman: University of Oklahoma Press, 1961.

Jinks, Roy G. *History of Smith & Wesson.* North Hollywood, CA: Beinfeld Publishing, 1977.

Jervis, Captain Jervis-White. *The Rifle-Musket.* London: Chapman & Hall, 1854.

Jesman, Czeslaw. "Egyptian Invasion of Ethiopia." *African Affairs* 58, no. 230 (January 1959): 75–78.

Jobbagy, Bill. "Ammunition Manufacturing in South Coventry, Connecticut." February 2017. https://www.coventryct.org/DocumentCenter/View/2077/Ammunition-Manufacturing-in-Coventry?bidId=.

Johnson, Benjamin Pierce. *Report of Benj. P. Johnson: Agent of the State of New York, Appointed to Attend the Exhibition of the Industry of All Nations, Held in London, 1851.* Albany, NY: C. Van Benthuysen, 1852.

Johnson, John P. "Robbins & Lawrence Armory (American Precision Museum)." US Department of the Interior, National Park Service, HAER VT-39, 2009.

Johnson, Rossiter, ed. *Twentieth Century Biographical Dictionary of Notable Americans*. Vol. 1. Boston: Biographical Society, 1904.

Jones, Gordon L. *Confederate Odyssey: The George W. Wray Jr. Civil War Collection at the Atlanta History Center*. Athens: University of Georgia Press, 2014.

Karakoç, Ercan, and Ali Serdar Mete. "The Effects of the Firearm Purchasings on the Ottoman Financial Structure During the Military Modernization (1853–1908)." *SUTAD* 49 (Ağustos 2020): 293–312 (e-ISSN: 2458-9071).

Kirchner, Walther. "One Hundred Years Krupp and Russia, 1818–1918." *VSWG: Vierteljahrschrift Für Sozial-Und Wirtschaftsgeschichte* 69, no. 1 (1982): 75–108.

Knight, Edward H. *Knight's American Mechanical Dictionary*. Vol. 1. Boston: Houghton Osgood & Co., 1880.

Laidley, Theodore T. S. "Breech-Loading Musket" *United States Service Magazine* 3 (1865): 67–70.

———. *The Ordnance Manual for the Use of the Officers of the United States Army*. Philadelphia: J. B. Lippincott & Co., 1862.

Lathrop, William G. *The Brass Industry of Connecticut: A Study of the Origin and the Development of the Brass Industry of the Naugatuck Valley*. New Haven, CT: Price, Lee & Adkins, 1909.

Layman, George. *The Military Remington Rolling Block Rifle*. 4th ed. Union City, NJ: Pioneer Press, 1999.

Lee, Andrew J. B. "The U.S. Armory at Harpers Ferry Historic Resource Study." Harpers Ferry National Historical Park Archeology Program, 2006.

LeFroy, Brig. Gen. J. H. *Official Catalogue of the Museum of Artillery in the Rotunda Woolwich*. London: George Eyre & William Spottiswoode, 1864.

Lewis, Col. Berkeley. *1972 Small Arms Ammunition at the International Exposition Philadelphia, 1876*. Smithsonian Studies in History and Technology 11. Washington, DC: Smithsonian Institution Press, 1972.

———. *Notes on Ammunition of the American Civil War 1861–1865*. Washington, DC: American Ordnance Association, 1959.

———. *Small Arms and Ammunition in the United States Service*. Washington, DC: Smithsonian Institution, 1956.

London Daily News. *The War Correspondence of the "Daily News," 1877, with a Connecting Narrative Forming a Continuous History of the War Between Russia and Turkey*. 2nd ed. London: Macmillan and Co., 1878.

———. *The War Correspondence of the "Daily News," 1877–78, Continued from the Fall of Kars to the Signature of the Preliminaries of Peace, with a Connecting Narrative Forming a Continuous History of the War Between Russia and Turkey*. London: Macmillan and Co., 1878.

Lorain, Pierre, and Jean Boudrio. *Les Armes Américaines de la Défense Nationale 1870–1871*. Paris: Les Presses de l'Emancipatrice, 1970.

Lord, Robert Howard. "The Congress of Berlin." In *Three Peace Congresses of the Nineteenth Century*. Cambridge, MA: Harvard University Press, 1917.

Loring, William W. *A Confederate Soldier in Egypt*. New York: Dodd, Mead, 1884.

Luvaas, Jay. *The Military Legacy of the Civil War*. Lawrence: University Press of Kansas, 1988.

Lynch, Jacqueline T. *The Ames Manufacturing Company of Chicopee Massachusetts: A Northern Factory Town's Perspective on the Civil War*. Privately published, 2013.

Majende, Vivian Dering. *The Arms and Ammunition of the British Service*. London: Cassell, Petter & Galpin, 1874.

Manning, Stephen. *The Martini-Henry Rifle*. Oxford: Osprey, 2013.

Marcot, Roy. *U.S. Sharpshooters: Berdan's Civil War Elite*. Mechanicsburg, PA: Stackpole Books, 2007.

Maurice, Frederick. *The Russo-Turkish War, 1877: A Strategical Sketch*. London: S. Sonnenschein & Co., 1905.

Maynadier, William. *Reply to the Charges in the Potter Committee*. Washington, DC: H. S. Bowen, 1862.

McCoan, James Carlile. *Egypt as It Is*. New York: Henry Holt & Co., 1877.

———. *Egypt Under Ismail: A Romance of History*. London: Chapman and Hall, 1889.

McClellan, George Brinton. *McClellan's Own Story*. New York: Charles L Webster, 1887.

———. *Report of the Secretary of War, Communicating the Report of Captain George B. McClellan, One of the Officers Sent to the Seat of War in Europe, in 1855 and 1856*. Washington, DC: A. O. P. Nicholson, 1857.

———. "The War in the East." *North American Review* 125, no. 256 (July–August 1877): 35–59.

———. "The War in the East, Part II." *North American Review* 125, no. 258 (September–October, 1877): 246–70.

McKenna, Joseph. *The Gun Makers of Birmingham, 1660–1960*. Jefferson, NC: McFarland & Co., 2021.

McPherson, James H. *Battle Cry of Freedom*. Oxford: Oxford University Press, 1988.

McWhiney, Grady, and Perry D. Jamieson. *Attack and Die: Civil War Military Tactics and the Southern Heritage*. Tuscaloosa: University of Alabama Press, 1982.

Mermelstein, Robert. *Mermelstein's Guide to Metallic Cartridge Evolution*. Fort Wayne, IN: Sinclair International, 2004.

Meyer, David R. *Networked Machinists: High Technology Industries in Antebellum America*. Baltimore: Johns Hopkins University Press, 2006.

Miller, H. T. "Small Arms Procurement in the Civil War." *Military Engineer* 25, no. 139 (January–February 1933): 70–77.

Mirsky, Jeanette, and Allan Nevins. *The World of Eli Whitney*. New York: Macmillan, 1952.

Mordecai, Alfred. *Ordnance Manual for the Use of Officers of the United States Army*. Washington, DC: Gideon & Co., 1850.

Morris, Charles R. *The Dawn of Innovation*. New York: Public Affairs, 2012.

Muir, Diana. *Reflections in Bullough's Pond: Economy and Ecosystem in New England*. Hanover and London: University Press of New England, 2000.

Nasmyth, James A. *James Nasmyth, Engineer: An Autobiography*. New York: Harper & Brothers, 1883.

"The New Martini-Enfield Rifle." *The Engineer*, July 2, 1886: 15–16.

New York Board for Examination of Breech-Loading Small Arms. *Report of the Board for Examination of Breech-loading Small Arms*. Albany, NY: Weed, Parsons & Co., 1867.

Nicolay, John George. *An Oral History of Abraham Lincoln: John G. Nicolay's Interviews and Essays*. Carbondale: Southern Illinois University Press, 2006.

Norman, C. B. *Armenia and the Campaign of 1877*. London: Cassell, Petter & Galpin, 1878.

Norris, Samuel. "Facts About Small Arms." *New York Times*, July 31, 1898, 22.

North, S. N. D., and Ralph North. *Simeon North, First Official Pistol Maker of the United States*. Concord, NH: Rumford Press, 1913.

Norton, Charles R. *American Breech-Loading Small Arms*. New York: F. W. Christern, 1872.

———. *American Inventions and Improvements in Breech-Loading Small Arms*. Springfield, MA: Chapin & Gould, 1880.

O'Connell, Robert L. *Of Arms and Men: A History of War, Weapons, and Aggression*. Oxford: Oxford University Press, 1989.

O'Connor, Maureen P. "The Vision of Soldiers: Britain, France, Germany and the United States Observe the Russo-Turkish War." *War in History* 4, no. 3 (July 1997): 264–95.

Officer of the Royal Artillery. "Weapons of War." In *The Technical Educator, an Encyclopædia*. London: Cassell, Petter & Galpin, 1880.

Orcutt, Samuel. *A History of the Old Town of Stratford and the City of Bridgeport, Connecticut*. Vol. 2. Bridgeport, CT: Fairfield County Historical Society, 1886.

Padgett, James A. "The Life of Alfred Mordecai: As Related by Himself." *North Carolina Historical Review* 22, no. 1 (January, 1945): 58–108.

Paullin, Charles Oscar. "A Half Century of Naval Administration in America, 1861–1911." *United States Naval Institute Proceedings* 39, no. 3 (September 1913): 1217–46.

Pears, Sir Edwin. *Forty Years in Constantinople*. London: Herbert Jenkins, 1916.

Pegler, Martin. *Winchester Lever-Action Rifles*. Oxford: Osprey Publishing, 2015.

Pennsylvania Academy of the Fine Arts. *Catalogue of the Memorial Exhibition of Portraits by Thomas Sully*. 2nd ed. Philadelphia: Pennsylvania Academy of the Fine Arts, 1922.

Peterson, Harold L. *Notes on Ordnance of the American Civil War*. Washington, DC: American Ordnance Association, 1959.

Poore, Benjamin Perley. *Life and Public Service of Ambrose E. Burnside*. Providence, RI: J. A. & R. A. Reid, 1882.

Pridham, C. H. B. *Superiority of Fire: A Short History of Rifles and Machine Guns*. London, New York, and Melbourne: Hutchinson's Scientific & Technical Publications, 1945.

Priya, Satia. *Empire of Guns*. New York: Penguin Press, 2018.

"Providence Tool Company." *Army and Navy Journal* 8, no. 22 (January 14, 1871): 355.

Raber, Michael S. "Conservative Innovators, Military Small Arms, and Industrial History at Springfield Armory, 1794–1918." *IA: The Journal of the Society for Industrial Archeology* 14, no. 1 (1988).

Raber, Michael S., Patrick M. Malone, Robert B. Gordon, and Carolyn C. Cooper. *Conservative Innovators and Military Small Arms: An Industrial History of Springfield Armory, 1794–1968*. South Glastonbury, CT: Raber Associates, 1989.

Rasenberger, James. *Revolver: Sam Colt and the Six Shooter That Changed America.* New York: Scribner, 2020.

"Recent Deaths." *Army and Navy Journal* 30, no. 32 (April 8, 1893): 550.

Remington Arms–Union Metallic Cartridge Co. *A New Chapter in an Old Story.* New York: Remington Arms–Union Metallic Cartridge Co., 1912.

Rhode Island Historical Society. "Benjamin Francis Thurston." In *Proceedings of the Rhode Island Historical Society (1890–1891)*, 98–101. Providence: Rhode Island Historical Society, 1891.

Robins, Benjamin. *New Principles of Gunnery.* London: W. Wingrave, 1805.

Roe, Joseph W. *English and American Tool Builders.* New York: McGraw Hill Book Co., 1916

Rosenberg, Nathan. *The American System of Manufactures.* Edinburgh: Edinburgh University Press, 1969.

Royal Commission for the Great Exhibition of the Works of Industry of All Nations. *Official Catalogue.* London: W. Clowes & Sons, 1851.

Royal Commission for the Vienna Universal Exhibition of 1873. *Report, Part III.* London: HM Stationery Office, 1874.

Russell, Albert N. "Ilion and the Remingtons." In *Papers Read Before the Herkimer County Historical Society 1896, 1897 & 1898.* Herkimer and Ilion, NY: Citizen Publishing Company, 1899.

Ryan, Charles S. *Under the Red Crescent: Adventures of an English Surgeon with the Turkish Army at Plevna and Erzeroum.* New York: Charles Scribner's Sons, 1897.

Saul, Norman. *Distant Friends: The United States and Russia, 1763–1867.* Lawrence: University Press of Kansas, 1991.

Sawyer, Charles Winthrop. *Firearms in American History: 1600 to 1800.* Boston: privately printed, 1910.

———. *Our Rifles.* Boston: Williams Book Store, 1944.

Schulz, Warren E. *Ilion—The Town Remington Made.* Hicksville, NY: Exposition Press, 1977.

Scoffern, John. "Jacob Snider." *Belgravia* 1 (February 1867): 175–87.

Scott, Robert Nicholson. *Analytical Digest of the Military Laws of the United States.* Philadelphia: J. B. Lippincott & Co., 1873.

Shlakman, Vera. *Economic History of a Factory Town.* New York: Octagon Books, 1969.

Smalley, George W. *Anglo-American Memories.* 2nd series. New York and London: G. P. Putnam's Sons, 1912.

Smith, Merritt Roe. "Army Ordnance and the 'American System' of Manufacturing, 1815–1861." In *Military Enterprise and Technological Change.* Edited by Merritt Roe Smith. Cambridge, MA: MIT Press, 1985.

———. "Eli Whitney and the American System of Manufacturing." In *Technology in America: A History of Individuals and Ideas.* 6th ed. Edited by Carrol W. Pursell Jr. Cambridge, MA: MIT Press, 1986.

———. "George Washington and the Establishment of the Harpers Ferry Armory." *Virginia Magazine of History and Biography* 81, no. 4 (October 1973): 415–36.

SELECTED BIBLIOGRAPHY

———. *Harpers Ferry Armory and the New Technology: The Challenge of Change.* Ithaca, NY: Cornell University Press, 1980.

———. "John H. Hall, Simeon North, and the Milling Machine: The Nature of Innovation among Antebellum Arms Makers." *Technology and Culture* 14, no. 4 (October 1973): 573–91.

Smithurst, Peter G. *The Guns and Gun-making Machinery of Robbins & Lawrence.* Windsor, VT: American Precision Museum, 2007.

———. *The Pattern 1853 Enfield Rifle.* Oxford: Osprey Publishing 2011.

Spon, Edward, Ernest Spon, and Oliver Byrne. *Spons' Dictionary of Engineering, Civil, Mechanical, Military, and Naval.* Vol. 4. London: E. & F. N. Spon, 1871.

Stanley, Francis. *St. Petersburg to Plevna: Containing Interviews with Leading Russian Statesmen and Generals.* London: R. Bentley, 1878.

Steele, Brett D. "Muskets and Pendulums: Benjamin Robins, Leonhard Euler, and the Ballistics Revolution." *Technology and Culture* 35, no. 2 (April 1994): 348–82.

Stevens, Charles A. *Berdan's United States Sharpshooters in the Army of the Potomac, 1861–1865.* St. Paul, MN: Price-McGill Company, 1892.

Strachan, Hew F. A. *From Waterloo to Balaclava: Tactics, Technology, and the British Army, 1815–1854.* Cambridge: Cambridge University Press, 1985.

Sumner, Benedict Humphrey. "Ignatyev at Constantinople, 1864–1874." *Slavonic and East European Review* 11, no. 32 (January 1933): pp. 341–53.

Tarsaidze, Alexander. "Berdanka." *Russian Review* 9, no. 1 (January 1950): 30–36.

Tate, Thomas K. *From Under Iron Eyelids: The Biography of James Henry Burton, Armorer to Three Nations.* Bloomington, IN: Author House, 2005.

Taylor, Alan. *The Internal Enemy: Slavery and War in Virginia.* New York: W. W. Norton, 2013.

Taylor, Alan John Percivale. *The Struggle for Mastery in Europe: 1848–1918.* Oxford: Oxford University Press, 1971.

Tennant, Sir James Emerson. *The Story of the Guns.* London: Longman, Green, Longman, Roberts & Green, 1864.

Thomas, Emory M. "The Greatest Service I Rendered the State: J. E. B. Stuart's Account of the Capture of John Brown." *Virginia Magazine of History and Biography* 94, no. 3 (July 1986): 345–57.

Thomas-Anquetil, Achille. "Canons, Poudres, Engins, Armes Portative." In *Le Spectateur Militaire: Recueil de Science, d'art et d'Histoire Militaires,* 268–92. Paris: Direction du Spectateur Militaire, 1869.

Tousard, Louis de. *American Artillerist's Companion.* Vol. 2. New York: C. & A. Conrad and Company, 1809.

Treadwell, Major Thomas J. *Metallic Cartridges, as Manufactured and Tested at the Frankford Arsenal, Philadelphia, PA.* Washington, DC: Government Printing Office, 1873.

Trenk, Richard L. "The Plevna Delay." *Men at Arms Magazine* 19, no. 4 (1997): 29–36.

Trevelyan, Laura. *The Winchester: The Gun That Built an American Dynasty.* New Haven, CT: Yale University Press, 2016.

"Trial of Victor Place." *Bench and Bar* (New Series), October 1871–January 1872: 31–49. Chicago: Callaghan & Cockcroft, 1871.

312

Twain, Mark. *The Innocents Abroad*. Hartford, CT: American Publishing, 1869.

United Kingdom. *The Counter Case of Great Britain as Laid Before the Tribunal of Arbitration Convened at Geneva*. 42nd Cong., 2nd Sess., Exec. Doc. No. 324. Washington, DC: Government Printing Office, 1872.

———. *Treatise on Ammunition*. Eds. 1, 2, 4 [2 eds.], 5–8. London: HM Stationery Office, 1878.

United States Army. *Proceedings of a Court of Inquiry Convened at Washington D.C., November 9, 1868, by Special Orders No. 217 War Department to Examine into the Accusations against Brig. and Bvt. Major General A. B. Dyer, Chief of Ordnance*. Washington, DC: Government Printing Office, 1869.

United States Centennial Commission. *International Exhibition 1876, Official Catalogue*. Philadelphia: Nagle & Co., 1876.

United States National Park Service. "Historic Structure Report, Buildings 8 and 10, Coltsville National Historical Park, Hartford, Connecticut." National Park Service, 2017.

Upton, Emery. *The Military Policy of the United States*. Washington, DC: Government Printing Office, 1912.

Urban, Mark. *Fusiliers: The Saga of a British Redcoat Regiment in the American Revolution*. New York: Walker & Co., 2007.

Uselding, Paul. "Elisha K. Root, Forging, and the 'American System.'" *Technology and Culture* 15, no. 4 (October 1974): 543–68.

Virginia, Commonwealth of. *Journal of the House of Delegates, of the State of Virginia, for the Session of 1859–60*. Richmond, VA: William F. Ritche, 1859.

von Trotha, Thilo. *Tactical Studies on the Battles Around Plevna*. Translated by Carl Reichman. Kansas City, MO: Hudson-Kimberly Publishing Co., 1896.

Wallace, Lewis, Maj. Gen. "The Capture of Fort Donelson." In *Battles and Leaders of the Civil War*. New York: Century Co., 1887–1888.

Walter, John. "James Paris Lee." *Classic Arms & Militaria*, August/September 2016: 19.

———. "The Rise of the Piled Arms: A Short History of the Birmingham Small Arms Company, Part II." *Guns Review* 24 (June 1984): 397–99.

Waters, Asa. "Thomas Blanchard, The Inventor." *Harper's New Monthly Magazine* 43, no. 374 (July 1881): 254–60.

Watrous, George R. "History of Winchester Repeating Arms Company." Typescript, Winchester Arms Company records.

Watson, Lt. Henry Charles. *Eight Lectures Delivered at the School of Musketry, Hythe, Being an Explanation of the 'Theoretical Principles' as Laid Down in the Book of Musketry Instruction*. Hythe, UK: W. S. Payne, 1862.

Wawro, Geoffrey. *The Austro-Prussian War: Austria's War with Prussia and Italy in 1866*. Cambridge: Cambridge University Press, 1997.

———. *The Franco-Prussian War: The German Conquest of France in 1870–1871*. Cambridge: Cambridge University Press, 2005.

Wellesley, Sir Frederick Arthur. *With the Russians in Peace and War: Recollections of a Military Attaché*. London: E. Nash, 1905.

Wilcox, Cadmus Marcellus. *Rifles and Rifle Practice: An Elementary Treatise Upon the Theory of Rifle Firing, Explaining the Causes of Inaccuracy of Fire, and the Manner of Correcting It*. New York: D. Van Nostrand, 1859.

Wilford, Lt. Col. Earnest C. *Three Lectures Upon the Rifle*. London: John W. Parker & Son, 1859.

Williams, David. *The Birmingham Gun Trade*. Stroud, UK: History Press, 2009.

Woodbury, Robert S. "The Legend of Eli Whitney and Interchangeable Parts." *Technology and Culture* 1, no. 3 (Summer 1960): 235–53.

Woodcroft, Bennett. *Chronological Index of Patents Applied for and Granted for the Year 1862*. London: George Eyre & William Spottiswoode, 1863.

Young, John Russell. *Around the World with General Grant*. New York: American News Company, 1879.

Theses and Dissertations

Buxton, Robin Joy Love. "The American Efforts to Modernize the Egyptian Army under Khedive Ismail." Master's theses, Portland State University, 1978.

Davis, John C. "U.S. Army Rifle and Carbine Adoption between 1865 and 1900." Master's thesis, U.S. Army Command and General Staff College, Fort Leavenworth, 2007.

Heptinstall, Thomas. "From Snider-Enfield, to Martini-Henry, to the Magazine Lee Metford: An Historical and Technical Overview of the Development of British Military Rifles from 1866 to 1895." Master's thesis, University of Huddersfield, 2016.

Hoel, Margaret Stevens. "The *Ticaret Odasi*: Origins, Functions, and Activities of the Chamber of Commerce of Istanbul, 1885–1899." PhD dissertation, Ohio State University, 1973.

Lewis, James H. "The Development of the Royal Small Arms Factory (Enfield Lock) and Its Influence upon Mass Production Technology and Product Design C1820–C1880." Thesis, Middlesex University, 1996.

Maurice, Eric. "Send Forward Some Who Would Fight: How John T. Wilder and His 'Lightning Brigade' of Mounted Infantry Changed Warfare." Master's thesis, Butler University, 2016.

Smithurst, Peter G. "The Development, Technology and Application of Mechanised Manufacture to the Enfield Pattern 1853 Rifle and the Achievement of Interchangeability." Doctoral thesis, University of Huddersfield, 2020.

Weidenmier, Marc D. "The Politics of Selective Default: The Foreign Debts of the Confederate States of America." Claremont Colleges Working Papers in Economics, No. 2000-13, Claremont McKenna College, 2000.

Yiğit, Tarik Tansu. "Reconstructing the Self and the American: Civil War Veterans in Khedival Egypt." PhD dissertation, İhsan Doğramaci Bilkent University, 2020.

Ziegler, Vanessa Michelle. "The Revolt of 'the Ever-faithful Isle': The Ten Years' War in Cuba, 1868–1878." PhD dissertation, University of California Santa Barbara, 2007.

INDEX

Prosser, Gabriel, 50
Providence Tool Company
  Anthony's short review of,
    241–242
  arms agents for, 120
  author's initial interest in,
    xi–xii
  background, 71–72
  on bribery, 152
  dissolution of, 241
  domestic arms sales, 70,
    72–78
  end of arms manufacturing
    for, 184
  epilogue, 251
  exhibitions attended by,
    118–119, 237
  financial issues, 211–213,
    216–218, 239–241
  foreign contracts, 122,
    123–124, 125, 164, 187,
    203–204, 210–218, 222
  machinery sales, 126
  Peabody patents, 114, 203,
    205–206, 209–210
  post-peak of small-arms
    industry, 238–242
  subcontracts, 125, 206–209
  Turkey's debt to, 238–
    242, 245
  at Turkish gun trials, 199–
    201
Prussia, 36–37, 118, 126, 130,
  160–165, 172, 197, 212, 249–
  250

Puerto Rico, 185

Ramsey, George, 96
Ratib Pasha, 141, 145, 146
Remington, Eliphalet, 18,
  188, 245
Remington, Philo, 119, 165, 186,
  188, 245
Remington, Samuel
  as arms agent, 119, 120,
    123, 125, 140–141, 145,
    164–166, 183–184,
    199–201, 249
  business of (see Remington
    & Sons)
  death of, 245
  Navy Remingtons, 168–173
  suicide attempt by, 244
Remington & Sons
  arms agents for, 119, 120–
    121, 123, 125, 140–141,
    145, 164–166, 183–184,
    199–201, 244, 249
  ballistics, 115
  bolt-action rifle, 244–245
  British criticisms, 202
  diversification by, 245–247
  domestic contracts, 70,
    165–167
  exhibitions attended by,
    118–119, 237
  financial issues, 238, 242–
    250
  foreign contracts, 112,
    115, 122–123, 140–141,

Union Arms, 70
Union Metallic Cartridge
  Company (UMC)
    background, 105
    cartridge sales, 108, 209, 222
    exhibitions attended by, 237
    foreign contracts, 195,
      225–226
    machinery sales, 126, 127
    Russian inspection of,
      178–179
    Turkish ammunition
      contract, 229
Upton, Emory, 57
U.S. Cartridge Company, 143, 237
US Navy, 167–173, 187, 245

Venezuela, 186
Vetterli rifle, 123
Victoria (queen), 2, 3, 4,
  59–60, 130
Von Oppen, Frederick August
  Kunow Waldman, 120, 155–
  156

Wadsworth, Decius, 13
Walker, Samuel, 38
Wänzl, 111
Warner, Thomas, 39, 77, 117
Warner carbines, 166
War of 1812, 28
The War of the Rebellion (Scott), 53
Washington, George, 11–12
Waterman, Rufus, 73
Watrous, George, 224

Watson, Peter, 66, 67
Welch, W. W., 70
Welles, Gideon, 94
Wellington (duke), 5, 30
Wells, Gideon, 98–99
Wesson, Daniel, 40–41, 42, 43–44,
  106, 114, 175, 179
Wesson, Edwin, 42
Wesson gun company, 117
Westley-Richards, 135, 201
Wheeler, Artemus, 38
White, Rollin, 42–43, 154,
  175–176
Whitney, Amos, 126
Whitney, Eli, 12, 13
Whitney, Eli, Jr., 39
Whitney Arms Co., 114, 176,
  237–238, 250
Wilcox, Cadmus, 84, 86
Wilder, John, 95, 99
Wilkinson, James, 29
Willard, George L., 86
Wilson, Henry, 52
Wilson, Robert, 109
Winchester, Oliver F.
  as arms agent, 119, 120, 165,
    193–194, 226
  background, 42
  business of (*see* Winchester
    Repeating Arms
    Company)
  epilogue, 254
  Henry (Winchester) rifle,
    93, 94, 106, 114, 197

on Peabody patent issues,
205–206
at Turkish gun trials, 199–
201
Winchester Repeating Arms
Company
acquisitions by, 114
arms agents for, 119–120,
121, 143
background, 71
British opinion of, 202
comparisons, 222
exhibitions attended by, 237
foreign contracts, 122, 126,
143, 165, 193–194, 196–
198, 203–205, 225, 229

knockoffs, 123
machinery sales, 126, 127
Model 1866, 197–198, 222,
224–226
post-peak of small-arms
industry, 238, 247, 250
subcontracting, 206–209
Windsor Manufacturing Co., 119

"Yellow boy" (rifle), 197
Yohannes IV (emperor), 145–146

Zundnadelgewehr, 36–37, 126, 160
See also Needle-gun